REVIEWING HISTORIES:

SELECTIONS FROM NEW LATIN AMERICAN CINEMA

GLAUBER ROCHA

NELSON PEREIRA DOS SANTOS

RICHARD PENA

FERNANDO SOLANAS &
OCTAVIO GETINO

JEAN-LUC GODARD

ROBERT STAM

SUSANA MUNOZ &
LOURDES PORTILLO

COCO FUSCO

MIGUEL LITTIN

JULIANNE BURTON

RAOUL RUIZ

DON RANVAUD

CINE OJO COLLECTIVE

JORGE SANJINES

JULIO GARCIA ESPINOSA

TOMAS GUTIERREZ ALEA

SARA GOMEZ

OSVALDO SANCHEZ CRESPO

JORGE DENTI &
FRANK PINEDA

RADIO VENCEREMOS COLLECTIVE

PREFACE BY ARIEL DORFMAN
EDITED WITH AN INTRODUCTION BY COCO FUSCO

REVIEWING HISTORIES

SELECTIONS FROM NEW LATIN AMERICAN CINEMA

HALLWALLS

CONTEMPORARY ARTS CENTER

700 MAIN ST., BUFFALO, N.Y.

EDITED BY COCO FUSCO

"History of Cinema Novo" by Glauber Rocha is reprinted from *Framework* (London), No. 12, pp. 19-27. It originally appeared as "Cinema Novo and the Adventure of Creation," in *Cine del tercer mundo*, Vol. 1, No. 1, October 1969; "After *Barren Lives*: The Legacy of Cinema Novo" by Richard Pena originally appeared as "Nelson Pereira Dos Santos: Presentation And Interview," in *Framework*, No. 29, pp. 59-75; "An Interview With Raoul Ruiz" by Don Ranvaud originally appeared as "Raul Ruiz — An Interview," in *Framework*, No. 10, pp. 16-18; "Language And Popular Culture" by Jorge Sanjines originally appeared in *Framework*, No. 10, pp. 31-33; all are reprinted with permission.

"Envisioning Popular Form" by Michel Delahaye, Pierre Kast and Jean Narboni appeared as "An Interview [with Glauber Rocha]" in *Afterimage* (London), No. 1, April 1970, and is reprinted in a slightly abridged form with permission. It originally appeared in *Cahiers du Cinema*, No. 214.

"Toward A Third Cinema" by Fernando Solanas and Octavio Getino is reprinted from *Cineaste*, Vol. 4, No. 3, Winter 1970/71, pp. 1-10. It originally appeared in *Tricontinental*, No. 13, October 1969; "The Politics of Mothering" by Coco Fusco originally appeared as "Las Madres de la Plaza de Mayo," in *Cineaste*, Vol. 15, No. 1, 1986; both are reprinted with permission.

"*The Hour Of The Furnaces* And The Two Avant-Gardes" by Robert Stam originally appeared as "The Hour Of The Furnaces And The Two Avant Gardes" in *Millenium Film Journal*, No. 7/8/9, Fall/Winter, 1980-81, and is reprinted with permission.

"Filmmakers And The Popular Government: A Political Manifesto" appeared as "Appendix A" in Teshome H. Gabriel's *Third Cinema in the Third World: The Aesthetics of Liberation*, pp. 99-101, and is reprinted by permission of UMI Research Press. It was first published, together with an interview with Miguel Littin, in *Cahiers du Cinema*, No. 251-52, July/August 1974, pp. 59-69.

"Bridging Past And Present: Legend And Politics In *The Promised Land*" by Julianne Burton originally appeared as "The Promised Land," (©1970 The Regents of the University of California) in *Film Quarterly*, Vol. 24, No. 1, Fall 1970, pp. 27-30, and is reprinted by permission of the Regents of the University of California.

"For An Imperfect Cinema" by Julio Garcia Espinosa appeared in *Jump Cut*, May, 1979, and is reprinted with permission. It was first published in *Cine Cubano*, No. 66/67, 1970; "The Viewer's Dialectic," Part I, by Tomas Guiterrez Alea appeared in *Jump Cut*, No. 29, and is reprinted by permission of *Cineaste* (who are presently compiling a collection of essays by Alea, to be titled *Up To This Point*).

"Public Access Media And The Information War" by Coco Fusco originally appeared as "The Radio Venceremos Collective" in *Afterimage* (Rochester, NY), Vol. 14, No. 8, March 1987, pp. 15-17, and is reprinted with permission.

ISBN No. 0-936739-06-1

Hallwalls
Contemporary Arts Center
700 Main Street, 4th Floor
Buffalo, NY 14202
(716) 854-5828

This publication was designed to accompany a touring film exhibition of the same title, curated by Coco Fusco, and was made possible through the generous support of the New York State Council on the Arts, the National Endowment for the Arts, Partners' Press, Thorner-Sidney Press, the Buffalo and Erie County Public Library, and UUAB/Cultural and Performing Arts (SUNY at Buffalo).

Cover design: Paul Szpakowski

CONTENTS

ACKNOWLEDGEMENTS

THIS PUBLICATION WAS EDITED BY COCO FUSCO, AND WAS ORGANIZED AND DESIGNED BY STEVE GALLAGHER. THE MANUSCRIPT WAS TYPESET BY STEVE GALLAGHER WITH BYRON BROWN AND DAWN DUMPERT, WITH ASSISTANCE FROM ED CARDONI AND DON METZ. ADDITIONAL DESIGN WORK AND THE PUBLICATION'S COVER WERE SUPPLIED BY PAUL SZPAKOWSKI.

WE WOULD LIKE TO THANK GARY CROWDUS AND DAN GEORGAKAS (*CINEASTE*), JULIA LESAGE (*JUMP CUT*), SIMON FIELD (*AFTERIMAGE*, LONDON), PAUL WILLEMEN (*FRAMEWORK*), JULIANNE BURTON, ROBERT STAM AND THE *MILLENIUM FILM JOURNAL* FOR ALLOWING US TO REPRINT MATERIAL FOR THIS PUBLICATION, AND COCO FUSCO, ARIEL DORFMAN, RICHARD PENA, OSVALDO SANCHEZ AND JAIME BARRIOS FOR CONTRIBUTING ORIGINAL MATERIAL.

ADDITIONAL THANKS TO BARBARA BROUGHEL (FOR INTRODUCING HALLWALLS TO COCO FUSCO), NANCY GERSTMAN, BOB AARONSON, SARA TALBERT, FREDY RONCALLA, CATHERINE BENAMOU, INGRID ENRIQUEZ, ROBERTO ZEPEDA, JORGE DENTI, TIM HAZEL (ZANZIBAR PRODUCTIONS), L'INSTITUT NATIONAL DE LA COMMUNICATION AUDIOVISUELLE, JOHN MONTAGUE (NEW YORKER FILMS), NIGEL ALGAR (BRITISH FILM INSTITUTE), MARY KEOGH (ICARUS FILMS), WAYNE BURGOS (DIRECT CINEMA), AND TO HALLWALLS STAFF AND BOARD OF DIRECTORS FOR THEIR ASSISTANCE, ADVICE, AND SUPPORT.

THIS PROJECT WOULD NOT HAVE BEEN POSSIBLE, HOWEVER, WITHOUT THE SUPPORT OF THE NEW YORK STATE COUNCIL ON THE ARTS, ROBERT GURN/THE BUFFALO AND ERIE COUNTY PUBLIC LIBRARY, MIKE HUBER/UUAB CULTURAL AND PERFORMING ARTS (SUNY AT BUFFALO), THE FILM BUREAU AT FILM/VIDEO ARTS, THE NEW YORK COUNCIL FOR THE HUMANITIES, THE NATIONAL ENDOWMENT FOR THE ARTS, AL ABGOTT (PARTNERS' PRESS), AND ROBERT FREUDENHEIM (THORNER-SIDNEY PRESS).

LASTLY, I WOULD LIKE TO THANK COCO FUSCO WHO ASSEMBLED A MAGNIFICENT SELECTION OF MANUSCRIPTS TO ACCOMPANY WHAT WAS ALREADY AN EXCITING AND PROVOCATIVE PROGRAM OF FILMS.

STEVE GALLAGHER
FILM PROGRAM

BEYOND SATAN AND A SIESTA: A PREFACE

ARIEL DORFMAN

WHEN PEOPLE IN LATIN AMERICA THINK ABOUT LIFE IN THE UNITED STATES, THE IMAGES CONJURED UP PRIMARILY DERIVE FROM WHAT THE U.S. MEDIA ITSELF HAS PROJECTED ON INCESSANTLY ACCESSIBLE SCREENS—FILMS AT THE MOVIE THEATERS, T.V. SERIALS AND NEWS ON TELEVISION AT HOME.

IF THERE WERE SYMMETRY AND FAIRNESS IN THE DISTRIBUTION OF IMAGES WORLD-WIDE, WE MIGHT EXPECT, THEREFORE, THAT PEOPLE IN THE UNITED STATES WOULD HAVE EXPLORED LATIN AMERICA THROUGH THE EXPERIENCE THAT ARTISTS AND MEDIA PRODUCERS SOUTH OF THE RIO GRANDE HAVE BEEN CREATING WITH ENORMOUS DIFFICULTIES DURING THIS CENTURY.

THIS HAS NOT, UNFORTUNATELY, BEEN THE CASE. THE CONTACT MOST PEOPLE IN THIS COUNTRY HAVE WITH LATIN AMERICA IS CONSTRUCTED WITH SECOND-HAND, TWICE-REMOVED, OVERLY-DIGESTED VISIONS, MOST OF THEM ENGENDERED IN THE UNITED STATES. WHAT THEY LEARN ABOUT THE SPRAWLING CONTINENT TO THEIR SOUTH IS MADE UP, FOR THE MOST PART, OF CLICHES. THEY CAN CHOOSE AMONG THE CONFLICTING STEREOTYPES. THE SIESTA OR SATAN? IT DEPENDS. LATIN AMERICA CAN BE VACATIONLAND: FULL OF PALM TREES AND CAREFREE, RHUMBA-DANCING NATIVES, AGOG WITH EXOTIC CUSTOMS. OR VIOLENCE-LAND: INCOM-PREHENSIBLE REVOLUTIONS, RAVAGING MASSACRES, MAJESTIC EARTHQUAKES, WILD RIVERS; YOU NAME THE DANGER, THEY'VE GOT IT. IN EITHER VISION, A LAND BEYOND REDEMPTION AND BEYOND REASON, WHERE ANY ATTEMPT AT CHANGE WILL BE BUMBLING AND QUIXOTIC AND PROBABLY MAKE THE SITUATION WORSE.

A GOOD WAY TO START CHALLENGING THAT STUBBORN AND PREDATORY REPRESENTATION OF LATIN AMERICA IS, QUITE SIMPLY, TO WATCH SOME OF THE EXTRAORDINARY, VIBRANT FILMS THAT HAVE BEEN PRODUCED BY LATIN AMERICANS THEMSELVES.

THAT IS ENOUGH TO SHAKE ANYBODY OUT OF COMPLACENCY. BUT FOR THOSE WHO ARE NOT CONTENT WITH THE FILMS ALONE AND WHO WANT MORE REAL

Latino adventures, of the intellectual kind, this publication will do wonders. It is a chance to eavesdrop on the filmmakers as they struggle to come to terms with the problems of portraying misdeveloped societies with the technological instruments and genres imported from abroad. The spectator can now become a reader, watching the process whereby these films were created—not fundamentally in order to explain our own ideas to a world that did not seem to care, but as one more attempt to reconquer a reality which, complex and tyrannically hidden as it was, had remained outside discovery, at least in the popular media. The construction of these films, therefore, has been accompanied by constant debate, furious thought, whirlwind dialogue among the filmmakers themselves, whose search for the right images and the way to communicate them had to begin by self-questioning, the breaking down of the walls of their own mental captivity.

You are invited to participate.

REVIEWING HISTORIES: An INTRODUCTION

COCO FUSCO

SINCE I BEGAN TO THINK ABOUT HOW TO PLAN THIS FILM PROGRAM, IT SEEMED THAT INCORPORATING FILMMAKER'S WRITINGS AND COMMENTARY WAS VERY MUCH IN THE SPIRIT OF THE NEW LATIN AMERICAN CINEMA. AMONG THE MOVEMENT'S FIRST LEADERS WERE MANY CRITICS AND GIFTED POLEMICISTS WHO REJECTED TRADITIONAL FILM CRITICISM AS "SUPERFLUOUS," PREFERRING TO DEFINE THE TERMS OF THE CINEMATIC PRACTICE THEMSELVES. IN THE 1960'S AND EARLY '70'S, FILMMAKERS OFFERED ARGUMENTS FOR A "CINEMA NOVO," FOR "CINE DE LIBERACION," FOR "CINE IMPERFECTO," FOR AN "AESTHETIC OF HUNGER," FOR A "THIRD CINEMA" OF DECOLONIZATION, ALL TERMS THAT HAVE SINCE FRAMED MANY A DEBATE AT HOME AND ABROAD. WRITING ABOUT THEIR PRACTICE CREATED ANOTHER FORUM, ANOTHER WAY TO INTEGRATE CINEMA INTO SOCIAL LIFE. AND DISCUSSIONS OF THEIR CINEMA AND THE ISSUES IT RAISED WAS, AND CONTINUES TO BE, A KEY ELEMENT OF A MUCH BROADER PROJECT OF REDEFINING POLITICAL AND CULTURAL VALUES, WHETHER IT BE TIED TO A LIBERATION MOVEMENT, THE DEVELOPMENT OF NATIONAL CULTURE, OR TO PROVOKE AWARENESS OF LATIN AMERICA'S CHRONIC SOCIAL AND ECONOMIC PROBLEMS. TIMES HAVE CHANGED, AND MANIFESTOES HAVE GIVEN WAY TO DEEPER REFLECTION AND COMMENTARY, THE SIGNS OF A MOVEMENT IN THE PROCESS OF ASSESSING ITSELF. MORE RECENT FILMS ARE GENERALLY LESS SWEEPING, AND OFTEN LESS POLEMICAL, BUT THE FINEST OF THEM CONTINUE TO COMBINE AESTHETIC INNOVATION AND SOCIAL COMMITMENT.

NEW LATIN AMERICAN CINEMA FIRST RECEIVED ATTENTION IN THE U.S. IN THE LATE 1960'S, WHEN MANY AMERICAN INDEPENDENT CINEASTES SOUGHT A SIMILAR FUSION OF RADICAL FORM AND POLITICS. BY THE MID-1970'S, THE MICROPOLITICS OF PSYCHOLOGY AND LANGUAGE HAD DRAWN MANY AESTHETIC QUESTIONS AWAY FROM INTERNATIONALIST ISSUES IN THE U.S. IN LATIN AMERICA,

RIGHT-WING GOVERNMENTS MADE WORK VIRTUALLY IMPOSSIBLE FOR THE NEW LATIN AMERICAN DIRECTORS, MANY OF WHOM WERE FORCED INTO EXILE. (CUBA'S FILMMAKING TRAJECTORY IS DIFFERENT, THOUGH IT HAS ALSO BEEN SUBJECT TO THE COUNTRY'S CHANGING POLITICAL CLIMATE.) ONLY RECENTLY HAS IT BEEN POSSIBLE TO SPEAK OF A RESURGENCE OF NEW LATIN AMERICAN CINEMA, AND IN THE MEANTIME, THE NATURE OF FILMMAKING THERE HAS BEEN SIGNIFICANTLY ALTERED. SUPPORT FROM STATE FILM AGENCIES, EUROPEAN TELEVISION, AND THE CUBAN FILM INSTITUTE, I.C.A.I.C., PROVIDE MATERIAL BACKING FOR LARGER SCALE PRODUCTIONS WHICH ARE RELATIVELY EASIER TO PRODUCE UNDER LESS REPRESSIVE GOVERNMENTS, AND MANY OF WHICH ATTAIN COMMERCIAL SUCCESS AT HOME AND ABROAD. THE ALTERNATIVE DISTRIBUTION NETWORKS AND PROTECTIVE LEGISLATION THAT THE NEW LATIN AMERICAN FILMMAKERS ARGUED, AND STILL ARGUE, FOR IS PRECISELY THE INFRASTRUCTURE THAT HAS ENABLED MANY MORE TO WORK. THE INTRODUCTION OF VIDEO HAS FURTHERED ACCESS TO MEDIA PRODUCTION, ASSUMING MUCH OF THE SPACE CREATED FOR OPPOSITIONAL MEDIA BY THE EARLY MILITANT CINEMA OF THE SIXTIES. ON THE OTHER HAND, TELEVISION'S AUDIENCE IN LATIN AMERICA HAS GROWN SUBSTANTIALLY, WHILE CINEMA'S HAS DECREASED AND LITTLE AIR TIME, IF ANY, IS ALLOTTED TO INDEPENDENT, LOCAL PROGRAMMING.

YOUNGER GENERATIONS OF FILMMAKERS HAVE ADAPTED THEORETICAL MODELS FOR THEIR OWN PURPOSES. FERNANDO SOLANAS AND OCTAVIO GETINO'S GUERRILLA FILM TEAM, A MEDIA ADJUNCT TO CHE GUEVARA'S "FOCO," RESURFACES AS CLANDESTINE CREWS IN CHILE, EL SALVADOR AND PRE-REVOLUTIONARY NICARAGUA, NOW MORE CONSCIOUSLY DIRECTED TOWARD THE OUTSIDE WORLD. JORGE SANJINES' WORK WITH THE QUECHUA INDIANS IN BOLIVIA IS NOT FAR IN SPIRIT FROM THE COMMUNITY-BASED VIDEO PROJECTS THAT HAVE FLOURISHED IN BRAZIL, PERU, AND NICARAGUA. THOUGH FILM LABOR HAS BEEN DIVIDED AND STRATEGIES DIVERSIFIED, THE QUESTIONS THAT THIS MOVEMENT RAISED YEARS AGO REGARDING LATIN AMERICA'S NEOCOLONIAL SITUATION, AND THE FUNCTION OF CINEMA IN THAT CONTEXT, ARE STILL CURRENT, AND STILL BEING GRAPPLED WITH.

THOUGH THE FILMS AND THE WRITTEN MATERIALS FOR THIS PROGRAM ARE OSTENSIBLY ORGANIZED BY COUNTRY, THERE ARE MANY INTERCULTURAL WAYS THAT THEY CAN BE READ. THE QUESTION OF REVOLUTIONARY FORM, DEFINING POPULAR CINEMA AND INTELLECTUALS' ROLES, RECUR THROUGHOUT. WHILE NELSON PEREIRA DOS SANTOS' NEOREALIST ENTRY INTO THE LIVES OF MIGRANTS IN BRAZIL'S NORTHEAST SUCCEEDED IN STIRRING UP DEBATES AMONG THE URBAN MIDDLE-CLASS, SIMILAR SUCCESS GAINED BY SANJINES WITH HIS HISTORICAL REENACTMENT OF U.S. STERILIZATION CAMPAIGNS IN BOLIVIA CAUSED THE FILMMAKER TO RETHINK HIS STRATEGIES OF REPRESENTATION IN ORDER TO MAKE HIS FILMS MORE INTELLIGIBLE TO THE QUECHUA SUBJECTS THEMSELVES. SOLANAS AND GETINO'S *THE HOUR OF THE FURNACES* AND ITS ACCOMPANYING TRACT "TOWARD A THIRD CINEMA," FORM AN EPIC SCALE ATTEMPT TO CREATE A "FILM ACT," AN OPEN-ENDED FORM THAT WOULD DRAW THE DOCUMENTARY SUBJECTS AND AUDIENCES INTO THE PROCESS.

SARA GOMEZ'S *ONE WAY OR ANOTHER* ALSO ENGAGES IN FORMAL EXPERIMEN-TATION, PRYING OPEN CINEMA'S IDEOLOGICAL STRUCTURES OF PERCEPTION AND "REVOLUTIONARY" PERSPECTIVES ON POPULAR CULTURE. HER WORK, TOGETHER WITH TOMAS GUTIERREZ ALEA'S REFLECTIONS ON SOCIALLY PRODUCTIVE POPULAR CINEMA IN "THE VIEWER'S DIALECTIC," GO MUCH FURTHER THAN JULIO GARCIA ESPINOSA'S REJECTION OF HIGH ART AND ARTISTS IN FAVOR OF POPULAR ART AS THE SEED OF THE FUTURE LIBERATED CULTURE IN HIS ESSAY ON "IMPERFECT CINEMA."

RECOGNIZING THE STRENGTH OF LATIN AMERICA'S AFRICAN AND INDIAN-BASED CULTURES OF RESISTANCE, MANY FILMMAKERS ATTEMPTED TO LEGITIMIZE THEIR DISCURSIVE FORMS—LEGEND, DANCE, MUSIC AND ORAL HISTORY, WHICH BECAME A RICH SOURCE OF MATERIAL AND THE FOCUS OF MANY A DEBATE. GLAUBER ROCHA'S WORK IS ONE OF THE MOST CREATIVE INTERPRETATIONS OF POPULAR CULTURE AND BRECHTIAN TECHNIQUES IN THE EARLY NEW LATIN AMERICAN CINEMA. MIGUEL LITTIN'S *THE PROMISED LAND* AND JORGE DENTI'S *CULTURAL INSURRECTION* ALSO INCORPORATE POPULAR HISTORICAL DISCOURSES, WITH VARY-ING DEGREES OF AMBIVALENCE. THE NEVER ENDING DEBATES ON "REVOLUTIONARY REALISM" REVOLVE AROUND THE QUESTION OF POPULISM, WHICH UNCRITICAL USE OF THESE DISCOURSES MIGHT IMPLY.

RECOVERING AND REVISING PAST HISTORY IS ALMOST A GENRE UNTO ITSELF IN NEW LATIN AMERICAN CINEMA. HOWEVER, THE SUBJECT MATTER'S CHRONOLOGICAL DISTANCE DOES NOT SEPARATE THIS ENDEAVOR FROM CONCEP-TUAL PROBLEMS OF THE PRESENT. *THE LAST SUPPER, REED: INSURGENT MEXICO,* AND *THE PROMISED LAND*, RATHER THAN BEING STRAIGHTFORWARD PERIOD DRAMAS, EACH EXPLORE QUESTIONS OF HISTORICAL PERSPECTIVE THROUGH CLASHES OF CULTURES AND CLASSES, AND POINT TO THE MASKING PROCESS OF IDEALIZA-TION BY WHICH LEGEND, RELIGION AND EVEN YOUTHFUL REVOLUTIONARY ZEAL CONJURE THE PAST.

ATTUNED TO THE COMPLEXITIES OF THE REPRESENTATION PROCESS, THE FILM-MAKERS, FAR FROM CONVEYING A SENSE OF FUTILITY, PROPOSED A VARIETY OF MEANS FOR CRITICAL RECEPTION. THE RENEGADE CHILEAN EXILE RAOUL RUIZ IS PERHAPS MOST SKEPTICAL ON THIS ISSUE, AND HIS INCISIVE REMARKS ON THE MOVE-MENT'S WEAKNESSES EVOKE ANXIETIES AND AMBIGUITIES OF THE COLONIAL AND NEOCOLONIAL INTELLECTUAL EXPERIENCE THAT GO FAR BEYOND THE PROBLEMS OF EXILE. HE IS THE FIRST, HOWEVER, TO ADMIT THE DEGREE TO WHICH HIS WORK-ING IN A EUROPEAN CONTEXT HAS MODIFIED HIS OWN CONCERNS. OTHER FILM-MAKERS, MORE GROUNDED IN A SENSE OF NATIONAL CULTURE, AT TIMES HAVE BORDERED ON SELF-CONGRATULATORY POSTURES, CLAIMING TO HAVE "RESCUED" THE PAST FROM IGNOMINIOUS OBSCURITY. HEROISM ASIDE, THEY, AS WELL AS MANY OTHER LATIN AMERICANS, ARE ACUTELY AWARE OF "OFFICIAL" HISTORIOGRAPHY'S ELLISIONS AND ITS CONFORMITY TO RULING INTERESTS, BOTH PAST AND PRESENT.

IT IS IN DEFIANCE OF CURRENT ATTEMPTS TO ERASE THE PRESENCE OF RESISTANCE TO STATE POWER THAT THE PROGRAM'S CONTEMPORARY DOCUMENTARIES SITUATE

THEMSELVES. REVIVING NOTIONS OF "IMPERFECT CINEMA" IN TERMS OF THEIR NEED TO INTERVENE IN NATIONAL AND INTERNATIONAL MEDIA, THESE FILMS, LIKE THE MOVEMENTS THEY REPRESENT, FUNCTION AS AN ONGOING SYMBOLIC PROTEST AGAINST THE STATE'S POWER OF EFFACEMENT, FROM ITS NEGATION OF PARTICIPATORY POLITICS AND CIVIL LIBERTIES TO ITS OWN VERSION OF TERRORISM: DISAPPEARANCE. AS URGENT AS THEIR TONE MIGHT SEEM, THESE DOCUMENTARIES ARE THE RESULT OF PRESCIENT, LONG-TERM STRATEGIES. AND, AS MANY OF THE INTERVIEWS IN-DICATE, THE TERMS HAVE SHIFTED SINCE THE SIXTIES. THEY ARE LESS APOCALYPTIC, SPEAK LESS OF DECOLONIZATION AND FILMIC ARTILLERIES AND MORE ABOUT THE ONGOING PROJECT OF PRESERVING POPULAR MEMORY, BUILDING IMAGE ARCHIVES FOR PRESENT AND FUTURE USE. THE FILMS ARE STYLED TO FORMATS THAT INSURE GREATER ACCESS, BUT THEY CONTINUE TO OFFER POINTED CRITIQUES OF WESTERN NOTIONS OF OBJECTIVITY.

AT THE RISK OF CONFUSION, I HAVE PURPOSELY CHOSEN TO EMPHASIZE THE HETEROGENEITY OF RESPONSES TO NEW LATIN AMERICAN CINEMA'S CENTRAL QUES-TIONS. IT IS IMPORTANT TO REMEMBER THAT LATIN AMERICA, AS A SINGULAR, UNIFIED VOICE, CINEMA OR CULTURE, IS AN HISTORIOGRAPHICAL FICTION, A SHORT CUT TO UNDERSTANDING THAT WE USE TO FACILITATE OUR RECEPTION OF OTHER PARTS OF THE WORLD. NEW LATIN AMERICAN CINEMA'S WAYS OF MAKING FILM AND ENVISIONING "REALISM" HAVE ALSO EVOLVED OVER TIME. THESE ARE THE DIF-FERENCES AND HISTORICAL CONTRASTS A PROGRAM COVERING SEVERAL COUN-TRIES, PERIODS, AND GENRES CAN BRING OUT. HISTORICAL PERSPECTIVE GIVES A SENSE OF DIMENSION TO CONTEMPORARY LATIN AMERICAN CINEMA, AND TO OUR PRESENT QUESTIONS ABOUT LATIN AMERICA. IT IS CRUCIAL TO AN ONGOING CRITICAL REFLECTION ON "SOCIAL REALITY." AND IT IS ONE OF THE BEST MEANS WE HAVE TO QUESTION OUR OWN IMAGES OF LATIN AMERICA. AS A BRAZILIAN DIRECTOR PUT IT TO ME IN A RECENT INTERVIEW, "WHY SHOULD I HAVE TO EX-PLAIN MY FILMS TO AN AMERICAN AUDIENCE? WHY DON'T THEY KNOW AS MUCH ABOUT OUR HISTORY AND CULTURE AS WE MUST LEARN ABOUT THEIRS?" *REVIEW-ING HISTORIES* IS BUT A SMALL GESTURE TOWARDS A BETTER UNDERSTANDING.

BRAZIL

Antonio Das Mortes

HISTORY OF CINEMA NOVO [1969]

GLAUBER ROCHA

THERE IS NO ONE IN THIS WORLD DOMINATED BY TECHNOLOGY, WHO HAS NOT BEEN INFLUENCED BY THE CINEMA. EVEN WITHOUT HAVING BEEN TO THE CINEMA, MAN IS INFLUENCED BY IT. NATIONAL CULTURES GENERALLY HAVE NOT BEEN UNAFFECTED BY A CERTAIN WAY OF DOING THINGS, A CERTAIN SORT OF MORALITY, AND, ABOVE ALL, A TENDENCY TOWARDS THE FANTASTIC, ALL SUPPLIED BY THE CINEMA OF THE IMAGINATION.

WHEN ONE TALKS OF CINEMA, ONE TALKS OF *AMERICAN* CINEMA. THE IN-FLUENCE OF THE CINEMA IS *THE INFLUENCE OF AMERICAN CINEMA*, WHICH IS THE MOST AGGRESSIVE AND WIDESPREAD ASPECT OF AMERICAN CULTURE THROUGHOUT THE WORLD. AND THIS INFLUENCE HAS SO AFFECTED THE AMERICAN PUBLIC ITSELF, THAT, DESPITE ITS CONDITIONING, THE PUBLIC DEMANDS THAT THE CINEMA FUR-NISHES AN IMAGE IN ITS OWN LIKENESS.

FOR THIS REASON, EVERY DISCUSSION OF CINEMA MADE OUTSIDE HOLLYWOOD MUST BEGIN WITH HOLLYWOOD, ESPECIALLY AS FAR AS BRAZILIAN CINEMA IS CON-CERNED. BEING ECONOMICALLY AND CULTURALLY MUCH CLOSER TO THE UNITED STATES THAN TO EUROPE, OUR PUBLIC HAS CREATED AN IMAGE OF LIFE THROUGH THE AMERICAN CINEMA. THEREFORE WHEN A BRAZILIAN DECIDES TO MAKE A FILM, HE DECIDES TO MAKE AN "AMERICAN-TYPE" MOVIE, AND IT IS ESSENTIALLY BECAUSE OF THIS THAT THE BRAZILIAN AUDIENCE EXPECTS A BRAZILIAN FILM TO BE AN "AMERICAN-TYPE" BRAZILIAN MOVIE. IF A FILM IS NOT AMERICAN, SIMPLY BECAUSE IT IS BRAZILIAN, HE IS DISAPPOINTED. THE AUDIENCE DOES NOT ACCEPT THE BRAZILIAN FILMMAKERS' IMAGE OF BRAZIL BECAUSE THIS IMAGE DOES NOT COIN-CIDE WITH THE ONE OF A TECHNICALLY DEVELOPED AND MORALLY IDEAL WORLD SUPPLIED BY HOLLYWOOD MOVIES.

THUS IT IS NOT DIFFICULT TO SEE WHICH BRAZILIAN FILMS ENJOY POPULAR ACCLAIM: THEY ARE THOSE WHICH, WHILE DEALING WITH *NATIONAL* THEMES, DO SO BY MAKING USE OF A TECHNIQUE AND AN ART WHICH IMITATES THE AMERICANS.

TWO OBVIOUS EXAMPLES ARE *O CANGACEIRO* [1953] BY LIMA BARRETO, AND *O ASSALTO AO TREM PAGADOR* [*ASSAULT ON THE PAY TRAIN*, 1953] BY ROBERT FARIAS.

THE PLOT OF *O CANGACEIRO* IS TAKEN FROM AMERICAN WESTERNS AND TRANSPOSED TO A SETTING OF THE *CANGACO*[1]. TO DO THIS, IT HACKS OUT ALL ASPECTS OF THE SOCIAL LIFE OF THE *SERTAO* (A ZONE OF THE BRAZILIAN INTERIOR), AND, FOLLOWING THE TRADITIONS OF THE WESTERN, ONLY MAKES USE OF THAT IMAGERY WHICH IS PART OF THOSE TRADITIONS: LONG HAIR, AGGRESSIVE LANDSCAPES, FIRE-ARMS, HORSES (EVEN WHEN, AS IS WELL KNOWN, THE *CANGACEIROS*[2] RARELY WENT ON HORSEBACK), MUSIC AND FOLK DANCES. THE PLOT, AS WILL BE REMEMBERED, DIVIDED THE FOUR MEN INTO GOODIES AND BADDIES. WHEN TEODORO ESCAPES WITH THE YOUNG SCHOOLMA'AM, THE STORY FOLLOWS, STEP BY STEP, THE CLASSIC SCHEME BETWEEN THE PURSUED GOODIES AND THE BADDIE PURSUERS. IN THE FINAL SCENE, THE SCHOOLMA'AM, PURE GOOD ITSELF, IS SAVED. TEODORO, WHO HAD PREVIOUSLY BEEN BAD, HAS NO POSSIBILITY OF BECOMING GOOD AND DIES HEROICALLY. HE DIES, HOWEVER, WITH AN ACT OF NATIONALISTIC FERVOR, KISSING THE EARTH. THE FILM'S TECHNIQUE IS PROVIDED BY AMERICAN MODELS. AT NO TIME DOES THE CAMERA STOP TO ANALYZE A CHARACTER.

AS CAN BE SEEN, THIS *REALISM* IS COMPLETELY *UNREAL*. THE ILLUSION OF THE WORLD OF THE *CANGACO* IS CREATED IN TERMS IDENTICAL TO THOSE OF THE ILLUSION OF THE WORLD OF TEXAN OUTLAWS. BROUGHT UP ON HUNDREDS OF "COWBOY" FILMS, THE PUBLIC NEED MAKE NO EFFORT TO UNDERSTAND THE FILM, WHICH IS OFFERED TO IT AS A RICH IMITATION OF WHAT THE PUBLIC'S DEFORMED TASTE EXPECTS.

SATISFIED THAT THIS IMITATION IS POSSIBLE, THE AUDIENCE WILL NATURALLY REACT AGAINST ANY FILM WHATSOEVER, WHICH WANTING TO SHOW THAT BRAZIL IS NOT THE UNITED STATES, PROPOSES A DIFFERENT SORT OF CONFLICT, AND CONSEQUENTLY USES A DIFFERENT SORT OF LANGUAGE.

IN THE CONTEXT OF THE DETECTIVE GENRE, *O ASSALTO AO TREM PAGADOR* REPEATS SEVERAL ELEMENTS WHICH GO TO IMITATE THE AMERICAN "GANGSTER" MOVIE. SINCE, HOWEVER, THE DETECTIVE GENRE IS MUCH MORE REALISTIC THAN THAT OF THE WESTERN, AND FOR THIS VERY REASON CARRIES A BIGGER DOSE OF SOCIAL STATEMENT, ROBERTO FARIAS' FILM ACHIEVES A DISTINCTIVE CULTURAL LEVEL. IT DOES NOT, ALL THE SAME, AVOID MAKING USE OF THE TECHNIQUES OF "SUSPENSE" WHICH ARE FUNDAMENTAL TO THE GENRE.

THE SAME ROBERTO FARIAS DECIDED, IN ANOTHER FILM, TO CONFRONT A SOCIAL QUESTION. MAKING *SELVA TRAGICA* [*TRAGIC FOREST*, 1946] HE TRIED WITH GREAT EFFORT TO FREE HIMSELF FROM AMERICAN FORMULAE BY BROACHING THE PROBLEM OF SLAVERY IN THE FARMING OF *MATE* IN CENTRAL BRAZIL. HE CEASED DIVIDING SOCIETY INTO GOODIES AND BADDIES AND SOUGHT TO CARRY OUT A MORE PROFOUND ANALYSIS. BY PENETRATING A COMPLEX STRUCTURE AND ATTEMPTING TO ARTICULATE A LANGUAGE WHICH SUITED THIS STRUCTURE, ROBER-

TO MADE A FILM WHICH WAS REGARDED AT THAT TIME AS DISCONNECTED. THE LACK OF CONNECTION OF THIS FILM, HOWEVER, WAS MUCH MORE REALISTIC AND NATIONAL THAN THE CLOSED AND PREDETERMINED FORMULA ADOPTED FOR *O ASSALTO AO TREM PAGADOR*.

THE PUBLIC'S REJECTION OF THIS FILM MADE ROBERTO FARIAS REALIZE THAT HIS ABILITY TO COMMUNICATE TO THEM WAS NOT LINKED TO HIS TALENT AS DIRECTOR, BUT TO THE USE TO WHICH HE COULD PUT HIS TALENT IN FUNCTION OF A DETERMINED THEME. AND SO THE DIRECTOR ONCE MORE RESORTED TO THE THEME OF THE CITY AND MORALITY, WITH A VISION OF THE MIDDLE-CLASSES' ATTITUDE TO THE BOURGEOISIE, IN THE FILM *TODA DONZELA TEM PAI QUE É UMA FERA [ALL NICE YOUNG LADIES HAVE BEASTLY FATHERS]*. HE CONFIRMED THE NOTION WHEREBY THE FORMULA FOR SUCCESS CONSISTS IN APPLYING THE AMERICAN NARRATIVE FORM TO A THEME WHICH IS SOCIALLY AND MORALLY FALSE.

THE WELCOME ACCORDED INTERNATIONALLY TO *SELVA TRAGICA* BY THE CRITICS AND THE ARTS CINEMA CIRCUIT CREATED A DILEMMA FOR ROBERTO FARIAS, HOWEVER THE ARTISAN DIRECTOR FINALLY SUCCEEDED IN OVERSHADOWING THE AUTEUR DIRECTOR; HENCE HIS LATEST FILM *ROBERTO CARLOS EM RITMO DE AVENTURA [ROBERT CARLOS IN THE BEAT OF ADVENTURE]* REPRESENTS A BRAZILIAN CONCOCTION OF AMERICAN FORMULAE, AND IT SEEMS DESTINED TO BECOME OUR BIGGEST BOX-OFFICE HIT.

The Challenge

BUT BY EXPLOITING ALIENATION IN THIS WAY, WILL ROBERTO FARIAS REALLY SUCCEED IN *CONQUERING* THIS PUBLIC? DOES GIVING TO THE PUBLIC WHAT IT *WANTS* REPRESENT A FORM OF CONQUEST, OR RATHER A FORM OF COMMERCIAL EXPLOITATION OF THE A-CULTURAL CONDITIONING OF THIS PUBLIC? IS IT NOT, PERHAPS, IN *SELVA TRAGICA* THAT THE TRUE PATH RESIDES, THE PATH WHICH LEADS TO THE CONQUEST OF THE SPECTATOR?

ROBERTO WOULD UNDOUBTEDLY ANSWER THAT THE CINEMA IS AN INDUSTRY AND THAT BRAZIL NEEDS A FILM INDUSTRY WHICH MIGHT LATER GIVE HIM THE CHANCE OF CREATING AN ORIGINAL CINEMA CONCERNED WITH THE COUNTRY'S PROBLEMS.

BUT HOW TO CREATE A NATIONAL FILM INDUSTRY? THE CINEMA IS AN INDUSTRY WHICH GENERATES CULTURE. AMERICAN CINEMA HAS CREATED A TASTE FOR ITSELF, AND IF BRAZILIAN CINEMA, IN ORDER TO DEVELOP, WANTS TO FOLLOW THE EASIEST PATH, ALL IT HAS TO DO IS MAKE USE OF AMERICAN FORMULAE. BUT IN DOING SO, BRAZIL'S INDUSTRIAL CINEMA WILL BE NOTHING MORE THAN THE PROPAGATOR OF A GREATER FORCE, THAT OF THE DOMINANT CULTURE. THIS CULTURE MIGHT JUST AS EASILY BE FRENCH OR RUSSIAN OR BELGIAN—IT WOULD MAKE NO DIFFERENCE; BUT IN AN UNDERDEVELOPED COUNTRY, IT *DOES* MAKE A DIFFERENCE WHETHER OR NOT THE SOCIETY CAN OBTAIN A PRACTICE GENERATED OUT OF THE CONDITIONS OF ITS OWN SPECIFIC SOCIAL AND ECONOMIC STRUCTURE.

THE FIRST CHALLENGE IS TO PROPOSE TO THE BRAZILIAN FILMMAKER HOW TO CONQUER THE PUBLIC WITHOUT MAKING USE OF AMERICAN FORMULAE WHICH, ALREADY TODAY, HAVE SPREAD INTO EUROPEAN SUB-FORMS. IS IT WORTH FORCING ONESELF TO MAKE A CINEMA WHICH WOULD PASS ON NEITHER THE BAD NOR THE GOOD TO THE SPECIFIC CULTURE OF THE SOCIETY TO WHICH IT BELONGS? THIS "IMPASSE," WHICH REFLECTS THE MODERN CONCEPTION OF THE UNDERDEVELOPED SOCIETIES OF THE TROPICAL COUNTRIES, HAS A TWO-SIDED AND CONFLICTING MORAL REPERCUSSION: ON THE FILMMAKER WHO "PRODUCES THE IMITATION," TO HIS OBVIOUS DISCREDIT, AND ON THE PUBLIC WHICH "REJECTS THE ORIGINAL EFFORT" WITH MANIFEST ANNOYANCE.

FOR THE PUBLIC, HOWEVER, THE UNDERTAKING IS MORE ARDUOUS, BECAUSE IT IS UNAWARE OF THE PROCESS OF CREATING AN ORIGINAL CINEMA IN OPPOSITION TO AN IMITATIVE CINEMA WHICH MORE EASILY SATISFIES THE CONCEPT OF PERFECTION DEMANDED BY THE SPECTATOR. IT IS MORE DIFFICULT FOR AN ORIGINAL CINEMA TO REACH PERFECTION SINCE, BEING NEW, IT IS IMPERFECT AND THUS LESS WELL RECEIVED BY THE PUBLIC WHICH, BY CONSENTING TO AN IMITATIVE CINEMA, TENDS TO STIMULATE IMITATION.

OUT OF THE CONCEPT OF IMITATIVE CINEMA AND ORIGINAL CINEMA EMERGED IN BRAZIL THE TERM "CINEMA NOVO." BUT HAVING CHOSEN TO CONFRONT THE BRAZILIAN REALITY, "CINEMA NOVO" GIVES RISE TO A SECOND CHALLENGE: HAVING REJECTED THE LANGUAGE OF IMITATION, WHAT THEN WILL BE THE ORIGINAL FORM EMPLOYED?

"No" to Populism

CINEMA, AS AN ELEMENT IN A CULTURAL PROCESS, WILL NEED TO BE, IN THE FINAL ANALYSIS, THE LANGUAGE OF A SOCIETY. BUT OF WHICH SOCIETY? BRAZIL, A COUNTRY "IN TRANSITION," IS INDIGENIST/VAINGLORIOUS, ROMANTIC/ABOLITIONISTIC, SYMBOLISTIC/NATURALISTIC, REALISTIC/PARNASSIAN, REPUBLICAN/POSITIVISTIC, ANARCHIC/CANNIBALISTIC, NATIONAL-POPULIST/REFORMIST, CONCRETIST/UNDERDEVELOPED, REVOLUTIONARY/CONFORMIST, TROPICAL/STRUCTURALISTIC, ETC. AN AWARENESS OF THE OSCILLATIONS OF OUR CULTURE SO PACKED WITH SUPERSTRUCTURES (GIVEN THAT WE ARE REFERRING TO AN ART PRODUCED BY ELITES, VERY DIFFERENT FROM THE "POPULAR ART PRODUCED BY THE PEOPLE") IS NOT SUFFICIENT TO PROVIDE AN AWARENESS OF WHO WE ARE. WHO ARE WE? WHAT SORT OF CINEMA DO WE HAVE?

THE PUBLIC CANNOT BE BOTHERED WITH ALL THIS—IT GOES TO THE CINEMA TO BE ENTERTAINED BUT ALL OF A SUDDEN DISCOVERS THAT IT IS WATCHING A NATIONAL FILM WHICH DEMANDS AN ENORMOUS EFFORT TO ESTABLISH A DIALOGUE WITH THE FILMMAKER WHO, IN TURN, IS MAKING AN EFFORT TO TALK TO THE PUBLIC . . . IN A NEW LANGUAGE!

THE DISCUSSIONS ON THE TOPIC OF THIS LANGUAGE ARE INVOLVED AND REVEALING. BY REJECTING IMITATIVE CINEMA AND CHOOSING A DIFFERENT FORM

OF EXPRESSION, CINEMA NOVO HAS ALSO REJECTED THE EASIEST PATH REPRESENTED BY THE USUAL NEW LANGUAGE OF SO-CALLED NATIONALIST ART, "POPULISM," REFLECTED IN THE TYPICAL POLITICAL POSITION ADOPTED BY US. LIKE THE *CAUDILHO*, THE ARTIST FEELS HIMSELF FATHER OF THE PEOPLE: THE ORDER OF THE DAY IS "SPEAK SIMPLY SO THAT THE PEOPLE UNDERSTAND."

MY FEELING IS THAT "TO CREATE SIMPLE THINGS FOR SIMPLE PEOPLE" SHOWS A LACK OF RESPECT FOR THE PUBLIC, HOWEVER UNDERDEVELOPED THIS PUBLIC MAY BE. THE PEOPLE MAY BE DISEASED, STARVING AND ILLITERATE, THEY ARE NOT SIMPLE, THEY ARE COMPLEX. THE PATERNALISTIC ARTIST IDEALIZES POPULAR TYPES AS SUBJECTS OF FANTASY WHO, EVEN IN THEIR POVERTY, POSSESS A PHILOSOPHY AND POOR CREATURES, ONLY HAVE TO GET A BIT OF "POLITICAL CONSCIOUSNESS" IN ORDER, FROM ONE DAY TO THE NEXT, TO BE ABLE TO TURN THE HISTORICAL PROCESS AROUND.

THE PRIMITIVENESS OF THIS CONCEPT IS STILL MORE PERNICIOUS IN ITS EFFECTS THAN DERIVATIVE ART, SINCE DERIVATIVE ART HAS THE COURAGE, AT LEAST, TO KNOW ITSELF TO IMITATE AND TO JUSTIFY THE "INDUSTRY OF ARTISTIC TASTE" BY PUTTING FORWARD, AS ITS AIM, GAIN.

POPULIST ART, ON THE OTHER HAND, SEEKS TO JUSTIFY ITS PRIMITIVENESS WITH A "CLEAR CONSCIENCE." THE POPULIST ARTIST IS ALWAYS DECLARING, "I AM NOT AN INTELLECTUAL, I AM WITH THE PEOPLE, MY ART IS BEAUTIFUL BECAUSE IT COMMUNICATES," ETC. IT COMMUNICATES TO THE PEOPLE THEIR OWN ALIENATION, THEIR OWN ILLITERACY AND COARSENESS, BORN OUT OF THEIR STATE OF POVERTY WHICH MAKES THEM REGARD LIFE WITH CONTEMPT.

THE BRAZILIAN PEOPLE, WHILE ACCEPTING THEIR POVERTY, ARE ALWAYS CRITICAL OF IT. ONE FINDS IN POPULAR MUSIC A GREAT MANY *SAMBAS* THAT SAY: "I'VE GOT NO BEANS, I MAKE SOUP OUT OF STONES" AND "I'LL DIE ON THE SIDEWALK, BUT SMILING ALL THE WHILE" OR "THE *FAVELA* [URBAN SLUM] IS THE ENTRY TO PARADISE." POPULISM DRAWS FROM THESE SOURCES AND SERVES THEM BACK TO THE PEOPLE, UNGARNISHED BY ANY DEEPER INTERPRETATIONS. THE PEOPLE, SEEING HOW THE ART CLOTHES ITSELF IN THE PRIMITIVE COMICALNESS OF UNDERDEVELOPMENT, FIND THEIR MISFORTUNE HILARIOUS AND DIE LAUGHING.

THUS IS EXPLAINED THE SUCCESS OF THE *CHANCHADA*[3], BASED ON THE PRETTY POVERTY OF THE *CABOCLO*[4], OR THE MIDDLE-CLASS. THENCE IS DERIVED THE SUCCESS OF ANY DRAMA CONTAINING SOCIAL STATEMENT.

THE POPULIST WILL ALSO DEFEND THE IDEA ACCORDING TO WHICH "THE FORMS OF COMMUNICATION SHOULD BE USED . . . TO COUNTERACT ALIENATION." BUT THESE "FORMS OF COMMUNICATION" AS WE HAVE ALREADY SEEN ARE THE COLONIZING CULTURE'S INSTRUMENTS OF ALIENATION.

AN UNDERDEVELOPED COUNTRY IS NOT NECESSARILY OBLIGED TO HAVE UNDERDEVELOPED ARTS. IT IS NAIVE AND IN SOME WAYS REACTIONARY TO THINK THAT ART OFFENDS. SHARING THE GENERAL MALAISE OF BRAZILIAN CULTURE, CINEMA NOVO HAS REJECTED POPULISM THUS REDUCING THE POSSIBILITY FOR

IT TO MANEUVER THE PUBLIC. HAS IT CHOSEN THE WAY OF SUBTERFUGE?

WHILE THE PROBLEM OF COMMUNICATION GENERATES WIDESPREAD DISCUSSION, CINEMA NOVO CONSIDERS THE PROBLEM OF CREATING. ARE CREATIVITY AND CINEMATOGRAPHY RECONCILABLE?

THE MAJORITY OF OBSERVERS REPLY THAT CINEMA IS, AND CAN ONLY BE, THE ART OF COMMUNICATION. FOR THESE OBSERVERS, *CREATING* IS OPPOSED TO *COMMUNICATING*. THE APOSTLES OF COMMUNICATION WILL AVOID AT ANY COST, HOWEVER, ASKING THEMSELVES THIS: ON HOW MANY LEVELS IS COMMUNICATION PRODUCED, AND, MORE THAN THIS, WHAT IS REAL COMMUNICATION?

CINEMA NOVO CLAIMS TO HAVE BEEN SUCCESSFUL IN ATTAINING GENUINE COMMUNICATION. STATING THIS, IT FREES ITSELF FROM THE COMMUNICATIVE CERTAINTY OF "POPULISM." THIS IS A MISLEADING BOAST BECAUSE, DEEP DOWN, POPULISM HARDLY CULTIVATES THE "CULTURAL VALUES" OF AN UNDERDEVELOPED SOCIETY AT ALL. THESE "VALUES" ARE WORTHLESS—OUR CULTURE, A PRODUCT OF A LACK OF ABILITY AT THE LEVEL OF ARTISINAL SKILLS, OF LAZINESS, OF ILLITERACY, AND OF IMPOTENT POLITICS, OF SOCIAL STAGNATION, IS A "CULTURE OF THE YEAR ZERO." SO BURN DOWN THE LIBRARIES THEN!

WITH EVERY FILM, CINEMA NOVO, LIKE THE LUMIERES, STARTS FROM ZERO. WHEN FILMMAKERS ORGANIZE THEMSELVES TO START FROM ZERO, TO CREATE A CINEMA WITH NEW TYPES OF PLOT LINES, OF PERFORMANCE, OF RHYTHM, AND WITH A DIFFERENT POETRY, THEY THROW THEMSELVES INTO THE DANGEROUS REVOLUTIONARY ADVENTURE, OF *LEARNING WHILE THEY WORK*, OF SIMULTANEOUSLY SUSTAINING THEORY AND PRACTICE, OF REFORMULATING EVERY THEORY THROUGH EVERY PRACTICE, OF CONDUCTING THEMSELVES ACCORDING TO THE APT DICTUM COINED BY NELSON PEREIRA DOS SANTOS FROM SOME PORTUGUESE POET: "DON'T KNOW WHERE I'M GOING, BUT I KNOW I'M NOT GOING OVER THERE."

THE PUBLIC FEELS ITSELF PROPELLED INTO THE THEATERS. IT FEELS OBLIGED TO READ A NEW GENRE OF CINEMA: TECHNICALLY IMPERFECT, DRAMATICALLY DISSONANT, POETICALLY REBELLIOUS, SOCIOLOGICALLY IMPRECISE, JUST AS THE OFFICIAL BRAZILIAN SOCIOLOGY IS ITSELF IMPRECISE, POLITICALLY AGGRESSIVE AND INSECURE, JUST AS THE POLITICAL AVANT-GARDE IN BRAZIL IS ITSELF, VIOLENT AND SAD, RATHER MORE SAD THAN VIOLENT, LIKE OUR CARNIVAL WHICH IS MUCH MORE SAD THAN GAY.

FOR US, NEW DOES NOT MEAN *PERFECT*, SINCE THE NOTION OF PERFECTION IS A CONCEPT INHERITED FROM THE COLONIZING CULTURES WHICH HAVE DETERMINED THEIR CONCEPT OF *PERFECTION* TO TAKE UP THE INTERESTS OF A *POLITICAL IDEAL*.

MODERN ART WHICH IS TRULY REVOLUTIONARY IN ITS ETHICS AND AESTHETICS IS OPPOSED, THROUGH ITS LANGUAGE, TO A LANGUAGE OF DOMINATION. IF THE SUM OF GUILT FELT BY BOURGEOIS ARTISTS LEADS THEM TO BE OPPOSED TO THEIR OWN WORLD, IN THE NAME OF THAT AWARENESS WHICH THE PEOPLE NEED BUT DO NOT HAVE, THE ONLY WAY OUT IS TO TRULY OPPOSE THROUGH THE IMPURE

AGGRESSIVENESS OF TRUE MODERN ART ALL THE MORAL AND AESTHETIC HYPOCRISY THAT LEAD THE ARTISTS INTO ALIENATION.

THUS THE CINEMA NOVO'S AMBITION COMES TO BE CONSIDERED AS SOMETHING OVER AND ABOVE THE CINEMA. THE CINEMA, EVERYBODY SAYS, IS A FORM OF ENTERTAINMENT. THOSE WHO GO TO THE CINEMA, GO TO ENJOY THEMSELVES. NOBODY WANTS TO HAVE TO FACE PROBLEMS AT THE CINEMA. ART IS THE TERRITORY OF THE THEATER, OF PAINTING, OF POETRY. CINEMA, ON THE OTHER HAND, COSTS MONEY. THE FILMMAKER ARTIST IS AN IRRESPONSIBLE, A CRETIN, OR ELSE AN INTELLECTUAL.

IN BRAZIL, INTELLECTUAL IS SYNONYMOUS WITH HOMOSEXUAL. SO YOU NEED A LOT OF COURAGE TO BE AN INTELLECTUAL AND, AS AN INTELLECTUAL, TO SEIZE THE POWER OF CINEMA. I THINK THAT BRAZIL IS A COUNTRY WHICH DESPERATELY NEEDS THE CINEMA AND, ABOVE ALL, THAT THE CINEMA WILL BE THE ART OF BRAZIL PAR EXCELLENCE. ROME, HOWEVER, WAS NOT BUILT IN A DAY, AND CINEMA NOVO ONLY BEGAN IN 1962, AND, TO DATE [1969], HAS PRODUCED A MERE 32 FILMS.

The Distribution System

BECAUSE CINEMA IS A BUSINESS, THE SECRET LIES IN THE DISTRIBUTION. ONCE THE FILM IS READY, THE PRODUCER NEEDS TO SELL IT, BUT BEFORE IT GETS TO THE EXHIBITOR, IT MUST FIRST PASS THROUGH THE HANDS OF AN INTERMEDIARY, THE DISTRIBUTOR, WHO PAYS ONLY FOR THE DRAWING UP OF CONTRACTS AND THE ORGANIZATION. THE PUBLICITY COSTS ARE DIVIDED INTO THREE, BUT THE PRO-PORTION FOR WHICH THE PRODUCER IS RESPONSIBLE RUNS TO 80%. THE EXHIBITOR TAKES 50% OF THE GROSS EARNINGS, THE PRODUCERS BETWEEN 30-40% (PAY-ING 80% OF THE PUBLICITY COSTS), WHILE THE DISTRIBUTOR TAKES BETWEEN 10-15% HAVING TO LAY OUT ONLY THE MINIMUM NECESSARY. BUT THE DISTRIBUTOR BILLS THE EXHIBITOR AND THUS MANAGES THE PRODUCER'S CAPITAL OUTLAY.

USUALLY THE PRODUCER, ON COMPLETION OF A FILM, FINDS HIMSELF PEN-NILESS. SO . . . HE GOES TO THE DISTRIBUTOR FOR HELP. USUALLY, THE DISTRIBUTOR GIVES HIM AN ADVANCE, BUT THE MONEY LENT IS DEDUCTED AT SOURCE FROM THE FIRST RETURNS, SO THAT THE PRODUCER, WHO GIVES UP THE INITIAL INCOME TO THE DISTRIBUTOR, MUST PAY OFF THE BANK WITH THE SUBSEQUENT RETURNS . . . ALWAYS SMALLER THAN THE FIRST.

THE BRAZILIAN CINEMA WENT THROUGH THIS FOR YEARS. WHEN SOME SAO PAULO CAPITALISTS ORGANIZED THE LARGE-SCALE VERA CRUZ FILM VENTURE, THEY SAW TO EVERYTHING EXCEPT THE DISTRIBUTION WHICH WAS ENTRUSTED TO COL-UMBIA PICTURES. COLUMBIA ORGANIZED DISTRIBUTION, BUT WITH LESS PUBLICI-TY AND COMMERCIAL DRIVE THAN THEY GAVE THEIR OWN FILMS.

IN THAT "AGE OF TITANS," THE THEORISTS OF SAO PAULO (THE SAME ONES WHO, TODAY, ARE TO BE FOUND AT THE NATIONAL INSTITUTE OF CINEMA) BELIEVED THAT THE CINEMA OF "STUDIOS," STARS, WARDROBE MANAGERS, FLOODLIGHTS,

ASTRONOMICAL SALARIES, ITALIAN DIRECTORS, WAS AN IDEAL CINEMA. AFTER EIGHTEEN YEARS, VERA CRUZ COLLAPSED. NOT EVEN THE SUCCESS OBTAINED BY *O CANGACEIRO* COULD PREVENT THIS CINEMATOGRAPHIC EMPIRE FROM CRUMBLING. WERE THE BACKERS TO BLAME? I DON'T THINK SO, IT WAS THE FAULT OF AD-HOC PRODUCERS, IMPORTED DIRECTORS, IRRESPONSIBLE ACTORS, AND OF IDEALISTS WHO HOODWINKED THE SAO PAULO BOURGEOISIE BY DECLARING THAT ART COSTS MONEY AND THAT, THANKS TO ART, EVEN WITH A SMALL MARKET, SAO PAULO WOULD HAVE ACQUIRED AN INDUSTRY THAT COULD RIVAL THE UNITED STATES.

DISTRIBUTION, WE SHOULD ADD, CAN PERFORM NO MIRACLE TO MAKE THE PUBLIC ENJOY A BAD FILM OR TO ENABLE THEM TO UNDERSTAND A GOOD ART FILM. BUT DISTRIBUTION CAN, VIA INTELLIGENT AND PERSISTENT PROGRAMMING, AND VIA EFFICIENT CONTROL, MARKET A FILM THROUGHOUT THE BRAZILIAN TERRITORY AND STAND A VERY GOOD CHANCE TO RECOVER PRODUCTION/DISTRIBUTION COSTS AND EVEN MAKE A PROFIT. BY CONSOLIDATING AND EXTENDING THE DISTRIBUTION NETWORK IN BRAZIL ONE WOULD, AT A CONSERVATIVE ESTIMATE, CREATE A 35% INCREASE IN THE EARNING POTENTIAL OF FILMS IN BLACK AND WHITE THAT DO NOT EXCEED THE AVERAGE BUDGET OF 150,000 CRUZEIROS [ABOUT $26,000]. THUS, EVEN IF A FILM IS "UNSUCCESSFUL" IT CAN STILL PAY FOR ITSELF BY MEANS OF WHAT WE CALL MINIMAL "NATURAL" RETURNS.

The Heart of the Cinema

IT IS AT THIS POINT THAT DISTRIBUTION BECOMES THE HEART OF THE CINEMA. A WELL-ORGANIZED DISTRIBUTOR CAN CREATE A PUBLIC FOR A PARTICULAR TYPE OF PRODUCT. THE BEST EXAMPLE OF THIS IS PROVIDED BY THE BIRTH OF THE ART CINEMA MARKET, WHICH HAS COME TO BE A WORLDWIDE PHENOMENON. AS THE PUBLIC WAS ABSORBED INTO THE TELEVISION, THE CINEMA MARKET MADE INROADS INTO THAT PART OF THE PUBLIC WHICH EXPECTED SOMETHING GREATER FROM THE CINEMA. THUS AROSE THE ART CINEMA MARKET, WHICH IS CONSTANTLY GROWING AND NOW THREATENS TO COMPETE WITH THE MAJOR CINEMATOGRAPHIC MARKET.

THE MOST COURAGEOUS EXHIBITORS REALIZED THAT THE ONLY WAY TO ATTRACT THE SPECTATOR, GENERALLY ATTACHED TO THE TELEVISION, WAS TO SUMMON HIM TO SEE "ART" IN HIS THEATERS. AND SO WAS ESTABLISHED A BUSINESS THAT CAME TO BE CALLED THE "OLD BUSINESS" OF . . . ART. IN THIS MARKET THE FRENCH NEW WAVE, FELLINI AND ANTONIONI, INGMAR BERGMAN, LUIS BUNUEL, AND MANY OTHER OLD AND YOUNG DIRECTORS, ESTABLISHED THEMSELVES. IN THE WAY ART CINEMA WAS PRESENTED, ONE TENDED TO READ THE NAME OF THE DIRECTOR IN THE PLACE OF THAT OF THE ACTORS. AND WITH THE EXCEPTION OF THREE OR FOUR, THE WORK OF VERY FEW AMERICAN DIRECTORS WAS BEING SHOWN IN THESE CINEMAS.

Thus the auteur, and with him the Art Cinema, emerged. And we thus conclude without much effort that Cinema Novo's struggle with the public is not a regional but a universal struggle. This struggle has the dimensions of a cultural revolution, with all the risks that any revolution involves.

In 1964, Luis Carlos Barreto became aware of this phenomenon and, with great difficulty, managed to convince the producer-directors of Cinema Novo that it would only be possible to sustain an original film language through the direct control of the market. He argued that the films would take a long time to modify the public's moral and artistic conceptions. To do this, he added, the films would need to be supported by a self-sufficient distribution structure that could distribute this sort of product in a planned way. Thus DiFilm emerged which today competes on an equal footing with the other distributors in Brazil.

The increase in receipts has been fast, and the public attendance at Cinema Novo films jumped by 40% between 1964 and today. Each Cinema Novo film, thanks to efficient distribution, is seen by an average of 50,000 to 100,000 people, in Rio de Janeiro alone. A transitional film like *Todas as Mulheres do Mundo* [*All the Women in the World*], which betrays a spontaneous, if somewhat unrigorous maker, has been seen by around 40,000 people.

Today DiFilm has fifteen films in distribution and this year will add another ten titles. Without much effort, the profit on the gross income would be about 10% to 15%, automatically re-invested in the concern's organization and in film production. This profit margin has enabled the co-production of nearly ten films. The company has also started to export its films, through agents in Paris and Buenos Aires, which are the centers for international distribution.

The majority of Cinema Novo's films being accepted into the Art Cinema's circuits abroad, beyond constituting a supplementary market which nurtures big perspectives, have vested Cinema Novo with a prestige that enables it to confront pressures from all sides.

It is an undeniable fact that an artistic language cannot consolidate itself in the abstract, that is to say that without economic power there cannot be cultural power. DiFilm has managed to insert itself into the system by acknowledging the system's objective reality, that of *business*, and can thus sell a subjective product, that is...art. What is more, the growth of the Art Cinema market represents an increasing need felt by the public, to be informed about, and able to discuss, its own destiny. This need mirrors the mobilization, though still slow, of a real Brazilian culture, to which our avant-garde in the universities contributes, along with the publishing movement, popular music, the new theater, literature,

THE NEW PRESS . . . AND CINEMA NOVO. CINEMA NOVO IS INSERTING ITSELF IN-
TO OUR SOCIETY AS AN AGENT WHICH, BY PARTICIPATING IN THE CREATION OF
QUALITY PRODUCTS, IS STRIVING FOR A FORM OF EXPRESSION, DIFFERENT FROM,
AND MORE EFFECTIVE THAN, THAT OF AMERICAN CINEMA.

ALL THE SAME, THE IMPORTANT QUESTION REMAINS UNANSWERED: WHAT IS
THIS CINEMATOGRAPHIC LANGUAGE I HAVE DEFENDED, WHICH I HAVE DIFFEREN-
TIATED FROM THE OTHERS WITHOUT HAVING SO FAR DEFINED?

The Hero Without Character

MARIO DE ANDRADE, THE THEORETICIAN AND CREATOR OF GREAT IMPOR-
TANCE IN THE 1922 MODERN ART MOVEMENT, WROTE A BOOK *MACUNAIMA,
THE HERO WITHOUT CHARACTER*, WHICH, LIKE *OS SERTOES* [*REBELLION IN THE
BACKLAND*][5], IS FUNDAMENTAL WITH REGARD TO KNOWLEDGE AND UNDERSTAND-
ING OF BRAZIL. JOAQUIM PEDRO DE ANDRADE IS CURRENTLY INVOLVED IN PREPAR-
ING THE ADAPTATION OF THE BOOK, WHICH WILL HAVE THE TITLE *O HEROI DE
MAU CARACTER* [*THE HERO OF BAD CHARACTER*]. BEGINNING WITH THE CON-
CEPT OF "HERO," WE SHALL ATTEMPT TO ANALYZE, IN THE MOST OBJECTIVE WAY
POSSIBLE, WHAT THE *LANGUAGE OF CINEMA NOVO* IS.

THE HERO IS AN EXCEPTIONAL CHARACTER WHICH ANY NOVELIST, PLAYWRIGHT
OR FILMMAKER CHOOSES FOR HIS DRAMA. EVEN THE HERO WHO EMBODIES AND
EXPRESSES A SOCIAL GROUP, IS TRANSFORMED BY THAT SYNTHESIS, INTO SOMETHING
EXCEPTIONAL. A DRAMA WITHOUT HEROES WOULD BE A DRAMA WITHOUT MEN.
CLEVERLY USING THE KEY CHARACTERS OF THE NINETEENTH CENTURY NOVEL AND
PLAY, THE AMERICAN CINEMA CREATED HEROES WHO CORRESPONDED TO THE
CINEMA'S VISION, VIOLENT AND HUMANITARIAN AT THE SAME TIME, OF THE "WORLD
OF PROGRESS." HANDSOME, STRONG, HONEST, SENTIMENTAL AND IMPLACABLE MEN.
INDEPENDENT, MATERNAL, LOVING, SINCERE AND UNDERSTANDING WOMEN.

AMERICAN PRODUCERS HAVE ALWAYS MADE FILMS WHICH WERE ADAPTED TO
THE NEEDS OF THE MOMENT. ONLY A SMALL NUMBER OF FILMS HAVE EVER OB-
TAINED CRITICAL PENETRATION WHICH, HOWEVER, NEVER WENT OUTSIDE THE SPHERE
OF SOCIAL STATEMENT. EVEN COURAGEOUS AND TOPICAL SUBJECTS, AS IN JOHN
STEINBECK'S NOVEL *THE GRAPES OF WRATH*, COULD BE SUBMITTED TO FANTASTIC
CHANGES: JOHN FORD, A GREAT TECHNICIAN GIFTED WITH A SENSE OF HUMOR,
TRANSFORMED THE POLITICAL THEME OF THE BOOK INTO THE SOCIAL-SENTIMENTAL
THEME OF THE FILM.

THE EXAMPLE OF *THE GRAPES OF WRATH* HELPS ONE TO SEE THAT THE MOST
IMPORTANT THING ABOUT A FILM IS NEVER THE STORY BUT ALWAYS THE "MISE-EN-
SCENE." ONE OF THE MAIN ERRORS COMMITTED BY THE PUBLIC AND THE CRITICS
IS THAT OF CONSIDERING THE *STORY* TO BE *THE BASIS OF THE FILM*. IN CINEMA,
THE STORY IS ONLY ONE ELEMENT IN THE "MISE-EN-SCENE." THE DIRECTOR, THE
MAN WHO HAS THE JOB OF CREATING A WORLD OF IMAGES, MAKES USE OF THE

STORY, ACTORS, PHOTOGRAPHY, TECHNICAL EFFECTS, RHYTHM, LANDSCAPE, DIALOGUE AND TITLES TO REALIZE HIS WORK. AND HE WILL NEVER CREATE HIS WORK FROM THE VISION OF THE WRITER, BUT FROM HIS OWN.

TO UNDERSTAND A FILM PROPERLY, THE SPECTATOR MUST LOOK, SIMULTANEOUSLY, AT THE LANDSCAPE, THE TONALITY OF THE PHOTOGRAPHY, THE INTERPRETATION OF THE ACTORS; HE MUST LISTEN PROPERLY TO THE DIALOGUE AND THE SCORE AND MUST READ PROPERLY THE TITLES; HE MUST BE PROPERLY AWARE OF WHEN THE ACTOR'S FACE ALONE IS SHOWN IN A CLOSEUP, OR WHEN THE ACTOR IS SHOWN FULL-FRAME, ALONE IN THE LANDSCAPE, OR ELSE IN THE COMPANY OF OTHERS.

IN CLASSIC AMERICAN CINEMA, IN JOHN FORD'S *THE GRAPES OF WRATH* [1940] FOR EXAMPLE, EVERYTHING WAS CONCEIVED SO AS NOT TO CREATE CONFLICT FOR THE SPECTATOR. THE DIRECTOR SOUGHT TO BREAK EVERYTHING DOWN, TO THE SMALLEST PARTICULAR, INTO LITTLE PIECES. INTO THESE HE INSERTED HIS IDEOLOGY AND SERVED UP THE WHOLE ALL READY FOR THE SPECTATOR TO SWALLOW. THE PUBLIC GOES TO SEE THE FILM AND CAN UNDERSTAND IT WITHOUT HAVING TO THINK. IT COMES OUT OF THE CINEMA SATISFIED BECAUSE, REALLY, IT HAS NOTHING IN COMMON WITH WHAT IT HAS SEEN. IT FEELS ONLY THE STIMULUS WHICH ENABLES IT TO OBTAIN SOME OF THE PHYSICAL ATTRIBUTES OF THE HERO OR THE HEROINE: BEAUTY, WILL-POWER, COURAGE, INTEGRITY AND VICTORY. BECAUSE LIFE OFFERS NONE OF THESE THINGS TO THEM, THE PUBLIC TAKES REFUGE IN THE CINEMA.

A FRENCH CRITIC ONCE TOLD ME HOW MUCH HE LIKED METRO MOVIES IN COLOR BECAUSE, BEING SO UNHAPPY WITH REALITY, METRO, FOR HIM, WAS A NEW PARADISE.

TODAY THE AMERICAN CINEMA IS FULL OF SELF-DOUBT, JUST AS AMERICAN SOCIETY ITSELF IS PERPLEXED AS NEVER BEFORE. THE DEATH OF KENNEDY SEEMS TO HAVE OPENED THE GATES TO NEW QUESTIONS, AND TODAY AMERICAN COMMERCIAL FILMS NO LONGER REFLECT ON THE OLD IDEAS OF JOHN FORD OR HOWARD HAWKS. AT THE MOMENT IN WHICH THE AMERICAN CHARACTER ITSELF ENTERS A CRISIS, IT IS ONLY RIGHT THAT THE IDEA OF THE HERO CHANGES. THUS EMERGES THE ANTI-HERO.

One Who is Living the Crisis

THE BRAZILIAN FILMMAKER IS INTERESTED IN EVERYTHING THAT HAPPENS IN BRAZIL, IN THE WORLD, IN SOCIETY AND THE CINEMA. IT IS NOT POSSIBLE TO ISOLATE ART, STILL LESS THE CINEMA—THE FILMMAKER IS A MAN WHO IS CONSTANTLY MOVING. HE GOES FROM THE CORRIDORS OF BANKS TO THE LABYRINTHS OF LABORATORIES, FROM THE SOPHISTICATED WORLD OF ACTORS TO THE VIOLENT WORLD OF RENTERS, FROM LUXURY APARTMENTS TO THE MOST DISTANT CORNERS OF FORESTS, AND THROUGH THIS, IF HE HAS A GRAIN OF SENSITIVITY, HE WILL EXPERIENCE AT CLOSE QUARTERS A REALITY SO COMPLEX AS TO MAKE HIM CONSTANTLY UNSURE OF THE WORLD IN WHICH HE LIVES.

FOR THIS REASON, OUR HERO MUST BE THE *MULTIPLE BRAZILIAN MAN*, WHO IS LIVING EVERY CRISIS WHERE IT OCCURS. THE INSTABILITY OF THIS ACTIVE AND REFLEXIVE CHARACTER CANNOT BE FOUND IN OUR CINEMA, BUT MAY BE ENCOUNTERED IN OUR COUNTRY'S NOVELS AND PLAYS, AND IS BOUND TO THAT SAME CONSCIOUSNESS WHICH OUR WRITERS HAVE OF REALITY. AND WE CANNOT IGNORE THE PRECARIOUSNESS OF A CONCEPT OF REALISM. IN A *REVEALED*, DEVELOPED SOCIETY, IT IS A LOT EASIER TO CONCEIVE OF AND PRACTICE A DRAMATIC REALISM THAN, AS WE HAVE ALREADY SEEN, IT IS IN A SOCIETY WHICH LACKS ANY INFORMATION. OUR FILMMAKER TAKES PART IN THE DISCOVERY OF THE CONSCIOUSNESS OF WHAT IS BRAZILIAN, THROUGH HIS WISH TO RECORD VIA DIRECT IMAGES, AND HIS WISH TO DISCUSS IN THE LIGHT OF WHAT HE KNOWS (OR THINKS HE KNOWS) OF MAN, OURSELVES AND OTHERS.

VIDAS SECAS, THE FILM MADE BY NELSON PEREIRA DOS SANTOS IN 1963, TAKEN FROM THE NOVEL BY GRACILIANO RAMOS, DID NOT HAVE ANY POPULAR SUCCESS EVEN THOUGH IT WAS A WORK RICH IN CULTURAL POLEMICS. FABIANO, THE PROTAGONIST, IS A *RETIRANTE* (A MAN WHO EMIGRATES FROM THE ARID REGIONS IN THE NORTHEAST OF BRAZIL, TO ESCAPE THE DROUGHT); HE IS A WEAKLING, TIMID, UGLY AND STARVING; HE IS NOT A COWARD, BUT HE IS LED BY HIS FEAR OF AN UNKNOWN POLITICAL POWER WHICH OPPRESSES HIM, TO CONSIDER HIS HONOR, WHICH LACKS ANY IDEA OF REVENGE, TO BE THE COMPENSATION FOR HIS HUMILIATION.

FOR *VIDAS SECAS*, LUIS BARRETO DEVELOPED DIRECT CAMERA WORK. HE TRIED TO REPRESENT THE NORTHEASTERN SUN, ITS EFFECTS ON THE LANDSCAPE AND ON THE MEN. THE SCORCHED CHARACTERS, AT THE BEGINNING, MOVE ACROSS THE VAST FLAT *CAATINGA* (AN AREA OF SCRUB AT THE EDGE OF THE *SERTAO*). ALREADY, AT THE FIRST SHOT, A NEW CINEMA IS PROPOSED. FOR FOUR MINUTES, WE CONTEMPLATE THE SAME IMAGE. WE SEE THE CHARACTERS IN LONG SHOT, SLOWLY GETTING NEARER THE AUDIENCE. THEY ARE LED BY A DOG CALLED BALAIA (WHALE). AS A BACKGROUND THERE IS THE SAD CREAKING OF THE BULLOCK CART, THE SOUND GROWING LOUDER WITHOUT CHANGING PITCH.

THE SPECTATOR WHO HAS MADE HIS WAY TO THE CINEMA TO WATCH A DRAMA ABOUT THE DROUGHT IS ASSAILED BY THE OPENING SCENE WHICH ATTEMPTS TO OBLIGE HIM NOT TO WATCH, BUT TO PARTICIPATE IN THE TRAGEDY OF THE DROUGHT. THE WHOLE FILM TAKES PLACE IN THE SAME WAY: THE WHITE AND DAZZLING SHOTS FOLLOW ON ONE FROM ANOTHER, BUT EACH SHOT REVEALS SOME NEW ASPECT OF THIS WORLD: PARCHED WORLD, PARCHED LIVES. THE SPECTATOR IS MADE TO THINK ABOUT WHAT HE SEES, BUT THIS IRRITATES HIM: IF THE HERO HIMSELF, THE SPECTATOR ASKS HIMSELF, DOES NOTHING TO CHANGE THE SITUATION, IF FABIANO MERELY CONFINES HIMSELF TO RUNNING AWAY AT THE POINT WHEN THE DROUGHT THREATENS TO KILL HIM, THEN WHY SHOULD HE, THE SPECTATOR, BOTHER ABOUT FABIANO, LET ALONE GET BORED WATCHING THIS GOOD-FOR-NOTHING FABIANO ON THE SCREEN?

THE SPECTATOR CAN SEE THAT THIS FILM IS DIFFERENT—HE READ IN THE NEWSPAPERS THAT IT HAD AN ARTISTIC TOUCH—BUT IT DOES NOT HOLD UP AND, HE COMPLAINS, IF IT HAD AT LEAST BEEN MADE IN COLOR, HAD BEEN LESS SAD . . .

A POPULIST FILM WOULD HAVE SHOWN FABIANO SINGING HIS *XAXADO* (FOLK SONG) BY THE FIRE, CREATING A SUB-LITERARY GENRE AROUND HIS LITTLE BLADE OF GRASS; FABIANO, AT THE END, WOULD HAVE KILLED THE YELLOW SOLDIER. SINHA VITORIA, THE GRUMPY SOUR WOMAN, WOULD HAVE DIED, AND FABIANO WOULD HAVE MARRIED THE BEAUTIFUL PEASANT GIRL AFTER HAVING RECEIVED THE BIT OF LAND ALLOTTED TO HIM BY THE AGRARIAN REFORM, WHERE HE WOULD PLANT HIS VEGETABLES NEXT TO THE DYKE BUILT BY THE SUDENE (STATE ORGANIZATION FOR THE IRRIGATION OF NORTHEAST BRAZIL).

THE SPECTATOR OF *VIDAS SECAS* IS NOT SEEKING A FILM WHICH ELICITS HIS TAME MONKEY'S MENTALITY TO REACT IN A PREDETERMINED WAY—HE WILL REFUSE TO FOLLOW THE MOVEMENT OF THE FILM AS HE MUST DO, IF HE IS TO UNDERSTAND WHY FABIANO DOES NOT MAKE THE BEST OF ALL POSSIBLE WORLDS, THAT FOR FABIANO TO CHANGE, HE AND THE OTHERS MUST CHANGE THE WORLD, ETC.

THE PROTAGONIST IRRITATES US. NOBODY SYMPATHIZES WITH HIS FATE, JUST AS NOBODY SYMPATHIZES WITH OURS. LOST AND ABANDONED IN THE *SERTAO*, OR IN THE CITY, OUR DESTINY IS IN OUR OWN HANDS.

VIDAS SECAS IS A FILM WHICH IS ABSOLUTELY DRAMATIC. NELSON PEREIRA DOS SANTOS ANALYZES THROUGH IT AN ASPECT OF *SERTANEJA* (OF THE *SERTAO*) SOCIETY; HE TELLS THE TRUTH, BUT FEW PEOPLE CAN SEE OR HEAR IT: HAS THE DIRECTOR MADE A MISTAKE?

IN SHOOTING *OS FUZIS* [*THE GUNS*, 1964], RUY GUERRA HAS TAKEN ANOTHER POSITION. HE SHOWS US A GROUP OF *RITIRANTES* (MIGRANTS)—THIS TIME A GROUP OF MEN LIKE THE YELLOW SOLDIER WHO HUMILIATED AND BEAT UP FABIANO. THE SOLDIERS HAVE BEEN CALLED INTO THE REGION TO MAINTAIN ORDER: THEY SHOOT ANY *FLAGELADO* (DROUGHT VICTIM) WHO TRIES TO RAID THE FOOD STORE. THE SOLDIERS ARE HUMAN BEINGS, BUT THEY HAVE A WORLD OF THEIR OWN. FOR THEM, THE *FLAGELADO* IS AN INFERIOR BEING WHO, FOR SOME REASON, HAS NOT MANAGED TO GET OUT OF HIS MISERABLE STATE, PROBABLY BECAUSE HE IS LAZY. HE, THE SOLDIER, HAS ALREADY HAD HIS REVOLUTION.

IN A SMALL TOWN, THEY MEET GAUCHO, FORMERLY A SOLDIER, NOW A LORRY DRIVER. HE IS AN ADVENTURER, A SKEPTIC, READY FOR ANYTHING. HE IS A MAN WITHOUT MORAL VALUES, WHO IS FED UP WITH THEIR PASSIVITY, AND CAPABLE OF TAKING A GUN TO DEFEND THE *FLAGELADOS*. HE IS SHOT DOWN BY THE SOLDIERS. GAUCHO DOES NOT MANAGE TO PULL IT OFF QUITE LIKE A TEXAN SHERIFF, AND THE SPECTATOR GOES AGAINST A FILM, WHICH, IN THE FINAL ANALYSIS, HAS OFFERED HIM NEITHER ANY SOLUTIONS NOR A STORY WHICH IS EASY TO FOLLOW.

OS FUZIS IS QUITE A DIFFERENT SORT OF FILM FROM *VIDAS SECAS*, AND PRESENTS US WITH A DIFFERENT ASPECT OF THE PROBLEM OF THE NORTHEAST: THE RELATIONSHIP BETWEEN THE FORCES OF ORDER AND THE SUFFERING. TO EX-

PRESS ALL THE ASPECTS OF THIS TRAGEDY, IT REQUIRED A VIOLENT LANGUAGE.

FOR RUY GUERRA, THE STORY IS RELATIVELY UNIMPORTANT—THE SPECTATOR MUST DWELL, AS RUY GUERRA HAS DONE, ON A LENGTHY SHOT WHICH SHOWS A *SERTANEJO*[6] SCRATCHING THE EARTH FOR A ROOT TO EAT, OR ANOTHER WHERE A SOLDIER, THANKS TO THE TRAINING WHICH HAS DEFORMED HIM, LOADS A RIFLE BLINDFOLDED, AND KILLS BY REFLEX, WITHOUT KNOWING WHO OR WHY HE IS SHOOTING.

IN THIS EXUBERANT NATURAL SETTING WHERE THE ACTION TAKES PLACE, THE SPECTATOR WOULD LIKE A COWBOY FILM, WITH ITS GRADUAL AND NATURAL RHYTHM, SPARED THE CONFLICTS BETWEEN MAN, LANDSCAPE AND SOCIAL ENVIRONMENT.

IN *DEUS O DIABO NA TERRA DO SOL* [*BLACK GOD, WHITE DEVIL*, 1964], MADE AROUND THE SAME TIME, I TOOK AS A STARTING POINT SOME POPULAR LEGENDS TO SHOW STILL ANOTHER ASPECT OF THE DRAMA OF THE NORTHEAST. MANUEL, A DOWN-AND-OUT OX-DRIVER, KILLS HIS BOSS AND GOES OFF WITH THE BOSS'S WOMAN IN SEARCH OF TRUTH, AND FINISHES UP BY BECOMING THE *CABRA* (A HITMAN) FOR A *CANGACEIRO*. WITH THE DEATH OF THE *CANGACEIRO*, HE LOSES FAITH IN EVERYTHING AND GOES MAD, LEAVING HIS WIFE AND RUNNING OFF TO AN IMAGINARY SEA TO FREE HIMSELF.

THIS FILM, A CULTURAL POLEMIC LIKE *VIDAS SECAS* AND *OS FUZIS*, UPSET THE PUBLIC AND FAILED TO OBTAIN THE SUCCESS WHICH WAS HOPED FOR. A YOUNG FILM PROGRAMMER TOLD ME THAT HAD MANUEL JOINED UP WITH ANTONIO DAS MORTES TO KILL *CANGANCEIROS* AND THE "HOLY MEN," HAD HE AFTERWARDS BEEN REWARDED BY RECEIVING A *FAZENDA* (LAND HOLDING) FROM SOME RICH COLONEL, THEN THE FILM WOULD HAVE BEEN A SUCCESS. BUT TO HAVE CHANGED THE DIRECTION OF MANUEL'S PROGRESS WOULD HAVE MEANT CHANGING MANUEL'S VERY CHARACTER, FOR HE IS WEAK, STARVING AND PERPLEXED, LIKE FABIANO. FABIANO, BECAUSE OF HIS PERPLEXITY, GIVES UP AND STAYS. MANUEL, IN THE SAME STATE OF MIND, KEEPS ON GOING, ALONG THE PATHS INDICATED BY A BLOODY MYSTICISM, USING UP HIS ENERGIES THROUGH AN ABSTRACT MORALITY AND A PHYSICAL AND SPIRITUAL PURGE.

SO THE PROTAGONIST'S BEHAVIOR, DECIDED BEFOREHAND BY THE DIRECTOR AND DEVELOPED IN THE COURSE OF CONSTRUCTING THE FILM, IS DIRECTLY LINKED TO THE TECHNIQUE OF SHOOTING. WHEN THE DIRECTOR TELLS THE CAMERAMAN THAT HE WANTS A CLOSE-UP OR A DISTANCE SHOT OF THE PROTAGONIST, OR WHEN HE TELLS THE LEADING ACTOR TO WALK RIGHT OR LEFT, HE DOES SO BECAUSE ALL THIS HAS GOT TO DO WITH THE PROTAGONIST, BOTH OBJECTIVELY AND SUBJECTIVELY.

A Moral Problem

BUT IF THE BRAZILIAN HERO IS WITHOUT CHARACTER, LOST AND PERPLEXED, WITHOUT TRADITIONS OR A FUTURE, HOW IS HE TO BE FILMED? THE INSTABILITY

OF THE TECHNIQUE ADOPTED FOR SHOOTING IS LINKED TO THIS FACT. NEVER HAS GODARD'S IDEA, WHEREBY A "CAMERA MOVEMENT IS NOT A MATTER OF TECHNIQUE, BUT A MORAL QUESTION" BEEN SHOWN SO CLEARLY TO BE TRUE, AS IN THE CASE OF BRAZIL. IF SO FAR THE CHARACTER OF THE BRAZILIAN HAS NOT BEEN SUCCESSFULLY DEFINED, IT IS BECAUSE THE RESEARCH FOR OUR MAN HAS BEEN HAMPERED BY A GREAT DEAL OF MISTAKES.

THE PRICE OF THE RESEARCH FOR TRUTH IS INCOMPREHENSION ON THE PART OF THE PUBLIC. BUT BY PERFECTING METHODS THROUGH THE OVERCOMING OF MISTAKES, BY BUILDING A GREATER AWARENESS OF REALITY, STARTING FROM THAT WHICH WE KNOW, WE CAN FORGE THE KEY TO A LANGUAGE CAPABLE OF CIRCUMSCRIBING, ANALYZING, STATING AND DEMONSTRATING THE TRUTH. BUT ALL THIS LIES OUTSIDE OF THE CINEMA AND IS PART OF SOCIO-POLITICAL PHENOMENA. CINEMA NOVO IS INTIMATELY TIED TO THIS PHENOMENON, AND THOUGH IT WOULD RATHER BE AN AGENT OF THE PROCESS THAN A REFLECTION OF IT, IT IS MUCH MORE OF A REFLECTION THAN AN AGENT. FROM THIS IT CAN BE SEEN, AS WITH POLITICS AND ECONOMICS, THAT CINEMA NOVO DOES NOT ADHERE ANY LONGER TO TRADITIONAL VALUES. IT DOES NOT DEFINE CLEARLY OUR FUTURE AND IS NOT QUITE CLEAR WHAT SYSTEM IT SHOULD BE STRIVING FOR. A COUNTRY "IN TRANSITION," A CINEMA "IN TRANSITION."

IS IT ENOUGH TO PROPOSE THIS STATE OF TRANSITION, INDUCED BY UNDERDEVELOPMENT AND LIFE IN THE TROPICS, TO EXPLAIN BRAZILIAN CINEMA'S ISOLATION? THIS FOR ME IS THE MOST IMPORTANT QUESTION, SINCE THE CINEMA MUST OVERCOME THE TRANSITION STAGE IN ORDER TO REACH A STAGE OF LESSER NEUROSIS AND GREATER EFFECTIVENESS. THE PASSAGE FROM CULTURAL NEUROSIS TO CULTURAL ACTION WILL BE THE FIRST ACT OF THE "SHOW." AT THE MOMENT, WE ARE STILL IN THE OVERTURE, IN WHICH ALL THE THEMES ARE ORCHESTRATED IN SUCH A WAY AS TO ANNOUNCE THE MELODIES TO FOLLOW.

VARIOUS OTHER FILMS, SUCH AS *O DESAFIO* [*THE CHALLENGE*, 1966], *O PADRE E A MOCA* [*THE PRIEST AND THE GOD*, 1965], *A FALECIDA* [*THE DECEASED WOMAN*], *MENINO DE ENGENHO* [*MILL BOY*], AND *A OPINIAO PUBLICA* [*PUBLIC OPINION*], MET WITH SERIOUS COMPREHENSION AND COMMUNICATION PROBLEMS. BUT IN THE CASE OF EACH OF THESE FILMS, THE FILMMAKERS THREW THEMSELVES INTO THE TASK OF ANALYZING THE DARKER ASPECTS OF OUR REALITY: THESE FILMS, IN SHORT, SHOWED THE PAINFUL NATURE OF OUR UNDERDEVELOPMENT, AND, ABOVE ALL, DISMANTLED THE PRECONCEPTIONS OF AN OLD CULTURE. THE BRAVE SELF-CRITICISM IN *O DESAFIO*, THE REJECTION OF TRADITIONS AND UNDERDEVELOPMENT IN *O PADRE E A MOCA*, THE SADNESS EXPRESSED IN *A FALECIDA* (A DEBUT WORK OF INTERNATIONAL VALUE), DID NOT MANAGE TO COMMUNICATE THEMSELVES DIRECTLY, BUT WERE RELAYED, AT MORE COMPLEX LEVELS, TO THE EXTENT THAT THESE FILMS BECAME POLEMICAL WORKS CONSTITUTING A CULTURAL STATEMENT.

Watching and Listening

IN MANY STUDIES OF THE PROBLEMS OF COMMUNICATION, ONE FINDS THAT THE SPECIALISTS DO NOTHING OTHER THAN DESCRIBE THE STATE OF AFFAIRS BROUGHT ABOUT BY IMPERIALISM. AS PROPAGANDA, SOCIALISM FAILS, AND IT IS PUT ABOUT THAT THE BIG PUBLICITY GIVEN TO THE FIFTIETH ANNIVERSARY OF THE RUSSIAN REVOLUTION WAS THE WORK OF NEW YORK ADVERTISING AGENCIES . . .

THE CREATORS OF THE TECHNOLOGY TREAT THE PUBLIC AS IF THEY WERE IDIOTS, AND ARE EXPANDING THEIR ACTIVITIES OVER THE WHOLE WORLD. ARTICULATING THIS STRUCTURE IS NOT DIFFICULT FOR THE CAREFUL TECHNICIAN. THE PROBLEM THE BRAZILIAN FILMMAKER SETS FOR HIMSELF IS RATHER DIFFERENT; WE KNOW BETTER THAN ANYBODY THE COMMUNICATION STRUCTURE OF THE AMERICAN CINEMA, FROM ARTISTIC TECHNIQUES TO THE MECHANICS OF DISTRIBUTION. WE ARE ALL TOO FAMILIAR WITH THE STAR SYSTEM, THE NARRATIVE DEVICES, THE ATTRACTIONS OF THE GENRES AND PUBLICITY STUNTS: WE KNOW IT ALL, THE WHOLE WORKS.

BUT IF WE KNOW IT, DOES THIS MEAN THAT, FASCINATED BY ITS EFFECTIVENESS, WE SHOULD ACCEPT IT? THE ATTITUDE OF CERTAIN GROUPS OF INTELLECTUALS HAS MADE A MAJOR CONTRIBUTION TO OUR STATE OF UNDERDEVELOPMENT. THEY HAVE DECIDED TO IMPORT THEORY UPON THEORY FROM THE DEVELOPED WORLD, WITHOUT ANY DISINFECTING AT THE CUSTOMS. THEIR THEORETICAL SCHEMATIZATION HAS GENERATED A SUB-ART BASED ON IMITATION. WE WERE SO PREOCCUPIED BY WHAT THE DEVELOPED WORLD MIGHT THINK ABOUT US, THAT WE FORGOT TO WORRY ABOUT OURSELVES. CINEMA NOVO, ON THE OTHER HAND, ONLY WORRIES ABOUT ITSELF, AND ONLY REFERS TO WHAT THEY SAY ABROAD IN ORDER TO DRAW A COMPARISON BETWEEN FOREIGN OPINION AND NATIONAL INCOMPREHENSION.

THE FACT THAT CINEMA NOVO IS WELL RECEIVED ABROAD IN NO WAY JUSTIFIES THE DIFFICULTY IT HAS GETTING ACCEPTED IN BRAZIL. THE FUNDAMENTAL PROBLEM, A PROBLEM OF ECONOMIC AND CULTURAL FACTORS WHICH ARE CLOSELY INTERRELATED, LIES WITH THE PUBLIC. IN TRYING TO DEAL WITH THE ESSENTIAL ASPECTS OF OUR SOCIETY, CINEMA NOVO, AS WE HAVE SEEN, CAME UP AGAINST A PRECARIOUS CULTURE PRACTICE. SO IT TRIED TO ELABORATE A CULTURAL PRACTICE WHICH WAS BASED ON THAT PRECARIOUSNESS. AS GUSTAV DAHL SO FELICITOUSLY EXPRESSED IT, CINEMA NOVO IS FORCING ITSELF TO WREAK QUALITATIVE CHANGE TO OVERCOME CULTURAL UNDERDEVELOPMENT, A PROJECT UNDERTAKEN BY CERTAIN OTHER BRAZILIAN ARTISTS, ESPECIALLY THE 1922 MOVEMENT.

NEITHER IS FAMILIARITY WITH THE TECHNOLOGY OF COMMUNICATION, NOR PARTICIPATION IN IT, PARTICULARLY IMPORTANT. WHAT IS IMPORTANT IS TO ATTACK THAT TECHNOLOGY AND PROPOSE ALTERNATIVES TO IT. THE CINEMA IN BRAZIL HAS ONE GREAT ADVANTAGE: IN CREATING A STRUCTURE FOR ITSELF AIMED AT SELFSUFFICIENCY, IT BENEFITS, WITH THE EXCEPTION OF THE STRUGGLE AGAINST THE

CENSORS, FROM INFINITELY GREATER ROOM TO MANEUVER THAN THE TELEVISION HAS.

THE REAL TRIAL FOR THE CINEMA IS THAT, WITH A PUBLIC HOOKED ON FOREIGN FILMS AND SUFFOCATED BY TELEVISION, COMMUNICATION IS PROBLEMATIC. BUT IT IS NOT IMPOSSIBLE TO BREAK THROUGH THE BARRIER OF GENERAL INSENSITIVITY. THE IMMEDIATE AND PARTIAL FAILURE FOR CINEMA NOVO WITH THE PUBLIC IS PARTLY DUE TO THE IMMATURITY OF THE FILMMAKERS WHO, FLUNG INTO THE ABYSS, WITHOUT TECHNICAL EXPERTISE OR MUCH EXPERIENCE, HIT THIS BARRIER FACE ON WHILE MAKING CONTRADICTORY EFFORTS TO GET THROUGH IT.

BUT ONE THING HAS MANAGED TO BREAK THROUGH THIS BARRIER OF GLASS, SOMETHING SO IMPORTANT AS TO UPSET THE MONOLOGUE: CINEMA NOVO HAS TURNED ITSELF INTO POLITICAL PARTIES, BOTH LEGAL AND ILLEGAL, FROM SOLITARY CONFINEMENT. BUT CONTRARY TO WHAT THE CRITIC JEAN-CLAUDE BERNARDET ASSERTS IN HIS BOOK *BRAZIL EM TEMPO DE CINEMA* [*BRAZIL IN THE EPOQUE OF CINEMA*, EDITRICE CIVILIZACAO BRASILIERA], CINEMA NOVO DOES NOT TAKE AD-VANTAGE OF THE PRESTIGE ACCORDED TO IT BY THE OFFICIAL CULTURE, RATHER IT HOLDS THAT PRESTIGE IN CONTEMPT, AND THIS CONTEMPT MAKES ITSELF FELT ON THE SCREEN, IN THOSE FILMS WHICH ACQUIRE PRESTIGE FOR THE FACT THAT THEY ARE *FILMS*. IF THEY ARE FILMS, THAT IS TO SAY THAT THEY REPRESENT SOMETHING CONCRETE: A TECHNICAL PRODUCTION WHICH IS A CREATIVE AFFIR-MATION, ONE WHICH ACKNOWLEDGES AND DEFEATS THE CHALLENGE OFFERED BY THE OFFICIAL CULTURE ITSELF, ACCORDING TO WHICH "BRAZILIANS HAVE NOT THE KNOW-HOW TO DO CINEMA."

MOST OF THE BODIES WHO AWARD PRIZES TO CINEMA NOVO FILMS DO NOT UNDERSTAND THESE FILMS, THEY RESPECT THEM. THE SAME THING HAPPENED IN THE CASE OF LITERATURE. THE DRAMA OF MISUNDERSTANDING WHICH THE CINEMA IS EXPERIENCING TODAY IS THE SAME ONE MODERN ART EXPERIENCED IN THE 1930s. BUT THIS MISUNDERSTANDING SHOULD NOT BE SEEN AS THE DOOM OF ARTISTIC LIFE BUT AS THE PRODUCT OF THE IMMATURE STATE OF THE NATIONAL CON-SCIOUSNESS.

The Breaking-Point

THE PHASE OF PURE DISCOVERY AND INTUITION, WHICH BEGAN IN 1964 WITH CINEMA NOVO'S FIRST EXPERIENCES, RUY GUERRA'S *OS CAFAJESTES* [*THE HUSTLERS*, 1962], MY OWN *BARRAVENTO* [1962] AND *PORTO DAS CAIXAS* [*PORT OF CAIXAS*, 1962] BY PAIRO CESAR SARACENI, HAS DEVELOPED INTO THE PHASE OF REFLEC-TION AND A BREAK WITH CINEMA NOVO'S OWN ROOTS, MARKED BY THIS YEAR'S EXPERIENCES WHICH ARE BOUND TO GIVE RISE TO MUCH POLEMIC. CINEMA NOVO IS LOOKING FOR A LANGUAGE DERIVED FROM SOCIO-POLITICO-ECONOMIC FAC-TORS, *IN ORDER TO COMMUNICATE TO THE PUBLIC AND INFLUENCE IT ON ITS PATH TO LIBERATION*. IT HAS NO INTENTION OF PROVIDING *THE ORGANIZATION FOR A SCHOOL*, IN THE SENSE SO LOVED BY THE THEORETICIANS WHO WAIT ON GOD'S

SALVATION, BUT IT DOES WANT TO PROVIDE FOR A *PROLIFERATION OF PERSONAL STYLES* WHICH WILL PUT PERMANENTLY IN DOUBT THE CONCEPT OF A SPECIAL LANGUAGE AS A HIGHER LEVEL OF CONSCIOUSNESS. FROM A CULTURAL DYNAMIC WHICH IS *SELF-DESTRUCTIVE*, WE COULD DEVELOP ONE OF *DIALECTICS*.

THE AVANT-GARDE IN THE THIRD WORLD, AS THE POET FERREIRA GULLAR USED TO TELL ME, IS QUITE A DIFFERENT AFFAIR FROM THE AVANT-GARDE OF THE DEVELOPED WORLD. THE CINEMA HAS AN ADVANTAGE OVER LITERATURE, IN SO FAR AS IT HAS A MEDIUM AT ITS DISPOSAL—THE IMAGE—THAT HAS NO NEED OF TRANSLATION.

THE PROBLEM, THOUGH, IS NOT ONE OF DECIDING BETWEEN THE *NATIONAL* AND THE *UNIVERSAL*, AS SOME WOULD HAVE IT. THE PROBLEM IS TO CREATE FROM THE POSITION OF ONE'S INSUFFICIENCIES, AND BUILD OUT OF THE QUALITIES OF THESE, THE FLEXIBLE FOUNDATIONS OF A WAY OF THINKING WHICH IS IN THE PROCESS OF EVOLVING. THEREBY WE WOULD HAVE AN INTERNATIONAL STYLE OF ART: THAT OF THE AVANT-GARDE. THUS CREATION WILL BE THE ONLY STIMULUS FOR THE DEVELOPMENT OF STYLES IN THE THIRD WORLD.

CREATION, I WOULD STRESS, RESULTS FROM THE TACTICS OF PRODUCTION, IS CARRIED OUT THROUGH THE "DIALECTICALLY FREE" ACT OF CREATING, AND ASSERTS ITSELF IN THE STRATEGY AND TACTICS OF DISTRIBUTION.

A CINEMA THAT WANTS TO CREATE AND SEEKS CULTURAL QUALITY, OBTAINS, AT VARIOUS LEVELS, POLITICAL RESULTS. ALTHOUGH CINEMA NOVO LOST THE FIRST ROUND GOING INTO ONE OR TWO CLINCHES WITH THE PUBLIC, IT HAS WON ON POINTS, IF NOT ACTUALLY BY A KNOCK-OUT. THE REALITY BEHIND ALL THIS LIES IN THE EVER-IMPROVING PROFESSIONAL ORGANIZATION ON THE PART OF THE PRODUCERS, WHICH CAN BE SEEN IN THE INCREASE, BOTH IN QUANTITY AND QUALITY, OF THE FILMS IN PRODUCTION.

THE DISCUSSION WILL NOT STOP THERE: *GAROTA DE IPANEMA* [*THE GIRL FROM IPANEMA*, 1967] BY LEON HIRSZMAN, DISMISSED BY THE CRITICS AND THE INTELLECTUAL ELITES WHO HAVE ALWAYS ACCUSED CINEMA NOVO OF BEING ANTIPOPULAR, IS BEATING BOX-OFFICE RECORDS IN BRAZIL, AND ONLY *ROBERTO CARLOS EM RITMA DE AVENTURA* WILL MAKE MORE THIS YEAR. BUT *GAROTA DE IPANEMA* HAS THIS GREAT ADVANTAGE OVER ANY OTHER TYPE OF COMMERCIAL PRODUCTION MADE IN BRAZIL: IT IS A FILM WHICH REJECTS IMITATION. IT HAS OPTED FOR THE SOLITUDE OF AN ATTEMPTED CRITIQUE OF A WORLD, THAT OF IPANEMA, MYTHICIZED BY "SUN AND BEER LITERATURE"; IT HAS OPTED FOR THE SOLITUDE OF AN ATTEMPT AT CRITICISM RATHER THAN CONFORM TO THE LIE WHICH IS INHERENT IN THAT LITERATURE'S LANGUAGE, RATHER THAN IMITATE CLAUDE LELOUCH AND GIVE A FALSE IMPRESSION OF BEING LIKE OTHER FILMS BY MEANS OF SUB-ART.

LEON HIRSZMAN'S FILM DISPLAYS THE AUTHOR'S DISBELIEF IN HIS SUBJECT, A DISBELIEF NOT FOUND IN *A FALECIDA*. HIRSZMAN HERE SAW HIMSELF AS BEING SACRIFICED ON THE ALTAR OF PARADISE BY ITS PRIESTS, FOR DENYING THE EXISTENCE OF A HAPPY ATLANTIC SEABOARD SOCIETY (MIGHT NOT A REAL GOOD-

HUMOREDNESS EXIST IN IPANEMA, A POOR PART OF THE CITY, WHERE A SELECT FEW ARE WASHED AWAY BY THEIR ILLUSION OF HAPPINESS?). THIS DISBELIEF PREVENTS THE FILM FROM GETTING TO GRIPS WITH THE OTHER ASPECT OF IPANEMA, THE INEVITABLE AGGRESSIVENESS. BUT HIRSZMAN'S *DETACHMENT* CONFERS ON THE FILM A CULTURAL VALUE.

I THINK THAT THE *DEMYSTIFICATION* PHASE WILL BE SURPASSED IN THE COMING FILMS, BUT IT WILL BE BY NO MEANS ENTIRELY ABSENT. THE FILMMAKERS ARE CONVINCED THAT THE "CRITICAL EYE" IS NOT ENOUGH: ANOTHER WAY OF MAKING AN IMPACT IS NECESSARY, ONE CAPABLE OF SHAKING UP THE PUBLIC AS THEY SIT IN THE STALLS. MY OWN *TERRA EM TRANSE* [*LAND IN ANGUISH*, 1967] TOOK A STEP IN THIS DIRECTION AND A BITTER STRUGGLE WAS THE RESULT, A STRUGGLE WHICH ENABLED A DISCUSSION TO TAKE PLACE ON MANY LEVELS, THUS OPENING UP THE PATH FOR NEW WAYS OF COMMUNICATION. CERTAIN LEFT-WING CRITICS LABELLED THE FILM WHICH ENCOURAGED A DIALOGUE WITH THE PUBLIC. DIDACTIC OR RAISING AN ISSUE, AGGRESSIVE OR CRITICIZING, AGITATING OR ORGANIZING, DEMYSTIFYING OR FABULOUS—CINEMA NOVO HAS REALIZED THAT TO BE *REALIST* MEANS *DISCUSSING THE DIFFERENT ASPECTS OF THE REAL*, AND NOT EMPLOYING SOME FORMULA OF EUROPEAN REALISM (HAIL LUKACS!) IN ORDER TO DETERMINE, *A PRIORI*, A REALISM WITH A CLEAR CONSCIENCE.

FOR THE MOST PART, BRAZILIAN CRITICISM HAS NOT GRASPED THIS PHENOMENON, AND ONLY A FEW, SUCH AS PAULO EMILIO SALLES GOMES, ALEX VIANY, RUDA DE ANDRADE, ALMEIDA SALLES, WALTER DA SILVEIRA, COSME ALVES NETO, FABIANO CANOSA, WILSON CUNHA, SERGIO AUGUSTO AND MAURICIO GOMES LEITO HAVE WORKED, AS MEN OF THE CINEMA, FOR THE DISCUSSION, DEFENCE, PUBLICIZING AND RECORDING OF THE HISTORY, OF THE PHENOMENON.

THE OTHER CRITICAL PRACTICE, THE REACTIONARY ONE, REFUSES TO ACCEPT THE OBVIOUS. IN PRACTICE, IT IS WORKING TO UNDERMINE ITS OWN LONG-WINDED DECLARATIONS ON A NATIONAL CINEMA, BY PROPOSING IDEAS THAT MYSTIFY AND WHICH WERE BEING PUT FORWARD A LONG TIME AGO BY THE AUDIENCE AND FILMMAKERS WHOSE PRACTICE WAS DOMINANT.

THE BUREAUCRACY OF THE NATIONAL INSTITUTE OF CINEMA DOES ITS GOOD WORKS, IN THE FORM OF CHANNELLING 10% OF BOX-OFFICE RECEIPTS THROUGHOUT THE COUNTRY BACK TO THE PRODUCERS. HOWEVER IT SOWS THE SEEDS OF THE CINEMA'S DESTRUCTION IN ESTABLISHING A NETWORK OF CULTURAL SABOTAGE AGAINST CINEMA NOVO. THE COMPOSITION OF THE JURIES, WHO GIVE PRIZES AND WHO CLASSIFY BRAZILIAN FILMS TO BE SENT ABROAD, IS OPENLY BIASED AGAINST CINEMA NOVO, BECOMING EVEN MORE RADICAL WHEN IT FAILS TO FIND FILMS TO PUT UP AGAINST CINEMA NOVO'S.

TO THE DEFEATISTS AND DENIGRATORS, WHILST ACKNOWLEDGING THE SHORTCOMINGS OF CINEMA NOVO, I ADDRESS THE FOLLOWING QUESTION:

WHAT ARE THE ALTERNATIVES FOR BRAZILIAN CINEMA, IF THERE IS A BOYCOTT OF FUTURE FILMS BELONGING TO THIS TENDENCY, AND OF THOSE, MADE BY THEIR

DIRECTORS WHICH ARE TO BE RELEASED THIS YEAR?

THEORIES DIE IF THEY ARE NOT PUT INTO PRACTICE. CINEMA NOVO EXISTS; IT IS A CREATIVE RESPONSE, AN ACTIVE PRACTICE, IN A COUNTRY SO FULL OF POSSIBILITIES AND MISUNDERSTANDINGS.

IT IS NOT OUR INTENTION, HOWEVER, TO TURN CINEMA NOVO INTO A CLOSED CIRCLE OF FILMMAKERS. OUR STRUGGLE HAS AS ITS AIM THE IMPLANTING OF A MENTALITY—CINEMA NOVO IS FOR AN ASSAULT ON THE POWER OF THE CINEMA; CINEMA NOVO IS TO MAKE SURE THAT BRAZILIAN CINEMA REALLY BECOMES A NEW CINEMA, ONE WORTHY OF A NEW COUNTRY (EVEN IF A PREMATURE DECLINE MIGHT RAISE FEARS OVER THE COUNTRY'S FUTURE). BUT THE ROLE OF THE INTELLECTUALS, WHATEVER THEIR APPROACH, IS TO CREATE AND TURN AN ADULT CULTURE INTO A SOURCE FOR POPULAR INSPIRATION. YOU DO NOT, HOWEVER, CREATE AN ADULT CULTURE BY USING FEAR. IF THE CHOICE IS EITHER TO FOLLOW THE CULT OF DUBIOUS TRADITIONS, OR TAKE THE RISK OF MAKING A DISCOVERY, CINEMA NOVO WILL SOLDIER UP THE SECOND PATH.

TRANSLATED BY JON DAVIS

Antonio Das Mortes

Fight with your ideas.

Notes

1. The *cangaco* is the Brazilian hinterlands.
2. A *cangaceiro* is a Robin Hood type bandit, an outlaw in the Northeast of Brazil. *O Cangaceiro* was one of the first Brazilian films to achieve international recognition. A prize winner at Cannes, it was distributed in 22 countries, and represented a highpoint of filmmaking in Vera Cruz, where large scale film studios were set up in Sao Paulo in an attempt to create European style entertainment.
3. The *chanchada*, traditionally the highest grossing genre of the Brazilian film industry, is a banal and formulaic kind of musical comedy.
4. A *caboclo* is a Brazilian of mixed white and Indian blood.
5. *Os Sertoes,* a 19th-century publication by Euclydes Da Cunha.
6. A *sertanejo* is a person who lives in the *sertao,* or backlands.

Envisioning Popular Form [1970]

An Interview with Glauber Rocha

GLAUBER ROCHA WAS THE MOST PROMINENT AND POLEMICAL MEMBER OF THE CINEMA NOVO MOVEMENT AND ITS UNDISPUTED LEADER. HE BEGAN HIS CAREER AS A JOURNALIST AND FILM CRITIC AND WAS A LEADING CONTRIBUTOR TO LATIN AMERICAN FILM JOURNALS UNTIL HIS DEATH IN 1981. IN THE EARLY SIXTIES, ROCHA COINED THE TERM THE "AESTHETIC OF HUNGER" TO DESCRIBE THE KIND OF CRITICAL REALISM HE SAW AS SUITED TO HIS FILM PROJECT; AN AESTHETIC THAT REPRESENTED BRAZIL'S POLITICAL INSTABILITY, UNDERDEVELOPMENT AND IM-BALANCE OF MATERIAL WEALTH, WHILE ALSO DRAWING ON THE POPULAR CULTURES OF RESISTANCE AND INCORPORATING THEIR VERY STRUCTURES OF PERCEPTION IN-TO THE WORK. DEEPLY CONCERNED WITH THE POLITICAL AND SOCIOLOGICAL IM-PLICATIONS OF FILM FORMS, ROCHA AT TIMES REACHED THE POINT OF ANTI-RATIONALIST TROPICALISM IN HIS ATTEMPTS TO BREAK WITH DOMINANT MODES OF FILMMAKING.

THE FOLLOWING IS EXCERPTED FROM AN INTERVIEW WITH *CAHIERS DU CINEMA* EDITORS MICHEL DELAHAYE, PIERRE KAST AND JEAN NARBONI, WHICH WAS HELD IN 1969. IT FIRST APPEARED IN ENGLISH IN *AFTERIMAGE* (LONDON) IN 1970.

Q: WHY DID YOU MAKE *ANTONIO DAS MORTES*?

A: *ANTONIO DAS MORTES* REPRESENTED, FOR ME, MY FIRST TRULY CINEMATOGRAPHIC EFFORT. FURTHERMORE, IT INCORPORATES PROBLEMS OF MY NATIVE REGION. IT IS VERY CLOSE TO MY CHILDHOOD AND TO MY LIFE. *ANTONIO DAS MORTES* RE-JOINS A CERTAIN CULTURAL AND CINEMATIC TRADITION, AND REFLECTS A DISCIPLINE VERY DIFFERENT TO THAT WHICH LIES BEHIND *TERRA EM TRANSE*. IN BRAZIL THERE WAS ALREADY THE WHOLE HERITAGE OF THE WESTERN AND *ANTONIO DAS MORTES* GOES IN THIS DIRECTION.

The cangaceiro (standing) and the Saint, in Antonio Das Mortes.

Q: Do Antonio Das Mortes and the *cangaceiros*, the outlaws, belong to the past in Brazil, to an outmoded legend, or to a continuing force, an active myth?

A: They still correspond to a reality, to the point where I was able to find a concrete justification for making the film. The person on whom Antonio Das Mortes is modelled is still alive. His name is Jose Rufino and he is about seventy years old. I've met him and spoken to him. The actor who played the role also listened to him and used what he learned to create the part. You can see this person in a short film by Gil Soares. He killed several *cangaceiros*. Before making *Black God, White Devil* I was doing some research and met him. He told me everything, even the story of *Black God*—all the second part is based on what he told me. He is an amazing personality because he never tells a story in the same way twice. I was fascinated by him and, little by little, we became friends. When I wanted to make *Antonio Das Mortes* I learned that a new *cangaco* had risen in the region of Pemambouc, and I read in a newspaper that Rufino had gone there because the whole police force couldn't catch this *cangaceiro* called Ze Crispin.

Q: WHEN DID THIS HAPPEN?

A: LAST YEAR. HE WENT TO ARREST THE *PISTOLEIRO*. ANOTHER TIME HE TOOK ME TO A TOWN CALLED SANTA BRIGIDA. SEVERAL PROFESSIONAL BANDITS LIVED THERE, BUT HE CAN GO THERE. HE EXPLAINED TO ME THAT THESE BANDITS WERE HIS FRIENDS, THAT THEY KNEW HE DIDN'T KILL FOR MONEY AND THAT HE WAS THE ONLY POLICEMAN ABLE TO GO THERE. THAT'S HOW I CAME TO SEE THE BANDITS, AND NOW I WOULD LIKE TO MAKE A FILM ABOUT THEM. BUT THEY ARE DIFFERENT FROM *CANGACEIROS*; THEY ARE NOT GANGSTERS, THEY DON'T STAGE HOLD-UPS, THEY ARE NO LONGER LOOKING AROUND FOR MONEY. THEY ARE IN THE PAID SERVICE OF THE PRESENT DAY POLITICAL PARTIES. THE OLD LIBERAL PARTIES ENGAGE THEM TO OBSTRUCT THE ELECTIONS AND TO KILL CANDIDATES.[1]

Q: WASN'T MATA VACA, THE COLONEL'S GUNMAN IN *ANTONIO DAS MORTES,* REALLY OF THIS TYPE?

A: YES, HE WAS SOMEBODY I KNEW. HE KILLED ONE OF MY RELATIONS WHEN I WAS A CHILD, AND SOMETIME LATER ONE OF MY COUSINS KILLED HIM.

Q: IF THE MAN WHO SERVED AS THE MODEL FOR ANTONIO DAS MORTES SAW THIS FILM, IN WHICH ANTONIO CHANGES SIDES, HOW WOULD HE REACT?

A: HE WOULD REACT FAVORABLY BECAUSE HE, TOO, OFTEN CHANGED SIDES. HE HAS ALREADY SERVED SEVERAL CAUSES . . . I SPOKE JUST NOW OF THE TOWN OF SANTA BRIGIDA WHOSE CHIEF DIED LAST YEAR. HIS NAME WAS PEDRO AND SERGIO MUNIZ (ANOTHER BRAZILIAN FILMMAKER) MADE A DOCUMENTARY ABOUT HIM. ON THE LEVEL OF MYSTIC RELATIONS THERE IS A MIXTURE OF CATHOLICISM AND PROTESTANTISM, AND THESE ARE WELL INTEGRATED. THAT IS WHY ANTONIO SAYS TO THE PROFESSOR, "YOUR AFFAIRS ARE POLITICAL AFFAIRS, MINE ARE THE AFFAIRS OF GOD." HE DIDN'T BECOME A REVOLUTIONARY; HIS CHANGE WAS MORE A MATTER OF MORALITY THAN POLITICS. HE IS SIMPLY A PERSON OF THE MIDDLE CLASS. HE HAS ALL ITS COMPLEXES, GUILT, ETC. WHEN HE IS AFFECTED BY THE MYTH OF THE SAINT, THAT IS A REACTION WHICH I FIND DIFFICULT TO EXPLAIN, IT'S VERY SUBJECTIVE. ALTHOUGH I AM FROM A PROTESTANT BACKGROUND, I AM FASCINATED BY THE AESTHETICS OF CATHOLICISM. I AM AN ATHEIST, BUT EVERYTHING CONNECTED WITH BLACK RELIGION HAS A GREAT EFFECT ON ME, ITS "MISE EN SCENE." IN BAHIA, FOR EXAMPLE, THE BLACK CULTURE HAS SUCCEEDED IN IMPOSING ITS RELIGIONS, ITS FOODS, ITS MUSIC, ITS DANCING. EVEN POLITICALLY, IT HAS RESISTED THE DICTATORSHIP OF VARGAS BY A VERITABLE UNDERGROUND WAR.[2]

Q: SOMEONE WHO HAD JUST SEEN *BLACK GOD* ASKED HOW ONE COULD RECONCILE REVOLUTION AND FOLK LORE. IT'S BECAUSE REVOLUTION IS AN INSTRUMENT OF CULTURAL AS WELL AS POLITICAL RESISTANCE.

A: THE GREATEST REBELLIONS IN BRAZILIAN HISTORY ARE THOSE WARS WHICH THE BLACKS AND THE PEASANT MYSTICS FOUGHT AT THE TIME OF SLAVERY. THE MOST FAMOUS ARE THOSE OF "ZUMBI DE PALMARES" (BLACK) AND CANUDOS (PEASANT MYSTIC).

Q: THE BLACK FORCE EXISTS NOT BECAUSE IT IS DETATCHED FROM RELIGION, BUT, ON THE CONTRARY, BECAUSE IT RESURGES AROUND RELIGION AND ITS MYTHS. IN THE UNITED STATES, THE BLACKS HAVE HAD THEIR CULTURE DESTROYED. THEY WERE CONVERTED TO CHRISTIANITY, AND TRACES OF BLACK RELIGION REMAIN IN THE NEGRO SPIRITUAL, THOUGH NOT IN A CONSCIOUS AND ORGANIZED WAY. BUT THE MACUMBA HAVE ORGANIZED THIS RESISTANCE.

YOU WERE TALKING ABOUT THE PERSONALITY OF ANTONIO DAS MORTES AND YOU SAID THAT PEOPLE LIKE HIM CHANGE SIDES SEVERAL TIMES. BUT THEY ALWAYS CHANGE FROM THE SIDE OF REACTION.

A: A PEASANT DOESN'T HAVE A GREAT DEAL OF CHOICE. HE BECOMES A BANDIT, OR HE DIES OF HUNGER, OR HE BECOMES A LABORER IN SAO PAULO, AS IN GIANNI AMINO'S *TROPICI*. TO HIM, THE PROFESSION OF A KILLER IS QUITE NORMAL . . . HE DOESN'T KILL TO STEAL. HE IS PAID TO KILL AND AT THE SAME TIME HAS A KEEN SENSE OF HONOR WHICH IS SOMETIMES STRONGER THAN HIS PROFESSIONAL CONSCIENCE. FOR INSTANCE, IN THE GREAT WAR OF CANUDOS, A LARGE NUMBER OF *JAGUNCOS* ABANDONED THEIR PROFESSION TO JOIN THEIR CHIEF CONSEILHEIRA TO RESIST THE ARMY. THESE REACTIONS ARE VERY MORAL AND SENTIMENTAL, A LITTLE LIKE THOSE OF THE TRUCK DRIVER IN RUY GUERRA'S *THE GUNS*. WHAT'S MORE, I MADE MY FILM IN THE SAME REGION, AT MILAGRES,[3] BECAUSE SUCH STORIES ARE FREQUENT AROUND THERE.

THESE REACTIONS ARE AS SURPRISING AS THOSE WHICH ALLOW THE LEFT IN BRAZIL TO MOVE TO THE RIGHT, AND THE RIGHT TO MOVE TO THE LEFT. I AM NOT AN EXPERT IN POLITICAL SCIENCE, BUT I HAVE SPOKEN TO THOSE WHO ARE AND IT SEEMS THAT IN THIS SENSE BRAZIL IS THE MOST PECULIAR COUNTRY IN LATIN AMERICA, AND THAT ALL POLITICAL REACTIONS ARE EXTRAORDINARY. ALL ROUTES ARE VALID IF THEY OFFER MEANS OF LIBERATION. IN *ANTONIO DAS MORTES* I WANTED TO SHOW CLEARLY HOW MANY PEOPLE MAY ARRIVE AT ACTION BY QUITE DIFFERENT ROUTES. THE PROFESSOR AND ANTONIO COME TOGETHER IN A MASSACRE DIRECTED AGAINST OPPRESSION, BUT THEIR MOTIVES ARE TOTALLY DIFFERENT. THEY HAVE NO THEORETICAL NOTIONS, NO GUIDE LINES. I AM AGAINST PROSELYTISM.

Q: THIS COINCIDES WITH WHAT YOU SAID ABOUT *THE GUNS*. WHEN GUERRA SHOWS THE DRIVER—WHO IS FIRST PORTRAYED AS AN EXPLOITER—AT LAST TURNING AGAINST THE ARMY, IT IS A VERY PERSONAL, AND THEREFORE LIMITED, REACTION.

A: YES. I WANT IT UNDERSTOOD THAT POLITICAL THEORIES IN LATIN AMERICA ARE OFTEN THE SOURCE OF SERIOUS MISUNDERSTANDINGS AND DEMAGOGIC ATTITUDES.

THE PHRASEOLOGY OF THE LEFT, ITS MORALISM AND ITS PROCEDURES, OFTEN END UP WITH A DISTINCTLY FOLKLORIC FLAVOR. THE POLITICAL MATURITY OF THE BRAZILIAN PEOPLE WILL NOT BE REACHED, IN MY OPINION, BY MEANS OF A TRADITIONAL POLITICAL EDUCATION. ALLOWING, OF COURSE, FOR A CERTAIN LEVEL OF POLITICAL AWARENESS, THERE WILL BE A REVOLUTIONARY EXPLOSION IN SPITE OF ALL THE CONTRADICTIONS CHARACTERISTIC OF BRAZIL. BUT WE MUST NOT BELIEVE THAT WE WILL ARRIVE AT THAT STAGE BY EDUCATING THE PEOPLE. THE BLACK STRENGTH, WHICH IS A MYSTICAL STRENGTH, DOES NOT ONLY INVOLVE THE PEASANTS. WHETHER THEY BELONG TO THE BOURGEOISIE OR THE ARISTOCRACY, NO ONE IN BRAZIL IS A STRANGER TO THE MACUMBA AND MYSTICISM. THIS SENTIMENTAL, EMOTIONAL, AND BLOODTHIRSTY ASPECT OF BRAZIL IS, ADMITTEDLY, A DEFECT, AN OBSTACLE, BUT IT COULD BECOME A POSITIVE QUALITY.

Q: IN *ANTONIO DAS MORTES* THE BLACK WHO, AT THE BEGINNING, IS MOST RESPECTABLE AND THE MOST RESIGNED IS HE WHO, QUITE RIGHTLY AT THE END, YOU MAKE FIGHT THE DRAGON WITH THE LANCE.

A: THAT IS BECAUSE, IN BRAZIL, THE BLACKS STRUGGLING AGAINST SLAVERY HAVE ALWAYS BEEN THE BRAVEST FIGHTERS.

Q: HOW DO YOU JUSTIFY THE ALLUSION TO ST. GEORGE?

A: IN PORTUGUESE, THE FIRST TITLE WAS *O DRAGAO DA MALDADA CONTRA O SANTA GUERREIRO*. UNFORTUNATELY, I HAD TO CHANGE IT. BUT THE LEGEND OF ST. GEORGE AND THE DRAGON IS VERY POPULAR IN BRAZIL, AND THERE ARE SIMILARITIES WITH CERTAIN AFRICAN MYTHS. ST. GEORGE CORRESPONDS TO OXOSSE, THE GOD OF THE HUNT IN AFRICAN RELIGIONS. THE FILM IS A DISCOURSE ABOUT THE SAINTLY WARRIOR AND THE DRAGON OF WICKEDNESS. THAT'S WHY I IMPROVISED THE FILMING. I WANTED TO AVOID THE LIMITATIONS OF TRADITIONAL, DRAMATIC FICTION FILMS. I CHOSE ACTORS WHO WERE VERY AWARE OF THE PROBLEM AND TALKED TO THEM A GREAT DEAL. THE FACT THAT IT WAS IMPROVISED MEANT THAT THE FILM COULD DEVELOP AT THE LEVEL OF EACH CHARACTER. IT'S A PITY THAT YOU COULDN'T UNDERSTAND THE PORTUGUESE. EACH CHARACTER IMPROVISES AND DEVELOPS HIS DIALOGUE. THIS ALLOWED A DEEP RELATIONSHIP BETWEEN THE ACTOR AND HIS ROLE IN THE FRAMEWORK OF THE RELATIONSHIP BETWEEN ST. GEORGE AND THE DRAGON, AND AT THE SAME TIME GOT RID OF ALL THE DOGMATISM OF TRADITIONAL REVOLUTIONARY FILMS. I PERMITTED COMPLETE FREEDOM WITH DIALOGUE, BUT IN EDITING TOOK A VERY RIGOROUS APPROACH. I CHOSE SHOTS WHICH ARE INFORMATIONALLY LOADED. PERHAPS SOME OF THEM ARE OVER-LOADED, BUT I DIDN'T WANT TO SACRIFICE THIS INFORMATION, I WANTED TO DO THE OPPOSITE OF *TERRA EM TRANSE* [*LAND IN ANGUISH*], TO ESTABLISH OTHER DIALECTICAL RELATIONS BETWEEN EDITING AND DIALOGUE AND I THINK THE FILM IS FAR MORE EFFECTIVE IN THAT IT COMMUNICATES WITH LARGER AREAS OF THE PUBLIC.

To my mind, the political film should not be burdened with too grand a formulation, except where one wants to make a didactic film. Personally, I prefer a polemical cinema where everything is flexible. I still ask myself, a propos Eisenstein—and it's the same of Brecht's theater—if all directors can really use their theories. I'm afraid that in Brazil formulations could inhibit the creative drive, especially as creation is initially spontaneous and chaotic. I'm not sure of all this . . . I spoke to Godard about it, who said that we must destroy the cinema in Brazil. I don't agree with him. Here in France, and in Italy, you can destroy. But we have still to build at all levels, language, aesthetics, technique. To begin with, there is a misunderstanding. All the first films of Cinema Novo were very Eisensteinian. We were still suffering from various colonial complexes. When everybody talked about Bazin we became more discursive. I don't regret all this because it was part of our education. We were ignorant of all that had happened in the cinema and we were behind. We were criticized, too, from all sides. Hirszman, for example, has made a film called *Pedreira de Sao Diogo*, which I consider a magnificent illustration of certain of Eisenstein's theories. Following that he made another film *Maioria Absoluta*, which does not really correspond to his conceptions. He made a very fine film, *La Morte*, which was very close to Dreyer. *La Morte* is a masochistic and very beautiful film. In Brazil it was dismissed, then Europe discovered it. I like Eisenstein too, but to a lesser degree than Hirszman, whose sense of the dialectic is more profound than my own. I have been influenced by Eisenstein, the Italian cinema and the [French] New Wave.

Q: Eisenstein described clearly how his formal procedures were closely related to a particular socio-historical reality and warned us against the retention of mere formalities. From *Barravento* [*The Turning Wind*] to *Antonio Das Mortes* one can see that you have thrown off your Eisensteinian apprenticeship.

A: The same thing is happening in the Brechtian theater, especially in the underdeveloped countries. They say, that's Brecht, and all the plays are produced according to his principles of "mise en scene," of distancing. The actors are immobile, the "mise en scene" is poor. There is a director in Brazil called Martinez. He staged a play based on de Andrade's play *O Rei da Vela*[4]. He has studied street theater, forgotten Brecht, and the work is very Brechtian. He has regained everything while cutting himself off from this Brechtianism, yet presented this amazing and fantastic performance. And it's the same in cinema. At the festivals at Cannes and at Pesaro, even in critics' week, one feels that one has discovered the cinema of a society anonymous in style and thought. Godard*ism*,

FOR EXAMPLE, IS FOUND EVERYWHERE, AND EVEN FROM THE POINT OF VIEW OF TECHNIQUE IT IS UNSUCCESSFUL, SUPERFICIAL. THIS IS THE CASE WITH INDEPENDENT CINEMA IN SEVERAL COUNTRIES, IT IS WITHOUT SPIRIT, IT'S NOTHING. NOW THERE WILL BE THE STRAUB STYLE. I HAVE SPOKEN TO SEVERAL YOUNG FILMMAKERS WHO HAVE SAID THAT THEY ARE GOING TO MAKE THEIR FILMS WITH LONG TAKES OF THIRTY OR FORTY MINUTES. AFTER THE STRAUB STYLE, NO DOUBT, THERE WILL BE THE JANCSO STYLE. YOUNG FILMMAKERS MUST REALIZE THAT STRAUB IS IMPORTANT BECAUSE HE IS AN ORIGINAL ARTIST AND THAT PROLIFERATION OF INDIVIDUAL STYLES IS THE MOST IMPORTANT THING FOR THE DEVELOPMENT OF CINEMA.

Q: WHEN TALKING ABOUT THE CINEMA NOVO, PEOPLE TAKE ONE OF TWO LINES. THEY EITHER ARGUE THAT THE BRAZILIAN GOVERNMENT, IN LEAVING THESE FILMS ALONE, OR PERHAPS HINDERING THEIR DISTRIBUTION A LITTLE, JUDGES THEM AS HARMLESS; OR THEY ASK, IF THE GOVERNMENT REALIZES THAT YOUR FILMS REPRESENT A DANGER TO THE STATUS QUO, WHY DOES IT PLAY ALONG WITH YOU, AND YOU WITH THEM?

A: NEITHER AT THE TIME OF GOULART [1961-1964], NOR IN THAT OF KUBITSHEK [1955-1960], HAVE WE HAD ANY RAPPORT WITH THE STATE. GOULART NOMINATED NELSON DOS SANTOS AS PRESIDENT OF THE EXECUTIVE COMMITTEE OF THE CINEMA. HE REJECTED THE NOMINATION SAYING THAT WE MUST NOT WORK WITH THE STATE NOR EVEN CREATE AN INSTITUTION OF THE CINEMA IN BRAZIL. WE THEREFORE OPERATE OUTSIDE ALL THAT, FINANCED BY BANKS BELONGING TO THE PROGRESSIVE BOURGEOISIE WHO LENT US MONEY AT THE HIGH INTEREST RATE OF 4% PER MONTH. IT IS A QUESTION OF LOAN, NOT OF SUBSIDY. THE NATIONAL INSTITUTE OF THE CINEMA CONTINUES TO FIGHT US IN A SITUATION OF CONSTANT WAR. ON ONE SIDE WE ARE ATTACKED BY POLITICAL AND MORAL CENSORSHIP, AND ON THE OTHER SIDE THERE IS THE TERRORISM OF THE WORD-SLINGING LEFT WHO WANT TO GIVE US A POLITICAL ORIENTATION. FOR US, THE AVANT-GARDE BELONGS TO THE PRACTICAL. THE EXISTENCE OF THE CINEMA NOVO IN BRAZIL IS A CHALLENGE TO THE DEFEATISTS. WE ARE ORGANIZED AND CAPABLE OF CONTINUING THE STRUGGLE. THE NATIONAL INSTITUTE WANTS TO TAKE OUR DIRECTORS INTO ITS SERVICE, BUT AT THE SAME TIME REFUSES THE FILMS WE MAKE. WE HAVE NO RELATIONS WITH THE INSTITUTE EXCEPT THOSE NEEDED TO OBTAIN THE NECESSARY CERTIFICATES OF QUALITY FOR THE FILMS TO BE SHOWN.

Q: A PROPOS BLACK RELIGION, YOU SAID THAT ITS "STAGING" FASCINATES YOU. YOU ALSO SAID THAT YOU ARE FASCINATED BY CATHOLICISM. THE CONNECTION LIES IN THE FACT THAT CATHOLICISM ALSO INVOLVES A "STAGING" OF RELIGION. AND CHRISTIAN MYTH AND BLACK THEOLOGY ARE CEMENTED TOGETHER.

A: THE "STAGING" OF PROTESTANTISM IS VERY SCHEMATIC. I HOLD ONTO ITS PROPHETIC ASPECT, BUT IN TERMS OF "MISE EN SCENE" I FIND CATHOLICISM AND BLACK RELIGION MORE INTERESTING. THERE IS ALSO THE FACT THAT THE BLACK RELIGION

HAS CREATED ITS OWN THEATER IN BRAZIL, ITS OWN DRAMATIC STRUCTURES, TECHNI-
QUES OF INTERPRETATION, CULTURE AND MUSIC.

I AM NOT A MUSICIAN BUT LIKE ALL BRAZILIANS I AM RECEPTIVE TO MUSICAL
PHENOMENA. I WANT TO MAKE A COMPLETELY MUSICAL FILM; NOT SUNG, BUT
WITH A MUSICAL STRUCTURE. IN BRAZILIAN MUSIC ONE FINDS MORE OF THE HISTORY
AND SOCIOLOGY OF BRAZIL THAN IN BOOKS. YOU CAN EVEN FIND THE MENTAL
STRUCTURES OF THE PEOPLE IN THEIR MUSIC. VELOSO AND GIL— MUSICIANS OF
THE BOURGEOIS CULTURE—ARE AT THE FOCAL POINT OF THIS, AND THEY ARE THE
MOST ADVANCED ARTISTS IN BRAZIL. THEY HAVE DISCOVERED SOMETHING REALLY
NEW AND NOT ONLY WITHIN THE LIMITS OF BRAZILIAN MUSIC. THEY HAVE ALSO
SUCCEEDED IN FORMULATING A CRITIQUE OF BRAZILIAN MUSIC, AND OF AMERICAN
MUSIC, THE MUSIC OF COLONIZATION WHICH ARRIVED THROUGH THE MEDIUM
OF FILMS. THEY HAVE EMERGED AS THE GODARDS OF MUSIC. AND FOR THAT, THEY
ARE STILL IN PRISON.

WHAT PEOPLE CALL FOLK LORE IN MY FILMS IS NOT ALTOGETHER FOLK LORE
. . . ONCE MORE WE ARE BACK WITH BRECHT AND EISENSTEIN. WHEN *BLACK
GOD* CAME OUT, SOME CRITICS DECLARED THAT IT WAS NOH, OTHERS THAT IT
WAS KABUKI, BUT IT IS NEITHER. THE TRADITION OF POPULAR SPECTACLES, WHETHER
THEY BE INDIAN, JAPANESE OR THE MYSTERY PLAYS OF THE EUROPEAN MIDDLE
AGES, ARE ALL THE SAME THING. THERE ARE JUST VARIATIONS. IN BRAZIL, PAR-
TICULARLY AMONG THE BLACKS, THERE IS THIS THEATRICAL REPRESENTATION OF
THEIR OWN HISTORY. WHEN I PORTRAY THIS ASPECT IT IS NOT FOLK LORE NOR
IS IT TO APPLY PRECISELY BRECHT'S THEORIES . . . I AM TRYING TO MAKE A MUSICAL
FILM, IN TERMS OF STRUCTURE, NOT OF SOUNDTRACK. IT IS VERY DIFFICULT BUT
IT IS WHAT INTERESTS ME MOST IN THE CINEMA. THIS IS WHY I LIKE WHAT WE
MIGHT CALL "OPERA-CINEMA," WELLES, EISENSTEIN. IT IS NOT AN INTELLECTUAL
FASCINATION BUT A REAL AND DIRECT BOND. I LOVE *IVAN THE TERRIBLE*, *ALEX-
ANDER NEVSKY*, *THE GENERAL LINE*, BUT THEY HAVE NO MORE TO DO WITH US
THAN BRECHT, KABUKI, OR ANYTHING ELSE. WITH ACTORS, FOR INSTANCE, IF I
SO APPLY A TECHNIQUE OF INTERPRETATION, OF EPIC REPRESENTATION, IT IS ONLY
FOR THE POPULAR CHARACTERS WHO ARE INVOLVED IN SUCH A PROCEDURE.

IN *ANTONIO DAS MORTES* SOME ACTORS WORKED WITH A WRITTEN SCRIPT
AND OTHER IMPROVISED, TO AVOID BEING RESTRICTED AND SCHEMATIC. AT THAT
POINT, WE HAD ALMOST REACHED DOCUMENTARY. THIS WAS ALSO THE CASE WITH
TERRA EM TRANSE AND PEOPLE SAID IT WAS A SURREAL INVENTION, BUT IT IS A
REAL DOCUMENTARY. ALTHOUGH THE STYLE IS IRREGULAR YOU WILL SEE, IF YOU
STUDY THE TECHNIQUE, THAT THE CAMERA IS ALWAYS POSITIONED AS IN A
DOCUMENTARY. I WANT TO EMPHASIZE THIS POINT. THERE IS NO SURREALISM, IT
IS NOT BUNUELISM. I FILMED NEWSPAPERS AND TELEVISION BROADCASTS, YET EVEN
IN BRAZIL PEOPLE SAID THAT IT WAS MADE UP. IF THE FILM HAD BEEN IN
CHRONOLOGICAL ORDER, AS IN A REALIST FICTION, THAT WOULD HAVE BEEN FINE,
BUT BECAUSE I CHOSE AN ASYMMETRICAL REPRESENTATION THIS WAS CONFUSED

WITH THE "MISE EN SCENE" AND THE FILM WAS SEEN AS SOMETHING BAROQUE. THE EDITING IS CLEAR AND IT IS NEARER TO A PAINTING BY MONDRIAN THAN A BAROQUE SCULPTURE.

Q: WHEN I SAW *BARRAVENTO* I WAS STRUCK BY THE GENERAL IMPRESSION THAT IT WAS A VERY FORMAL FILM. PERHAPS IT IS VERY COMPOSED, INFLUENCED BY EISENSTEIN, BUT IT IS, ON THE CONTRARY, A DOCUMENTARY ON THE BODY, ON GESTURES, A FILM DIRECTLY OF THE PEOPLE WHO CREATE THEIR OWN PARTS. IT IS EVEN MORE EVIDENT WITH *ANTONIO DAS MORTES*, WITH THE FESTIVAL ON THE CLIFF.

A: IN *ANTONIO DAS MORTES*, THE SCENE I LIKE BEST IS THAT OF THE BATTLE BETWEEN ANTONIO AND THE *CANGACEIRO*. WELL, THAT WAS NO "MISE EN SCENE" CREATED BY ME. I WAS SCHEDULED TO FILM IT ONE AFTERNOON WHEN THERE WAS NO SUNSHINE, SO I DELAYED BECAUSE WE WERE ALL TIRED. THE NEXT DAY, AT SEVEN IN THE MORNING, WE DECIDED TO SHOOT THE BATTLE BETWEEN ST. GEORGE AND THE DRAGON. I DISCUSSED IT WITH THE CAST AND CREW, AND THERE WAS ONE OLD LADY WHO SAID, "WAIT, I KNOW A SONG." THE MOMENT SHE BEGAN TO SING, WE ALL BEGAN TO TAKE UP POSITIONS FOR THE BATTLE. AT THE SAME TIME, SOME ACTORS BEGAN TO MOVE IN TIME TO THE MUSIC AND I REALIZED HOW TO SHOOT THE SCENE. I WAS A SPECTATOR AND PARTICIPANT AT THE SAME TIME. THEY ALL FOUND THEIR POSITIONS VERY NATURALLY, WE SHOT IT ALL IN ONE TAKE AND IT WAS VERY REAL, EVEN AT THE POINT WHERE ANTONIO WOUNDS THE *CANGACEIRO*; THEY DECIDED IT WAS TO BE LIKE THAT, NO SPONTANEITY, BUT WORK LINKED TO PROFOUND REPRESENTATIONAL ROOTS. IT WAS GOOD FOR ME, AS WE REDISCOVERED THE TRADITIONS OF THE WESTERN IN THIS WAY. UNFORTUNATELY, I COULDN'T GET THE SAME RESULTS IN THE ENDING. I HAD A COMPLETELY DIFFERENT CONCEPTION OF THE FINAL DUEL, I WAS FORCED TO CUT A LITTLE. I HAD TO DO IT ALL IN LONG TAKES BUT I DIDN'T HAVE ENOUGH BLANK CARTRIDGES. THE ACTORS WERE AFRAID OF ANTONIO WHO WANTED TO USE REAL BULLETS. THAT COMPLICATED THINGS AS HE MAY HAVE WOUNDED SOMEBODY. AND I HAD ANOTHER IDEA. I WANTED TO DO A SHOT OF THE CHURCH OF ST. GEORGE WITH ALL SORTS OF THINGS EMERGING FROM IT.

Q: WHY COULDN'T YOU DO IT?

A: WE HADN'T ENOUGH BULLETS AND THE EXTRAS WERE AFRAID OF THE HORSE. I COULDN'T DO IT AS I WANTED TO. I WANTED TO RECAPTURE THE SPIRIT OF A WESTERN I HAD SEEN, *GUNS IN THE AFTERNOON*, AS I WAS VERY ATTACHED TO THE IMAGE OF RANDOLPH SCOTT AND JOEL MCCREA FIRING SIDE BY SIDE AT THE END OF THE FILM.

Q: BUT IN THE DUEL SCENE, THE SWORD WHICH BUCKLES . . . WAS THAT AN ACCIDENT?

Antonio Das Mortes and the dead *cangaceiro*.

A: YES, BUT THE ACTOR TRIED TO CORRECT IT. THERE IS A MOUNTING VIOLENCE WHEN THE WOMAN KILLS THE COMMISSAR, THEN THERE IS THE BURIAL AND THE LOVE SCENE. ALL THIS WAS SHOT IN ONE DAY, A SUNDAY, IT WAS ONE OF THE LAST THINGS TO BE SHOT AND THE ACTORS WERE ALL IN A PARTICULAR MOOD. I SUCCEEDED IN THIS FILM IN DOING SOMETHING I HADN'T BEEN ABLE TO DO BEFORE BECAUSE OF PRODUCTION PROBLEMS. I SHUT THE ACTORS AWAY IN THE VILLAGE. THEY HAD NO SCRIPT TO READ, BUT WE TALKED AND IT WORKED VERY NATURALLY. IN FACT, IT WAS NECESSARY TO RID THE ACTORS OF THEIR TRAINING. I DID SEVERAL TAKES WITH ACTORS BEHIND THE CAMERA WHO COULD ENTER THE ACTION AT ANY TIME. NOTHING WAS PLANNED, BUT THINGS WERE ALREADY DETERMINED BY THE MOOD WHICH HAD BEEN CREATED. WE SHOT, RESTRICTED EACH TIME BECAUSE IT WAS IMPOSSIBLE TO REPEAT. THE SEQUENCE WAS BORN OF THE STATE OF THE ACTORS AND NOT PLANNED IN THE "MISE EN SCENE." I HAVE AN ASSISTANT CALLED CALMON AND I GIVE HIM COMPLETE FREEDOM. THEN I SEND THE MATERIAL TO THE EDITOR, ESCOREL, WHO ORGANIZES ALL MY FILMS. THEN I LOOK AT THE FILM WITH FRIENDS, DIEGUES FOR EXAMPLE, AND ALSO DISCUSS IT WITH ESCOREL WHO HAS THE VERY IMPORTANT WORK OF CUTTING THE LONG DRAWN-OUT SCENES. IT MIGHT BECOME UNBEARABLE TO SHOW FILMS JUST AS THEY WERE SHOT. BUT THIS GUY CUTS TIGHTLY AND HAS A VERY SHARP CRITICAL SENSE. I ALWAYS WORK A LOT WITH THE CREW AND WITH BEATO, THE CAMERA OPERATOR AS WELL. I EXPLAIN VARIOUS PRINCIPLES TO HIM, I CHOOSE THE COLORS AND ONLY TWO OR THREE LENSES WERE USED IN THIS FILM. I SHOW HIM THE DISTANCE FROM THE CAMERA, BUT I RARELY LINED UP THE CAMERA IN ORDER TO AVOID COMPOSING THE SHOT. AS THE "MISE EN SCENE" WAS ALREADY SOPHISTICATED, ALTHOUGH CONCERNED WITH PRIMITIVE THINGS, I PREFERRED TO AVOID COMPOSITION AT THE LEVEL OF THE FRAME. THE OPERATOR WAS A VERY GOOD TECHNICIAN, BUT A VERY SIMPLE TYPE, NOT AN AESTHETE OF THE CINEMA. IT WAS MY ASSISTANT WHO DID ALL THE WORK ANALYZING THE CHARACTERS, BUT AT EVERY LEVEL THERE WAS DISCUSSION.

Q: IN *ANTONIO DAS MORTES,* ANTONIO HIMSELF IS PORTRAYED AS A MYTHICAL FIGURE WHILE ALL THE OTHERS ARE REALISTIC. DID YOU INTEND THAT?

A: YES, BECAUSE HE IS CLOSE TO HIS OWN CULTURAL TRADITION, THAT OF A KILLER, AND THIS IS ALSO A REFERENCE TO THE WHOLE TRADITION OF THE WESTERN. ALL THAT MAKES HIM A HERO IS TRUE NO MATTER WHAT THE COUNTRY, JAPAN, BRAZIL, THE UNITED STATES, SICILY . . . THIS RATHER DISTURBING MYSTIQUE OF THE FAR WESTERN HEROES IS TRADITION. THERE IS ALWAYS A REALITY AND A SORT OF QUESTIONING WHICH GOES BEYOND. FOR US IT IS MORE COMPLICATED. IN THE AMERICAN WESTERN THERE IS AN ESTABLISHED LANGUAGE. WHEN THE HERO APPEARS YOU KNOW WHO HE IS BY HIS HORSE AND BY WHAT HE WEARS, HE BRINGS ALL THE INFORMATION WITH HIM. IN OUR CASE THIS CANNOT BE DONE; WE HAVE NO CINEMATIC OR LITERARY TRADITION WHICH SPEAKS OF THIS. AND PERHAPS THIS

IS A LIMITATION ON CINEMA.

Q: YOU WERE SPEAKING OF THE INFLUENCE OF EISENSTEIN AND SAID THAT YOU WOULD LIKE TO MAKE A FILM IN WHICH EACH SHOT WOULD CARRY MUCH INFORMATION. HERE, IN CONTRAST TO *TERRA EM TRANSE* THE SCENE FULL OF INFORMATION IS ABANDONED FOR THE SHOT GIVING ALL THE INFORMATION. IT'S THE SAME PROGRESSION ONE FINDS IN GODARD FROM HIS FIRST FILMS TO HIS LAST. THERE IS NO LONGER A DIALECTIC WITHIN THE SCENE BUT WITHIN THE SHOT. IT'S VERY NOTICEABLE IN *ANTONIO DAS MORTES*.

A: YES, BUT MY PREOCCUPATIONS WITH THIS DID NOT ORIGINATE WITH FILM, BUT WITH A STUDY I MADE OF FAULKNER. I NOTICED THE CINEMATIC QUALITY OF HIS WORK WHICH MAKES HIM A REMARKABLE NOVELIST. IT IS AN IMMEDIACY TAKING PLACE WITHIN A SORT OF PERPETUAL MOTION PACKED WITH CONTRADICTIONS. IT IS A FORM BOTH OPEN AND CLOSED AT THE SAME TIME. I WAS DISAPPOINTED NOT TO FIND THIS IN FILMS DERIVED FROM FAULKNER'S WORK; THESE FILMS ARE RIDICULOUS. LATER, IN ORSON WELLES' *TOUCH OF EVIL*, I FOUND THIS FAULKNERIAN SPIRIT. IN A WAY, IT'S VERY AMERICAN. I EVEN TRIED, AS AN EXERCISE, TO ADAPT CERTAIN SENTENCES OF FAULKNER'S. THE PAROXYSM IN JOYCE IS THAT OF GREAT LITERARY STASIS SET AGAINST THE MOBILITY OF IMAGES. I DON'T KNOW IF GODARD IS AWARE OF IT BUT *A BOUT DE SOUFFLE* [*BREATHLESS*] IS VERY CLOSE TO THE FIRST CHAPTER OF *ULYSSES*. WHETHER HE MEANT IT OR NOT, IT SHOWS GREAT INSIGHT. WHAT INTERESTS ME IN FAULKNER ESPECIALLY IS THE VIOLENCE WHICH IS PUSHED RIGHT TO THE LIMIT WITHOUT CENSORSHIP. THIS EXORCISM, THIS LUCID PRAXIS, CORRESPONDS TO A COLLECTIVE UNCONSCIOUS OF THE UNITED STATES, THERE IS COMPLETE INTEGRATION OF INDIVIDUAL AND SOCIAL ACTION. THIS IS WHAT INSPIRED ME IN *BARRAVENTO*, THIS IMMEDIACY, THIS SEARCH FOR COMPLETE SHOTS CARRYING ALL THE INFORMATION.

Q: THAT'S TO SAY THERE ARE VARIOUS LEVELS WITHIN THE SHOT . . .

A: I THINK THIS IS THE WHOLE PROBLEM OF MODERN ART, THE DIALECTIC BETWEEN SYMMETRY AND ASYMMETRY WHICH CAN BECOME MERE CONVENTION AT ANY MOMENT. IT'S NECESSARY TO PRACTICE THE ART OF BREAKING THINGS OFF . . .

Q: YOU MENTIONED *GUNS IN THE AFTERNOON*, BUT ONE CAN THINK OF ANOTHER FILM APROPOS *ANTONIO DAS MORTES*, NAMELY, *THE MAN WHO SHOT LIBERTY VALENCE*. THESE ARE THE FILMS WHICH INVOLVE AN EXISTING REALITY AND VIOLENTLY CRITICIZE IT. THIS IS APPARENT IN *ANTONIO DAS MORTES*. THE FILM EXISTS WITHOUT BEING REMOTE, ONE IS WITHIN IT YET FEELS AT THE SAME TIME THAT THE ERA OF THE *CANGACEIROS*, OF DAS MORTES, HAS PASSED. THE LAST SHOT SHOWS THAT REPRESSION TAKES MORE SUBTLE FORMS: SHELL, PETROL, MONEY, THE UNITED STATES . . . THE PROBLEM IS POSED DIFFERENTLY.

A: ALTHOUGH IT WASN'T A GREAT FILM, SAM PECKINPAH'S *GUNS IN THE AFTERNOON*

MOVED ME VERY MUCH. THE STRUCTURE IS VERY CALCULATED, BUT IT GOES FURTHER THAN THAT. IN *ANTONIO DAS MORTES*, BY COMPARISON, I WANTED TO MAKE A MORE OBJECTIVE WESTERN, I CHOSE FOUR OR FIVE WESTERNS WHICH I SAW AGAIN AND AGAIN TO REACH CERTAIN CONCLUSIONS. I SAW *RED RIVER*, *RIO BRAVO* AND *EL DORADO*. I HAD TO RECOVER THEIR FEELING, THOSE GESTURES IN HAWKS, WHICH ARE MADE WITH SUCH UNDERSTATEMENT. IT IS REAL ANTI-EXPRESSIONIST REPRESENTATION. BUT AT THE MOMENT OF SHOOTING, EVERYTHING CHANGED AND I COULDN'T STICK TO WHAT I HAD LEARNED. BUT I WANT VERY MUCH TO RETURN TO MY REFERENCE TO *GUNS IN THE AFTERNOON*, AND THE TWO MEN FIRING. IT WAS AN UNCONSCIOUS THING, BECAUSE WHEN DAS MORTES DEFIES THE COLONEL I HAD FORGOTTEN THE REFERENCE TO PECKINPAH, EXCEPT THAT IT WAS A SHORT TAKE WHEREAS MINE WAS LONG, ABOUT FORTY SECONDS. AT CANNES PEOPLE DIDN'T NOTICE THE REFERENCE. BUT YESTERDAY SOMEONE SPOKE ABOUT *GUNS IN THE AFTERNOON* A PROPOS *ANTONIO DAS MORTES* AND I WAS VERY MOVED.

Q: WHEN THE COLONEL SAYS TO MATA VACA, "YOU WILL RID ME OF THIS VERMIN," YOU CUT TO THE DANCE AND WE SEE ALL THE PEOPLE WHO HAVE BEEN KILLED. DID YOU NOT FILM THE SHOOTING, OR DID YOU CUT IT?

A: I didn't shoot it.

Q: That, too, is a very Eisensteinian principle.

A: I was wondering how to film the massacre. I told the people who were to act it, "You are going to die, they are going to kill you." And they began to sing. They sang for an hour. In Brazil there is a very violent dance, the Xaxado. I said to the others, "You are going to kill them, but you must tease them first." They sang the Xaxado and Mata Vaca, who is the theater actor, and of a bourgeois family, also began to get into the mood. I wanted to do two long four minute takes of this. But after a minute I had to stop. They became so involved that they had taken out their knives and were beginning to slash at people's feet. If I had let it go on, the would have wounded somebody. People reached a complete truth because it was within the tradition. Even in 1969 they could rediscover that spirit. Afterwards I filmed the massacre, but not the actual killing. I preferred to film the people dead. These were complete shots.

Q: Could you tell us a little about the color?

A: When Barreto did the photography for *Vidas Secas* he made the first discovery of a lighting which corresponds to a particular Brazilian climate. Barreto always said that the camera must keep its distance and remain in that tradition of early photographs and engravings. He had a great influence on the cameraman who is working with us now. To make this color film, I chose Alfonso Beato who had spoken with Barreto and he knew Brazil well having worked there for years as a photographer. Our principles were not to compose shots and not to add to the natural color which was already very sophisticated. But I did make certain preparations in terms of "mise en scene," and choice of colors for costumes.

Now I want to make something clear about independent filmmaking. The cinema is an industry, an existing economic phenomenon be it in either a capitalist or socialist system. Filmmakers cannot behave like the artists of past centuries. They often engage in polemics against producers when they are unable to make and distribute their films, and these are often false arguments. When a producer gives a young director money to make a film, he believes that the director is capable of making that film. Afterwards, when the finished film does not resemble at all the film which the director had described, the producer is left with all the responsibility for distributing a film unsuited to the market. It is not a question of talent, but of a certain literary, marginal, masochistic frame of mind. New methods must be found for making films successful. Not all producers are commercially minded, ill natured or dictatorial.

EVERY FILM EVER MADE IS ONE WHICH HAS FOUND FINANCIAL BACKING. FILM-MAKERS, HOWEVER MUCH THEY CONSIDER THEMSELVES ARTISTS AND INTELLECTUALS, MUST ALSO REALIZE THAT THEY ARE BOUND TO THE CINEMA AS AN ECONOMIC PHENOMENON. EITHER HE MAKES "AUTEUR" FILMS, VERY BEAUTIFUL, VERY POLITICAL, WHICH CAN BE SHOWN IN ALL THE LARGE THEATERS QUESTIONING ALL THE PRIN-CIPLES OF COMMERCIALISM, OR HE MAKES MARGINAL FILMS AND MUST ORGANIZE AN UNDERGROUND MEANS OF DISTRIBUTION. IN LATIN AMERICA, THE THIRD WORLD, AND AT THE FESTIVALS, A PECULIAR DEMAGOGIC POLITICS COMBINES WITH CINEMATIC PRACTICES. BAD FILMS TRY TO JUSTIFY THEMSELVES BY THE FILM ITSELF, AND ARE VERY SUBJECTIVE SINCE THEY HAVE NOT SUCCEEDED IN MAKING THEIR OWN REVOLUTION AT THE LEVEL OF PRODUCTION. THEY TALK A LOT, BUT THERE ARE NO CONCRETE RESULTS. THIS CRISIS WHICH IS COMMON TO ALL COUNTRIES, STEMS, THEN, FROM THE FILMMAKERS' OWN ALIENATION. CINEMA IS AN ACTUAL, MODERN ENTITY AND ITS THEORY AND PRACTICE MUST BE BOUND TOGETHER. FILM-MAKERS ARE ALSO RESPONSIBLE, NOT ONLY THE PRODUCERS AND DISTRIBUTORS. IF YOU MAKE ANTI-ESTABLISHMENT FILMS WHICH CANNOT BE DISTRIBUTED, THE ESTABLISHMENT DOESN'T CARE A DAMN. THE CINEMA MUST BE MASS COMMUNICA-TION IN THE MOST OPEN WAY POSSIBLE, NOT JUST A HISTORY OF SECRET SOCIETIES. AND TO BRAVE THE SYSTEM YOU MUST BE ORGANIZED.

TRANSLATED BY SIMON FIELD, JO LEVY AND PETER SAINSBURY. THIS INTERVIEW IS REPRINTED FROM *AFTERIMAGE* (LONDON), NO. 1, APRIL 1970, AND IS SLIGHT-LY ABRIDGED.

Notes
1. The military coup of 1964 broke up several civilian parties but the monied land owners continued to use the *juguncos* to maintain their power. The social framework is reflected accurately in *Antonio Das Mortes*.
2. The Vargas dictatorship banned the practice of African religions.
3. Milagres, a town open to the cinema. *Entre o Amor e o Cangaco, Os Fuzis, Tropici, Antonio Das Mortes* were all shot there. Farias, Coutinho, Lima Junior and Hirszman are all going to make there to make films this year. Milagres is close to Salvador, the capital of Bahia, a province. The popula-tion is poor and forgotten. A young peasant approached the camera operator on *Antonio Das Mortes*, who was calculating the light, and said, "2.8. At this time of day, if the camera is here and the sun there, it's always 2.8. I've noticed that with the other films." From that moment he was made assistant.

4. Oswald de Andrade, the greatest Brazilian poet and writer, now dead, says, "Tupi or not Tupi"—to be primitive or not to be primitive; the Tupi were an Indian race destroyed by white civilization. Our generation of filmmakers is writing the pre-history of Brazilian cinema and in this everything is valid; fiction films and the hundreds of documentaries that Thomas Farkas is currently producing with a large team of young directors. I am sure that all the predictions of Cinema Novo will be surpassed.

AFTER *BARREN LIVES:* THE LEGACY OF CINEMA NOVO [1985]

AN INTERVIEW WITH NELSON PEREIRA DOS SANTOS

RICHARD PEÑA ◆◇◆◇◆◇◆◇◆◇◆◇◆◇◆◇◆◇

NELSON PEREIRA DOS SANTOS HAS BEEN AT THE FOREFRONT OF BRAZILIAN CINEMA SINCE THE 1950'S. THE MORE THAN TWENTY FILMS HE HAS MADE IN THE LAST 35 YEARS CONSTITUTE ONE OF THE MOST IMPORTANT BODIES OF WORK IN LATIN AMERICAN FILM. LIKE MANY OF THE DIRECTORS OF HIS GENERATION, DOS SANTOS STUDIED FILM IN EUROPE (AT FRANCE'S I.D.H.E.C.) AFTER WORLD WAR II. HE RETURNED TO BRAZIL WHERE HE, WITH A GROUP OF FILMMAKERS AND CRITICS, ATTEMPTED TO REFRAME THE DEBATES AND DEVELOPMENTS AROUND THE ITALIAN NEOREALISTS AND THE *CAHIERS* GROUP WITHIN THE SOCIAL AND CULTURAL CONTEXT OF BRAZIL. *BARREN LIVES* WAS HIS FOURTH FILM, MADE IN 1963, AND IT ESTABLISHED HIS INTERNATIONAL REPUTATION. PORTRAYING THE HARSH REALITIES OF EXISTENCE FOR A MIGRANT FAMILY IN THE NORTHEAST, THE COUNTRY'S MOST UNDERDEVELOPED REGION, THE FILM IMMEDIATELY BECAME PART OF THE POLITICAL DEBATES OF THE PERIOD OVER GOVERNMENT POLICIES IN THAT REGION. STYLISTICAL-LY, IT MARKS THE TRANSITION IN BRAZILIAN CINEMA FROM NEOREALISM TO CINEMA NOVO.

BELOW ARE EXCERPTS FROM AN INTERVIEW HELD IN ROTTERDAM IN 1985, IN WHICH DOS SANTOS DISCUSSES HIS CAREER AND THE DEVELOPMENT OF BRAZILIAN CINEMA.

Richard Peña: Can you speak a little bit about the filmmaking situation in Brazil in the fifties, when you began making films?

Nelson Pereira Dos Santos: There were two basic film producing companies in Brazil at that time, Vera Cruz in Sao Paulo and Atlantida in Rio. I was living in Rio and began work at a small competitor of Atlantida's, Flama Films, which had a huge success with a comedy called *Tudo Azul*. Anyway, it was at Flama that I met Alex Viany and others who were interested in trying to work on independent productions. There were several people trying to set up production on their own, away from Atlantida or even Flama—many of them were rather ambitious. There was a lot of hope, and a lot of talk, but then all of a sudden everything began to collapse. Vera Cruz went bankrupt, and Atlantida began to reduce its production. It was an extremely difficult moment for anyone involved in cinema.

RP: What do you think were the reasons for this collapse of the industry in the early fifties?

NP: Television was certainly one of them. Television began taking over the cultural position which the most successful Brazilian films—the *chanchadas* of Atlantida—used to occupy. In fact, several of Atlantida's biggest stars moved over to television. So, anyway, it became sort of every man for himself, and I worked on a few independent productions—*Blanca Mais Nao Cai*, which was based on a famous radio show, *Amei Um Bicheiro*, and a few others. It was at this time that I began organizing the production of *Rio 40 Graus*; at that time—'53, '54—there were extremely few Brazilian films in production, but there were a couple of influential national meetings on the state of the Brazilian cinema, at which all the "great questions" about finance and distribution and government involvement were raised. These meetings, in a way, were a response to the failure of Vera Cruz; Vera Cruz, at that time, was what Embrafilme is today—any filmmaker who was given the opportunity would attack it.

RP: At this time, did you see yourself as working out of a tradition in Brazilian culture, a tradition which went back to the work of Graciliano Ramos and the other major figures of the thirties and forties?

NP: Yes, very much. Actually, this was the level of debate that I myself liked to enter in on. I've never been much for getting involved in discussions of whether or not the government should open up a factory for producing raw film stock. Even today there are people who believe that Brazil will only be able to develop a great national cinema when there's

A DOMESTIC FACTORY FOR PRODUCING RAW STOCK! I MYSELF WAS INTERESTED IN THE ROLE WHICH THE CINEMA COULD PLAY WITHIN BRAZILIAN CULTURE, OR IN HOW WE COULD CREATE A TRULY NATIONAL CINEMA OF WORLD CALIBRE. SO ALL THOSE FIGURES FROM THE THIRTIES AND FROM BEFORE—MARIO DE ANDRADE, OSWALD DE ANDRADE, ETC.—WERE EXTREMELY IMPORTANT FOR US. WE HAD TO FIGHT AGAINST A WHOLE SERIES OF RIDICULOUS PREJUDICES AND BELIEFS—THERE WERE THOSE WHO CLAIMED THAT THE BRAZILIAN LANGUAGE "WASN'T CINEMATIC," OR THAT BRAZILIAN SKIN TONES WOULD BE TOO CONTRASTY. RIDICULOUS THINGS LIKE THAT, THAT CAME DOWN FROM VERA CRUZ OR EVEN ATLANTIDA.

RP: DID YOUR DISCUSSIONS ABOUT NATIONAL CINEMA EVER INCLUDE DEBATE ABOUT FILM LANGUAGE OR STYLE? WAS THERE TALK OF ESTABLISHING A BRAZILIAN FILM STYLE?

NP: THERE WAS SOME . . . IT DEPENDED ON WHAT YOUR BACKGROUND WAS. MINE, FOR EXAMPLE, IS DOMINATED BY THE AMERICAN CINEMA—YOU MIGHT SAY THAT I WAS BROUGHT UP ON THE HOLLYWOOD CINEMA. MY FATHER WAS A GREAT FILM FAN, AND WE'D GO TOGETHER OFTEN. LATER ON, WHEN I WENT TO FRANCE, I WAS EXPOSED TO EUROPEAN CINEMA—FRENCH, SOVIET, ITALIAN, ALL THE CLASSICS. THERE, ALL THE DISCUSSION CENTERED ON ITALIAN NEOREALISM; WHAT IMPRESS-ED ME ABOUT THE NEOREALIST FILMS WAS NOT THEIR THEMES OR THEIR STYLE BUT THEIR PRODUCTION MODEL—THEY DEMONSTRATED HOW YOU COULD MAKE FILMS WITHOUT ANY MONEY. HOW ALL YOU HAD TO DO WAS GO OUT ON THE STREET. HOW YOU DIDN'T NEED STUDIOS, AND EXPENSIVE LIGHTING EQUIPMENT OR COSTUMES. EVEN AT FLAMA OR ATLANTIDA, THE SET-UP WAS LIKE A HOLLYWOOD STUDIO, EVEN IF NOT AS WELL EQUIPPED. BUT WITH NEOREALISM—WELL, LIGHT WE HAVE PLENTY OF IN BRAZIL. NON-PROFESSIONAL ACTORS? THE SAME. WE WERE YOUNG AND NAIVE, BUT WITH A LOT OF ENERGY; NEOREALISM SEEMED TO OPEN UP NEW POSSIBILITIES FOR US.

I THINK IT WASN'T THE SAME FOR THE GROUP THAT WOULD LATER BECOME CINEMA NOVO; THEIR CINEMATIC EDUCATION WAS MUCH MORE INTERNATIONAL CINEMA, THEY WEREN'T AS INFLUENCED PERHAPS BY THE AMERICAN CINEMA AS I WAS. GODARD, OF COURSE, WAS ALSO A HUGE INFLUENCE ON EVERYONE.

RP: COULD YOU TALK A BIT ABOUT THE RELATIONSHIP BETWEEN BRAZILIAN CINEMA AND POPULAR CULTURE?

NP: WELL, FIRST OF ALL, "POPULAR CULTURE" ISN'T JUST ONE THING—THERE ARE MANY KINDS OF POPULAR CULTURE IN BRAZIL, MANY LEVELS. I THINK THAT MANY OF THE FILMMAKERS OF MY GENERATION WERE ALL FASCINATED BY ANTHROPOLOGY—MY WIFE IS AN ANTHROPOLOGIST—AND THAT WE TRIED TO BE AMATEUR AN-THROPOLOGISTS IN OUR FILMS. TO USE OUR FILMS REALLY TO DISCOVER BRAZIL, FOR OURSELVES AND FOR OUR AUDIENCES, AS SO MUCH HAD BEEN HIDDEN OR FORBIDDEN. POPULAR CULTURE IN BRAZIL EXISTS AS A KIND OF DEFENSE AGAINST

OFFICIAL CULTURE—IT'S A PRIVATE SPACE FOR THE PEOPLE TO RETREAT TO. PAR-
TIALLY BECAUSE IT IS SO PRIVATE, IT'S DIFFICULT FOR OUTSIDERS TO ENTER INTO
IT. ONE PLACE WHERE I TRIED WAS IN *O Amuleto de Ogum* [*The Amulet of
Ogum*]; I THINK I WAS AT LEAST PARTIALLY SUCCESSFUL THERE BECAUSE THE
PHENOMENON THAT IT WAS DESCRIBING, UMBANDA, OR AFRO-BRAZILIAN RELIGION,
IS SO INCREDIBLY PERVASIVE IN CONTEMPORARY BRAZIL THAT IT'S NO LONGER SUCH
A SECRET PRACTICE. BUT IT WAS THE FIRST BRAZILIAN FILM TO TREAT IT AS ANYTHING
MORE THAN FOLKLORE OR BACKGROUND; I TRIED TO SHOW HOW IT ENTERS THE
LIVES OF THESE PEOPLE ON A DAILY BASIS. IT'S HARD, THOUGH, TO SHOW "POPULAR
CULTURE" AS IT REALLY EXISTS, WITHOUT BEING IRONIC OR CONDESCENDING. IN
Na Estrada da Vida, MOST OF THE JOKES WERE BASED ON THE FALSE INNOCENCE
OF MILIONARIO AND ZE RICO—WE KNOW THEY'RE NOT SERIOUS, AND THEY KNOW
THAT WE KNOW THEY'RE NOT SERIOUS.

RP: COULD YOU SPEAK A BIT ABOUT THE POLITICAL CLIMATE FOR MAKING FILMS IN BRAZIL TODAY? HOW CAN YOU COMPARE IT TO THE SITUATION 10 OR 15 YEARS AGO?

NP: WELL, OF COURSE, THINGS HAVE CHANGED QUITE A LOT RECENTLY. TEN OR FIFTEEN YEARS AGO THERE WAS AN EXTREMELY STRICT CENSORSHIP AND WE NEVER KNEW WHAT COULD OR COULDN'T BE SAID IN A FILM. IT WAS AN ESPECIALLY DIFFICULT TIME FOR THOSE OF US WHO WANTED TO CONTINUE THE SOCIALLY ENGAGED CINEMA OF THE EARLY SIXTIES. BUT, BIT BY BIT, THE RESTRICTIONS WERE RELAXED, UNTIL TODAY WE REALLY DO HAVE A LOT OF FREEDOM.

RP: DID THE FILMS OF CINEMA NOVO EVER REALLY REACH THE PUBLIC? DO ANY OF THE CHANGES IN YOUR OWN WORK OVER THE YEARS REFLECT AN INCREASED DESIRE FOR A GREATER AUDIENCE FOR YOUR WORK?

NP: THERE'S ONE FACT, RIGHT AT THE START, WHICH I SHOULD MENTION BEFORE WE BEGIN THIS DISCUSSION: THE GREAT MAJORITY OF BRAZILIANS HAVE NEVER BEEN TO SEE A MOVIE. EVEN IN THE GREAT DAYS OF THE HOLLYWOOD CINEMA, THE '30S AND '40S, THE MOVIE THEATERS WERE ONLY LOCATED IN THOSE DISTRICTS WHERE PEOPLE WHO COULD AFFORD TO GO LIVED—THE MIDDLE-CLASS OR ABOVE. I REMEMBER THAT, WHEN I WAS YOUNG, YOU HAD TO WEAR A TIE AND SHOES— YOU COULDN'T GET IN IF YOU HAD ON SNEAKERS, OR SANDALS. ANYWAY, THIS IS AN IMPORTANT FACT TO REMEMBER— THE MAJORITY OF BRAZILIANS HAVE NEVER SEEN ANY MOVIE— BRAZILIAN, AMERICAN OR OTHERWISE. CINEMA NOVO GREW UP FROM THE SAME ROOTS AS BRAZILIAN LITERATURE AND PAINTING—THAT IS, OUT OF A KIND OF ANTI-COLONIALIST FEELING AND, BASICALLY, THEIR PROBLEM WAS THAT THEY HAD TO REACH A MIDDLE-CLASS AUDIENCE THAT DIDN'T WANT TO DEAL WITH THE ROLE OF BLACKS OR INDIANS IN THE FORMATION OF BRAZILIAN CULTURE OR HISTORY. THIS WAS ONE OF THE REASONS WHY THERE WAS NEVER REALLY AN IMPORTANT RELATIONSHIP BETWEEN THE CINEMA NOVO AND THE MOVIEGOING PUBLIC; ANOTHER REASON IS THE RADICAL "ELITISM" OF SOME OF THE CINEMA NOVO FILMMAKERS, THE FEELING THAT THEY DIDN'T HAVE TO REACH OUT TO THE AUDIENCE, BUT THAT THE AUDIENCE HAD TO CATCH UP WITH THEM. THIS FEELING ALSO GOT IN THE WAY OF THE FILMS REACHING A GREATER PUBLIC. FORTUNATELY, I THINK THE ERA OF "THE DIRECTOR C'EST MOI" IS OVER. AFTER THAT FIRST PHASE, I THINK THERE WAS A REAL ATTEMPT TO CREATE A POPULAR CINEMA THAT WAS ALSO CULTURALLY BRAZILIAN; BEFORE THAT, FILMS CONSIDERED "POPULAR" WERE ESSENTIALLY MIMETIC IMITATIONS OF HOLLYWOOD FILMS.

RP: WHAT HAS BEEN THE EFFECT OF HAVING EMBRAFILME—AN OFFICIAL, GOVERNMENT AGENCY—INVOLVED IN THE PRODUCTION AND DISTRIBUTION OF BRAZILIAN FILMS?

NP: EMBRAFILME WAS ACTUALLY FOUNDED AT THE SUGGESTION OF THE FILMMAKERS THEMSELVES AND WAS SET UP VERY MUCH TO PROTECT THE INTERESTS OF BRAZILIAN FILMS. FOR EXAMPLE, ONE OF THEIR FIRST ACTS WAS TO SET A MINIMUM NUMBER

OF DAYS EACH YEAR FOR EACH MOVIE THEATER IN WHICH BRAZILIAN FILMS HAD TO BE SHOWN. THIS LAW, WHICH HAS CHANGED AND BEEN EXPANDED SOMEWHAT OVER THE YEARS, WASN'T OFTEN OBEYED, BUT IT DID REPRESENT AN ATTEMPT BY THE GOVERNMENT TO HELP THE FILM INDUSTRY ON THE COMMERCIAL LEVEL. IN ALL HONESTY, THOUGH, THE SITUATION OF EMBRAFILME IN THE GOVERNMENT WAS ALWAYS RATHER DELICATE—SOME ELEMENTS IN THE GOVERNMENT FELT THAT BRAZILIAN CINEMA WAS GOOD FOR THE IMAGE OF THE COUNTRY. OTHERS MERELY SAW IT AS A WAY OF PACIFYING SOME OF THE MORE RADICAL CULTURAL ELEMENTS IN THE COUNTRY. IT'S A VERY BRAZILIAN WAY OF THINKING, AND A VERY CYNICAL ONE. ON THE ONE HAND, EMBRAFILME GAVE DIRECTORS TOTAL FREEDOM—FOR EXAMPLE, EMBRAFILME NEVER ITSELF PROHIBITED A SINGLE SCREENPLAY WHICH WAS SUBMITTED TO IT; ON THE OTHER HAND, FILMS WHICH THEY HAD PRODUCED WERE LATER PROHIBITED BY THE POLICE.

RP: IF THE VAST MAJORITY OF BRAZILIANS DON'T GO TO THE MOVIES, THEN WHO ARE YOU MAKING MOVIES FOR? THE MIDDLE-CLASS?

NP: IN A SENSE, YES, MY PRIMARY AUDIENCE IS THE MIDDLE-CLASS, AND CIRCUMSTANCES AREN'T SUCH THAT THIS REALITY WILL CHANGE SIGNIFICANTLY RIGHT NOW. WHAT MY FILMS CAN DO, PERHAPS, IN THE SAME WAY AS CINEMA NOVO FILMS, IS MAKE THE MIDDLE-CLASS REFLECT A BIT ON ITS OWN REALITY AND ROLE IN BRAZIL RIGHT NOW. OPEN UP A DEBATE, WITHIN THE MIDDLE-CLASS, ABOUT ITS RELATIONSHIP TO THE GREAT MASSES OF BRAZILIANS. FOR EXAMPLE, A FILM LIKE *VIDAS SECAS* REALLY HAD A KIND OF NATIONAL EFFECT; IT WAS SEEN AS PART OF A NATIONAL DISCUSSION ABOUT THE CONDITIONS OF THE NORTHEAST OF BRAZIL, AND THE PLACE WHICH ECONOMIC DEVELOPMENT OF THAT REGION MIGHT HAVE WITHIN NATIONAL DEVELOPMENT PROGRAMS. OF COURSE, I MAKE THESE FILMS ALSO TO EXPRESS MY OWN FEELINGS AND THOUGHTS ABOUT DIFFERENT ISSUES. IN BRAZIL I'VE BEEN ASKED WHETHER I'LL STILL BE ABLE TO MAKE MY FILMS LIVING IN A DEMOCRACY.

RP: HOW WOULD YOU CHARACTERIZE THE MAJORITY OF BRAZILIAN FILMS MADE TODAY?

NP: WELL, CINEMA NOVO, OF COURSE, NO LONGER EXISTS. THERE'S NO LONGER THE CULTURAL NEED FOR THAT KIND OF MILITANT, COHESIVE MOVEMENT. NOW THAT BRAZILIAN CINEMA HAS BECOME ACCEPTED AS A CULTURAL FACT, IT'S BECOME EXTREMELY DIVERSIFIED, AND THUS DIFFICULT TO CHARACTERIZE AS ONE THING OR THE OTHER.

THERE'S A VERY LARGE NUMBER OF PORNO-*CHANCHADAS*—SOFT-CORE EROTIC COMEDIES—AND MANY BRAZILIAN EXHIBITORS WOULD RATHER SHOW THESE FILMS TO COMPLY WITH THE LAW OF "OBLIGATORY SCREENINGS OF BRAZILIAN FILMS" THAN, SAY, THE FILMS MADE BY THOSE DIRECTORS WHO CAME OUT OF CINEMA NOVO. I SHOULD ALSO MENTION THAT THERE IS A VERY IMPORTANT DOCUMENTARY MOVEMENT IN BRAZIL NOW; IMPORTANT FROM BOTH A CULTURAL AND

POLITICAL STANDPOINT. THESE FILMS ARE RARELY SHOWN ANYWHERE, OUTSIDE OF THE FILM CLUBS OR UNIVERSITY SETTINGS—THEY HAVE NO ACCESS EITHER TO THE COMMERCIAL THEATERS OR TO TELEVISION. THE CENTER FOR THE DOCUMENTARY PRODUCTION IS SAO PAULO.

RP: WOULD YOU SAY THAT BRAZIL IS STILL UNDER THE CULTURAL DOMINATION OF THE U.S.?

NP: VERY MUCH SO. WHERE WE SEE THIS ESPECIALLY IS IN THE AREA OF TELEVISION. LAST YEAR, ON TV GLOBO, WELL OVER 1,000 HOLLYWOOD FILMS WERE SHOWN AND NOT A SINGLE BRAZILIAN FILM. WHAT COULD BE A GREAT MARKET FOR US IS TOTALLY CLOSED TO US.

Vidas Secas

ARGENTINA

LA APARICION CON VIDA
DETENIDOS - DESAPARECIDOS
...RES DE PLAZA DE MAYO

TOWARD A THIRD CINEMA [1969]

FERNANDO SOLANAS AND OCTAVIO GETINO

JUST A SHORT TIME AGO IT WOULD HAVE SEEMED LIKE A QUIXOTIC ADVEN-
TURE IN THE COLONIALIZED, NEOCOLONIALIZED, OR EVEN THE IMPERIALIST NA-
TIONS THEMSELVES TO MAKE ANY ATTEMPT TO CREATE *FILMS OF DECOLONIZATION*
THAT TURNED THEIR BACK ON OR ACTIVELY OPPOSED THE SYSTEM. UNTIL RECENT-
LY, FILM HAD BEEN SYNONYMOUS WITH SHOW OR AMUSEMENT: IN A WORD, IT
WAS ONE MORE *CONSUMER GOOD*. AT BEST, FILMS SUCCEEDED IN BEARING WITNESS
TO THE DECAY OF BOURGEOIS VALUES AND TESTIFYING TO SOCIAL INJUSTICE. AS
A RULE, FILMS ONLY DEALT WITH EFFECT NEVER WITH CAUSE; IT WAS CINEMA OF
MYSTIFICATION OR ANTI-HISTORICISM. IT WAS *SURPLUS VALUE* CINEMA. CAUGHT
UP IN THESE CONDITIONS, FILMS, THE MOST VALUABLE TOOL OF COMMUNICATION
OF OUR TIMES, WERE DESTINED TO SATISFY ONLY THE IDEOLOGICAL AND ECONOMIC
INTERESTS OF THE *OWNERS OF THE FILM INDUSTRY*, THE LORDS OF THE WORLD
FILM MARKET, THE GREAT MAJORITY OF WHOM WERE FROM THE UNITED STATES.

WAS IT POSSIBLE TO OVERCOME THIS SITUATION? HOW COULD THE PROBLEM
OF TURNING OUT LIBERATION FILMS BE APPROACHED WHEN COSTS CAME TO SEVERAL
THOUSAND DOLLARS AND THE DISTRIBUTION AND EXHIBITION CHANNELS WERE
IN THE HANDS OF THE ENEMY? HOW COULD THE CONTINUITY OF THE WORK
BE GUARANTEED? HOW COULD THE PUBLIC BE REACHED? HOW COULD SYSTEM-
IMPOSED REPRESSION AND CENSORSHIP BE VANQUISHED? THESE QUESTIONS, WHICH
COULD BE MULTIPLIED IN ALL DIRECTIONS, LED AND STILL LEAD MANY PEOPLE TO
SKEPTICISM OR RATIONALIZATION: "REVOLUTIONARY FILMS CANNOT BE MADE BEFORE
THE REVOLUTION"; "REVOLUTIONARY FILMS HAVE BEEN POSSIBLE ONLY IN THE
LIBERATED COUNTRIES"; "WITHOUT THE SUPPORT OF REVOLUTIONARY POLITICAL
POWER, REVOLUTIONARY FILMS OR ART IS IMPOSSIBLE." THE MISTAKE WAS DUE TO
TAKING THE SAME APPROACH TO REALITY AND FILMS AS DID THE BOURGEOISIE.
THE MODELS OF PRODUCTION, DISTRIBUTION, AND EXHIBITION CONTINUED TO
BE *THOSE OF HOLLYWOOD* PRECISELY BECAUSE, IN IDEOLOGY AND POLITICS, FILMS
HAD NOT YET BECOME THE VEHICLE FOR A CLEARLY DRAWN DIFFERENTIATION BET-
WEEN BOURGEOIS IDEOLOGY AND POLITICS. A REFORMIST POLICY, AS MANIFESTED
IN DIALOGUE WITH THE ADVERSARY, IN COEXISTENCE, AND IN THE RELEGATION
OF NATIONAL CONTRADICTIONS TO THOSE BETWEEN TWO SUPPOSEDLY UNIQUE

BLOCS—THE U.S.S.R. AND THE U.S.A.—WAS AND IS UNABLE TO PRODUCE ANYTHING BUT A CINEMA WITHIN THE SYSTEM ITSELF. AT BEST, IT CAN BE THE *"PROGRESSIVE" WING OF ESTABLISHMENT CINEMA*. WHEN ALL IS SAID AND DONE, SUCH CINEMA WAS DOOMED TO WAIT UNTIL THE WORLD CONFLICT WAS RESOLVED PEACEFULLY IN FAVOR OF SOCIALISM IN ORDER TO CHANGE QUALITATIVELY. THE MOST DARING ATTEMPTS OF THOSE FILMMAKERS WHO STROVE TO CONQUER THE FORTRESS OF OFFICIAL CINEMA ENDED, AS JEAN-LUC GODARD ELOQUENTLY PUT IT, WITH THE FILMMAKERS THEMSELVES "TRAPPED INSIDE THE FORTRESS."

BUT THE QUESTIONS THAT WERE RECENTLY RAISED APPEARED PROMISING: THEY AROSE FROM A NEW HISTORICAL SITUATION TO WHICH THE FILMMAKER, AS IS OFTEN THE CASE WITH THE EDUCATED STRATA OF OUR COUNTRIES, WAS RATHER A LATE-COMER: TEN YEARS OF THE CUBAN REVOLUTION, THE VIETNAMESE STRUGGLE, AND THE DEVELOPMENT OF A WORLDWIDE LIBERATION MOVEMENT WHOSE FORCE IS TO BE FOUND IN THE THIRD WORLD COUNTRIES. *THE EXISTENCE OF MASSES ON THE WORLDWIDE REVOLUTIONARY PLANE WAS THE SUBSTANTIAL FACT WITHOUT WHICH THOSE QUESTIONS COULD NOT HAVE BEEN POSED.* A NEW HISTORICAL SITUATION AND A NEW MAN BORN IN THE PROCESS OF THE ANTI-IMPERIALIST STRUGGLE DEMANDED A NEW, REVOLUTIONARY ATTITUDE FROM THE FILMMAKERS OF THE WORLD. THE QUESTION OF WHETHER OR NOT MILITANT CINEMA *WAS POSSIBLE* BEFORE THE REVOLUTION BEGAN TO BE REPLACED, AT LEAST WITHIN SMALL GROUPS, BY THE QUESTION OF *WHETHER OR NOT SUCH A CINEMA WAS NECESSARY TO CONTRIBUTE TO THE POSSIBILITY OF REVOLUTION.* AN AFFIRMATIVE ANSWER WAS THE STARTING POINT FOR THE FIRST ATTEMPTS TO CHANNEL THE PROCESS OF SEEKING POSSIBILITIES IN NUMEROUS COUNTRIES. EXAMPLES ARE NEWSREEL, A U.S. NEW LEFT FILM GROUP, THE *CINEGIORNALI* OF THE ITALIAN STUDENT MOVEMENT, THE FILMS MADE BY THE *ETATS GENERAUX DU CINEMA FRANCAIS*, AND THOSE OF THE BRITISH AND JAPANESE STUDENT MOVEMENTS, ALL A CONTINUATION AND DEEPENING OF THE WORK OF A JORIS IVENS OR A CHRIS MARKER. LET IT SUFFICE TO OBSERVE THE FILMS OF SANTIAGO ALVAREZ IN CUBA, OR THE CINEMA BEING DEVELOPED BY DIFFERENT FILMMAKERS IN "THE HOMELAND OF ALL," AS BOLIVAR WOULD SAY, AS THEY SEEK A REVOLUTIONARY LATIN AMERICAN CINEMA.

A PROFOUND DEBATE ON THE ROLE OF INTELLECTUALS AND ARTISTS BEFORE LIBERATION TODAY IS ENRICHING THE PERSPECTIVES OF INTELLECTUAL WORK ALL OVER THE WORLD. HOWEVER, THIS DEBATE OSCILLATES BETWEEN TWO POLES: ONE WHICH PROPOSES TO *RELEGATE* ALL INTELLECTUAL WORK CAPACITY TO A *SPECIFICALLY* POLITICAL OR POLITICAL-MILITARY FUNCTION, DENYING PERSPECTIVES TO ALL ARTISTIC ACTIVITY WITH THE IDEA THAT SUCH ACTIVITY MUST INELUCTABLY BE ABSORBED BY THE SYSTEM, AND THE OTHER WHICH MAINTAINS AN INNER DUALITY OF THE INTELLECTUAL: ON THE ONE HAND, THE "WORK OF ART," "THE PRIVILEGE OF BEAUTY," AN ART AND A BEAUTY WHICH ARE NOT NECESSARILY BOUND TO THE NEEDS OF THE REVOLUTIONARY POLITICAL PROCESS, AND, ON THE OTHER, A POLITICAL COMMITMENT WHICH GENERALLY CONSISTS IN SIGNING CERTAIN ANTI-

IMPERIALIST MANIFESTOES. IN PRACTICE, THIS POINT OF VIEW MEANS THE *SEPARATION OF POLITICS AND ART*.

THIS POLARITY RESTS, AS WE SEE IT, ON TWO OMISSIONS: FIRST, THE CONCEPTION OF CULTURE, SCIENCE, ART, AND CINEMA AS UNIVOCAL AND UNIVERSAL TERMS; SECOND, AN INSUFFICIENTLY CLEAR IDEA OF THE FACT THAT THE REVOLUTION DOES NOT BEGIN WITH THE TAKING OF POLITICAL POWER FROM IMPERIALISM AND THE BOURGEOISIE, BUT RATHER BEGINS AT THE MOMENT WHEN THE MASSES SENSE THE NEED FOR CHANGE AND THEIR INTELLECTUAL VANGUARDS BEGIN TO STUDY AND CARRY OUT THIS CHANGE *THROUGH ACTIVITIES ON DIFFERENT FRONTS*.

CULTURE, ART, SCIENCE AND CINEMA ALWAYS RESPOND TO CONFLICTING CLASS INTERESTS. IN THE NEOCOLONIAL SITUATION TWO CONCEPTS OF CULTURE, ART, SCIENCE, AND CINEMA COMPETE: *THAT OF THE RULERS AND THAT OF THE NATION*. AND THIS SITUATION WILL CONTINUE, AS LONG AS THE NATIONAL CONCEPT IS NOT IDENTIFIED WITH THAT OF THE RULERS, AS LONG AS THE STATUS OF COLONY OR SEMI-COLONY CONTINUES IN FORCE. MOREOVER, THE DUALITY WILL BE OVERCOME AND WILL REACH A SINGLE AND UNIVERSAL CATEGORY ONLY WHEN THE BEST VALUES OF MAN EMERGE FROM PROSCRIPTION TO ACHIEVE HEGEMONY, WHEN THE LIBERATION OF MAN IS UNIVERSAL. IN THE MEANTIME, THERE EXISTS *OUR* CULTURE AND *THEIR* CULTURE, *OUR* CINEMA AND *THEIR* CINEMA. BECAUSE OUR CULTURE IS AN IMPULSE TOWARD EMANCIPATION, IT WILL REMAIN IN EXISTENCE UNTIL EMANCIPATION IS A REALITY: *A CULTURE OF SUBVERSION* WHICH WILL CARRY WITH IT AN ART, A SCIENCE, AND *A CINEMA OF SUBVERSION*.

THE LACK OF AWARENESS IN REGARD TO THESE DUALITIES GENERALLY LEADS THE INTELLECTUAL TO DEAL WITH ARTISTIC AND SCIENTIFIC EXPRESSIONS AS THEY WERE UNIVERSALLY CONCEIVED BY THE CLASSES THAT RULE THE WORLD, AT BEST INTRODUCING SOME CORRECTION INTO THESE EXPRESSIONS. WE HAVE NOT GONE DEEPLY ENOUGH INTO DEVELOPING A REVOLUTIONARY THEATER, ARCHITECTURE, MEDICINE, PSYCHOLOGY, AND CINEMA; INTO DEVELOPING A CULTURE *BY AND FOR US*. THE INTELLECTUAL TAKES EACH OF THESE FORMS OF EXPRESSION AS A UNIT TO BE CORRECTED *FROM WITHIN THE EXPRESSION ITSELF, AND NOT FROM WITHOUT, WITH ITS OWN NEW METHODS AND MODELS*.

AN ASTRONAUT OR A RANGER MOBILIZES ALL THE SCIENTIFIC RESOURCES OF IMPERIALISM. PSYCHOLOGISTS, DOCTORS, POLITICIANS, SOCIOLOGISTS, MATHEMATICIANS, AND EVEN ARTISTS ARE THROWN INTO THE STUDY OF EVERYTHING THAT SERVES, *FROM THE VANTAGE POINT OF DIFFERENT SPECIALTIES*, THE PREPARATION OF AN ORBITAL FLIGHT, OR THE MASSACRE OF VIETNAMESE; IN THE LONG RUN, ALL OF THESE SPECIALTIES ARE EQUALLY EMPLOYED TO SATISFY THE NEEDS OF IMPERIALISM. IN BUENOS AIRES THE ARMY ERADICATES *VILLAS MISERIA* (URBAN SHANTY TOWNS) AND IN THEIR PLACE PUTS UP "STRATEGIC HAMLETS" WITH URBANIZED SETUPS AIMED AT FACILITATING MILITARY INTERVENTION WHEN THE TIME COMES. THE REVOLUTIONARY ORGANIZATIONS LACK SPECIALIZED FRONTS IN *THE ESTABLISHMENT'S* MEDICINE, ENGINEERING, PSYCHOLOGY, AND ART—NOT TO MENTION THE

DEVELOPMENT OF *OUR OWN REVOLUTIONARY* ENGINEERING, PSYCHOLOGY, ART AND CINEMA. IN ORDER TO BE EFFECTIVE, ALL THESE FIELDS MUST RECOGNIZE THE *PRIORITIES* OF EACH STAGE; THOSE REQUIRED BY THE STRUGGLE FOR POWER OR THOSE DEMANDED BY THE ALREADY VICTORIOUS REVOLUTION. EXAMPLES: CREATING A POLITICAL SENSITIVITY AS AWARENESS OF THE NEED TO UNDERTAKE A POLITICAL-MILITARY STRUGGLE IN ORDER TO TAKE POWER; INTENSIFYING ALL THE MODERN RESOURCES OF MEDICAL SCIENCE TO PREPARE PEOPLE WITH OPTIMUM LEVELS OF HEALTH AND PHYSICAL EFFICIENCY, READY FOR COMBAT IN RURAL AND URBAN ZONES; OR ELABORATING AN ARCHITECTURE, A CITY PLANNING, THAT WILL BE ABLE TO WITHSTAND THE MASSIVE AIR RAIDS THAT IMPERIALISM CAN LAUNCH AT ANY TIME. THE SPECIFIC STRENGTHENING OF EACH SPECIALTY AND FIELD SUBORDINATE TO COLLECTIVE PRIORITIES CAN FILL THE EMPTY SPACES CAUSED BY THE STRUGGLE FOR LIBERATION AND CAN DELINEATE WITH GREATEST EFFICACY THE ROLE OF THE INTELLECTUAL IN OUR TIME. IT IS EVIDENT THAT REVOLUTIONARY MASS-LEVEL CULTURE AND AWARENESS CAN ONLY BE ACHIEVED AFTER THE TAKING OF POLITICAL POWER, BUT IT IS NO LESS TRUE THAT THE USE OF SCIENTIFIC AND ARTISTIC MEANS, TOGETHER WITH POLITICAL-MILITANCY, PREPARES THE TERRAIN FOR THE REVOLUTION TO BECOME REALITY AND FACILITATES THE SOLUTION OF THE PROBLEMS THAT WILL ARISE WITH THE TAKING OF POWER.

THE INTELLECTUAL MUST FIND THROUGH HIS ACTION THE FIELD IN WHICH HE CAN RATIONALLY PERFORM THE MOST EFFICIENT WORK. ONCE THE FRONT HAS BEEN DETERMINED, HIS NEXT TASK IS TO FIND OUT *WITHIN THAT FRONT* EXACTLY WHAT IS THE ENEMY'S STRONGHOLD AND WHERE AND HOW HE MUST DEPLOY HIS FORCES. IT IS IN THIS HARSH AND DRAMATIC DAILY SEARCH THAT A CULTURE OF THE REVOLUTION WILL BE ABLE TO EMERGE, THE BASIS WHICH WILL NURTURE, *BEGINNING RIGHT NOW*, THE *NEW MAN* EXEMPLIFIED BY CHE [GUEVARA]—NOT MAN IN THE ABSTRACT, NOT THE "LIBERATION OF MAN," BUT *ANOTHER MAN*, CAPABLE OF ARISING FROM THE ASHES OF THE OLD, ALIENATED MAN THAT WE ARE AND WHICH THE NEW MAN WILL DESTROY—BY STARTING TO STOKE THE FIRE *TODAY*.

THE ANTI-IMPERIALIST STRUGGLE OF THE PEOPLES OF THE THIRD WORLD AND OF THEIR EQUIVALENTS INSIDE THE IMPERIALIST COUNTRIES CONSTITUTES TODAY THE AXIS OF WORLD REVOLUTION. *THIRD CINEMA* IS, IN OUR OPINION, THE CINEMA THAT *RECOGNIZES IN THAT STRUGGLE THE MOST GIGANTIC CULTURAL, SCIENTIFIC, AND ARTISTIC MANIFESTATION OF OUR TIME*, THE GREAT POSSIBILITY OF CONSTRUCTING A LIBERATED PERSONALITY WITH EACH PEOPLE AS THE STARTING POINT—IN A WORD, THE *DECOLONIZATION OF CULTURE*.

THE CULTURE, INCLUDING THE CINEMA, OF A NEOCOLONIALIZED COUNTRY IS JUST THE EXPRESSION OF AN OVERALL DEPENDENCE THAT GENERATES MODELS AND VALUES BORN FROM THE NEEDS OF IMPERIALIST EXPANSION.

IN ORDER TO IMPOSE ITSELF, NEOCOLONIALISM NEEDS TO CONVINCE THE PEOPLE OF A DEPENDENT COUNTRY OF THEIR OWN INFERIORITY. SOONER OR LATER, THE INFERIOR MAN RECOGNIZES MAN WITH A CAPITAL M; THIS RECOGNITION MEANS THE DESTRUCTION OF HIS DEFENSES. IF YOU WANT TO BE A MAN, SAYS THE OPPRESSOR, YOU HAVE TO BE LIKE ME, SPEAK MY LANGUAGE, DENY YOUR OWN BEING, TRANSFORM YOURSELF INTO ME. AS EARLY AS THE 17TH CENTURY THE JESUIT MISSIONARIES PROCLAIMED THE APTITUDE OF THE [SOUTH AMERICAN] NATIVE FOR COPYING EUROPEAN WORKS OF ART. COPYIST, TRANSLATOR, INTERPRETER, AT BEST A SPECTATOR, THE NEOCOLONIALIZED INTELLECTUAL WILL ALWAYS BE ENCOURAGED TO REFUSE TO ASSUME HIS CREATIVE POSSIBILITIES. INHIBITIONS, UPROOTEDNESS, ESCAPISM, CULTURAL COSMOPOLITANISM, ARTISTIC IMITATION, METAPHYSICAL EXHAUSTION, BETRAYAL OF COUNTRY—ALL FIND FERTILE SOIL IN WHICH TO GROW.[1]

CULTURE BECOMES BILINGUAL, NOT DUE TO THE USE OF TWO LANGUAGES, BUT BECAUSE OF THE CONJUNCTURE OF TWO CULTURAL PATTERNS OF THINKING. ONE IS NATIONAL, THAT OF THE PEOPLE, AND THE OTHER IS ESTRANGING, THAT OF THE CLASSES SUBORDINATE TO OUTSIDE FORCES. THE ADMIRATION THAT THE UPPER CLASSES EXPRESS FOR THE U.S. OR EUROPE IS THE HIGHEST EXPRESSION OF THEIR SUBJECTION. WITH THE COLONIALIZATION OF THE UPPER CLASSES THE CULTURE OF IMPERIALISM INDIRECTLY INTRODUCES AMONG THE MASSES KNOWLEDGE WHICH CANNOT BE SUPERVISED.[2]

JUST AS THEY ARE NOT MASTERS OF THE LAND UPON WHICH THEY WALK, THE NEOCOLONIALIZED PEOPLE ARE NOT MASTERS OF THE IDEAS THAT ENVELOP THEM. A KNOWLEDGE OF NATIONAL REALITY PRESUPPOSES GOING INTO THE WEB OF LIES AND CONFUSION THAT ARISE FROM DEPENDENCE. THE INTELLECTUAL IS OBLIGED TO *REFRAIN FROM SPONTANEOUS THOUGHT*; IF HE DOES THINK, HE GENERALLY RUNS THE RISK OF DOING SO IN FRENCH OR ENGLISH—NEVER IN THE LANGUAGE OF A CULTURE OF HIS OWN, WHICH, LIKE THE PROCESS OF NATIONAL AND SOCIAL LIBERATION, IS STILL HAZY AND INCIPIENT. EVERY PIECE OF DATA, EVERY CONCEPT THAT FLOATS AROUND US, IS PART OF A FRAMEWORK OF MIRAGES THAT IS DIFFICULT TO TAKE APART.

THE NATIVE BOURGEOISIE OF THE PORT CITIES SUCH AS BUENOS AIRES, AND THEIR RESPECTIVE INTELLECTUAL ELITES, CONSTITUTED, FROM THE VERY ORIGINS OF OUR HISTORY, THE TRANSMISSION BELT OF NEOCOLONIAL PENETRATION. BEHIND SUCH WATCHWORDS AS "CIVILIZATION OR BARBARISM!", MANUFACTURED IN ARGEN-

TINA BY EUROPEANIZING LIBERALISM, WAS THE ATTEMPT TO IMPOSE A CIVILIZA-
TION FULLY IN KEEPING WITH THE NEEDS OF IMPERIALIST EXPANSION AND THE DESIRE
TO DESTROY THE RESISTANCE OF THE NATIONAL MASSES, WHICH WERE SUCCESSIVELY
CALLED THE "RABBLE," A "BUNCH OF BLACKS," AND "ZOOLOGICAL DETRITUS" IN
OUR COUNTRY, AND "THE UNWASHED HORDES" IN BOLIVIA. IN THIS WAY THE
IDEOLOGISTS OF THE SEMI-COUNTRIES, PAST MASTERS IN "THE PLAY OF BUG WORDS,
WITH AN IMPLACABLE, DETAILED, AND RUSTIC UNIVERSALISM,"[3] SERVED AS
SPOKESMAN OF THOSE FOLLOWERS OF DISRAELI WHO INTELLIGENTLY PROCLAIM-
ED: "I PREFER THE RIGHTS OF THE ENGLISH TO THE RIGHTS OF MAN."

THE MIDDLE-CLASS WERE AND ARE THE BEST RECIPIENTS OF CULTURAL
NEOCOLONIALISM. THEIR AMBIVALENT CLASS CONDITION, THEIR BUFFER POSITION
BETWEEN SOCIAL POLARITIES, AND THEIR BROADER POSSIBILITIES OF ACCESS TO
CIVILIZATION OFFER IMPERIALISM A BASE OF SOCIAL SUPPORT WHICH HAS ATTAIN-
ED CONSIDERABLE IMPORTANCE IN SOME LATIN AMERICAN COUNTRIES.

> *IT SERVES TO INSTITUTIONALIZE AND GIVE A NORMAL APPEARANCE
> TO DEPENDENCE. THE MAIN OBJECTIVE OF THIS CULTURAL DEFORMATION
> IS TO KEEP THE PEOPLE FROM REALIZING THEIR NEOCOLONIALIZED POSI-
> TION AND ASPIRING TO CHANGE IT. IN THIS WAY PEDAGOGICAL COL-
> ONIALIZATION IS AN EFFECTIVE SUBSTITUTE FOR THE COLONIAL POLICE.*[4]

MASS COMMUNICATIONS TEND TO COMPLETE THE DESTRUCTION OF A NA-
TIONAL AWARENESS AND OF A COLLECTIVE SUBJECTIVITY ON THE WAY TO ENLIGHTEN-
MENT, A DESTRUCTION WHICH BEGINS AS SOON AS THE CHILD HAS ACCESS TO
THESE MEDIA, THE EDUCATION AND CULTURE OF THE RULING CLASSES. IN ARGEN-
TINA 26 TELEVISION CHANNELS, ONE MILLION TELEVISION SETS, MORE THAN 50
RADIO STATIONS, HUNDREDS OF NEWSPAPERS, PERIODICALS, AND MAGAZINES, AND
THOUSANDS OF RECORDS, FILMS ETC., JOIN THEIR ACCULTURATING ROLE ON THE
COLONIALIZATION OF TASTE AND CONSCIOUSNESS TO THE PROCESS OF NEOCOLONIAL
EDUCATION WHICH BEGINS IN THE UNIVERSITY. "MASS COMMUNICATIONS ARE MORE
EFFECTIVE FOR NEOCOLONIALISM THAN NAPALM. WHAT IS REAL, TRUE, AND RA-
TIONAL IS TO BE FOUND ON THE MARGIN OF THE LAW, JUST AS ARE THE PEOPLE.
VIOLENCE, CRIME, AND DESTRUCTION COME TO BE PEACE, ORDER, AND NOR-
MALITY."[5] *TRUTH, THEN, AMOUNTS TO SUBVERSION.* ANY FORM OF EXPRESSION
OR COMMUNICATION THAT TRIES TO SHOW NATIONAL REALITY IS *SUBVERSION.*

CULTURAL PENETRATION, PEDAGOGICAL COLONIALIZATION, AND MASS COM-
MUNICATIONS ALL JOIN FORCES TODAY IN A DESPERATE ATTEMPT TO ABSORB,
NEUTRALIZE, OR ELIMINATE ANY EXPRESSION THAT RESPONDS TO AN ATTEMPT AT
DECOLONIALIZATION. NEOCOLONIALISM MAKES A SERIOUS ATTEMPT TO CASTRATE,
TO DIGEST, THE CULTURAL FORMS THAT ARISE BEYOND THE BOUNDS OF ITS OWN
AIMS. ATTEMPTS ARE MADE TO REMOVE FROM THEM PRECISELY WHAT MAKES THEM
EFFECTIVE AND DANGEROUS, THEIR *POLITICIZATION.* OR, TO PUT IT ANOTHER WAY,
TO SEPARATE THE CULTURAL MANIFESTATION FROM THE FIGHT FOR NATIONAL IN-

DEPENDENCE.

IDEAS SUCH AS "BEAUTY IN ITSELF IS REVOLUTIONARY" AND "ALL NEW CINEMA IS REVOLUTIONARY" ARE IDEALISTIC ASPIRATIONS THAT DO NOT TOUCH THE NEOCOLONIAL CONDITION, SINCE THEY CONTINUE TO CONCEIVE OF CINEMA, ART, AND BEAUTY AS UNIVERSAL ABSTRACTIONS AND NOT AS AN INTEGRAL PART OF THE NATIONAL PROCESSES OF DECOLONIALIZATION.

ANY DISPUTE, NO MATTER HOW VIRULENT, WHICH DOES NOT SERVE TO MOBILIZE, AGITATE, AND POLITICIZE SECTORS OF THE PEOPLE TO ARM THEM RATIONALLY AND PERCEPTIBLY, IN ONE WAY OR ANOTHER, FOR THE STRUGGLE, IS RECEIVED WITH INDIFFERENCE OR EVEN WITH PLEASURE. VIRULENCE, NONCONFORMISM, PLAIN REBELLIOUSNESS, AND DISCONTENT ARE JUST SO MANY MORE PRODUCTS ON THE CAPITALIST MARKET; THEY ARE *CONSUMER GOODS*. THIS IS ESPECIALLY TRUE IN A SITUATION WHERE THE BOURGEOISIE IS IN NEED OF A DAILY DOSE OF SHOCK AND EXCITING ELEMENTS OF CONTROLLED VIOLENCE[6]—THAT IS, VIOLENCE WHICH ABSORPTION BY THE SYSTEM TURNS INTO PURE STRIDENCY. EXAMPLES ARE THE WORKS OF A SOCIALIST-TINGED PAINTING AND SCULPTURE WHICH ARE GREEDILY SOUGHT AFTER BY THE NEW BOURGEOISIE TO DECORATE THEIR APARTMENTS AND MANSIONS; PLAYS FULL OF ANGER AND AVANT-GARDISM WHICH ARE NOISILY APPLAUDED BY THE RULING CLASSES; THE LITERATURE OF PROGRESSIVE WRITERS CONCERNED WITH SEMANTICS AND MAN ON THE MARGIN OF TIME AND SPACE, WHICH GIVES AN AIR OF DEMOCRATIC BROAD-MINDEDNESS TO THE SYSTEM'S PUBLISHING HOUSES AND MAGAZINES; AND THE CINEMA OF "CHALLENGE," OF "ARGUMENT," PROMOTED BY THE DISTRIBUTION MONOPOLIES AND LAUNCHED BY THE BIG COMMERCIAL OUTLETS.

IN REALITY THE AREA OF "PERMITTED PROTEST" OF THE SYSTEM IS MUCH GREATER THAN THE SYSTEM IS WILLING TO ADMIT. THIS GIVES THE ARTISTS THE ILLUSION THAT THEY ARE ACTING "AGAINST THE SYSTEM" BY GOING BEYOND CERTAIN NARROW LIMITS; THEY DO NOT REALIZE THAT EVEN ANTI-SYSTEM ART CAN BE ABSORBED AND UTILIZED BY THE SYSTEM, AS BOTH A BRAKE AND A NECESSARY SELF-CORRECTION.[7]

LACKING AN AWARENESS OF HOW TO *UTILIZE WHAT IS OURS FOR OUR TRUE LIBERATION*—IN A WORD, LACKING *POLITICIZATION*— ALL OF THESE "PROGRESSIVE" ALTERNATIVES COME TO FORM THE LEFTISH WING OF THE SYSTEM, THE IMPROVEMENT OF ITS CULTURAL PRODUCTS. THEY WILL BE DOOMED TO CARRY OUT THE BEST WORK ON THE LEFT THAT THE RIGHT IS ABLE TO ACCEPT TODAY AND WILL THUS ONLY SERVE THE SURVIVAL OF THE LATTER. "RESTORE WORDS, DRAMATIC ACTIONS, AND IMAGES TO THE PLACES WHERE THEY CAN CARRY OUT A REVOLUTIONARY ROLE, WHERE THEY WILL BE USEFUL, WHERE THEY WILL BECOME *WEAPONS*

IN THE STRUGGLE."[8] INSERT THE WORK AS AN ORIGINAL FACT IN THE PROCESS OF LIBERATION, PLACE IT FIRST AT THE SERVICE OF LIFE ITSELF, AHEAD OF ART; *DISSOLVE AESTHETICS IN THE LIFE OF SOCIETY*: ONLY IN THIS WAY, AS FANON SAID, CAN DECOLONIALIZATION BECOME POSSIBLE AND CULTURE, CINEMA, AND BEAUTY—AT LEAST, WHAT IS OF GREATEST IMPORTANCE TO US—BECOME *OUR CULTURE, OUR FILMS, AND OUR SENSE OF BEAUTY*.

THE HISTORICAL PERSPECTIVES OF LATIN AMERICA AND OF THE MAJORITY OF THE COUNTRIES UNDER IMPERIALIST DOMINATION ARE HEADED NOT TOWARDS A LESSENING OF REPRESSION BUT TOWARDS AN INCREASE. WE ARE HEADING NOT FOR BOURGEOIS-DEMOCRATIC REGIMES BUT FOR DICTATORIAL FORMS OF GOVERNMENT. THE STRUGGLES FOR DEMOCRATIC FREEDOMS, INSTEAD OF SEIZING CONCESSIONS FROM THE SYSTEM, MOVE TO CUT DOWN ON THEM, GIVEN ITS NARROW MARGIN FOR MANEUVERING.

THE BOURGEOIS-DEMOCRATIC FACADE CAVED IN SOME TIME AGO. THE CYCLE OPENED DURING THE LAST CENTURY IN LATIN AMERICA WITH THE FIRST ATTEMPTS AT SELF-AFFIRMATION OF A NATIONAL BOURGEOISIE DIFFERENTIATED FROM THE METROPOLIS (EXAMPLES ARE ROSAS' FEDERALISM IN ARGENTINA, THE LOPEZ AND FRANCIA REGIME IN PARAGUAY, AND THOSE OF BENGIDO AND BALMACEDA IN CHILE) WITH A NEW TRADITION THAT HAS CONTINUED WELL INTO OUR CENTURY: NATIONAL-BOURGEOIS, NATIONAL-POPULAR, AND DEMOCRATIC-BOURGEOIS ATTEMPTS WERE MADE BY CARDENAS, YRIGOYEN, HAYA DE LA TORRE, VARGAS, AGUIRRE CERDA, PERON, AND ARBENZ. BUT AS FAR AS REVOLUTIONARY PROSPECTS ARE CONCERNED, THE CYCLE HAS DEFINITELY BEEN COMPLETED. THE LINES ALLOWING FOR THE DEEPENING OF THE HISTORICAL ATTEMPT OF EACH OF THOSE EXPERIENCES TODAY PASS THROUGH SECTORS THAT UNDERSTAND THE CONTINENT'S SITUATION AS ONE OF WAR AND THAT ARE PREPARING, UNDER THE FORCE OF CIRCUMSTANCES, TO MAKE THAT REGION THE VIETNAM OF THE COMING DECADE. A WAR IN WHICH NATIONAL LIBERATION CAN ONLY SUCCEED WHEN IT IS SIMULTANEOUSLY POSTULATED AS SOCIAL LIBERATION—SOCIALISM AS THE ONLY VALID PERSPECTIVE OF ANY NATIONAL LIBERATION PROCESS.

AT THIS TIME IN LATIN AMERICA THERE IS ROOM FOR NEITHER PASSIVITY NOR INNOCENCE. THE INTELLECTUAL'S COMMITMENT IS MEASURED IN TERMS OF RISKS AS WELL AS WORDS AND IDEAS; WHAT HE DOES TO FURTHER THE CAUSE OF LIBERATION IS WHAT COUNTS. THE WORKER WHO GOES ON STRIKE AND THUS RISKS LOSING HIS JOB OR EVEN HIS LIFE, THE STUDENT WHO JEOPARDIZES HIS CAREER, THE MILITANT WHO KEEPS SILENT UNDER TORTURE: EACH BY HIS OR HER ACTION COMMITS US TO SOMETHING MUCH MORE IMPORTANT THAN A VAGUE GESTURE OF SOLIDARITY.[9]

IN A SITUATION IN WHICH THE "STATE OF LAW" IS REPLACED BY THE "STATE OF FACTS," THE INTELLECTUAL, WHO IS *ONE MORE WORKER*, FUNCTIONING ON A CULTURAL FRONT, MUST BECOME INCREASINGLY RADICALIZED TO AVOID DENIAL OF SELF AND TO CARRY OUT WHAT IS EXPECTED OF HIM IN OUR TIMES. THE IMPOTENCE OF ALL REFORMIST CONCEPTS HAS ALREADY BEEN EXPOSED SUFFICIENTLY, NOT ONLY IN POLITICS BUT ALSO IN CULTURE AND FILMS—AND ESPECIALLY IN THE LATTER, *WHOSE HISTORY IS THAT OF IMPERIALIST DOMINATION—MAINLY YANKEE.*

WHILE, DURING THE EARLY HISTORY (OR THE PREHISTORY) OF THE CINEMA, IT WAS POSSIBLE TO SPEAK OF A GERMAN, AN ITALIAN, OR A SWEDISH CINEMA CLEARLY DIFFERENTIATED AND CORRESPONDING TO SPECIFIC NATIONAL CHARACTERISTICS, TODAY SUCH DIFFERENCES HAVE DISAPPEARED. THE BORDERS WERE WIPED OUT ALONG WITH THE EXPANSION OF U.S. IMPERIALISM AND THE FILM MODEL THAT IT IMPOSED: *HOLLYWOOD MOVIES.* IN OUR TIMES IT IS HARD TO FIND A FILM WITHIN THE FIELD OF COMMERCIAL CINEMA, INCLUDING WHAT IS KNOWN AS "AUTHOR'S CINEMA"—IN BOTH THE CAPITALIST AND SOCIALIST COUNTRIES—THAT MANAGES TO AVOID THE MODELS OF HOLLYWOOD PICTURES. THE LATTER HAVE SUCH A FAST HOLD THAT MONUMENTAL WORKS SUCH AS THE U.S.S.R.'s BONDARCHUK'S *WAR AND PEACE* ARE ALSO MONUMENTAL EXAMPLES OF THE SUBMISSION TO ALL THE PROPOSITIONS IMPOSED BY THE U.S. MOVIE INDUSTRY (STRUCTURE, LANGUAGE, ETC.) AND, CONSEQUENTLY, TO ITS CONCEPTS.

THE PLACING OF THE CINEMA WITHIN U.S. MODELS, EVEN IN THE FORMAL ASPECT, IN LANGUAGE, LEADS TO THE ADOPTION OF THE IDEOLOGICAL FORMS THAT *GAVE RAISE TO PRECISELY THAT LANGUAGE AND NO OTHER.* EVEN THE APPROPRIATION OF MODELS WHICH APPEAR TO BE ONLY TECHNICAL, INDUSTRIAL, SCIENTIFIC, ETC., LENDS TO A CONCEPTUAL DEPENDENCY SITUATION, DUE TO THE FACT THAT THE CINEMA IS AN INDUSTRY, BUT DIFFERS FROM OTHER INDUSTRIES IN THAT IT HAS BEEN CREATED AND ORGANIZED IN ORDER *TO GENERATE CERTAIN IDEOLOGIES.* THE 35MM CAMERA, 24 FRAMES PER SECOND, ARC LIGHTS, AND A COMMERCIAL PLACE OF EXHIBITION FOR AUDIENCES WERE CONCEIVED NOT TO GRATUITOUSLY TRANSMIT ANY IDEOLOGY, BUT TO SATISFY, IN THE FIRST PLACE, THE CULTURAL AND SURPLUS VALUE NEEDS *OF A SPECIFIC IDEOLOGY, OF A SPECIFIC WORLD-VIEW: THAT OF U.S. FINANCIAL CAPITAL.*

THE MECHANISTIC TAKEOVER OF A CINEMA CONCEIVED AS A SHOW TO BE EXHIBITED IN LARGE THEATERS WITH A STANDARD DURATION, HERMETIC STRUCTURES THAT ARE BORN AND DIE ON THE SCREEN, SATISFIES, TO BE SURE, THE *COMMERCIAL INTERESTS* OF THE PRODUCTION GROUPS, BUT IT ALSO LEADS TO THE *ABSORPTION OF FORMS OF THE BOURGEOIS WORLD-VIEW* WHICH ARE THE CONTINUATION OF 19TH CENTURY ART, OF BOURGEOIS ART: MAN IS ACCEPTED ONLY AS A PASSIVE AND CONSUMING OBJECT; *RATHER THAN HAVING HIS ABILITY TO MAKE HISTORY RECOGNIZED, HE IS ONLY PERMITTED TO READ HISTORY, CONTEMPLATE IT, LISTEN TO IT, AND UNDERGO IT.* THE CINEMA, AS A SPECTACLE AIMED AT A DIGESTING OBJECT, IS THE HIGHEST POINT THAT CAN BE REACHED BY BOURGEOIS FILMMAK-

ING. THE WORLD, EXPERIENCE, AND THE HISTORIC PROCESS ARE ENCLOSED WITHIN THE FRAME OF A PAINTING, THE SAME STAGE OF A THEATER, AND THE MOVIE SCREEN; MAN IS VIEWED AS A *CONSUMER OF IDEOLOGY*, AND NOT AS THE CREATOR OF IDEOLOGY. THIS NOTION IS THE STARTING POINT FOR THE WONDERFUL INTERPLAY OF BOURGEOIS PHILOSOPHY AND THE OBTAINING OF SURPLUS VALUE. THE RESULT IS A CINEMA STUDIED BY MOTIVATIONAL ANALYSTS, SOCIOLOGISTS AND PSYCHOLOGISTS, BY THE ENDLESS RESEARCHERS OF THE DREAMS AND FRUSTRATIONS OF THE MASSES, ALL AIMED AT SELLING *MOVIE-LIFE*, REALITY AS IT IS CONCEIVED BY THE RULING CLASS.

THE FIRST ALTERNATIVE TO THIS TYPE OF CINEMA, WHICH WE COULD CALL THE *FIRST CINEMA*, AROSE WITH THE SO-CALLED "AUTHOR'S CINEMA," "EXPRESSION CINEMA," "*NOUVELLE VAGUE*," "*CINEMA NOVO*," OR, CONVENTIONALLY, THE *SECOND CINEMA*. THIS ALTERNATIVE SIGNIFIED A STEP FORWARD INASMUCH AS IT DEMANDED THAT THE FILMMAKER BE FREE TO EXPRESS HIMSELF IN NON-STANDARD LANGUAGE AND INASMUCH AS IT WAS AN ATTEMPT AT CULTURAL DECOLONIZATION. BUT SUCH ATTEMPTS HAVE ALREADY REACHED, OR ARE ABOUT TO REACH, THE OUTER LIMITS OF WHAT THE SYSTEM PERMITS. THE *SECOND CINEMA FILMMAKER* HAS REMAINED "TRAPPED INSIDE THE FORTRESS" AS GODARD PUT IT, OR IS ON HIS WAY TO BECOMING TRAPPED. THE SEARCH FOR A MARKET OF 200,000 MOVIEGOERS IN ARGENTINA, A FIGURE THAT IS SUPPOSED TO COVER COSTS OF AN INDEPENDENT LOCAL PRODUCTION, THE PROPOSAL OF DEVELOPING A MECHANISM OF INDUSTRIAL PRODUCTION PARALLEL TO THAT OF THE SYSTEM BUT WHICH WOULD BE DISTRIBUTED BY THE SYSTEM ACCORDING TO ITS OWN NORMS, THE STRUGGLE TO STRENGTHEN THE LAWS PROTECTING THE CINEMA AND REPLACING "BAD OFFICIALS" BY "LESS BAD," ETC., IS A SEARCH LACKING IN VIABLE PROSPECTS, UNLESS YOU CONSIDER VIABLE THE PROSPECT OF BECOMING INSTITUTIONALIZED AS "THE YOUTHFUL, ANGRY WING OF SOCIETY"—THAT IS, OF NEOCOLONIALIZED OR CAPITALIST SOCIETY.

REAL ALTERNATIVES DIFFERING FROM THOSE OFFERED BY THE SYSTEM ARE ONLY POSSIBLE IF ONE OF TWO REQUIREMENTS IS FULFILLED: *MAKING FILMS THAT THE SYSTEM CANNOT ASSIMILATE AND WHICH ARE FOREIGN TO ITS NEEDS, OR MAKING FILMS THAT ARE DIRECTLY AND EXPLICITLY SET OUT TO FIGHT THE SYSTEM.* NEITHER OF THESE REQUIREMENTS FITS WITHIN THE ALTERNATIVES THAT ARE STILL OFFERED BY THE *SECOND CINEMA*, BUT THEY CAN BE FOUND IN THE REVOLUTIONARY OPENING TOWARDS A CINEMA OUTSIDE AND AGAINST THE SYSTEM, IN A CINEMA OF LIBERATION: THE *THIRD CINEMA*.

ONE OF THE MOST EFFECTIVE JOBS DONE BY NEOCOLONIALISM IS ITS CUTTING OFF OF INTELLECTUAL SECTORS, ESPECIALLY ARTISTS, FROM NATIONAL REALITY BY LINING THEM UP BEHIND "UNIVERSAL ART AND MODELS." IT HAS BEEN VERY COMMON FOR INTELLECTUALS AND ARTISTS TO BE FOUND AT THE TAIL END OF POPULAR STRUGGLE, WHEN THEY HAVE NOT ACTUALLY TAKEN UP POSITIONS AGAINST IT. THE SOCIAL LAYERS WHICH HAVE MADE THE GREATEST CONTRIBUTION TO THE

BUILDING OF A NATIONAL CULTURE (UNDERSTOOD AS AN IMPULSE TOWARDS DECOLONIALIZATION) HAVE NOT BEEN PRECISELY THE ENLIGHTENED ELITES BUT RATHER THE MOST EXPLOITED AND UNCIVILIZED SECTORS. POPULAR ORGANIZATIONS HAVE VERY RIGHTLY DISTRUSTED THE "INTELLECTUAL" AND THE "ARTIST." WHEN THEY HAVE NOT BEEN OPENLY USED BY THE BOURGEOISIE OR IMPERIALISTS, THEY HAVE CERTAINLY BEEN THEIR INDIRECT TOOLS; MOST OF THEM DID NOT GO BEYOND SPOUTING A POLICY IN FAVOR OF "PEACE AND DEMOCRACY," FEARFUL OF ANYTHING THAT HAD A NATIONAL RING TO IT, AFRAID OF CONTAMINATING ART WITH POLITICS AND THE ARTISTS WITH THE REVOLUTIONARY MILITANT. THEY THUS TENDED TO OBSCURE THE INNER CAUSES DETERMINING NEOCOLONIALIZED SOCIETY AND PLACED IN THE FOREGROUND THE OUTER CAUSES, WHICH, WHILE "THEY ARE THE CONDITION FOR CHANGE, THEY CAN NEVER BE THE BASIS FOR CHANGE";[10] IN ARGENTINA THEY REPLACED THE STRUGGLE AGAINST IMPERIALISM AND THE NATIVE OLIGARCHY WITH THE STRUGGLE OF DEMOCRACY AGAINST FASCISM, SUPPRESSING THE FUNDAMENTAL CONTRADICTION OF A NEOCOLONIALIZED COUNTRY AND REPLACING IT WITH "A CONTRADICTION THAT WAS A COPY OF THE WORLD-WIDE CONTRADICTION."[11]

THIS CUTTING OFF OF THE INTELLECTUAL AND ARTISTIC SECTORS FROM THE PROCESSES OF NATIONAL LIBERATION—WHICH, AMONG OTHER THINGS, HELPS US TO UNDERSTAND THE LIMITATIONS IN WHICH THESE PROCESSES HAVE BEEN UNFOLDING—TODAY TENDS TO DISAPPEAR TO THE EXTENT THAT ARTISTS AND INTELLECTUALS ARE BEGINNING TO DISCOVER THE IMPOSSIBILITY OF DESTROYING THE ENEMY WITHOUT FIRST JOINING IN A BATTLE FOR THEIR COMMON INTERESTS. THE ARTIST IS BEGINNING TO DISCOVER THE INSUFFICIENCY OF HIS NONCONFORMISM AND INDIVIDUAL REBELLION. AND THE REVOLUTIONARY ORGANIZATIONS, IN TURN, ARE DISCOVERING THE VACUUMS THAT THE STRUGGLE FOR POWER CREATES IN THE CULTURAL SPHERE. THE PROBLEMS OF FILMMAKING, THE IDEOLOGICAL LIMITATIONS OF A FILMMAKER IN A NEOCOLONIALIZED COUNTRY, ETC., HAVE THUS FAR CONSTITUTED OBJECTIVE FACTORS IN THE LACK OF ATTENTION PAID TO THE CINEMA BY THE PEOPLE'S ORGANIZATIONS. NEWSPAPERS AND OTHER PRINTED MATTER, POSTERS AND WALL PROPAGANDA, SPEECHES AND OTHER VERBAL FORMS OF INFORMATION, ENLIGHTENMENT, AND POLITICIZATION ARE STILL THE MAIN MEANS OF COMMUNICATION BETWEEN THE ORGANIZATIONS AND THE VANGUARD LAYERS OF THE MASSES. BUT THE NEW POLITICAL POSITIONS OF SOME FILMMAKERS AND THE SUBSEQUENT APPEARANCE OF FILMS USEFUL FOR LIBERATION HAVE PERMITTED CERTAIN POLITICAL VANGUARDS TO DISCOVER THE IMPORTANCE OF MOVIES. THIS IMPORTANCE IS TO BE FOUND IN THE SPECIFIC MEANING OF FILMS AS A FORM OF COMMUNICATION AND BECAUSE OF *THEIR PARTICULAR CHARACTERISTICS*, CHARACTERISTICS THAT ALLOW THEM TO DRAW AUDIENCES OF DIFFERENT ORIGINS, MANY OF THEM PEOPLE WHO MIGHT NOT RESPOND FAVORABLY TO THE ANNOUNCEMENT OF A POLITICAL SPEECH. FILMS OFFER AN EFFECTIVE PRETEXT FOR GATHERING AN AUDIENCE, IN ADDITION TO THE IDEOLOGICAL MESSAGE THEY CONTAIN.

THE CAPACITY FOR SYNTHESIS AND THE PENETRATION OF THE FILM IMAGE, THE POSSIBILITIES OFFERED BY THE LIVING DOCUMENT AND NAKED REALITY, AND THE POWER OF ENLIGHTENMENT BY AUDIOVISUAL MEANS MAKE THE FILM FAR MORE EFFECTIVE THAN ANY OTHER TOOL FOR COMMUNICATION. IT IS HARDLY NECESSARY TO POINT OUT THAT THOSE FILMS WHICH ACHIEVE AN INTELLIGENT USE OF THE POSSIBILITIES OF THE IMAGE, ADEQUATE DOSAGE OF CONCEPTS, LANGUAGE AND STRUCTURE THAT FLOW NATURALLY FROM EACH THEME, AND COUNTERPOINTS OF AUDIOVISUAL NARRATION ACHIEVE EFFECTIVE RESULTS IN THE POLITICIZATION AND MOBILIZATION OF CADRES AND EVEN IN WORK WITH THE MASSES, WHERE THIS IS POSSIBLE.

THE STUDENTS WHO RAISED BARRICADES ON THE *AVENIDA 18 DE JULIO* IN MONTEVIDEO AFTER THE SHOWING OF *ME GUSTAN LOS ESTUDIANTES* (*I LIKE STUDENTS*) (MARIO HANDLER), THOSE WHO DEMONSTRATED AND SANG THE "INTERNATIONALE" IN MERIDA AND CARACAS AFTER THE SHOWING OF *LA HORA DE LOS HORNOS* (*THE HOUR OF THE FURNACES*), THE GROWING DEMANDS FOR FILMS SUCH AS THOSE MADE BY SANTIAGO ALVAREZ AND THE CUBAN DOCUMENTARY FILM MOVEMENT, AND THE DEBATES AND MEETINGS THAT TAKE PLACE AFTER THE UNDERGROUND OR SEMIPUBLIC SHOWINGS OF *THIRD CINEMA* FILMS ARE THE BEGINNING OF A TWISTING AND DIFFICULT ROAD BEING TRAVELED IN THE CONSUMER SOCIETIES BY THE MASS ORGANIZATIONS (*CINEGIORNALI LIBERI* IN ITALY, *ZENGAKUREN* DOCUMENTARIES IN JAPAN, ETC.). FOR THE FIRST TIME IN LATIN AMERICA, ORGANIZATIONS ARE READY AND WILLING TO EMPLOY FILMS FOR POLITICAL-CULTURAL ENDS: THE CHILEAN *PARTIDO SOCIALISTA* PROVIDES ITS CADRES WITH REVOLUTIONARY FILM MATERIAL, WHILE ARGENTINE REVOLUTIONARY PERONIST AND NON-PERONIST GROUPS ARE TAKING AN INTEREST IN DOING LIKEWISE. MOREOVER, O.S.P.A.A.A.L. (ORGANIZATION OF SOLIDARITY OF THE PEOPLES OF AFRICA, ASIA AND LATIN AMERICA) IS PARTICIPATING IN THE PRODUCTION AND DISTRIBUTION OF FILMS THAT CONTRIBUTE TO THE ANTI-IMPERALIST STRUGGLE. THE REVOLUTIONARY ORGANIZATIONS ARE DISCOVERING THE NEED FOR CADRES WHO, AMONG OTHER THINGS, KNOW HOW TO HANDLE A FILM CAMERA, TAPE RECORDERS, AND PROJECTORS IN THE MOST EFFECTIVE WAY POSSIBLE. THE STRUGGLE TO SEIZE POWER FROM THE ENEMY IS THE MEETING GROUND OF THE POLITICAL AND ARTISTIC VANGUARDS ENGAGED IN A COMMON TASK WHICH IS ENRICHING TO BOTH.

SOME OF THE CIRCUMSTANCES THAT DELAYED THE USE OF FILMS AS A REVOLUTIONARY TOOL UNTIL A SHORT TIME AGO WERE LACK OF EQUIPMENT, TECHNICAL DIFFICULTIES, THE COMPULSORY SPECIALIZATION; THE SIMPLIFICATION OF MOVIE CAMERAS AND TAPE RECORDERS; IMPROVEMENTS IN THE MEDIUM ITSELF, SUCH AS RAPID FILM THAT CAN BE PRINTED IN A NORMAL LIGHT; AUTOMATIC LIGHT METERS; IMPROVED AUDIOVISUAL SYNCHRONIZATION; AND THE SPREAD OF KNOW-HOW BY MEANS OF SPECIALIZED MAGAZINES WITH LARGE CIRCULATIONS AND EVEN THROUGH NONSPECIALIZED MEDIA, HAVE HELPED TO DEMYSTIFY FILMMAKING AND

DIVEST IT OF THAT ALMOST MAGIC AURA THAT MADE IT SEEM THAT FILMS WERE ONLY WITHIN THE REACH OF "ARTISTS," "GENIUSES," AND "THE PRIVILEGED." FILM-MAKING IS INCREASINGLY WITHIN THE REACH OF LARGER SOCIAL LAYERS. CHRIS MARKER EXPERIMENTED IN FRANCE WITH GROUPS OF WORKERS WHOM HE PRO-VIDED WITH 8MM EQUIPMENT AND SOME BASIC INSTRUCTION IN ITS HANDLING. THE GOAL WAS TO HAVE THE WORKER FILM *HIS WAY OF LOOKING AT THE WORLD, JUST AS IF HE WERE WRITING IT.* THIS HAS OPENED UP UNHEARD-OF-PROSPECTS FOR THE CINEMA; ABOVE ALL, *A NEW CONCEPTION OF FILMMAKING AND THE SIGNIFICANCE OF ART IN OUR TIMES.*

IMPERIALISM AND CAPITALISM, WHETHER IN THE CONSUMER SOCIETY OR IN THE NEOCOLONIALIZED COUNTRY, VEIL EVERYTHING BEHIND A SCREEN OF IMAGES AND APPEARANCES. *THE IMAGE OF REALITY* IS MORE IMPORTANT THAN REALITY ITSELF. IT IS A WORLD PEOPLED WITH FANTASIES AND PHANTOMS IN WHICH WHAT IS HIDEOUS IS CLOTHED IN BEAUTY, WHILE BEAUTY IS DISGUISED AS THE HIDEOUS. ON THE ONE HAND, FANTASY, THE IMAGINARY BOURGEOIS UNIVERSE REPLETE WITH COMFORT, EQUILIBRIUM, SWEET REASON, ORDER, EFFICIENCY, AND THE POSSIBILI-TY TO "BE SOMEONE." AND, ON THE OTHER, THE PHANTOMS, WE THE LAZY, WE THE INDOLENT AND UNDERDEVELOPED, WE WHO CAUSE DISORDER. WHEN A NEOCOLONIALIZED PERSON ACCEPTS HIS SITUATION, HE BECOMES A GUNGHA DIN, A TRAITOR AT THE SERVICE OF THE COLONIALIST, AN UNCLE TOM, A CLASS AND RACIAL RENEGADE, OR A FOOL, THE EASY-GOING SERVANT AND BUMPKIN; BUT, WHEN HE REFUSES TO ACCEPT HIS SITUATION OF OPPRESSION, THEN HE TURNS INTO A RESENTFUL SAVAGE, A CANNIBAL. THOSE WHO *LOSE SLEEP FROM FEAR OF THE HUNGRY,* THOSE WHO COMPRISE THE SYSTEM, SEE THE REVOLUTIONARY AS A BANDIT, ROBBER, AND RAPIST; THE FIRST BATTLE WAGED AGAINST THEM IS THUS NOT ON A POLITICAL PLANE, BUT RATHER IN THE POLICE CONTEXT OF LAW, AR-RESTS, ETC. THE MORE EXPLOITED A MAN IS, THE MORE HE IS PLACED ON A PLANE OF INSIGNIFICANCE. THE MORE HE RESISTS, THE MORE HE IS VIEWED AS BEAST. THIS CAN BE SEEN IN *AFRICA ADDIO*, MADE BY THE FASCIST JACOPETTI: THE AFRICAN SAVAGES, KILLER ANIMALS, WALLOW IN ABJECT ANARCHY ONCE THEY ESCAPE FROM WHITE PROTECTION. TARZAN DIED AND IN HIS PLACE WERE BORN LUMUMBAS AND LOBEGULAS, NKOMOS, AND THE MASZIMBAMUTOS, AND THIS IS SOMETHING THAT NEOCOLONIALISM CANNOT FORGIVE. FANTASY HAS BEEN REPLACED BY PHANTOMS AND MAN IS TURNED INTO AN EXTRA WHO DIES SO JACOPETTI CAN COMFORTABLY FILM HIS EXECUTION.

I MAKE THE REVOLUTION; THEREFORE, I EXIST. THIS IS THE STARTING POINT FOR THE DISAPPEARANCE OF FANTASY AND PHANTOM TO MAKE WAY FOR LIVING HUMAN BEINGS. THE CINEMA OF THE REVOLUTION IS AT THE SAME TIME ONE OF *DESTRUCTION AND CONSTRUCTION*: DESTRUCTION OF THE IMAGE THAT NEOCOLONIALISM HAS CREATED OF ITSELF AND OF US, AND CONSTRUCTION OF A THROBBING, LIVING REALITY WHICH RECAPTURES TRUTH IN ANY OF ITS EX-PRESSIONS.

THE RESTITUTION OF THINGS TO THEIR REAL PLACE AND MEANING IS AN EMINENTLY SUBVERSIVE FACT BOTH IN THE NEOCOLONIAL SITUATION AND IN THE CONSUMER SOCIETIES. IN THE FORMER, THE SEEMING AMBIGUITY OR PSEUDO-OBJECTIVITY IN NEWSPAPERS, LITERATURE, ETC., AND THE RELATIVE FREEDOM OF THE PEOPLE'S ORGANIZATIONS TO PROVIDE THEIR OWN INFORMATION CEASE TO EXIST, GIVING WAY TO OVERT RESTRICTION, WHEN IT IS A QUESTION OF TELEVISION AND RADIO, THE TWO MOST IMPORTANT SYSTEM-CONTROLLED OR MONOPOLIZED COMMUNICATIONS MEDIA. LAST YEAR'S MAY EVENTS IN FRANCE ARE QUITE EXPLICIT ON THIS POINT.

IN A WORLD WHERE THE UNREAL RULES, ARTISTIC EXPRESSION IS SHOVED ALONG THE CHANNELS OF FANTASY, FICTION, LANGUAGE IN CODE, SIGN LANGUAGE, AND MESSAGES WHISPERED BETWEEN THE LINES. ART IS CUT OFF FROM THE CONCRETE FACTS—WHICH, FROM THE NEOCOLONIALIST STANDPOINT, ARE ACCUSATORY TESTIMONIES— TO TURN BACK ON ITSELF, STRUTTING ABOUT IN A WORLD OF ABSTRACTIONS AND PHANTOMS, WHERE IT BECOMES "TIMELESS" AND HISTORY-LESS. VIETNAM CAN BE MENTIONED, BUT ONLY FAR FROM VIETNAM; LATIN AMERICA CAN BE MENTIONED, BUT ONLY FAR ENOUGH AWAY FROM THE CONTINENT TO BE INEFFECTIVE, *IN PLACES WHERE IT IS DEPOLITICIZED* AND WHERE IT DOES NOT LEAD TO ACTION.

THE CINEMA KNOWN AS DOCUMENTARY, WITH ALL THE VASTNESS THAT THE CONCEPT HAS TODAY, FROM EDUCATIONAL FILMS TO THE RECONSTRUCTION OF A FACT OR A HISTORICAL EVENT, IS PERHAPS THE MAIN BASIS OF REVOLUTIONARY FILMMAKING. EVERY IMAGE THAT DOCUMENTS, BEARS WITNESS TO, REFUTES OR DEEPENS THE TRUTH OF A SITUATION IS SOMETHING MORE THAN A FILM IMAGE OR PURELY ARTISTIC FACT; IT BECOMES SOMETHING WHICH THE SYSTEM FINDS INDIGESTIBLE.

TESTIMONY ABOUT A NATIONAL REALITY IS ALSO AN INESTIMABLE MEANS OF DIALOGUE AND KNOWLEDGE ON THE WORLD PLANE. NO INTERNATIONALIST FORM OF STRUGGLE CAN BE CARRIED OUT SUCCESSFULLY IF THERE IS NOT A MUTUAL EXCHANGE OF EXPERIENCES AMONG THE PEOPLE, IF THE PEOPLE DO NOT SUCCEED IN BREAKING OUT OF THE BALKANIZATION ON THE INTERNATIONAL, CONTINENTAL, AND NATIONAL PLANES WHICH IMPERIALISM IS STRIVING TO MAINTAIN.

THERE IS NO KNOWLEDGE OF A REALITY AS LONG AS THAT REALITY IS NOT ACTED UPON, *AS LONG AS ITS TRANSFORMATION IS NOT BEGUN ON ALL FRONTS OF STRUGGLE.* THE WELL-KNOWN QUOTE FROM MARX DESERVES CONSTANT REPETITION: "IT IS NOT SUFFICIENT TO INTERPRET THE WORLD; IT IS NOW A QUESTION OF TRANSFORMING IT."

WITH SUCH AN ATTITUDE AS HIS STARTING POINT, IT REMAINS FOR THE FILMMAKER TO DISCOVER HIS OWN LANGUAGE, A LANGUAGE WHICH WILL ARISE FROM A MILITANT AND TRANSFORMING WORLD-VIEW AND FROM THE THEME BEING DEALT WITH. HERE IT MAY WELL BE POINTED OUT THAT CERTAIN POLITICAL CADRES STILL MAINTAIN OLD DOGMATIC POSITIONS, WHICH ASK THE ARTIST OR FILMMAKER TO

PROVIDE AN APOLOGETIC VIEW OF REALITY, *ONE WHICH IS MORE IN LINE WITH WISHFUL THINKING THAN WITH WHAT ACTUALLY IS.* SUCH POSITIONS, WHICH AT BOTTOM MASK A LACK OF CONFIDENCE IN THE POSSIBILITIES OF REALITY ITSELF, HAVE IN CERTAIN CASES LED TO THE USE OF FILM LANGUAGE AS A MORE IDEALIZED ILLUSTRATION OF A FACT, TO THE DESIRE TO REMOVE REALITY'S DEEP CONTRADICTIONS, ITS DIALECTIC RICHNESS, WHICH IS PRECISELY THE KIND OF DEPTH WHICH CAN GIVE A FILM BEAUTY AND EFFECTIVENESS. THE REALITY OF THE REVOLUTIONARY PROCESSES ALL OVER THE WORLD, IN SPITE OF THEIR CONFUSED AND NEGATIVE ASPECTS, POSSESSES A DOMINANT LINE, A SYNTHESIS WHICH IS SO RICH AND STIMULATING THAT IT DOES NOT NEED TO BE SCHEMATIZED WITH PARTIAL OR SECTARIAN VIEWS.

PAMPHLET FILMS, DIDACTIC FILMS, REPORT FILMS, ESSAY FILMS, WITNESS-BEARING FILMS—ANY MILITANT FORM OF EXPRESSION IS VALID, AND IT WOULD BE ABSURD TO LAY DOWN A SET OF AESTHETIC WORK NORMS. *BE RECEPTIVE TO ALL THAT THE PEOPLE HAVE TO OFFER, AND OFFER THEM THE BEST*; OR, AS CHE PUT IT, *RESPECT THE PEOPLE BY GIVING THEM QUALITY.* THIS IS A GOOD THING TO KEEP IN MIND IN VIEW OF THOSE TENDENCIES WHICH ARE ALWAYS LATENT IN THE REVOLUTIONARY ARTIST TO LOWER THE LEVEL OF INVESTIGATION AND THE LANGUAGE OF A THEME, IN A KIND OF *NEOPOPULISM,* DOWN TO LEVELS WHICH, WHILE THEY MAY BE THOSE UPON WHICH THE MASSES MOVE, DO NOT HELP THEM TO GET RID OF THE STUMBLING BLOCKS LEFT BY IMPERIALISM. THE EFFECTIVENESS OF THE BEST FILMS OF MILITANT CINEMA SHOW THAT SOCIAL LAYERS CONSIDERED BACKWARD ARE ABLE TO CAPTURE THE EXACT MEANING OF AN ASSOCIATION OF IMAGES, AN EFFECT OF STAGING, AND ANY LINGUISTIC EXPERIMENTATION PLACED WITHIN THE CONTEXT OF A GIVEN IDEA. FURTHERMORE, REVOLUTIONARY CINEMA IS NOT FUNDAMENTALLY ONE WHICH ILLUSTRATES, DOCUMENTS, OR PASSIVELY ESTABLISHES A SITUATION: *RATHER, IT ATTEMPTS TO INTERVENE IN THE SITUATION AS AN ELEMENT PROVIDING THRUST OR RECTIFICATION.* TO PUT IT ANOTHER WAY, IT PROVIDES *DISCOVERY THROUGH TRANSFORMATION.*

THE DIFFERENCES THAT EXIST BETWEEN ONE AND ANOTHER LIBERATION PROCESS MAKE IT IMPOSSIBLE TO LAY DOWN SUPPOSEDLY UNIVERSAL NORMS. A CINEMA WHICH IN THE CONSUMER SOCIETY DOES NOT ATTAIN THE LEVEL OF THE REALITY IN WHICH IT MOVES CAN PLAY A STIMULATING ROLE IN AN UNDERDEVELOPED COUNTRY, JUST AS A REVOLUTIONARY CINEMA IN THE NEOCOLONIAL SITUATION WILL NOT NECESSARILY BE REVOLUTIONARY IF IT IS MECHANICALLY TAKEN TO THE METROPOLIS COUNTRY.

TEACHING THE HANDLING OF GUNS CAN BE REVOLUTIONARY WHERE THERE ARE POTENTIALLY OR EXPLICITLY VIABLE LAYERS READY TO THROW THEMSELVES INTO THE STRUGGLE TO TAKE POWER, BUT CEASES TO BE REVOLUTIONARY WHERE THE MASSES STILL LACK SUFFICIENT AWARENESS OF THEIR SITUATION OR WHERE THEY ALREADY HAVE LEARNED TO HANDLE GUNS. THUS, A CINEMA WHICH INSISTS UPON THE DENUNCIATION OF THE *EFFECTS* OF NEOCOLONIAL POLICY IS CAUGHT

UP IN A REFORMIST GAME IF THE CONSCIOUSNESS OF THE MASSES HAS ALREADY ASSIMILATED SUCH KNOWLEDGE; THEN THE REVOLUTIONARY THING IS TO EXAMINE THE *CAUSES*, TO INVESTIGATE THE WAYS OF ORGANIZING AND ARMING FOR THE CHANGE. THAT IS, IMPERIALISM CAN SPONSOR FILMS THAT FIGHT ILLITERACY, AND SUCH PICTURES WILL ONLY BE INSCRIBED WITHIN THE CONTEMPORARY NEED OF IMPERIALIST POLICY, BUT, IN CONTRAST, THE MAKING OF SUCH FILMS IN CUBA AFTER THE TRIUMPH OF THE REVOLUTION WAS CLEARLY REVOLUTIONARY. ALTHOUGH THEIR STARTING POINT WAS JUST THE FACT OF TEACHING READING AND WRITING, THEY HAD A GOAL WHICH WAS RADICALLY DIFFERENT FROM THAT OF IMPERIALISM: THE TRAINING OF PEOPLE FOR LIBERATION, NOT FOR SUBJECTION. THE MODEL OF THE PERFECT WORK OF ART, THE FULLY-ROUNDED FILM STRUCTURED ACCORDING TO THE METRICS IMPOSED BY BOURGEOIS CULTURE, ITS THEORETICIANS AND CRITICS, HAS SERVED TO INHIBIT THE FILMMAKER IN THE DEPENDENT COUNTRIES, ESPECIALLY WHEN HE HAS ATTEMPTED TO ERECT SIMILAR MODELS IN A REALITY WHICH *OFFERED HIM NEITHER THE CULTURE, THE TECHNIQUES, NOR THE MOST PRIMARY ELEMENTS FOR SUCCESS*. THE CULTURE OF THE METROPOLIS KEPT THE AGE-OLD SECRETS THAT HAD GIVEN LIFE TO ITS MODELS; THE TRANSPOSITION OF THE LATTER TO THE NEOCOLONIAL REALITY WAS ALWAYS A MECHANISM OF ALIENATION, *SINCE IT WAS NOT POSSIBLE FOR THE ARTIST OF THE DEPENDANT COUNTRY TO ABSORB, IN A FEW YEARS, THE SECRETS OF A CULTURE AND SOCIETY ELABORATED THROUGH THE CENTURIES IN COMPLETELY DIFFERENT HISTORICAL CIRCUMSTANCES*. THE ATTEMPT IN THE SPHERE OF FILMMAKING TO MATCH THE PICTURES OF THE RULING COUNTRIES GENERALLY ENDS IN FAILURE, GIVEN THE EXISTENCE OF TWO DISPARATE HISTORICAL REALITIES. AND SUCH UNSUCCESSFUL ATTEMPTS LEAD TO FEELINGS OF FRUSTRATION AND INFERIORITY. BOTH THESE FEELINGS ARISE IN THE FIRST PLACE FROM THE FEAR OF TAKING RISKS ALONG COMPLETELY NEW ROADS *WHICH ARE ALMOST A TOTAL DENIAL OF "THEIR CINEMA."* A FEAR OF RECOGNIZING THE PARTICULARITIES AND LIMITATIONS OF A DEPENDENCY SITUATION IN ORDER TO DISCOVER THE *POSSIBILITIES INHERENT IN THAT SITUATION* BY FINDING WAYS OF OVERCOMING IT *WHICH WOULD OF NECESSITY BE ORIGINAL*.

THE EXISTENCE OF A REVOLUTIONARY CINEMA IS INCONCEIVABLE WITHOUT THE CONSTANT AND METHODICAL EXERCISE OF PRACTICE, SEARCH, AND EXPERIMENTATION. IT EVEN MEANS COMMITTING THE NEW FILMMAKER TO TAKE CHANCES ON THE UNKNOWN, TO LEAP INTO SPACE AT TIMES, EXPOSING HIMSELF TO FAILURE AS DOES THE GUERRILLA WHO TRAVELS ALONG PATHS THAT HE HIMSELF OPENS UP WITH MACHETE BLOWS. THE POSSIBILITY OF DISCOVERING AND INVENTING FILM FORMS AND STRUCTURES THAT SERVE A MORE PROFOUND VISION OF OUR REALITY RESIDES IN THE ABILITY TO PLACE ONESELF ON THE OUTSIDE LIMITS OF THE FAMILIAR, TO MAKE ONE'S WAY AMID CONSTANT DANGERS.

OUR TIME IS ONE OF HYPOTHESIS RATHER THAN OF THESIS, A TIME OF WORKS IN PROCESS—UNFINISHED, UNORDERED, VIOLENT WORKS MADE WITH THE CAMERA IN ONE HAND AND A ROCK IN THE OTHER. SUCH WORKS CANNOT BE ASSESSED

ACCORDING TO THE TRADITIONAL THEORETICAL AND CRITICAL CANONS. THE IDEAS FOR *OUR* FILM THEORY AND CRITICISM WILL COME TO LIFE THROUGH INHIBITION-REMOVING PRACTICE AND EXPERIMENTATION. "KNOWLEDGE BEGINS WITH PRAC-TICE. AFTER ACQUIRING THEORETICAL KNOWLEDGE THROUGH PRACTICE, IT IS NECESSARY TO RETURN TO PRACTICE."[12] ONCE HE HAS EMBARKED UPON THIS PRAC-TICE, THE REVOLUTIONARY FILMMAKER WILL HAVE TO OVERCOME COUNTLESS OBSTACLES; HE WILL EXPERIENCE THE LONELINESS OF THOSE WHO ASPIRE TO THE PRAISE OF THE SYSTEM'S PROMOTION MEDIA ONLY TO FIND THAT THOSE MEDIA ARE CLOSED TO HIM. AS GODARD WOULD SAY, HE WILL CEASE TO BE A BICYCLE RIDER, VIETNAMESE STYLE, SUBMERGED IN A CRUEL AND PROLONGED WAR. BUT HE WILL ALSO DISCOVER THAT THERE IS A RECEPTIVE AUDIENCE THAT LOOKS UPON HIS WORK AS SOMETHING OF ITS OWN EXISTENCE, AND THAT IS READY TO DEFEND HIM IN A WAY THAT IT WOULD NEVER DO WITH ANY WORLD BICYCLE CHAMPION.

Implementation

IN THIS LONG WAR, WITH THE CAMERA AS OUR RIFLE, WE DO IN FACT MOVE INTO A GUERRILLA ACTIVITY. THIS IS WHY THE WORK OF A *FILM-GUERRILLA* GROUP IS GOVERNED BY STRICT DISCIPLINARY NORMS AS TO BOTH WORK METHODS AND SECURITY. A REVOLUTIONARY FILM GROUP IS IN THE SAME SITUATION AS A GUER-RILLA UNIT: IT CANNOT GROW STRONG WITHOUT MILITARY STRUCTURES AND COM-MAND CONCEPTS. THE GROUP EXISTS AS A NETWORK OF COMPLEMENTARY RESPONSIBILITIES, AS THE SUM AND SYNTHESIS OF ABILITIES, INASMUCH AS IT OPERATES HARMONICALLY WITH A LEADERSHIP THAT CENTRALIZES PLANNING WORK AND MAIN-TAINS ITS CONTINUITY. EXPERIENCE SHOWS THAT IT IS NOT EASY TO MAINTAIN THE COHESION OF A GROUP WHEN IT IS BOMBARDED BY THE SYSTEM AND ITS CHAIN OF ACCOMPLICES FREQUENTLY DISGUISED AS "PROGRESSIVES," WHEN THERE ARE NO IMMEDIATE AND SPECTACULAR OUTER INCENTIVES AND THE MEMBERS MUST UNDERGO THE DISCOMFORTS AND TENSIONS OF WORK THAT IS DONE UNDERGROUND AND DISTRIBUTED CLANDESTINELY. MANY ABANDON THEIR RESPON-SIBILITIES BECAUSE THEY UNDERESTIMATE THEM OR BECAUSE THEY MEASURE THEM WITH VALUES APPROPRIATE TO SYSTEM CINEMA AND NOT UNDERGROUND CINEMA. THE BIRTH OF INTERNAL CONFLICTS IS A REALITY PRESENT IN ANY GROUP, WHETHER OR NOT IT POSSESSES IDEOLOGICAL MATURITY. THE LACK OF AWARENESS OF SUCH AN INNER CONFLICT ON THE PSYCHOLOGICAL OR PERSONALITY PLANE, ETC., THE LACK OF MATURITY IN DEALING WITH PROBLEMS OF RELATIONSHIPS, AT TIMES LEADS TO ILL FEELING AND RIVALRIES THAT IN TURN CAUSE REAL CLASHES GOING BEYOND IDEOLOGICAL OR OBJECTIVE DIFFERENCES. ALL OF THIS MEANS THAT A BASIC CON-DITION IS AN AWARENESS OF THE PROBLEMS OF INTERPERSONAL RELATIONSHIPS, LEADERSHIP AND AREAS OF COMPETENCE. WHAT IS NEEDED IS TO SPEAK CLEARLY, MARK OFF WORK AREAS, ASSIGN RESPONSIBILITIES AND TAKE ON THE JOB AS A RIGOROUS MILITANCY.

GUERRILLA FILMMAKING PROLETARIANIZES THE FILM WORKER AND BREAKS DOWN THE INTELLECTUAL ARISTOCRACY THAT THE BOURGEOISIE GRANTS TO ITS FOLLOWERS. IN A WORD, IT *DEMOCRATIZES*. THE FILMMAKER'S TIE WITH REALITY MAKES HIM MORE A PART OF HIS PEOPLE. VANGUARD LAYERS AND EVEN MASSES PARTICIPATE COLLECTIVELY IN THE WORK WHEN THEY REALIZE THAT IT IS THE CONTINUITY OF THEIR DAILY STRUGGLE. *LA HORA DE LOS HORNOS* SHOWS HOW A FILM CAN BE MADE IN HOSTILE CIRCUMSTANCES WHEN IT HAS THE SUPPORT AND COLLABORATION OF MILITANTS AND CADRES FROM THE PEOPLE.

THE REVOLUTIONARY FILMMAKER ACTS WITH A RADICALLY NEW VISION OF THE ROLE OF THE PRODUCER, TEAMWORK, TOOLS, DETAILS, ETC. ABOVE ALL, HE SUPPLIES HIMSELF AT ALL LEVELS, HE LEARNS HOW TO HANDLE THE MANIFOLD TECHNIQUES OF HIS CRAFT. HIS MOST VALUABLE POSSESSIONS ARE THE TOOLS OF HIS TRADE, WHICH FORM PART AND PARCEL OF HIS NEED TO COMMUNICATE. THE CAMERA IS THE INEXHAUSTIBLE *EXPROPRIATOR OF IMAGE-WEAPONS*; THE PROJECTOR, *A GUN THAT CAN SHOOT 24 FRAMES A SECOND*.

EACH MEMBER OF THE GROUP SHOULD BE FAMILIAR, AT LEAST IN A GENERAL WAY, WITH THE EQUIPMENT BEING USED: HE MUST BE PREPARED TO REPLACE ANOTHER IN ANY OF THE PHASES OF THE PRODUCTION. THE MYTH OF IRREPLACEABLE TECHNICIANS MUST BE EXPLODED.

THE WHOLE GROUP MUST GRANT GREAT IMPORTANCE TO THE MINOR DETAILS OF THE PRODUCTION AND THE SECURITY MEASURES NEEDED TO PROTECT IT. A LACK OF FORESIGHT WHICH IN CONVENTIONAL FILMMAKING WOULD GO UNNOTICED CAN RENDER VIRTUALLY USELESS WEEKS OR MONTHS OF WORK. AND A FAILURE IN GUERRILLA CINEMA, JUST AS IN THE GUERRILLA STRUGGLE ITSELF, CAN MEAN THE LOSS OF A WORK OR A COMPLETE CHANGE OF PLANS. "IN A GUERRILLA STRUGGLE THE CONCEPT OF FAILURE IS PRESENT A THOUSAND TIMES OVER, AND VICTORY A MYTH THAT ONLY A REVOLUTIONARY CAN DREAM."[13] EVERY MEMBER OF THE GROUP MUST HAVE AN ABILITY TO TAKE CARE OF DETAILS; DISCIPLINE; SPEED; AND, ABOVE ALL, THE WILLINGNESS TO OVERCOME THE WEAKNESSES OF COMFORT, OLD HABITS, AND THE WHOLE CLIMATE OF PSEUDONORMALITY BEHIND WHICH THE WARFARE OF EVERYDAY LIFE IS HIDDEN. EACH FILM IS A DIFFERENT OPERATION, A DIFFERENT JOB REQUIRING VARIATIONS IN METHODS IN ORDER TO CONFUSE OR REFRAIN FROM ALERTING THE ENEMY, ESPECIALLY AS THE PROCESSING LABORATORIES ARE STILL IN HIS HANDS.

THE SUCCESS OF THE WORK DEPENDS TO A GREAT EXTENT ON THE GROUP'S ABILITY TO REMAIN SILENT, ON ITS PERMANENT WARINESS, A CONDITION THAT IS DIFFICULT TO ACHIEVE IN A SITUATION IN WHICH APPARENTLY NOTHING IS HAPPENING AND THE FILMMAKER HAS BEEN ACCUSTOMED TO TELLING ALL AND SUNDRY ABOUT EVERYTHING THAT HE'S DOING BECAUSE THE BOURGEOISIE HAS TRAINED HIM PRECISELY ON SUCH A BASIS OF PRESTIGE AND PROMOTION. THE WATCHWORD "CONSTANT VIGILANCE, CONSTANT WARINESS, CONSTANT MOBILITY" HAS PROFOUND VALIDITY FOR GUERRILLA CINEMA. YOU HAVE TO GIVE THE APPEARANCE OF WORKING

ON VARIOUS PROJECTS, SPLIT UP MATERIALS, PUT IT TOGETHER, TAKE IT APART, CON-
FUSE, NEUTRALIZE, AND THROW OFF THE TRACK. ALL OF THIS IS NECESSARY AS
LONG AS THE GROUP DOESN'T HAVE ITS OWN PROCESSING EQUIPMENT, NO MAT-
TER HOW RUDIMENTARY, AND THERE REMAIN CERTAIN POSSIBILITIES IN THE TRADI-
TIONAL LABORATORIES.

GROUP-LEVEL COOPERATION BETWEEN DIFFERENT COUNTRIES CAN SERVE TO
ASSURE THE COMPLETION OF A FILM OR THE EXECUTION OF CERTAIN PHASES OF
WORK THAT MAY NOT BE POSSIBLE IN THE COUNTRY OF ORIGIN. TO THIS SHOULD
BE ADDED THE NEED FOR A RECEPTION CENTER FOR FILE MATERIALS TO BE USED
BY THE DIFFERENT GROUPS AND THE PERSPECTIVE OF COORDINATION, ON A
CONTINENT-WIDE OR EVEN A WORLD-WIDE SCALE, OF THE CONTINUITY OF WORK
IN EACH COUNTRY: PERIODIC REGIONAL OR INTERNATIONAL GATHERINGS TO EX-
CHANGE EXPERIENCES, CONTRIBUTIONS, JOINT PLANNING OF WORK, ETC.

AT LEAST IN THE EARLIEST STAGES, THE REVOLUTIONARY FILMMAKER AND THE
WORK GROUPS WILL BE THE SOLE PRODUCERS OF THEIR FILMS. THEY MUST BEAR
THE RESPONSIBILITY OF FINDING WAYS TO FACILITATE THE CONTINUITY OF WORK.
GUERRILLA CINEMA STILL DOESN'T HAVE ENOUGH EXPERIENCE TO SET DOWN STAN-
DARDS IN THIS AREA; WHAT EXPERIENCE THERE IS HAS SHOWN, ABOVE ALL, THE
ABILITY TO MAKE USE OF THE CONCRETE SITUATION OF EACH COUNTRY. BUT,
REGARDLESS OF WHAT THESE SITUATIONS MAY BE, THE PREPARATION OF A FILM
CANNOT BE UNDERTAKEN WITHOUT A PARALLEL STUDY OF ITS FUTURE AUDIENCE
AND, CONSEQUENTLY, A PLAN TO RECOVER THE FINANCIAL INVESTMENT. HERE,
ONCE AGAIN, THE NEED ARISES OF CLOSER TIES BETWEEN POLITICAL AND ARTISTIC
VANGUARDS, SINCE THIS ALSO SERVES FOR THE JOINT STUDY OF FORMS OF PRO-
DUCTION, EXHIBITION, AND CONTINUITY.

A GUERRILLA FILM CAN BE AIMED ONLY AT THE DISTRIBUTION MECHANISMS
PROVIDED BY THE REVOLUTIONARY ORGANIZATIONS, INCLUDING THOSE INVENTED
OR DISCOVERED BY THE FILMMAKER HIMSELF. PRODUCTION, DISTRIBUTION, AND
ECONOMIC POSSIBILITIES FOR SURVIVAL MUST FORM PART OF A SINGLE STRATEGY.
THE SOLUTION OF THE PROBLEMS FACED IN EACH OF THESE AREAS WILL ENCOURAGE
OTHER PEOPLE TO JOIN IN THE WORK OF GUERRILLA FILMMAKING, WHICH WILL
ENLARGE ITS RANKS AND THUS MAKE IT LESS VULNERABLE.

THE DISTRIBUTION OF GUERRILLA FILMS IN LATIN AMERICA IS STILL IN SWAD-
DLING CLOTHES, WHILE SYSTEM REPRISALS ARE ALREADY A LEGALIZED FACT. SUF-
FICE IT TO NOTE IN ARGENTINA THE RAIDS THAT HAVE OCCURRED DURING SOME
SHOWINGS AND THE RECENT FILM SUPPRESSION LAW OF A CLEARLY FASCIST
CHARACTER, IN BRAZIL THE EVER-INCREASING RESTRICTIONS PLACED UPON THE
MOST MILITANT COMRADES OF *CINEMA NOVO*, AND IN VENEZUELA THE BANNING
AND LICENSE CANCELLATION OF *LA HORA DE LOS HORNOS*; ALMOST ALL OVER
THE CONTINENT CENSORSHIP PREVENTS ANY POSSIBILITY OF PUBLIC DISTRIBUTION.

WITHOUT REVOLUTIONARY FILMS AND A PUBLIC THAT ASKS FOR THEM, ANY
ATTEMPT TO OPEN UP NEW WAYS OF DISTRIBUTION WOULD BE DOOMED TO FAILURE.

BUT BOTH OF THESE ALREADY EXIST IN LATIN AMERICA. THE APPEARANCE OF THE FILMS OPENED UP A ROAD WHICH IN SOME COUNTRIES, SUCH AS ARGENTINA, OCCURS THROUGH SHOWINGS IN APARTMENTS AND HOUSES TO AUDIENCES OF NEVER MORE THAN 25 PEOPLE; IN OTHER COUNTRIES, SUCH AS CHILE, FILMS ARE SHOWN IN PARISHES, UNIVERSITIES, OR CULTURAL CENTERS (OF WHICH THERE ARE FEWER EVERY DAY); AND, IN THE CASE OF URUGUAY, SHOWINGS WERE GIVEN IN MONTEVIDEO'S BIGGEST MOVIE THEATER TO AN AUDIENCE OF 2500 PEOPLE, WHO FILLED THE THEATER AND MADE EVERY SHOWING AN IMPASSIONED ANTI-IMPERIALIST EVENT.[14] BUT THE PROSPECTS ON THE CONTINENTAL PLANE INDICATE THAT THE POSSIBILITY FOR THE CONTINUITY OF A REVOLUTIONARY CINEMA RESTS UPON THE *STRENGTHENING OF RIGOROUSLY UNDERGROUND BASE STRUCTURES*.

PRACTICE IMPLIES MISTAKES AND FAILURES.[15] SOME COMRADES WILL LET THEMSELVES BE CARRIED AWAY BY THE SUCCESS AND IMPUNITY WITH WHICH THEY PRESENT THE FIRST SHOWINGS AND WILL TEND TO RELAX SECURITY MEASURES, WHILE OTHERS WILL GO IN THE OPPOSITE DIRECTION OF EXCESSIVE PRECAUTIONS OR FEAR-FULNESS, TO SUCH AN EXTENT THAT DISTRIBUTION REMAINS CIRCUMSCRIBED, LIMITED TO A FEW GROUPS OF FRIENDS. ONLY CONCRETE EXPERIENCE IN EACH COUNTRY WILL DEMONSTRATE WHICH ARE THE BEST METHODS THERE, WHICH DO NOT ALWAYS LEND THEMSELVES TO APPLICATION IN OTHER SITUATIONS.

IN SOME PLACES IT WILL BE POSSIBLE TO BUILD INFRASTRUCTURES CONNECTED TO POLITICAL, STUDENT, WORKER, AND OTHER ORGANIZATIONS, WHILE IN OTHERS IT WILL BE MORE SUITABLE TO SELL PRINTS TO ORGANIZATIONS WHICH WILL TAKE CHARGE OF OBTAINING THE FUNDS NECESSARY TO PAY FOR EACH PRINT (THE COST OF THE PRINT PLUS A SMALL MARGIN). THIS METHOD, WHEREVER POSSIBLE, WOULD APPEAR TO BE THE MOST VIABLE, BECAUSE IT PERMITS THE DECENTRALIZATION OF DISTRIBUTION; MAKES POSSIBLE A MORE PROFOUND POLITICAL USE OF THE FILM; AND PERMITS THE RECOVERY, THROUGH THE SALE OF MORE PRINTS, OF THE FUNDS INVESTED IN THE PRODUCTION. IT IS TRUE THAT IN MANY COUNTRIES THE ORGANIZA-TIONS STILL ARE NOT FULLY AWARE OF THE IMPORTANCE OF THIS WORK OR, IF THEY ARE, MAY LACK THE MEANS TO UNDERTAKE IT. IN SUCH CASES OTHER METHODS CAN BE USED: THE DELIVERY OF PRINTS TO ENCOURAGE DISTRIBUTION AND A BOX-OFFICE CUT TO THE ORGANIZERS OF EACH SHOWING, ETC. THE IDEAL GOAL TO BE ACHIEVED WOULD BE PRODUCING AND DISTRIBUTING GUERRILLA FILMS WITH FUNDS OBTAINED FROM EXPROPRIATIONS OF THE BOURGEOISIE—THAT IS, *THE BOURGEOISIE WOULD BE FINANCING GUERRILLA CINEMA WITH A BIT OF THE SURPLUS VALUE THAT IT GETS FROM THE PEOPLE*. BUT, AS LONG AS THE GOAL IS NO MORE THAN A MIDDLE OR LONG-RANGE ASPIRATION, THE ALTERNATIVES OPEN TO REVOLU-TIONARY CINEMA TO RECOVER PRODUCTION AND DISTRIBUTION COSTS ARE TO SOME EXTENT SIMILAR TO THOSE OBTAINED FOR CONVENTIONAL CINEMA: EVERY SPECTATOR SHOULD PAY THE SAME AMOUNT THAT HE PAYS TO SEE THE SYSTEM CINEMA. FINANCING, SUBSIDIZING, EQUIPPING, AND SUPPORTING REVOLUTIONARY CINEMA ARE POLITICAL RESPONSIBILITIES FOR REVOLUTIONARY ORGANIZATIONS AND

MILITANTS. A FILM CAN BE MADE, BUT IF ITS DISTRIBUTION DOES NOT ALLOW FOR THE RECOVERY OF THE COSTS, IT WILL BE DIFFICULT OR IMPOSSIBLE TO MAKE A SECOND FILM.

THE 16MM FILM CIRCUITS IN EUROPE (20,000 EXHIBITION CENTERS IN SWEDEN, 30,000 IN FRANCE, ETC.) ARE NOT THE BEST EXAMPLES FOR THE NEOCOLONIALIZED COUNTRIES, BUT THEY ARE NEVERTHELESS A COMPLEMENT TO BE KEPT IN MIND FOR FUND RAISING, ESPECIALLY IN A SITUATION IN WHICH SUCH CIRCUITS CAN PLAY AN IMPORTANT ROLE IN PUBLICIZING THE STRUGGLES IN THE THIRD WORLD, INCREASINGLY RELATED AS THEY ARE TO THOSE UNFOLDING IN THE METROPOLIS COUNTRIES. A FILM ON THE VENEZUELAN GUERRILLAS WILL SAY MORE TO A EUROPEAN PUBLIC THAN 20 EXPLANATORY PAMPHLETS, AND THE SAME IS TRUE FOR US WITH A FILM ON THE MAY EVENTS IN FRANCE OR THE BERKELEY, U.S.A. STUDENT STRUGGLE.

A *GUERRILLA FILMS INTERNATIONAL?* AND WHY NOT? ISN'T IT TRUE THAT A KIND OF NEW INTERNATIONAL IS ARISING THROUGH THE THIRD WORLD STRUGGLES; THROUGH O.S.P.A.A.A.L. AND THE REVOLUTIONARY VANGUARDS OF THE CONSUMER SOCIETIES.

A GUERRILLA CINEMA, AT THIS STAGE STILL WITHIN THE REACH OF LIMITED LAYERS OF THE POPULATION, IS, NEVERTHELESS, *THE ONLY CINEMA OF THE MASSES POSSIBLE TODAY*, SINCE IT IS THE ONLY ONE INVOLVED WITH THE INTERESTS, ASPIRATIONS, AND PROSPECTS OF THE VAST MAJORITY OF THE PEOPLE. EVERY IMPORTANT FILM PRODUCED BY A REVOLUTIONARY CINEMA WILL BE, EXPLICIT OR NOT, *A NATIONAL EVENT OF THE MASSES*.

THIS *CINEMA OF THE MASSES*, WHICH IS PREVENTED FROM REACHING BEYOND THE SECTORS REPRESENTING THE MASSES, PROVOKES WITH EACH SHOWING, AS IN A REVOLUTIONARY MILITARY INCURSION, A LIBERATED SPACE, *A DECOLONIZED TERRITORY*. THE SHOWING CAN BE TURNED INTO A KIND OF POLITICAL EVENT, WHICH, ACCORDING TO FANON, COULD BE "A LITURGICAL ACT, A PRIVILEGED OCCASION FOR HUMAN BEINGS TO HEAR AND BE HEARD."

MILITANT CINEMA MUST BE ABLE TO EXTRACT THE INFINITY OF NEW POSSIBILITIES THAT OPEN UP FOR IT FROM THE CONDITIONS OF PROSCRIPTION IMPOSED BY THE SYSTEM. THE ATTEMPT TO OVERCOME NEOCOLONIAL OPPRESSION CALLS FOR THE INVENTION OF FORMS OF COMMUNICATION; *IT OPENS UP THE POSSIBILITY*.

BEFORE AND DURING THE MAKING OF *LA HORA DE LOS HORNOS* WE TRIED OUT VARIOUS METHODS FOR THE DISTRIBUTION OF REVOLUTIONARY CINEMA— THE LITTLE THAT WE HAD MADE UP TO THEN. EACH SHOWING FOR MILITANTS, MIDDLE-LEVEL CADRES, ACTIVISTS, WORKERS, AND UNIVERSITY STUDENTS BECAME— WITHOUT OUR HAVING SET OURSELVES THIS AIM BEFOREHAND—A KIND OF ENLARGED CELL MEETING OF WHICH THE FILMS WERE A PART OF BUT NOT THE MOST IMPORTANT FACTOR. WE THUS DISCOVERED A NEW FACET OF CINEMA: THE *PARTICIPATION* OF PEOPLE WHO, UNTIL THEN, WERE CONSIDERED *SPECTATORS*. AT TIMES, SECURITY REASONS OBLIGED US TO TRY TO DISSOLVE THE GROUP OF PAR-

TICIPANTS AS SOON AS THE SHOWING WAS OVER, AND WE REALIZED THAT THE DISTRIBUTION OF THAT KIND OF FILM HAD LITTLE MEANING IF IT WAS NOT COMPLEMENTED BY THE PARTICIPATION OF THE COMRADES, IF A DEBATE WAS NOT OPENED ON THE THEMES SUGGESTED BY THE FILMS.

WE ALSO DISCOVERED THAT EVERY COMRADE WHO ATTENDED SUCH SHOWINGS DID SO WITH FULL AWARENESS THAT HE WAS INFRINGING ON THE SYSTEM'S LAWS AND EXPOSING HIS PERSONAL SECURITY TO EVENTUAL REPRESSION. THIS PERSON WAS NO LONGER A SPECTATOR; ON THE CONTRARY, FROM THE MOMENT HE DECIDED TO ATTEND THE SHOWING, *FROM THE MOMENT HE LINED HIMSELF UP ON THIS SIDE* BY TAKING RISKS AND CONTRIBUTING HIS LIVING EXPERIENCE TO THE MEETING, HE BECAME AN ACTOR, A MORE IMPORTANT PROTAGONIST THAN THOSE WHO APPEARED IN THE FILMS. SUCH A PERSON WAS SEEKING OTHER COMMITTED PEOPLE LIKE HIMSELF, WHILE HE, IN TURN, BECAME COMMITTED TO THEM. *THE SPECTATOR MADE WAY FOR THE ACTOR, WHO SOUGHT HIMSELF IN OTHERS.*

OUTSIDE THIS SPACE WHICH THE FILMS MOMENTARILY HELPED TO LIBERATE, THERE WAS NOTHING BUT SOLITUDE, NONCOMMUNICATION, DISTRUST, AND FEAR; WITHIN THE FREED SPACE THE SITUATION TURNED EVERYONE INTO ACCOMPLICES OF THE ACT THAT WAS UNFOLDING. THE DEBATES AROSE SPONTANEOUSLY. AS WE GAINED IN EXPERIENCE, WE INCORPORATED INTO THE SHOWING VARIOUS ELEMENTS (A STAGE PRODUCTION) TO REINFORCE THE THEMES OF THE FILMS, THE CLIMATE OF THE SHOWING, THE "DISINHIBITING" OF THE PARTICIPANTS, AND THE DIALOGUE: RECORDED MUSIC OR POEMS, SCULPTURE AND PAINTINGS, POSTERS, A PROGRAM DIRECTOR WHO CHAIRED THE DEBATE AND PRESENTED THE FILM AND THE COMRADES WHO WERE SPEAKING, A GLASS OF WINE, A FEW *MATES*, ETC. WE REALIZED THAT WE HAD AT HAND THREE VERY VALUABLE FACTORS:

1) *THE PARTICIPANT COMRADE*, THE MAN-ACTOR-ACCOMPLICE WHO RESPONDED TO THE SUMMONS;

2) *THE FREE SPACE* WHERE THAT MAN EXPRESSED HIS CONCERNS AND IDEAS, BECAME POLITICIZED, AND STARTED TO FREE HIMSELF; AND

3) *THE FILM*, IMPORTANT ONLY AS A DETONATOR OR PRETEXT.

WE CONCLUDED FROM THESE DATA THAT A FILM COULD BE MUCH MORE EFFECTIVE IF IT WERE FULLY AWARE OF THESE FACTORS AND TOOK ON THE TASK OF SUBORDINATING ITS OWN FORM, STRUCTURE, LANGUAGE, AND PROPOSITIONS TO THAT ACT AND TO THOSE ACTORS—TO PUT IT ANOTHER WAY, *IF IT SOUGHT ITS OWN LIBERATION IN THE SUBORDINATION AND INSERTION IN THE OTHERS, THE PRINCIPAL PROTAGONISTS OF LIFE.* WITH THE CORRECT UTILIZATION OF THE *TIME* THAT THAT GROUP OF ACTOR-PERSONAGES OFFERED US WITH THEIR DIVERSE HISTORIES, THE USE OF THE *SPACE* OFFERED BY CERTAIN COMRADES, AND OF THE *FILMS* THEMSELVES, *IT WAS NECESSARY TO TRY TO TRANSFORM TIME, ENERGY, AND WORK INTO FREEDOM-GIVING ENERGY.* IN THIS WAY THE IDEA BEGAN TO GROW

OF STRUCTURING WHAT WE DECIDED TO CALL THE *FILM ACT*, THE *FILM ACTION*, ONE OF THE FORMS WHICH WE BELIEVE ASSUMES GREAT IMPORTANCE IN AFFIRMING THE LINE OF A *THIRD CINEMA*. A CINEMA WHOSE FIRST EXPERIMENT IS TO BE FOUND, PERHAPS ON A RATHER SHAKY LEVEL, IN THE SECOND AND THIRD PARTS OF *LA HORA DE LOS HORNOS* ("*ACTO PARA LA LIBERACION*"; ABOVE ALL, STARTING WITH "*LA RESISTENCIA*" AND "*VIOLENCIA Y LIBERACION*").

COMRADES [WE SAID AT THE START OF "ACTO PARA LA LIBERACION"] *THIS IS NOT JUST A FILM SHOWING, NOR IS IT A SHOW; RATHER, IT IS, ABOVE ALL,* **a meeting***—AN ACT OF ANTI-IMPERIALIST UNITY; THIS IS A PLACE ONLY FOR THOSE WHO FEEL IDENTIFIED WITH THIS STRUGGLE, BECAUSE HERE THERE IS NO ROOM FOR SPECTATORS OR FOR ACCOMPLICES OF THE ENEMY; HERE THERE IS ROOM ONLY FOR THE AUTHORS AND PROTAGONISTS OF THE PROCESS TO WHICH THE FILM ATTEMPTS TO BEAR WITNESS AND TO DEEPEN. THE FILM IS THE PRETEXT FOR DIALOGUE, FOR THE SEEKING AND FINDING OF WILLS. IT IS A REPORT THAT WE PLACE BEFORE YOU FOR YOUR CONSIDERATION, TO BE DEBATED AFTER THE SHOWING.*

THE CONCLUSIONS [WE SAID AT ANOTHER POINT IN THE SECOND PART] *TO WHICH YOU MAY ARRIVE AS THE REAL AUTHORS AND PROTAGONISTS OF THIS HISTORY ARE IMPORTANT. THE EXPERIENCES AND CONCLUSIONS THAT WE HAVE ASSEMBLED HAVE A RELATIVE WORTH; THEY ARE OF USE TO THE EXTENT THAT THEY ARE USEFUL TO YOU, WHO ARE THE PRESENT AND FUTURE OF LIBERATION. BUT MOST IMPORTANT OF ALL IS THE ACTION THAT MAY ARISE FROM THESE CONCLUSIONS, THE UNITY ON THE BASIS OF THE FACTS. THIS IS WHY THE FILM STOPS HERE; IT OPENS OUT TO YOU SO THAT YOU CAN CONTINUE IT.*

THE FILM ACT MEANS AN OPEN-ENDED FILM; IT IS ESSENTIALLY A WAY OF LEARNING.

THE FIRST STEP IN THE PROCESS OF KNOWLEDGE IS THE FIRST CONTACT WITH THE THINGS OF THE OUTSIDE WORLD, THE STAGE OF SENSATIONS [IN A FILM, THE LIVING FRESCO OF IMAGE AND SOUND]. *THE SECOND STEP IS THE SYNTHESIZING OF THE DATA PROVIDED BY THE SENSATIONS; THEIR ORDERING AND ELABORATION; THE STAGE OF CONCEPTS, JUDGMENTS, OPINIONS, AND DEDUCTIONS* [IN THE FILM, THE ANNOUNCER, THE REPORTINGS, THE DIDACTICS, OR THE NARRATOR WHO LEADS THE PROJECTION ACT]. *AND THEN COMES THE THIRD STAGE, THAT OF KNOWLEDGE. THE ACTIVE ROLE OF KNOWLEDGE IS EXPRESSED NOT ONLY IN THE ACTIVE LEAP FROM SENSORY TO RATIONAL KNOWLEDGE, BUT, AND WHAT IS EVEN MORE IMPORTANT, IN THE LEAP FROM RATIONAL KNOWLEDGE TO REVOLUTIONARY PRACTICE. . . . THE PRACTICE OF THE TRANSFORMATION OF THE WORLD. . . . THIS, IN GENERAL TERMS, IS THE DIALECTICAL MATERIALIST THEORY*

OF THE UNITY OF KNOWLEDGE AND ACTION[16] [IN THE PROJECTION OF THE FILM ACT, THE PARTICIPATION OF THE COMRADES, THE ACTION PROPOSALS THAT ARISE, AND THE ACTIONS THEMSELVES THAT WILL TAKE PLACE LATER].

MOREOVER, EACH PROJECTION OF A FILM ACT PRESUPPOSES A *DIFFERENT SETTING*, SINCE THE SPACE WHERE IT TAKES PLACE, THE MATERIALS THAT GO TO MAKE IT UP (ACTORS-PARTICIPANTS), AND THE HISTORIC TIME IN WHICH IT TAKES PLACE ARE NEVER THE SAME. THIS MEANS THAT THE RESULT OF EACH PROJECTION ACT WILL DEPEND ON THOSE WHO ORGANIZE IT, ON THOSE WHO PARTICIPATE IN IT, AND ON THE TIME AND PLACE; THE POSSIBILITY OF INTRODUCING VARIATIONS, ADDITIONS, AND CHANGES IS UNLIMITED. THE SCREENING OF A FILM ACT WILL ALWAYS EXPRESS IN ONE WAY OR ANOTHER THE HISTORICAL SITUATION IN WHICH IT TAKES PLACE; ITS PERSPECTIVES ARE NOT EXHAUSTED IN THE STRUGGLE FOR POWER BUT WILL INSTEAD CONTINUE AFTER THE TAKING OF POWER TO STRENGTHEN THE REVOLUTION.

THE MAN OF THE *THIRD CINEMA*, BE IT *GUERRILLA CINEMA* OR A *FILM ACT*, WITH THE INFINITE CATEGORIES THAT THEY CONTAIN (FILM LETTER, FILM POEM, FILM ESSAY, FILM PAMPHLET, FILM REPORT, ETC.), ABOVE ALL COUNTERS THE FILM INDUSTRY OF A CINEMA OF CHARACTERS WITH ONE OF THEMES, THAT OF INDIVIDUALS WITH THAT OF MASSES, THAT OF THE AUTHOR WITH THAT OF THE OPERATIVE GROUP, ONE OF NEOCOLONIAL MISINFORMATION WITH ONE OF INFORMATION, ONE OF ESCAPE WITH ONE THAT RECAPTURES THE TRUTH, THAT OF PASSIVITY WITH THAT OF AGGRESSIONS. TO AN INSTITUTIONALIZED CINEMA, HE COUNTERPOSES A GUERRILLA CINEMA; TO MOVIES AS SHOWS, HE OPPOSES A FILM ACT OR ACTION; TO A CINEMA MADE FOR THE OLD KIND OF HUMAN BEING, FOR THEM, HE OPPOSES A *CINEMA FIT FOR A NEW KIND OF HUMAN BEING, FOR WHAT EACH ONE OF US HAS THE POSSIBILITY OF BECOMING.*

THE DECOLONIZATION OF THE FILMMAKER AND OF FILMS WILL BE SIMULTANEOUS ACTS TO THE EXTENT THAT EACH CONTRIBUTES TO COLLECTIVE DECOLONIZATION. THE BATTLE BEGINS WITHOUT, AGAINST THE ENEMY WHO ATTACKS BUT ALSO WITHIN, *AGAINST THE IDEAS AND MODELS OF THE ENEMY TO BE FOUND INSIDE EACH ONE OF US.* DECONSTRUCTION AND CONSTRUCTION. DECOLONIZING ACTION RESCUES WITH ITS PRACTICE THE PUREST AND MOST VITAL IMPULSES. IT OPPOSES TO THE COLONIALIZATION OF MINDS THE REVOLUTION OF CONSCIOUSNESS. THE WORLD IS SCRUTINIZED, UNRAVELED, REDISCOVERED. PEOPLE ARE WITNESS TO A CONSTANT ASTONISHMENT, A KIND OF SECOND BIRTH. THEY RECOVER THEIR EARLY INGENUITY, THEIR CAPACITY FOR ADVENTURE; THEIR LETHARGIC CAPACITY FOR INDIGNATION COMES TO LIFE.

FREEING A FORBIDDEN TRUTH MEANS SETTING FREE THE POSSIBILITY OF INDIGNATION AND SUBVERSION. OUR TRUTH, THAT OF THE NEW MAN WHO BUILDS

HIMSELF BY GETTING RID OF ALL THE DEFECTS THAT STILL WEIGH HIM DOWN, IS A BOMB OF INEXHAUSTIBLE POWER AND, AT THE SAME TIME, *THE ONLY REAL POSSIBILITY OF LIFE*. WITHIN THIS ATTEMPT, THE REVOLUTIONARY FILMMAKER VENTURES WITH *HIS SUBVERSIVE OBSERVATION, SENSIBILITY, IMAGINATION, AND REALIZATION*. THE GREAT THEMES—THE HISTORY OF THE COUNTRY, LOVE AND UNLOVE BETWEEN COMBATANTS, THE EFFORTS OF A PEOPLE THAT AWAKENS—ALL THIS IS REBORN BEFORE THE LENS OF THE DECOLONIZED CAMERA. HE DISCOVERS THAT, WITHIN THE SYSTEM, NOTHING FITS, WHILE OUTSIDE OF AND AGAINST THE SYSTEM, EVERYTHING FITS, *BECAUSE EVERYTHING REMAINS TO BE DONE*. WHAT APPEARED YESTERDAY AS A PREPOSTEROUS ADVENTURE, AS WE SAID AT THE BEGINNING, IS POSED TODAY AS *AN INESCAPABLE NEED AND POSSIBILITY*.

THUS FAR, WE HAVE OFFERED IDEAS AND WORKING PROPOSITIONS, WHICH ARE THE SKETCH OF A HYPOTHESIS ARISING FROM OUR PERSONAL EXPERIENCE AND WHICH WILL HAVE ACHIEVED SOMETHING POSITIVE EVEN IF THEY DO NO MORE THAN SERVE TO OPEN A HEATED DIALOGUE ON THE NEW REVOLUTIONARY FILM PROSPECTS. THE VACUUMS EXISTING IN THE ARTISTIC AND SCIENTIFIC FRONTS OF THE REVOLUTION ARE SUFFICIENTLY WELL KNOWN SO THAT THE ADVERSARY WILL NOT TRY TO APPROPRIATE THEM, WHILE WE ARE STILL UNABLE TO DO SO.

WHY FILMS AND NOT SOME OTHER FORM OF ARTISTIC COMMUNICATION? IF WE CHOOSE FILMS AS THE CENTER OF OUR PROPOSITIONS AND DEBATE, IT IS BECAUSE THAT IS OUR WORK FRONT AND BECAUSE THE BIRTH OF A *THIRD CINEMA* MEANS, AT LEAST FOR US, *THE MOST IMPORTANT REVOLUTIONARY ARTISTIC EVENT OF OUR TIMES*.

Notes

1. *The Hour of the Furnaces*—"Neocolonialism and Violence."
2. Juan Jose Hernandez Arregui, *Imperialism and Culture.*
3. Rene Zavaleta Mercado, *Bolivia: Growth of the National Concept.*
4. *Hour of the Furnaces,* ibid.

5. Ibid.
6. Observe the new customs of some groups of the upper bourgeoisie from Rome and Paris who spend their weekends travelling to Saigon to get a close-up view of the Vietcong offensive.
7. Irwin Silber, "USA: The Alienation of Culture," *Tricontinental* 10.
8. The organization Vanguard Artists of Argentina.
9. *The Hour of the Furnaces,* ibid.
10. Mao Tse-tung, *On Practice.*
11. Rodolfo Pruigross, *The Proletariat and National Revolution.*
12. Mao Tse-tung, op. cit.
13. Che Guevara, *Guerrilla Warfare.*
14. The Uruguayan weekly *Marcha* organizes latenight and Sunday morning exhibitions that are widely and well received.
15. The raiding of a Buenos Aires union and the arrests of dozens of persons resulting from a bad choice of projection site and the large number of people invited.
16. Mao Tse-tung, op. cit.

Godard On Solanas/Solanas On Godard [1969]

An Interview

The work of the French New Wave, particularly that of Jean-Luc Godard made an enormous impact on New Latin American filmmakers. Directors continuously alluded to Godard's techniques and influence, at times shunning him as a European, at times condemning him as a rebel without a real revolution, but always acknowledging the centrality of his contributions to radical filmmaking.

This interview was held shortly after *The Hour of the Furnaces* began to be shown in the U.S. and Europe, but was never published in English. The style, language and concerns of the interview reveal as much about the spirit of 1968 as they do about the transformations both directors have undergone in the two decades that followed. It appears here in a slightly abridged form.

Jean-Luc Godard: How would you define your film, *The Hour of the Furnaces?*

Fernando Solanas: As an ideological and political film-essay. Some people have talked about a film-book and this is correct, because we supply information, elements for reflection, titles, and didactic forms . . . The structure of the narration is constructed as it is in a book: prologue, chapters, and the epilogue. It is a film absolutely free in its form and its language. We have used everything that was necessary or useful for our educational ends: from direct sequences or interviews to others whose form approaches that of a story, or tale, or a song, or even

MONTAGE OF CONCEPTS AS IMAGES. THE SUB-TITLE OF THE FILM SHOWS ITS DOCUMENTARY CHARACTER, IT IS INTENDED TO BE A PROOF, A TESTIMONY, CONCRETE EVIDENCE OF A PARTICULAR REALITY: "NOTES AND TESTIMONIES ON NEOCOLONIALISM, VIOLENCE AND LIBERATION." IT IS A DOCUMENTARY FILM OF ACCUSATION BUT AT THE SAME TIME IT IS A FILM THAT WANTS TO EDUCATE AND TO RESEARCH. IT IS A FILM WHOSE CONTRIBUTION LIES IN ITS ORIENTATION; IT POINTS A DIRECTION, IT POINTS A WAY. BECAUSE THE FILM IS NOT ADDRESSED TO ANYONE, IT IS NOT ADDRESSED TO AN AUDIENCE THAT BELIEVES IN "CULTURAL COEXISTENCE," BUT, ON THE OTHER HAND, IT IS ADDRESSED TO THE MASSES WHO SUFFER THE GREAT NEOCOLONIAL OPPRESSION. THIS IS SHOWN MAINLY IN THE SECOND AND THIRD PART, BECAUSE THE FIRST TELLS THAT WHICH THE MASSES ALREADY KNOW, INTUITIVELY FEEL AND LIVE; THE FIRST PART PLAYS THE ROLE OF A PROLOGUE. *THE HOUR OF THE FURNACES* IS ALSO A FILM "ACT," AN ANTI-SHOW, BECAUSE IT DENIES ITSELF AS FILM AND OPENS ITSELF TO THE PUBLIC FOR DEBATE, DISCUSSION AND FURTHER DEVELOPMENTS. EACH SHOW BECOMES A PLACE OF LIBERATION, AN ACT IN WHICH MAN TAKES CONSCIENCE OF HIS SITUATION AND OF THE NEED FOR A DEEPER PRAXIS TO CHANGE THAT SITUATION.

JLG: HOW DOES THE "ACT" TAKE PLACE?

FS: THERE ARE PAUSES IN THE FILM, INTERRUPTIONS SO THAT THE FILM AND THE TOPICS PRESENTED CAN PASS FROM THE SCREEN TO THE THEATER, THAT IS TO LIFE, TO THE PRESENT. THE OLD SPECTATOR, THE SUBJECT WHO BEHOLDS, THE ONLOOKER, ACCORDING TO THE TRADITIONAL FILM THAT DEVELOP THE BOURGEOIS CONCEPTS OF THE ARTS OF THE 1800'S, THAT NON-PARTICIPANT, BECOMES THE LIVE PROTAGONIST, A REAL ACTOR IN THE STORY OF THE FILM AND IN THE HISTORY ITSELF, SINCE THE FILM IS ABOUT OUR CONTEMPORARY HISTORY. AND IT IS A FILM ABOUT LIBERATION, ABOUT AN UNFINISHED STAGE IN OUR HISTORY; IT CANNOT BE ANYTHING BUT AN UNFINISHED FILM, A FILM OPEN TO THE PRESENT AND TO THE FUTURE OF THIS ACT OF LIBERATION. THAT IS WHY THE FILM MUST BE COMPLETED BY THE PROTAGONISTS, AND WE ARE NOT DISCARDING THE POSSIBILITY OF ADDING NEW NOTES AND FILM TESTIMONIES IF WE WERE TO FIND IN THE FUTURE NEW OCCURRENCES THAT NEEDED TO BE INCORPORATED. THE "ACTS" END WHEN THE PARTICIPANTS DECIDE TO END THEM. THE FILM HAS BEEN THE DETONATOR OF THE ACT, THE AGENT THAT MOBILIZES THE OLD SPECTATOR. FURTHERMORE, WE BELIEVE IN WHAT FANON SAID: "IF WE MUST INVOLVE EVERYONE IN THE FIGHT FOR OUR COMMON SALVATION, THERE ARE NO SPECTATORS, THERE ARE NO INNOCENTS. WE ALL DIRTY OUR HANDS IN THE SWAMPS OF OUR SOIL AND IN THE EMPTINESS OF OUR MINDS. EVERY SPECTATOR IS EITHER A COWARD OR A TRAITOR." THAT IS TO SAY, THAT WE ARE NOT FACING A FILM FOR EXPRESSION, NOR A FILM FOR COMMUNICATION, BUT A FILM FOR ACTION, A FILM FOR LIBERATION.

JLG: WHAT SORT OF PROBLEMS DID YOU HAVE?

FS: BESIDES ALL THE PROBLEMS COMMON TO ANY ECONOMIC PRODUCTION, I COULD SAY THAT THE BIGGEST PROBLEM WAS TO OVERCOME OUR DEPENDENCE ON FOREIGN CINEMATOGRAPHIC MODELS. MEANING THAT WE HAD TO LIBERATE OURSELVES AS CREATORS. IT IS THIS DEPENDENCE, FUNDAMENTALLY AESTHETIC, OF OUR FILM VIS-A-VIS THE AMERICAN AND EUROPEAN FILM, WHICH IS ITS BIGGEST LIMITATION. AND THIS COULD NOT BE UNDERSTOOD SEPARATELY FROM THE ANALYSIS OF THE ARGENTINE CULTURAL SITUATION. THE OFFICIAL ARGENTINE CULTURE, THE CULTURE OF THE NEOCOLONIAL BOURGEOISIE, IS A CULTURE OF IMITATION, SECOND-HAND, OLD AND DECADENT. A CULTURE BUILT WITH THE CULTURAL MODELS OF THE OPPRESSIVE, IMPERIALIST BOURGEOISIES. A CULTURE EUROPEAN-STYLE, TODAY AMERICANIZED. THAT IS WHY THE GREATEST PART OF ARGENTINE FILMS MADE TODAY ARE BUILT UPON THE PRODUCTIVE, ARGUMENTATIVE AND AESTHETIC MODELS OF YANKEE FILMS, OR ON THE SO-CALLED "AUTHOR-ORIENTED" EUROPEAN FILMMAKING. THERE ARE NO INVENTIONS, NO SEARCH OF OUR OWN. THERE IS TRANSLATION, DEVELOPMENT OR COPY. THERE IS DEPENDENCE . . .

JLG: AMERICAN FILM IS FILM TO BE SOLD . . .

FS: EXACTLY, A FILM TIED UP WITH SHOWS AND BUSINESS; SUBSERVIENT TO AND CONDITIONED BY CAPITALIST EXPLOITATION. OF THIS PROFIT-SEEKING MODE OF PRODUCTION ARE BORN ALL GENRES, TECHNIQUES, LANGUAGE AND EVEN THE DURATION OF PRESENT DAY FILMS. IT WAS TO BREAK WITH THESE CONCEPTIONS, WITH THIS CONDITIONING WHICH GAVE US THE MOST DIFFICULTY. WE HAD TO LIBERATE OURSELVES: FILM MADE SENSE IF WE COULD USE IT AS A WRITER OR A PAINTER DO TO ACCOMPLISH THEIR TASK, IF WE COULD BRING ABOUT OUR EXPERIENCE STARTING FROM OUR NEEDS. SO WE DECIDED TO RISK, TO TRY, TO SEARCH BEFORE CONDITIONING OURSELVES TO THE MASTERS OF THE "SEVENTH ART," WHO COULD ONLY EXPRESS THEMSELVES THROUGH THE NOVEL, THE SHORT STORY OR DRAMA. WE STARTED TO LIBERATE OURSELVES OF THE "VISCONTIS, RENOIRS, GIOCONDAS, RESNAIS, PAVESES, ETC." . . . COMMITTED TO FIND A NEW FORM, OUR FORM, OUR LANGUAGE, OUR STRUCTURE . . . THAT WHICH WOULD COINCIDE WITH THE NEEDS OF OUR AUDIENCES AND WITH THE NEEDS OF THE TOTAL LIBERATION OF THE ARGENTINE MAN; MEANING THAT THIS SEARCH IN THE FILM MEDIA DID NOT COME AS AN AESTHETIC CATEGORY, BUT AS A CATEGORY OF THE LIBERATION OF OUR PEOPLE AND OUR COUNTRY. THIS WAY A NEW FILM WAS BORN THAT GAVE UP THE HOLDING OF THE THEME-NOVEL, OR THE FILM THAT IS A FILM OF ACTORS, STORIES AND FEELINGS, TO BECOME A FILM OF CONCEPTS, OF THOUGHTS, OF TOPICS. HISTORY AS A NOVEL GAVE WAY TO HISTORY TOLD WITH IDEAS, TO A FILM TO SEE AND TO READ, TO FEEL AND TO THINK, A FILM OF RESEARCH EQUIVALENT TO THE IDEOLOGICAL ESSAY . . .

JLG: WHAT ROLE CAN THIS FILM PLAY IN THE PROCESS OF LIBERATION?

FS: FIRST OF ALL, TO TRANSMIT THE INFORMATION THAT WE DO NOT HAVE. THE MEANS OF COMMUNICATION, THE MECHANISM OF CULTURE ARE IN THE HANDS OR ARE CONTROLLED BY THE SYSTEM. THE INFORMATION THAT IS MADE AVAILABLE IS THAT WHICH THE SYSTEM WANTS TO MAKE AVAILABLE. THE ROLE OF THE FILM OF LIBERATION IS, ABOVE ALL, TO PREPARE AND TO PROPAGATE OUR INFORMATION. BRINGING UP ONCE AGAIN: THAT WHICH IS THEIRS AND THAT WHICH IS OURS. FROM ANOTHER POINT OF VIEW, THE WHOLE CONCEPT OF OUR FILM—OPEN FILM, FILM OF PARTICIPATION, ETC.—POINTS TO ONE AND ONLY ONE FUNDAMENTAL OBJECTIVE: TO HELP SET FREE, TO LIBERATE MAN. A MAN WHO IS OPPRESSED, REPRESSED, INHIBITED AND MANACLED. IT IS A FILM FOR THIS COMBAT. TO RAISE THE LEVEL OF CONSCIOUSNESS AND UNDERSTANDING OF THOSE SECTORS OF THE PEOPLE WHO ARE THE MOST UNEASY ABOUT THEIR CONDITION. WILL IT JUST REACH A LIMITED CIRCLE? MAYBE. BUT THE SO- CALLED FILM OF THE MASSES ONLY TRANSMITS THAT WHICH THE SYSTEM ALLOWS, THAT IS, IT BECOMES AN INSTRUMENT OF ESCAPE, OF EVASION, OF MYSTIFICATION. FILM OF LIBERATION, ON THE OTHER HAND, REACHES, AT THIS STAGE, SMALLER GROUPS, BUT REACHES THEM IN GREATER DEPTH. IT COMES WITH THE TRUTH, IT IS BETTER TO DISSEMINATE IDEAS THAT HELP LIBERATE A SINGLE MAN, THAN TO CONTRIBUTE TO THE MASS COLONIZATION OF THE PEOPLE.

JLG: THE CUBANS SAY THAT THE DUTY OF EVERY REVOLUTIONARY IS TO MAKE THE REVOLUTION. WHAT IS THE DUTY OF THE REVOLUTIONARY FILMMAKER?

FS: TO USE FILM AS A WEAPON, OR AS A GUN, TO TRANSFORM THE WORK ITSELF IN AN ACT, IN A REVOLUTIONARY ACT. *WHAT IS FOR YOU THIS DUTY OR COMMITMENT?*

JLG: TO WORK FULLY AS A MILITANT, TO MAKE LESS FILMS AND BE MORE MILITANT. THIS IS VERY DIFFICULT BECAUSE THE FILMMAKER HAS BEEN EDUCATED IN THE REALM OF INDIVIDUALISM. BUT IN FILMS TOO IT IS NECESSARY TO START ANEW . . .

FS: YOUR EXPERIENCE AFTER THE "MAY EVENTS" [MAY '68] ARE PARAMOUNT; I'D LIKE YOU TO SHARE THEM WITH OUR LATIN AMERICAN COLLEAGUES . . .

JLG: THE "MAY EVENTS" HAVE BROUGHT US A FANTASTIC LIBERATION. "MAY" HAS IMPOSED ITS TRUTH, IT HAS FORCED US TO TALK AND TO ARTICULATE THE PROBLEMS IN A DIFFERENT LIGHT. BEFORE "MAY" HERE IN FRANCE ALL THE INTELLECTUALS HAD AN ALIBI WHICH PERMITTED THEM TO LIVE COMFORTABLY, THAT IS, TO HAVE A CAR, AN APARTMENT . . . BUT "MAY" HAS CREATED A VERY SIMPLE PROBLEM, THAT OF CHANGING OUR LIFE STYLES, OF BREAKING WITH THE SYSTEM. TO THE SUCCESSFUL INTELLECTUALS "MAY" USHERED IN A SITUATION ANALOGOUS TO THAT OF A WORKER WHO MUST ABANDON THE STRIKE BECAUSE HE OWES FOUR MONTHS TO THE GROCER. THERE ARE FILMMAKERS, LIKE TRUFFAUT, WHO SINCERELY SAY THAT THEY ARE NOT GOING TO CHANGE THEIR LIFE STYLES, AND OTHERS JUST KEEP PLAYING A DUAL GAME, LIKE THOSE OF *CAHIERS* . . .

FS: IS THE "AUTHOR-ORIENTED" FILM A BOURGEOIS FILM CATEGORY?

JLG: Exactly. The "author" is something like a professor in a university . . .

FS: How do you ideologically define this type of "author" film?

JLG: Objectively, today's "author" films are allied with the reaction.

FS: Who stand out as examples?

JLG: Fellini, Antonioni, Visconti, Bresson, Bergman . . .

FS: What about young ones?

JLG: In France, Godard before "May"; Truffaut, Rivette, Demy, Resnais . . . everyone . . . In England, Lester, Brooks . . . In Italy, Passolini, Bertolucci . . . lastly, Polanski . . . everyone.

FS: Do you think these filmmakers are integrated within the system?

JLG: Yes. They are integrated and they do not want to be de-integrated . . .

FS: And the more critical filmmaking, is it also recovered by the system?

JLG: Yes, these films are also recovered by the system because they are not strong enough in relation to their integrating potentialities. For example, the American "Newsreels" are as poor as you and me, but if CBS offered them $10,000 to project one of their films, they would refuse because they would be integrated . . . and why would they be integrated? Because the structure of American television is so strong that it recuperates for the system everything that it shows. The only way in which we could get back at t.v in the U.S.A. would be not to project anything during two or four hours that the t.v. station pays precisely for showing and recuperating. In Hollywood they are now preparing a film about Che Guevara, and there is even a film with Gregory Peck about Mao Tse Tung . . . Those Newsreel films, if they were to be shown by French t.v., they would not be recuperative, at least not totally, because they are coming from another country . . . Similarly, my films, which here are recuperated, maintain certain value in Latin America.

FS: I don't agree with the last thing you said. I believe that when a national film deals with a subject from the point of view of the oppressed classes, when it is clear and deep, it becomes practically indigestible for the system . . . I do not believe that CBS would buy a film about "Black Power," or a film with Carmichael talking to Blacks about violence, or that French t.v. would show a film about Cohn-Bendit saying everything he believes . . . In our countries there are a lot of things allowed when they refer to foreign problems, but when these same problems are international, because of their political nature, they cannot be absorbed . . .

A FEW MONTHS BACK, CENSORSHIP PREVENTED *STRIKE* AND *OCTOBER* BY EISEN-
STEIN . . . ON THE OTHER HAND, THE GREATEST PART OF ALL "AUTHOR-ORIENTED"
FILMS DEAL WITH BOURGEOIS PROBLEMS FROM THE POINT OF VIEW OF THE
BOURGEOISIE. THEY ARE NOT ONLY RECUPERATED BY THE SYSTEM, THEY ACTUALLY
BECOME IN OUR COUNTRIES THE AESTHETIC AND THEMATIC MODELS FOR OUR
NEOCOLONIZED "AUTHOR" FILMMAKING.

JLG: I AGREE. BUT WHEN, HERE IN FRANCE, THE POLITICAL BECOMES DIFFICULT FOR
THEM, [THE SYSTEM] CAN NO LONGER RECUPERATE LIKE BEFORE . . . THIS IS THE
CASE WITH YOUR FILM, WHICH I AM SURE WILL NOT BE RECUPERATED, AND WILL
BE CENSORED . . . BUT IT IS NOT ONLY IN THE POLITICAL SCENE THAT RECUPERA-
TION OCCURS, IT ALSO HAPPENS IN THE AESTHETIC FIELD.

MY MOST DIFFICULT FILMS TO RECUPERATE WERE THE LAST ONES THAT I MADE
WITHIN THE SYSTEM, WHERE THE AESTHETIC WAS TURNED POLITICAL, LIKE IN
WEEKEND AND *LA CHINOISE* . . . A POLITICAL POSITION MUST CORRESPOND TO
AN AESTHETIC POSITION. WE MUST NOT MAKE AN "AUTHOR-ORIENTED" CINEMA,
BUT A SCIENTIFIC CINEMA. AESTHETICS MUST ALSO BE STUDIED SCIENTIFICALLY. EVERY
INVESTIGATION IN SCIENCE, AS IN ART, CORRESPONDS TO A POLITICAL LINE, EVEN
IF YOU IGNORE IT. IN THE SAME MANNER AS THERE ARE SCIENTIFIC DISCOVERIES,
THERE ARE AESTHETIC DISCOVERIES. THIS IS WHY WE MUST CONSCIOUSLY CLEAR
THE ROLE WE HAVE CHOSEN AND TO WHICH WE ARE COMMITTED. ANTONIONI,
FOR EXAMPLE, AT A CERTAIN MOMENT REALIZED SOME VALID WORK, BUT HE NO
LONGER DOES . . . HE DID NOT RADICALIZE HIMSELF. HE MAKES A FILM ABOUT
STUDENTS AS IT WOULD BE DONE IN THE UNITED STATES, BUT HE DOES NOT MAKE
A FILM COMING FROM THE STUDENTS . . . PASOLINI HAS TALENT, LOTS OF TALENT,
HE KNOWS HOW TO MAKE FILMS ON A PARTICULAR TOPIC AS ONE LEARNS TO MAKE
COMPOSITIONS AT SCHOOL . . . FOR EXAMPLE, HE CAN MAKE A BEAUTIFUL POEM
ABOUT THE THIRD WORLD . . . BUT IT IS NOT THE THIRD WORLD THAT HAS MADE
THE POEM. THEN, I BELIEVE IT IS NECESSARY TO BE THE THIRD WORLD, AND THEN
ONE DAY IT IS THE THIRD WORLD WHO HAS MADE THE POEM, AND IF YOU ARE
THE ONE WHO SINGS IT, IT IS SIMPLY BECAUSE YOU ARE A POET AND YOU KNOW
HOW TO DO IT . . . IT'S AS YOU SAY, A FILM MUST BE A WEAPON, A GUN . . .
BUT THERE ARE STILL PEOPLE IN THE DARK AND THEY NEED MORE THAN A POCKET
FLASHLIGHT TO BRING LIGHT AROUND THEMSELVES, AND THIS IS PRECISELY THE
ROLE OF THEORY . . . WE NEED A MARXIST ANALYSIS OF IMAGE AND SOUND. EVEN
LENIN, WHEN HE TALKED ABOUT FILM, DID NOT MAKE A THEORETICAL ANALYSIS,
BUT RATHER AN ANALYSIS IN TERMS OF PRODUCTION, SO THAT THERE COULD BE
FILMS EVERYWHERE. ONLY EISENSTEIN AND DZIGA VERTOV OCCUPIED THEMSELVES
WITH THIS TOPIC.

FS: HOW DO YOU FILM NOW? DO YOU HAVE A PRODUCER?

JLG: I HAVE NEVER HAD A PRODUCER. I HAD ONE OR TWO PRODUCER FRIENDS OF

MINE, BUT I NEVER WORKED WITH THE USUAL PRODUCTION HOUSES. WHEN I DID IT, ONCE OR TWICE, IT WAS AN ERROR . . . IT IS NOW IMPOSSIBLE FOR ME. I DON'T KNOW HOW THE OTHERS DO IT. I SEE SOME OF MY COMRADES, LIKE COURNOT OR BERTOLUCCI, FOR EXAMPLE, WHO ARE FORCED TO RING THE BELL AT THE HOUSE OF A CRETIN TO SAVE THEIR WORK. BUT I NEVER DID THIS. NOW I AM THE PRODUCER WITH WHATEVER I HAVE . . . AND I FILM MUCH MORE THAN BEFORE, BECAUSE I FILM IN A DIFFERENT WAY, IN 16MM, OR WITH MY SMALL T.V. EQUIPMENT . . . AND DIFFERENT ALSO IN ANOTHER SENSE, EVEN IF IT SOUNDS PREPOSTEROUS TO USE THE VIETNAMESE EXAMPLE. I REFER TO THE USE THE VIETNAMESE GIVE TO THE BICYCLE IN COMBAT OR RESISTANCE. HERE A CHAMPION CYCLIST COULD NOT MAKE USE OF THE BICYCLE AS A VIETNAMESE DOES. WELL, I WANT TO LEARN TO USE THE BICYCLE AS A VIETNAMESE. I HAVE A LOT TO DO WITH MY BICYCLE, A LOT OF WORK AHEAD, AND THIS IS WHAT I HAVE TO DO, AND THIS IS WHAT I MUST DO. THIS IS WHY NOW I FILM SO MUCH. THIS YEAR I MADE FOUR FILMS.

FS: WHAT IS THE DIFFERENCE BETWEEN WHAT YOU USED TO DO AND THE SORT OF FILM YOU MAKE NOW?

JLG: NOW I TRY TO MAKE A FILM THAT CONSCIOUSLY TRIES TO PARTICIPATE IN THE POLITICAL STRUGGLE. BEFORE IT WAS UNCONSCIOUS, A SENTIMENTALIST . . . I WAS IN THE LEFT, IF YOU WANT, ALTHOUGH I STARTED FROM A POSITION IN THE RIGHT, AND ALSO BECAUSE I WAS BOURGEOIS, AN INDIVIDUALIST. AFTERWARDS I EVOLVED PSYCHOLOGICALLY TO THE LEFT, UNTIL I REACHED NOT THE POSITION OF A "PARLIAMENTARY LEFT," BUT A REVOLUTIONARY LEFT, RADICALIZED, WITH ALL THE CONTRADICTIONS THAT THIS PRESUPPOSES . . .

FS: AND CINEMATOGRAPHICALLY?

JLG: CINEMATOGRAPHICALLY, I ALWAYS TRIED TO DO THAT WHICH WAS NEVER DONE, EVEN WHEN I WORKED WITH THE SYSTEM. NOW I TRY TO TIE UP "WHAT IS NEVER DONE" WITH THE REVOLUTIONARY STRUGGLE. BEFORE, MY SEARCH WAS AN INDIVIDUAL'S STRUGGLE. NOW I WANT TO KNOW IF I AM WRONG, WHY I AM WRONG, AND IF I AM RIGHT, WHY I AM RIGHT. I TRY TO DO THAT WHICH IS NOT DONE BECAUSE EVERYTHING THAT IS DONE IS ALMOST TOTALLY IMPERIALIST. THE CINEMA OF THE EAST IS IMPERIALIST CINEMA; THE CUBAN CINEMA—WITH THE EXCEPTION OF SANTIAGO ALVAREZ AND ONE OR TWO DOCUMENTARY FILMMAKERS—IS A CINEMA THAT FUNCTIONS HALF-WAY WITH AN IMPERIALIST MODEL. ALL THE RUSSIAN CINEMA HAS TURNED RAPIDLY INTO IMPERIALIST, IT HAS BEEN BUREAUCRATIZED, WITH THE EXCEPTION OF TWO OR THREE PERSONS WHO HAVE STRUGGLED AGAINST THIS: EISENSTEIN, DZIGA VERTOV AND METREKIN, WHO IS ABSOLUTELY UNKNOWN . . . NOW I MAKE CINEMA WITH THE WORKERS, I DO THAT WHICH IDEOLOGICALLY THEY WANT, BUT I ALSO SAY: "CAREFUL!" . . . IT IS NECESSARY THAT IN ADDITION TO MAKING THIS TYPE OF FILM, THEY DO NOT ON SUNDAYS

PATRONIZE THE SYSTEM'S CRAPPY FILMS. THIS IS OUR OBLIGATION AND OUR WAY TO HELP "THE STRUGGLE OF THE FILMMAKERS." IN SHORT, I HAVE REACHED THE CONCLUSION THAT THE MOVIE SCENE BEING SO CONFUSED AND COMPLICATED, IT IS IMPORTANT TO MAKE FILMS WITH PEOPLE WHO ARE NOT FILMMAKERS, WITH PEOPLE WHO ARE INTERESTED WITH WHAT THEY SEE ON THE SCREEN HAVING A RELATIONSHIP WITH THEMSELVES . . .

FS: WHY DO YOU WORK WITH PEOPLE WHO DO NOT BELONG TO FILMMAKING?

JLG: BECAUSE IN REGARDS TO THE LANGUAGE OF FILMMAKING IT IS A SMALL HANDFUL OF INDIVIDUALS, IN HOLLYWOOD OR IN MOSFILM, OR WHEREVER, THAT IMPOSES THEIR LANGUAGE, THEIR SPEECH, TO THE WHOLE POPULATION, AND IT IS NOT SUFFICIENT TO GET AWAY FROM THIS SMALL GROUP AND SAY "I MAKE A DIFFERENT CINEMA" . . . BECAUSE ONE STILL HAS THE SAME IDEALS ABOUT FILMMAKING. THIS IS WHY TO OVERCOME THIS ONE MUST GIVE THE OPPORTUNITY TO MAKE CINEMATOGRAPHIC SPEECH TO THOSE PEOPLE WHO, UP TO NOW, NEVER HAD THIS OPPORTUNITY . . . A VERY EXTRAORDINARY THING ABOUT THE EVENTS OF LAST MAY IN PARIS HAPPENED WHEN ALL THE PEOPLE STARTED TO WRITE ON THE WALLS . . . THE ONLY ONES WHO HAD THE RIGHT TO WRITE ON THE WALLS WERE ADVERTISERS . . . PEOPLE WERE MADE TO BELIEVE THAT WRITING ON THE WALLS WAS DIRTY AND UGLY, BUT I ALSO HAD THE IMPULSE TO WRITE ON THE WALLS AND I HAVE KEPT IT UP SINCE "MAY" . . . IT WAS NO LONGER AN ANARCHISTIC IDEA BUT A DEEP DESIRE . . . ALSO FOR FILMMAKING IT IS NECESSARY TO BEGIN ANEW . . . I MADE A FILM WITH STUDENTS TALKING TO WORKERS AND IT WAS VERY CLEAR: THE STUDENTS TALKED ALL THE TIME AND THE WORKERS NEVER . . . THE WORKERS AMONG THEMSELVES TALKED A LOT . . . BUT WHERE ARE THEIR WORDS? NOT IN THE NEWSPAPERS, NOT IN THE FILMS. WHERE ARE THE WORDS OF THE PEOPLE WHO CONSTITUTE THE 80%? WE MUST ALLOW THE WORD OF THE MAJORITY TO BE EXPRESSED. THAT IS WHY I DO NOT WANT TO BELONG TO THE MINORITY WHO TALKS AND TALKS ALL THE TIME, OR THE MINORITY WHO MAKES FILM, BUT I WANT MY LANGUAGE TO EXPRESS WHAT THE 80% WANT TO SAY . . . THIS IS WHY I DO NOT WANT TO MAKE FILMS WITH FILM PEOPLE BUT WITH THE PEOPLE WHO CONSTITUTE THE GREAT MAJORITY OF HUMANITY . . .

THE HOUR OF THE FURNACES AND THE TWO AVANT-GARDES
[1980]

〜〜〜 ROBERT STAM

THE STRUGGLE TO SEIZE POWER FROM THE ENEMY IS THE MEETING-GROUND OF THE POLITICAL AND ARTISTIC VANGUARDS ENGAGED IN A COMMON TASK WHICH IS ENRICHING TO BOTH.

—FERNANDO SOLANAS AND OCTAVIO GETINO IN "TOWARD A THIRD CINEMA."

IF THERE ARE TWO AVANT-GARDES—THE FORMAL AND THE THEORETICO-POLITICAL—THEN *LA HORA DE LOS HORNOS* (*THE HOUR OF THE FURNACES*), 1968, SURELY MARKS ONE OF THE HIGH POINTS OF THEIR CONVERGENCE. FUSING THIRD-WORLD RADICALISM WITH ARTISTIC INNOVATION, THE SOLANAS-GETINO FILM REVIVES THE HISTORICAL SENSE OF AVANT-GARDE AS CONNOTING POLITICAL AS WELL AS CULTURAL MILITANCY. IT TEASES TO THE SURFACE THE MILITARY METAPHOR SUBMERGED IN THE VERY EXPRESSION "AVANT-GARDE"—THE IMAGE OF AN ADVANCED CONTINGENT RECONNOITERING UNEXPLORED AND DANGEROUS TERRITORY. IT RESUSCITATES THE VENERABLE ANALOGY (AT LEAST AS OLD AS MAREY'S "FUSIL PHOTOGRAPHIQUE") OF CAMERA AND GUN, CHARGING IT WITH A PRECISE REVOLUTIONARY SIGNIFICATION. ART BECOMES, AS WALTER BENJAMIN SAID OF THE DADAISTS, "AN INSTRUMENT OF BALLISTICS." AT THE SAME TIME, *LA HORA'S* EXPERIMENTAL LANGUAGE IS INDISSOLUBLY WEDDED TO ITS POLITICAL PROJECT; THE ARTICULATION OF ONE WITH THE OTHER GENERATES THE FILM'S MEANING AND SECURES IT RELEVANCE.

IT IS IN THIS EXEMPLARY TWO-FRONTED STRUGGLE, RATHER THAN IN THE HISTORICAL SPECIFICITY OF ITS POLITICS, THAT *LA HORA* RETAINS VITALITY AS A MODEL FOR CINEMATIC PRACTICE. EVENTS SUBSEQUENT TO 1968 HAVE, IF NOT WHOLLY DISCREDITED, AT LEAST RELATIVIZED THE FILM'S ANALYSIS. UNMOORED AND SET ADRIFT ON THE CURRENTS OF HISTORY, *LA HORA* HAS BEEN SEVERED FROM ITS ORIGINAL CONTEXT, AS ITS AUTHORS HAVE BEEN EXILED FROM THEIR COUN-

TRY. THE LATE SIXTIES WERE, VIRTUALLY EVERYWHERE, THE HOUR OF THE FURNACES, AND *LA HORA*, QUINTESSENTIAL PRODUCT OF THE PERIOD, FORGED THE INCANDESCENT EXPRESSION OF THEIR GLOW. TRICONTINENTAL REVOLUTION, UNDER THE SYMBOLIC AEGIS OF FRANTZ FANON, CHE GUEVARA, AND HO CHI MINH, WAS DEEMED IMMINENT, WAITING TO SURPRISE US AROUND THE NEXT BEND OF THE DIALECTIC. BUT DESPITE SALIENT VICTORIES (VIETNAM, MOZAMBIQUE, NICARAGUA), MANY FLAMES HAVE DWINDLED INTO EMBERS, AS SOME OF THE THIRD WORLD HAS SETTLED INTO THE ERA OF DIMINISHED EXPECTATIONS. IN MOST OF SOUTH AMERICA, THE CIA, MULTINATIONAL CORPORATIONS, AND NATIVE RULING ELITES CONSPIRED TO INSTALL WHAT NOAM CHOMSKY CALLS "SUB-FASCIST" REGIMES, I.E., REGIMES WHOSE POLITICS AND PRACTICES ARE FASCIST BUT WHO LACK ANY POPULAR BASE. IN ARGENTINA, CLASS STRUGGLE IN A RELATIVELY LIBERAL CONTEXT GAVE WAY TO VIRTUAL CIVIL WAR. PERON—THE LAST HOPE OF THE REVOLUTIONARIES *AND* THE BOURGEOISIE—RETURNED, BUT ONLY TO DIE. HIS POLITICAL HEIRS VEERED RIGHTWARD, DEFYING THE HOPES OF THOSE WHO RETURNED HIM TO POWER, UNTIL A PUTSCH INSTALLED A QUASI-FASCIST REGIME. RATHER THAN BEING SURPRISED BY REVOLUTION, ARGENTINA, AND *LA HORA* WITH IT, WAS AMBUSHED BY AN HISTORICAL EQUIVOCATION.

LA HORA IS STRUCTURED AS A TRIPARTITE POLITICAL ESSAY. THE FIRST SECTION, "NEOCOLONIALISM AND VIOLENCE," SITUATES ARGENTINA INTERNATIONALLY, REVEALING IT AS A PALIMPSEST OF EUROPEAN INFLUENCES: "BRITISH GOLD, ITALIAN HANDS, FRENCH BOOKS." A SERIES OF "NOTES"—"THE DAILY VIOLENCE," "THE OLIGARCHY, "DEPENDENCY"—EXPLORE THE VARIEGATED FORMS OF NEOCOLONIAL OPPRESSION. THE SECOND SECTION, "AN ACT FOR LIBERATION," IS SUBDIVIDED INTO A " CHRONICLE OF PERONISM," COVERING PERON'S RULE FROM 1945 THROUGH HIS DEPOSITION BY COUP IN 1955, AND "CHRONICLE OF RESISTANCE," DETAILING THE OPPOSITION STRUGGLE DURING THE PERIOD OF PERON'S EXILE. THE THIRD SECTION, "VIOLENCE AND LIBERATION," CONSISTS OF AN OPEN-ENDED SERIES OF INTERVIEWS, DOCUMENTS AND TESTIMONIALS CONCERNING THE BEST PATH TO A REVOLUTIONARY FUTURE FOR LATIN AMERICA. MUCH OF THIS SECTION IS TAKEN UP BY TWO INTERVIEWS, ONE WITH AN OCTOGENARIAN, ORAL ARCHIVIST OF THE NATIONAL MEMORY OF RESISTANCE, WHO RECOUNTS PAST COMBATS AND PREDICTS IMMINENT SOCIALIST REVOLUTION, THE OTHER WITH LABOR ORGANIZER JULIO TROXLER, THEN LIVING AND WORKING UNDERGROUND, WHO DESCRIBES MASS EXECUTIONS AND VOWS STRUGGLE UNTIL VICTORY.

WHILE REAWAKENING THE MILITARY METAPHOR DORMANT IN "AVANT-GARDE," *LA HORA* ALSO LITERALIZES THE NOTION OF THE "UNDERGROUND." FILMED CLANDESTINELY IN CONJUNCTION WITH MILITANT CADRES, IT WAS MADE IN THE INTERSTICES OF THE SYSTEM AND AGAINST THE SYSTEM. IT SITUATES ITSELF ON THE PERIPHERY OF THE PERIPHERY—A KIND OF OFF-OFF-HOLLYWOOD—AND BRASHLY DISPUTES THE HEGEMONY OF BOTH THE DOMINANT MODEL ("FIRST CINEMA") AND OF AUTERISM ("SECOND CINEMA"), PROPOSING INSTEAD A "THIRD CINEMA," IN-

DEPENDENT IN PRODUCTION, MILITANT IN POLITICS, AND EXPERIMENTAL IN LANGUAGE.[1] AS A POETIC CELEBRATION OF THE ARGENTINE NATION, IT IS "EPIC" IN THE CLASSICAL AS WELL AS THE BRECHTIAN SENSE, WEAVING DISPARATE MATERIALS—NEWSREELS, EYEWITNESS REPORTS, TV COMMERCIALS, PHOTOGRAPHS— INTO A SPLENDID HISTORICAL TAPESTRY. A CINEMATIC SUMMA, WITH STRATEGIES RANGING FROM STRAIGHTFORWARD DIDACTICISM TO OPERATIC STYLIZATION, BOR- ROWING FROM AVANT-GARDE AND MAINSTREAM, FICTION AND DOCUMENTARY, CINEMA VERITE AND ADVERTISING, IT INHERITS AND PROLONGS THE WORK OF EISENS- TEIN, VERTOV, JORIS IVENS, GLAUBER ROCHA, FERNANDO BIRRI, RESNAIS, BUNUEL AND GODARD.

LA HORA'S MOST STRIKING FEATURE IS ITS OPENNESS. BUT WHEREAS "OPEN- NESS" IN ART USUALLY EVOKES PLURISIGNIFICATON, POLYSEMY, THE AUTHORIZA- TION OF A PLURALITY OF EQUALLY LEGITIMATE READINGS, THE SOLANAS-GETINO FILM IS NOT OPEN IN THIS SENSE: IT MESSAGES ARE STRIDENTLY UNEQUIVOCAL. ITS AMBIGUITIES, SUCH AS THEY ARE, DERIVE MORE FROM THE VICISSITUDES OF HISTORY THAN FROM THE INTENTIONS OF ITS AUTHORS. THE FILM'S OPENNESS LIES ELSEWHERE, AND FIRST OF ALL IN ITS PROCESS OF PRODUCTION. COMING FROM THE TRADI- TIONAL EUROPEANIZED LEFT, SOLANAS AND GETINO SET OUT TO MAKE A SOCIALLY- MINDED SHORT DOCUMENTARY ABOUT THE WORKING CLASS IN ARGENTINA. THROUGH THE FILMMAKING EXPERIENCE, HOWEVER, THEY EVOLVED TOWARD A LEFT PERONIST POSITION. THE PRODUCTION PROCESS, IN OTHER WORDS, INFLECTED THEIR OWN IDEOLOGICAL TRAJECTORY IN WAYS THAT THEY THEMSELVES COULD NOT HAVE FULLY PREDICTED. (ONE NEED NOT ENDORSE THE SPECIFIC NATURE OF THIS INFLECTION TO APPRECIATE THE *FACT* OF THE INFLECTION.) ONCE AWARE OF THE TENUOUS NATURE OF THEIR INITIAL "CERTAINTIES," THEY OPENED THEIR PRO- JECT TO THE CRITICISMS AND SUGGESTIONS OF THE WORKING CLASS. AS A RESULT, THE FILM UNDERWENT A PROCESS OF CONSTANT MUTATION, NOT BECAUSE OF AUTHORIAL WHIMS (A LA *8 1/2*) BUT UNDER THE PRESSURE OF PROLETARIAN CRITI- QUE. RATHER THAN PERFORMING THE "MISE-EN-SCENE" OF PRECONCEIVED OPI- NIONS, THE FILM'S MAKING ENTAILED INQUIRY AND SEARCH. THE REFORMIST SHORT BECAME A REVOLUTIONARY MANIFESTO.[2]

LA HORA IS OPEN, SECONDLY, IN ITS VERY STRUCTURE AS A TEXT, OPERATING BY WHAT MIGHT BE CALLED TENDENTIOUSLY ALEATORY PROCEDURES.[3] AT KEY POINTS, THE FILM RAISES QUESTIONS—"WHY DID PERON FALL WITHOUT A STRUGGLE? SHOULD HE HAVE ARMED THE PEOPLE?"—AND PROPOSES THAT THE AUDIENCE DEBATE THEM, INTERRUPTING THE PROJECTION TO ALLOW FOR DISCUSSION. ELSEWHERE, THE AUTHORS APPEAL FOR SUPPLEMENTARY MATERIAL ON THE THEME OF VIOLENCE AND LIBERATION, SOLICITING COLLABORATION IN THE FILM'S WRITING. THE "END" OF THE FILM REFUSES CLOSURE BY INVITING THE AUDIENCE TO PROLONG THE TEXT: "NOW IT IS UP TO YOU TO DRAW CONCLUSIONS, TO CONTINUE THE FILM. YOU HAVE THE FLOOR." THIS CHALLENGE, MORE THAN RHETORICAL, WAS CONCRETELY TAKEN UP BY ARGENTINE AUDIENCES, AT LEAST UNTIL THE EXPERIMENT WAS CUT

SHORT BY MILITARY RULE.

CINE-SEMIOLOGISTS DEFINE THE CINEMA AS A SYSTEM OF SIGNIFICATION RATHER THAN COMMUNICATION, ARGUING THAT THE GAP BETWEEN THE RECEPTION AND THE PRODUCTION OF AN ANSWERING MESSAGE, ALLOWS ONLY FOR *DEFERRED* COMMUNICATION. *LA HORA*, BY OPENING ITSELF UP TO PERSON-TO-PERSON DEBATE, TESTS AND "STRETCHES" THIS DEFINITION TO ITS VERY LIMITS. IN A PROVOCATIVE AMALGAM OF CINEMA/THEATER/POLITICAL RALLY, IT JOINS THE SPACE OF REPRESENTATION TO THE SPACE OF THE SPECTATOR, THUS MAKING "REAL" AND IMMEDIATE COMMUNICATION POSSIBLE. THE PASSIVE CINEMATIC EXPERIENCE, THAT *RENDEZVOUS MANQUE* BETWEEN EXHIBITIONIST AND VOYEUR, IS TRANSFORMED INTO A "THEATRICAL" ENCOUNTER BETWEEN HUMAN BEINGS PRESENT IN THE FLESH. THE TWO-DIMENSIONAL SPACE OF THE SCREEN GIVES WAY TO THE THREE-DIMENSIONAL SPACE OF THEATER AND POLITICS. THE FILM MOBILIZES, FOSTERING MOTOR AND MENTAL ACTIVITY RATHER THAN SELF-INDULGENT FANTASY. RATHER THAN VIBRATE TO THE SENSIBILITY OF AN AUTEUR, THE SPECTATORS BECOME THE AUTHORS OF THEIR OWN DESTINY. RATHER THAN A MASS HERO *ON THE SCREEN*, THE PROTAGONISTS OF HISTORY ARE *IN THE AUDIENCE*. RATHER THAN A WOMB TO REGRESS IN, THE CINEMA BECOMES A POLITICAL STAGE ON WHICH TO ACT.

BRECHT CONTRASTED ARTISTIC INNOVATION EASILY ABSORBED BY THE APPARATUS WITH THE KIND WHICH THREATENS ITS VERY EXISTENCE. *LA HORA* WARDS OFF COOPTATION BY A STANCE OF RADICAL INTERVENTIONISM. RATHER THAN BEING HERMETICALLY SEALED OFF FROM LIFE, THE TEXT IS PERMEABLE TO HISTORY AND PRAXIS, CALLING FOR ACCOMPLICES RATHER THAN CONSUMERS. THE THREE MAJOR SECTIONS BEGIN WITH *OUVERTURES*—ORCHESTRATED QUOTATIONS, SLOGANS. RALLYING CRIES—WHICH SUGGEST THAT THE SPECTATORS HAVE COME NOT TO ENJOY A SHOW BUT TO PARTICIPATE IN AN ACTION. EACH SCREENING IS MEANT TO CREATE WHAT THE AUTHORS CALL A "LIBERATED SPACE, A DECOLONIZED TERRITORY." BECAUSE OF THIS ACTIVIST STANCE, *LA HORA* WAS DANGEROUS TO MAKE, TO DISTRIBUTE, AND, NOT INFREQUENTLY, TO *SEE*. WHEN A REPRESSIVE SITUATION MAKES FILMGOING A CLANDESTINE ACTIVITY PUNISHABLE BY PRISON OR TORTURE, THE MERE ACT OF VIEWING COMES TO ENTAIL POLITICAL COMMITMENT. CINEPHILIA, AT TIMES A SURROGATE FOR POLITICAL ACTION IN THE UNITED STATED AND EUROPE, BECAME IN ARGENTINA A LIFE-ENDANGERING FORM OF PRAXIS, PLACING THE SPECTATOR IN A BOOBYTRAPPED SPACE OF POLITICAL COMMITMENT. INSTEAD OF THE MERE FIRECRACKER-UNDER-THE-SEATS OF THE DADAISTS, THE SPECTATOR WAS FACED WITH THE DISTANT POSSIBILITY OF MACHINE-GUN FIRE IN THE CINEMA. ALL THE CELEBRATED "ATTACKS ON THE VOYEURISM OF THE SPECTATOR" PALE IN VIOLENCE NEXT TO THIS THREATENED INITIATION INTO POLITICAL BRUTALITY.

IN ITS FRONTAL ASSAULT ON PASSIVITY, *LA HORA* DEPLOYS A NUMBER OF TEXTUAL STRATEGIES. THE SPOKEN AND WRITTEN COMMENTARY, ADDRESSED DIRECTLY TO THE SPECTATOR, FOSTERS A DISCURSIVE RELATIONSHIP, THE I-YOU OF *DISCOURS* RATHER THAN THE HE-SHE VOYEURISM OF *HISTOIRE*. THE LANGUAGE, FURTHER-

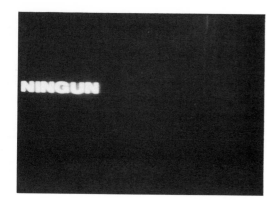 

MORE, IS UNABASHEDLY PARTISAN, ESCHEWING ALL FACTITIOUS "OBJECTIVITY."
DIVERSE CLASSES, THE FILM REMINDS US, SPEAK DIVERGENT LANGUAGES. THE 1955
PUTSCH, FOR THE ELITE, IS A "LIBERATING REVOLUTION," FOR THE PEOPLE, "THE
GORILLA COUP." EVERYTHING IN THE FILM, FROM THE INITIAL DEDICATION TO CHE
GUEVARA THROUGH THE FINAL EXHORTATION TO ACTION, OBEYS THE BRECHTIAN
INJUNCTION TO "DIVIDE THE AUDIENCE," FORCING THE AUDIENCE TO "TAKE SIDES."
THE ARGENTINE INTELLECTUAL MUST DECIDE TO BE WITH THE PERONIST MASSES
OR AGAINST THEM. THE AMERICAN MUST REJECT THE PHRASE "YANKEE IMPERIALISM"
OR ACKNOWLEDGE THAT IT CORRESPONDS, ON SOME LEVEL, TO THE TRUTH. AT
TIMES, THE CALL FOR COMMITMENT REACHES DISCOMFORTING EXTREMES FOR THE
SPECTATOR HOPING FOR A WARM BATH OF ESCAPISM. QUOTING FANON'S "ALL
SPECTATORS ARE COWARDS OR TRAITORS" (NEITHER OPTION FLATTERS), THE FILM
CALLS AT TIMES FOR VIRTUAL READINESS FOR MARTYRDOM—"TO CHOOSE ONE'S
DEATH IS TO CHOOSE ONE'S LIFE"—AT WHICH POINT THE LUKEWARM ENTERTAINMENT-
SEEKER MIGHT FEEL THAT THE DEMANDS FOR COMMITMENT HAVE ESCALATED UNAC-
CEPTABLY.

LA HORA ALSO SHORT-CIRCUITS PASSIVITY BY MAKING INTENSE INTELLECTUAL
DEMANDS. THE WRITTEN TITLES AND SPOKEN COMMENTARY TAKEN TOGETHER FORM
A MORE OR LESS CONTINUOUS ESSAY, ONE WHICH RANKS IN RHETORICAL POWER
WITH THOSE OF THE AUTHORS IT CITES—FANON, CESAIRE, SARTE. AT ONCE BROADLY
DISCURSIVE AND VIVIDLY IMAGISTIC, ABSTRACT AND CONCRETE, THIS ESSAY-TEXT,
RATHER THAN SIMPLY COMMENTING ON THE IMAGES, ORGANIZES THEM AND PRO-
VIDES THEIR PRINCIPLE OF COHERENCE. THE ESSAY CONSTITUTES THE FILM'S CONTROL-
CENTER, ITS BRAIN. THE IMAGES TAKE ON MEANING IN RELATION TO IT RATHER
THAN THE REVERSE. DURING PROLONGED PERIODS, THE SCREEN BECOMES AN AUDIO-
VISUAL BLACKBOARD AND THE SPECTATOR A READER OF TEXT. THE STACCATO IN-
TERCUTTING OF BLACK FRAMES AND INCENDIARY TITLES GENERATES A DYNAMIC
CINE-ECRITURE; THE FILM WRITES ITSELF. VERTOVIAN TITLES EXPLODE AROUND THE
SCREEN, RUSHING TOWARD AND RETREATING FROM THE SPECTATOR, THEIR GRAPHIC

PRESENTATION OFTEN MIMICKING THEIR SIGNIFICATION. THE WORD "LIBERATION," FOR EXAMPLE, PROLIFERATES AND MULTIPLIES, IN STRIKING VISUAL AND KINETIC REMINISCENCE OF CHE'S CALL FOR "TWO, THREE, MANY VIETNAMS." AT OTHER TIMES, IN A RUDE CHALLENGE TO THE SACROSANCT "PRIMACY OF THE VISUAL," THE SCREEN REMAINS BLANK WHILE A DISEMBODIED VOICE ADDRESSES US IN THE DARKNESS.

THE COMMENTARY PARTICIPATES MIGHTILY IN THE FILM'S WORK OF DEMYSTIFICATION. AS THE CAPTION, FOR WALTER BENJAMIN, COULD TEAR PHOTOGRAPHY AWAY FROM FASHIONABLE CLICHES AND GRANT IT "REVOLUTIONARY USE-VALUE," SO THE COMMENTARY SHATTERS THE OFFICIAL IMAGE OF EVENTS. AN IDEALIZED PAINTING CELEBRATING ARGENTINE POLITICAL INDEPENDENCE IS UNDERCUT BY THE OFF-SCREEN ACCOUNT OF THE FINANCIAL DEALS WHICH BETRAYED *ECONOMIC* INDEPENDENCE. FORMAL SOVEREIGNTY IS EXPOSED AS THE FACADE MASKING THE REALITIES OF MATERIAL SUBJUGATION. SHOTS OF THE BUSTLING, PROSPEROUS PORT OF BUENOS AIRES, SIMILARLY, ARE ACCOMPANIED BY AN ANALYSIS OF A GENERAL SYSTEMATIC POVERTY: "WHAT CHARACTERIZES LATIN AMERICAN COUNTRIES IS, FIRST OF ALL, THEIR DEPENDENCE—ECONOMIC DEPENDENCE, POLITICAL DEPENDENCE, CULTURAL DEPENDENCE." THE SPECTATOR IS TAUGHT TO DISTRUST IMAGES, OR BETTER, TO SEE THROUGH THEM TO THEIR UNDERLYING STRUCTURES. THE FILM STRIVES TO ENABLE THE SPECTATOR TO PENETRATE THE VEIL OF APPEARANCES, TO DISPEL THE MISTS OF IDEOLOGY THROUGH AN ACT OF REVOLUTIONARY DECODING.

MUCH OF *LA HORA'S* PERSUASIVE POWER DERIVES FROM ITS ABILITY TO RENDER IDEAS VISUAL. ABSTRACT CONCEPTS ARE GIVEN CLEAR AND ACCESSIBLE FORM. THE SOCIOLOGICAL ABSTRACTION "OLIGARCHY" IS CONCRETIZED BY SHOTS OF THE "FIFTY FAMILIES" THAT MONOPOLIZE MUCH OF ARGENTINA'S WEALTH. "HERE THEY ARE . . ." SAYS THE TEXT; THE "OLIGARCHY" COMES INTO FOCUS AS THE ACTUAL FACES OF REAL PEOPLE, RECOGNIZABLE AND ACCOUNTABLE. "CLASS SOCIETY" BECOMES THE IMAGE ("QUOTED" FROM BIRRI'S *TIRE DIE*) OF DESPERATE CHILD BEGGARS RUNNING ALONGSIDE TRAINS IN HOPE OF A FEW PENNIES FROM BLASE PASSENGERS.

"Systematic violence" is rendered by images of the state's apparatus of repression—prisons, armored trucks, bombers. The title "No Social Order Commits Suicide" yields to four quick-cut shots of the military. Cesaire's depiction of the colonized—"Dispossessed, Marginalized, Condemned"—gives way to shots of workers, up against the wall, undergoing police interrogation. Thus *La Hora* engraves ideas on the mind of the spectator. The images do not explode harmlessly, dissipating their energy. They fuse with ideas in order to detonate in the minds of the audience.

Parody and satire form part of the strategic arsenal of *La Hora de los Hornos*. One sequence, a sight-seeing excursion through Buenos Aires, compares in irreverence to Bunuel's sardonic tour of Rome in *L'Age d'Or*. The images are those customary in travelogues—government buildings, monuments, busy thoroughfares—but the accompanying text is dipped in acid. Rather than exalt the cosmopolitan charm or the bustling energy of Buenos Aires, the commentary disengages its class structure: the highly-placed *comprador* bourgeoisie, the middle-class ("eternal in-betweens, both protected and used by the oligarchy") and the petite bourgeoisie, "eternal crybabies, for whom change is necessary, but impossible." Monuments, symbols of national pride, are treated as petrified emblems of servility. As the camera zooms out from an equestrian statue of one of Argentina's founding fathers (Carlos de Alvear), an off-screen voice ironizes: "Here monuments are erected to the man who said: `These provinces want to belong to Great Britain, to accept its laws, obey its government, live under its powerful influence.'"

Satiric vignettes pinpoint the reactionary nostalgia of the Argentine ruling class. We see them in an antique car acting out their fantasy of *la belle epoque*. We see "La Recoleta," their cemetery, baroque testimonial to an atrophied way of life, where the oligarchy tries to "freeze time" and "crystallize history." Just as Vertov destroys (via split screen) the Bolshoi Theater in *Man with the Movie Camera*, Solanas-Getino annihilate the cemetery's neoclassical statues, creating a completely artificial time and space. The statue's "dialogue" in shot/reaction shot to the music of an Argentine opera whose words ("I shall bring down the rebel flag in blood") remind us of the aristocracy's historical capacity for savage repression. Still another vignette pictures the oligarchy at its annual cattle show in Buenos Aires. The sequence interweaves shots of the crowned heads of the prize bulls with the faces of the aristocracy. The bulls—inert, sluggish, well pedigreed—present a perfect

ANALOGUE TO THE OLIGARCHS THAT BREED THEM. METONYMIC CONTIGUITY COIN-
CIDES WITH METAPHORIC TRANSFER AS THE AUCTIONEER'S PHRASE DESCRIBING THE
BULLS ("ADMIRE THE EXPRESSION, THE BONE STRUCTURE") ARE YOLKED, IN A STUN-
NING CINEMATIC XEUGMA, TO THE LOOKS OF BOVINE SELF-SATISFACTION ON THE
FACES OF THEIR OWNERS.

ON OCCASION, SOLANAS-GETINO ENLIST THE UNWITTING COOPERATION OF
THEIR SATIRIC TARGETS BY HAVING RULING-CLASS FIGURES CONDEMN THEMSELVES
BY THEIR OWN DISCOURSE. NEWSREEL FOOTAGE SHOWS AN ARGENTINE WRITER,
SURROUNDED BY JEWELRY-LADEN DOWAGERS, AT AN OFFICIAL RECEPTION, AS A
PARODIC OFF-SCREEN VOICE SETS THE TONE: "AND NOW LET'S GO TO THE PEPSI
COLA SALON, WHERE MANUEL MUJICA LAINEZ, MEMBER OF THE ARGENTINE
ACADEMY OF LETTERS, IS PRESENTING HIS LATEST BOOK *ROYAL CHRONICLES*." LAINEZ
THEN BOASTS, IN NON-SYNCHRONOUS SOUND, OF HIS INTERNATIONAL PRIZES, HIS
EUROPEAN FORMATION, HIS "DEEP SYMPATHY FOR THE ELIZABETHAN SPIRIT." NO
PROFESSIONAL ACTOR COULD BETTER INCARNATE THE INTELLECTUAL BANKRUPTCY
OF THE ELITE, WITH ITS FOSSILIZED ATTITUDES, ITS NOSTALGIA FOR EUROPE, ITS
HAND-ME-DOWN CULTURE, AND ITS SNIDE INGRATITUDE TOWARD THE COUNTRY
AND PEOPLE THAT MADE POSSIBLE ITS PRIVILEGES.

RECORDED NOISES AND MUSIC ALSO PLAY A DISCURSIVE AND DEMYSTIFICATORY
ROLE. THE SOUND OF A TIME CLOCK PUNCTUATES SHOTS OF WORKERS HURRYING
TO THEIR JOBS, AN AURAL REMINDER OF THE DAILY VIOLENCE OF "WAGE SLAVERY."
GODARDIAN FRONTAL SHOTS OF OFFICE BUILDINGS WITH THEIR ABSTRACT
GEOMETRICALITY ARE SUPERIMPOSED WITH SIRENS; INNOCUOUS IMAGES TAKE ON
OVERTONES OF URBAN ANXIETY. A VERITABLE COMPENDIUM OF MUSICAL STYLES—
TANGO, OPERA, POP—MAKE MORDANT COMMENT ON THE IMAGE. A SEGMENT
ON CULTURAL COLONIALISM HAS RAY CHARLES SINGING "I DON'T NEED A DOC-
TOR" AS A POP-MUSIC JUNKIE NODS HIS HEAD IN RHYTHM IN A BUENOS AIRES
RECORD STORE. A MEDLEY OF NATIONAL AND PARTY ANTHEMS ("LA MARSEILLAISE,"
"THE INTERNATIONAL") LAMPOONS THE EUROPEAN ALLEGIANCES TO THE TRADI-
TIONAL LEFT PARTIES. AND ONE OF THE MOST POIGNANTLY TELLING SEQUENCES
SHOWS A SMALL-TOWN PROSTITUTE, PUBIC HAIR EXPOSED, EATING LUNCH WHILE
SAD-LOOKING MEN WAIT IN LINE FOR HER FAVORS. THE MUSICAL ACCOMPANIMENT
(THE PATRIOTIC "FLAG-RAISING" SONG) SUGGESTS THAT ARGENTINA HAS BEEN REDUC-
ED TO EXACTLY THIS—A HUNGRY PROSTITUTE WITH HER JOYLESS CLIENTELE.

SOLANAS-GETINO PROLONG AND CRITICALLY REELABORATE THE AVANT-GARDE
HERITAGE. ONE SEQUENCE FUSES EISENSTEIN WITH WARHOL BY INTERCUTTING
SCENES FROM A SLAUGHTERHOUSE WITH POP-CULTURE ADVERTISING ICONS. THE
SEQUENCE OBVIOUSLY QUOTES EISENSTEIN'S CELEBRATED NON-DIEGETIC METAPHOR
IN *STRIKE*, BUT ALSO INVESTS IT WITH SPECIFICALLY ARGENTINE RESONANCES. IN
ARGENTINA, WHERE LIVESTOCK IS A BASIC INDUSTRY, THE SAME WORKERS WHO
CAN BARELY AFFORD THE MEAT THAT THEY THEMSELVES PRODUCE ARE
SIMULTANEOUSLY ENCOURAGED BY ADVERTISING TO CONSUME THE USELESS PRO-

DUCTS OF THE MULTINATIONAL COMPANIES. THE LIVESTOCK METAPHOR, ANTICIPATED IN THE EARLIER PRIZE-BULL SEQUENCE, IS SUBSEQUENTLY "DIEGETIZED" WHEN A SHOT OF THE EXTERIOR OF A SLAUGHTERHOUSE COINCIDES WITH AN ACCOUNT OF THE POLICE REPRESSION OF ITS STRIKING WORKERS. THE ADVERTISING/SLAUGHTER JUXTAPOSITION, MEANWHILE, EVOKES ADVERTISING ITSELF AS A KIND OF SLAUGHTER WHOSE NUMBING EFFECT IS IMAGED BY THE MALLET STRIKING THE OX UNCONSCIOUS. THE VAPID ACCOMPANYING MUSIC BY THE SWINGLE SINGERS (BACH GROTESQUE-LY METAMORPHOSED INTO RAY CONNIFF) COUNTERPOINTS THE BRUTALITY OF THE IMAGES, WHILE UNDERLINING THE SHALLOWLY PLASTIC GOOD CHEER OF THE ADS.

IN *LA HORA*, MINIMALISM—THE AVANT-GARDE AESTHETIC MOST APPROPRIATE TO THE EXIGENCIES OF FILM PRODUCTION IN THE THIRD WORLD—REFLECTS PRAC-TICAL NECESSITY AS WELL AS ARTISTIC STRATEGY. TIME AND AGAIN ONE IS STRUCK BY THE CONTRAST BETWEEN THE POVERTY OF THE ORIGINAL MATERIALS AND THE POWER OF THE FINAL RESULT. UNPROMISING FOOTAGE IS TRANSMOGRIFIED INTO ART, AS THE ALCHEMY OF MONTAGE TRANSFORMS THE BASE METALS INTO TITLES, BLANK FRAMES AND PERCUSSIVE SOUNDS INTO THE GOLD AND SILVER OF RHYTHMIC VIRTUOSITY. STATIC TWO-DIMENSIONAL IMAGES (PHOTOS, POSTERS, ADS, ENGRAV-INGS) ARE DYNAMIZED BY EDITING AND CAMERA MOVEMENT. STILL PHOTOS AND MOVING IMAGES SWEEP BY AT SUCH VELOCITY THAT WE LOSE TRACK OF WHERE MOVEMENT STOPS AND STASIS BEGINS. THE MOST STRIKING MINIMALIST IMAGE—A CLOSE-UP OF CHE GUEVARA'S FACE IN DEATH—IS HELD FOR A FULL FIVE MINUTES. THE EFFECT OF THIS INSPIRATIONAL DEATH MASK IS PARADOXICAL. THROUGH THE HAVING-BEEN-THERE OF PHOTOGRAPHY, CHE GUEVARA RETURNS OUR GLANCE FROM BEYOND THE GRAVE. HIS FACE EVEN IN DEATH SEEMS MESMERIZINGLY PRESENT, HIS EXPRESSION ONE OF DEFIANT UNDEFEAT. AT THE SAME TIME, THE PHOTO GRADUALLY ASSUMES THE LOOK OF A CRACKED REVOLUTIONARY ICON. THE LONG CONTEMPLA-TION OF THE PHOTOGRAPH DEMYSTIFIES AND UNMASKS: WE BECOME CONSCIOUS OF THE FRAME, THE TECHNICAL IMPERFECTIONS, THE FILMIC MATERIAL ITSELF.[4]

THE MOST ICONOCLASTIC SEQUENCE, ENTITLED "MODELS," BEGINS BY CITING FANON'S CALL FOR AN AUTHENTICALLY THIRD-WORLD CULTURE: "LET US NOT PAY TRIBUTE TO EUROPE BY CREATING STATES, INSTITUTIONS AND SOCIETIES IN ITS MOULD. HUMANITY EXPECTS MORE FROM US THAN THIS CARICATURAL AND GENERALLY OBSCENE IMITATION." AS THE COMMENTARY DERIDES EUROPE'S "RACIST HUMANISM," THE IMAGE TRACK PARADES THE MOST HIGHLY PRIZED ARTIFACTS OF EUROPEAN HIGH CULTURE: THE PARTHENON, *DÉJEUNER SUR L'HERBE*, ROMAN FRESCOES, PORTRAITS OF BYRON AND VOLTAIRE. IN AN ATTACK ON THE IDEOLOGICAL HIERARCHIES OF THE SPECTATOR, HALOED ART WORKS ARE INEXORABLY LAP-DISSOLVED INTO MEANINGLESSNESS. AS IN THE POSTCARD SEQUENCE OF *LES CARABINERS*, THAT LOCUS CLASSICUS OF ANTI-HIGH-ART SEMIOCLASM, THE MOST CHERISHED MONUMENTS OF WESTERN CULTURE ARE IMPLICITLY EQUATED WITH THE COMMERCIALIZED FETISHES OF CONSUMER SOCIETY. CLASSICAL PAINTING AND TOOTHPASTE ARE LEVELLED AS TWO KINDS OF IMPERIAL EXPORT. THE PRETENDED

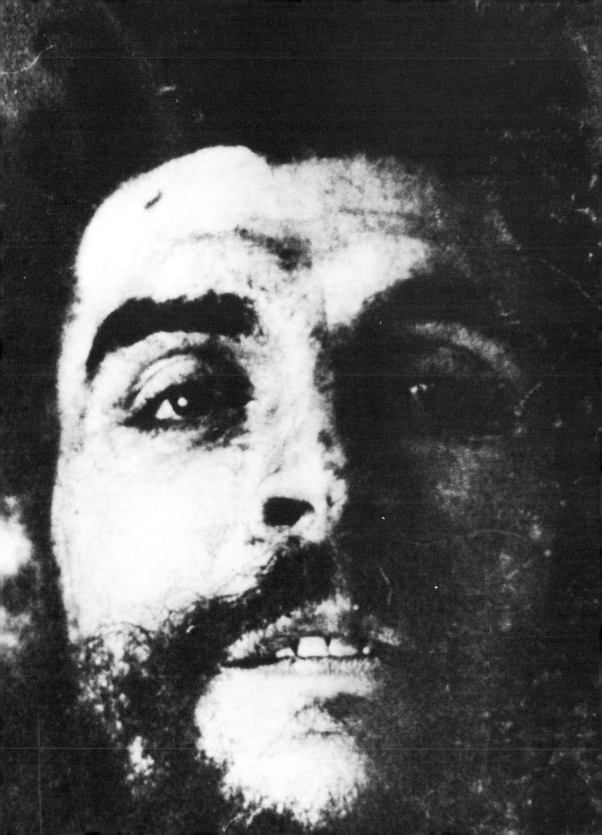

"UNIVERSALITY" OF EUROPEAN CULTURE IS EXPOSED AS A MYTH MASKING THE FACT OF DOMINATION.

THIS DEMOLITION JOB ON WESTERN CULTURE IS NOT WITHOUT ITS AMBIGUITIES, HOWEVER; FOR SOLANAS AND GETINO, LIKE FANON BEFORE THEM, ARE IMBUED WITH THE VERY CULTURE THEY SO VEHEMENTLY DENIGRATE. LA HORA BETRAYS A CULTIVATED FAMILIARITY WITH FLEMISH PAINTING, ITALIAN OPERA, FRENCH CINEMA; IT ALLUDES TO THE ENTIRE SPECTRUM OF HIGHBROW CULTURE. THEIR AT-TACK IS ALSO AN EXORCISM, THE PRODUCT OF A LOVE-HATE RELATIONSHIP TO THE EUROPEAN PARENT CULTURE. THE SAME LAP DISSOLVES THAT OBLITERATE CLASSICAL ART ALSO HIGHLIGHT ITS BEAUTY. THE FILM'S SCORN FOR "CULTURE," FURTHER-MORE, FINDS AMPLE PRECEDENT WITHIN THE ANTI-TRADITIONALIST MODERNISM OF EUROPE ITSELF. MAYAKOVSKY ASKED, EVEN BEFORE THE REVOLUTION, THAT THE CLASSICS BE "CAST FROM THE STEAMBOAT OF MODERNITY." THE DISMISSAL OF ALL ANTECEDENT ART AS SIMPLY A WASTE OF TIME RECALLS THE ANTEPASSATISMO OF THE FUTURISTS. "WE MUST SPIT EACH DAY," SAID MARINETTI, "ON THE ALTAR OF ART." AND BOTH MAYAKOVSKY AND GODARD HAVE EVOKED THE SYMBOLIC DESTRUCTION OF THE SHRINES OF HIGH CULTURE. "MAKE BOMBARDMENT ECHO ON THE MUSEUM WALLS," SHOUTED MAYAKOVSKY, AND GODARD, IN LA CHINOISE, HAS VERONIQUE CALL FOR THE BOMBING OF THE LOUVRE AND THE COMEDIE FRANCAISE.

WHILE DRAWING ON A CERTAIN AVANT-GARDE, LA HORA CRITIQUES WHAT IT SEES AS THE APOLITICAL AVANT-GARDE. REVOLUTIONARY FILMS, IN THEIR VIEW, MUST BE AESTHETICALLY AVANT-GARDE—REVOLUTIONARY ART MUST FIRST OF ALL BE REVOLUTIONARY AS ART (BENJAMIN)—BUT AVANT-GARDE FILMS ARE NOT NECESSARILY REVOLUTIONARY. LA HORA ELUDES WHAT IT SEES AS THE VACUITY OF A CERTAIN AVANT-GARDE BY POLITICIZING WHAT MIGHT HAVE BEEN PURELY FOR-MALISTIC EXERCISES. THE IRONIC PAGEANT OF HIGH ART IMAGES IN THE "MODELS" SEQUENCE, FOR EXAMPLE, IS ACCOMPANIED BY A DISCOURSE ON THE COLONIZA-TION OF THIRD-WORLD CULTURE. ANOTHER SEQUENCE, SUPERIMPOSING SHOTS OF ARGENTINEANS LOUNGING AT POOLSIDE WITH VAPID COCKTAIL DIALOGUE ABOUT THE PRESTIGE VALUE OF BEING FAMILIAR WITH OP ART AND POP ART, ABSTRACT ART AND CONCRETE ART, HIGHLIGHTS THE BOURGEOIS FONDNESS FOR A POLITICALLY INNOCUOUS AVANT-GARDE WHICH IS AS MUCH THE PRODUCT OF FASHION AND COMMODITY FETISHISM AS STYLES IN SHIRTS AND JEANS. IN ARGENTINA, ITS PRO-MOTION FORMED PART OF A PATTERN OF UNITED STATES CULTURAL INTERVEN-TION IN WHICH ORGANIZATIONS SUCH AS THE U.S.I.S. EXHIBITED MODERNIST PAINTING AS PART OF A LARGER IMPERIALIST STRATEGY.

AN APOLITICAL AVANT-GARDE RISKS BECOMING AN INSTITUTIONALIZED LOYAL OPPOSITION, THE PROGRESSIVE WING OF ESTABLISHMENT ART. SUPPLYING A DAILY DOSE OF NOVELTY TO A SATIATED SOCIETY, IT GENERATES SURFACE TURMOIL WHILE LEAVING THE DEEP STRUCTURES INTACT. THE ARTISTS, AS GODARD ONCE POINTED OUT, ARE INMATES WHO BANG THEIR DISHES AGAINST THE BARS OF THEIR PRISON.

RATHER THAN DESTROY THE PRISON, THEY MERELY MAKE A NOISE WHICH, ULTIMATELY, REASSURES THE WARDEN. THE NOISE IS THEN COOPTED BY A MECHANISM OF REPRESSIVE DESUBLIMATION AND CITED AS PROOF OF THE SYSTEM'S LIBERALITY. *LA HORA* HAS NOTHING TO DO WITH SUCH AN AVANT-GARDE, AND TO TREAT IT AS SUCH WOULD BE TO TRIVIALIZE IT BY DETACHING IT FROM THE REVOLUTIONARY IMPULSE THAT DRIVES AND INFORMS IT.

EMBRACING ELEMENTS OF THIS CRITIQUE OF AN APOLITICAL AVANT-GARDE DOES NOT ENTAIL ENDORSING ALL FEATURES OF THE FILM'S GLOBAL POLITICS. WITHOUT DIMINISHING THE DIRECTORS' ACHIEVEMENT OR DISRESPECTING THE SACRIFICE OF THOUSANDS OF ARGENTINEANS, ONE FEELS OBLIGED TO POINT OUT CERTAIN POLITICAL AMBIGUITIES IN THE FILM. *LA HORA* SHARES WITH WHAT ONE MIGHT CALL THE HEROIC-MASOCHISTIC AVANT-GARDE A VISION OF ITSELF AS ENGAGED IN A KIND OF APOCALYPTIC SELF-SACRIFICE IN THE NAME OF FUTURE GENERATIONS. THE ARTISTIC AVANT-GARDE, AS RENATO POGGIOLI AND MASSIMO BONTEMPELLI HAVE SUGGESTED, OFTEN CULTIVATES THE IMAGE, AND SYMBOLICALLY SUFFERS THE FATE, OF MILITARY AVANT-GARDES: THEY SERVE AS ADVANCED CADRES "SLAUGHTERED" (IF ONLY BY THE CRITICS) TO PREPARE THE WAY FOR THE REGULAR ARMY OR THE NEW SOCIETY. THE SPIRIT OF SELF-IMMOLATION ON THE ALTAR OF THE FUTURE ("PITIE POUR NOUS QUI COMBATTONS TOUJOURS AUX FRONTIERES/DE L'ILLIMITE ET DE L'AVENIR") MERGES IN *LA HORA* WITH A QUASI-RELIGIOUS SUBTEXT WHICH DRAWS ON THE LANGUAGE AND IMAGERY OF MARTYRDOM, DEATH AND RESURRECTION. ONE MIGHT EVEN POSIT A SUBLIMINAL DANTESQUE STRUCTURING WHICH ASCENDS FROM THE *INFERNO* OF NEOCOLONIAL OPPRESSION THROUGH THE *PURGATORIO* OF REVOLUTIONARY VIOLENCE TO THE *PARADISIO* OF NATIONAL LIBERATION. WITHOUT REVIVING THE FACILE CARICATURE OF MARXISM AS "SECULAR RELIGION," ONE CAN REGRET THE FILM'S OCCASIONAL CONFUSION OF POLITICAL CATEGORIES WITH MORAL-RELIGIOUS ONES. THE SUBSURFACE MILLENARIANISM OF THE FILM, WHILE IT PARTIALLY EXPLAINS THE FILM'S POWER (AND ITS APPEAL FOR EVEN SOME BOURGEOIS CRITICS), IN SOME WAYS UNDERMINES ITS POLITICAL INTEGRITY.

EQUIPPED WITH THE LUXURY OF RETROSPECTIVE LUCIDITY, ONE CAN ALSO BETTER DISCERN THE DEFICIENCIES OF THE FANONIAN AND GUEVARIST IDEAS INFORMING THE FILM. *LA HORA* IS DEEPLY IMBUED WITH FANON'S FAITH IN THE THERAPEUTIC VALUE OF VIOLENCE. BUT WHILE IT IS TRUE TO SAY THAT VIOLENCE IS AN EFFECTIVE POLITICAL LANGUAGE, THE KEY TO RESISTANCE OR THE TAKING OF POWER, IT IS QUITE ANOTHER TO VALUE IT AS THERAPY FOR THE OPPRESSED. *LA HORA* MISAPPLIES A THEORY ASSOCIATED WITH A SPECIFIC POINT IN FANON'S IDEOLOGICAL TRAJECTORY (THE POINT OF MAXIMUM DISENCHANTMENT WITH THE EUROPEAN LEFT) AND WITH A PRECISE HISTORICAL SITUATION (FRENCH SETTLER COLONIALISM IN ALGERIA). SOLANAS AND GETINO ALSO PLAY RIGHTFUL TRIBUTE TO CHE GUEVARA AS MODEL REVOLUTIONARY. SUBSEQUENT EVENTS, HOWEVER, HAVE MADE IT OBVIOUS THAT CERTAIN OF CHE'S POLICIES WERE MISTAKEN. GUEVARISM IN LATIN AMERICA GAVE IMPETUS TO AN ULTRA-VOLUNTARIST STRATEGY

WHICH OFTEN TURNED OUT TO BE INEFFECTIVE OR EVEN SUICIDAL. ONE MIGHT
EVEN LINK THE VESTIGIAL MACHISMO OF THE FILM'S LANGUAGE ("EL HOMBRE":
MAN) TO THIS IDEAL OF THE HEROIC WARRIOR WHO PERSONALLY EXPOSES HIMSELF
TO COMBAT.[5] GUERRILLA STRATEGISTS OFTEN UNDERESTIMATED THE REPRESSIVE
POWER OF THE GOVERNMENTS IN PLACE AND OVERESTIMATED THE OBJECTIVE AND
SUBJECTIVE READINESS OF THE LOCAL POPULATIONS FOR REVOLUTION.

AS A LEFT PERONIST FILM, *LA HORA* ALSO PARTAKES OF THE HISTORICAL
STRENGTHS AND WEAKNESSES OF THAT MOVEMENT.[6] SOLANAS-GETINO RIGHTLY
IDENTIFY PERON AS A THIRD-WORLD NATIONALIST *AVANT LA LETTRE* RATHER THAN
THE "FASCIST DICTATOR" OF EUROCENTRIC MYTHOLOGY.[7] ("PERON WAS A FASCIST
AND A DICTATOR DETESTED BY ALL GOOD MEN . . . EXCEPT ARGENTINES," SAID
DEAN ACHESON, SLYLY INSINUATING THAT ARGENTINES WERE NOT GOOD MEN.)
WHILE *LA HORA* DOES SCORE THE FAILURES OF PERONISM—ITS REFUSAL TO AT-
TACK THE POWER BASES OF THE OLIGARCHY, ITS FAILURE TO ARM THE PEOPLE AGAINST
RIGHT-WING COUPS, ITS CONSTANT OSCILLATION BETWEEN "DEMOCRACY OF THE
PEOPLE" AND THE "DICTATORSHIP OF BUREAUCRACY"—THE FILMMAKERS SEE PERON
AS THE MAN THROUGH WHOM ARGENTINE WORKING CLASS BECAME GROP-
INGLY AWARE OF ITS COLLECTIVE DESTINY. PERONISM, FOR THEM, WAS "OBJECTIVE-
LY REVOLUTIONARY," BECAUSE IT EMBODIED THIS PROLETARIAN MOVEMENT. BY
BREAKING THE IMPERIAL STRANGLEHOLD ON ARGENTINA'S ECONOMY, PERONISM
WOULD PREPARE THE WAY FOR AUTHENTIC SOCIALIST REVOLUTION. THE FILM FAILS
MOST CRUCIALLY, HOWEVER, IN NOT PLACING PERONISM IN ITS MOST APPROPRIATE
CONTEXT—LATIN AMERICA POPULISM. IN THIS VERSION, POPULISM REPRESENTS
A STYLE OF POLITICAL REPRESENTATION BY WHICH CERTAIN PROGRESSIVE AND NA-
TIONALISTIC ELEMENTS OF THE BOURGEOISIE ENLIST THE SUPPORT OF THE PEOPLE
IN ORDER TO ADVANCE THEIR OWN INTERESTS. LATIN AMERICAN POPULISTS, LIKE
POPULISTS EVERYWHERE, FLIRT WITH THE RIGHT WITH ONE HAND AND CARESS
THE LEFT WITH THE OTHER, MAKING PACTS WITH GOD AND THE DEVIL. LIKE THE
INHABITANTS OF ALPHAVILLE, THEY MANAGE TO SAY YES AND NO AT THE SAME

Hour of the Furnaces

TIME. AS A TACTICAL ALLIANCE, PERONISM CONSTITUTED A LABYRINTHINE TANGLE OF CONTRADICTIONS, A FRAGILE MOSAIC WHICH SHATTERED, NOT SURPRISINGLY, WITH ITS LEADER'S DISAPPEARANCE.

PERONISM WAS PLAGUED BY AT LEAST TWO MAJOR CONTRADICTIONS, BOTH OF WHICH ARE INSCRIBED, TO A CERTAIN EXTENT, IN THE FILM. WHOLEHEARTEDLY ANTI-IMPERIALIST, PERONISM WAS ONLY HALF HEARTEDLY ANTI-MONOPOLIST SINCE THE INDUSTRIAL BOURGEOISIE ALLIED WITH IT WAS MORE FRIGHTENED OF THE WORKING CLASS THAN IT WAS OF IMPERIALISM. ALTHOUGH SOLANAS-GETINO AT ONE POINT EXPLICITLY CALL FOR SOCIALIST REVOLUTION, THERE IS AMBIGUITY IN THE FILM AND IN THE CONCEPT OF "THIRD CINEMA." THE "THIRD," WHILE OBVIOUSLY REFERRING TO THE "THIRD WORLD," ALSO ECHOES PERON'S CALL FOR A "THIRD WAY," FOR AN INTERMEDIATE PATH BETWEEN SOCIALISM AND CAPITALISM. THAT *LA HORA* SEEMS MORE RADICAL THAN IT IS IN FACT LARGELY DERIVES FROM ITS SKILLFUL ORCHESTRATION OF WHAT ONE MIGHT CALL THE REVOLUTIONARY INTERTEXT, I.E., ITS AURAL AND VISUAL EVOCATION OF TRICONTINENTAL REVOLUTION. THE STRATEGICALLY PLACED ALLUSIONS TO CHE GUEVARA, FANON, HO CHI MINH AND STOKELY CARMICHAEL CREATE A KIND OF *"EFFET DE RADICALITE"* RATHER LIKE THE *"EFFET DE REEL"* CITED BY BARTHES IN CONNECTION WITH THE STRATEGIC DETAILS OF CLASSICAL REALIST FICTION.

PERONISM'S SECOND MAJOR CONTRADICTION HAS TO DO WITH ITS CONSTANT SWING BETWEEN DEMOCRACY AND AUTHORITARIANISM, PARTICIPATION AND MANIPULATION. WITH POPULISM, A PLEBIAN STYLE AND PERSONAL CHARISMA OFTEN MASK A DEEP SCORN FOR THE MASSES. EGALITARIAN MANNERS CREATE AN APPARENT EQUALITY BETWEEN THE REPRESENTATIVE OF THE ELITE AND THE PEOPLE WHO ARE THE OBJECT OF MANIPULATION. THE FILM, AT ONCE MANIPULATIVE AND PARTICIPATORY, STRONG-ARMED AND EGALITARIAN, SHARES IN THIS AMBIGUITY. IT SPEAKS THE LANGUAGE OF POPULAR EXPRESSION ("YOUR IDEAS ARE AS IMPORTANT AS OURS") BUT ALSO RESORTS TO HYPERBOLIC LANGUAGE AND SLEDGEHAMMER PERSUASION.

LA HORA IS BRILLIANT IN ITS CRITIQUE. AND HISTORY HAS NOT SHOWN ITS AUTHORS TO BE TOTALLY FAILED PROPHETS. IT IS FACILE FOR US, EQUIPPED WITH HINDSIGHT AND PROTECTED BY DISTANCE, TO POINT UP MISTAKEN PREDICTIONS OR FAILED STRATEGIES. THE FILM'S INDICTMENT OF NEOCOLONIALISM REMAINS SHATTERINGLY RELEVANT. THE CRITIQUE OF THE TRADITIONAL LEFT, AND ESPECIALLY OF THE ARGENTINE COMMUNIST PARTY, HAS BEEN BORNE OUT AS THE PCA OFFERS ITS CRITICAL SUPPORT TO A RIGHT-WING REGIME, LARGELY BECAUSE IT CONCENTRATES IS REPRESSION ON THE NON-STALINIST LEFT AND MAKES GRAIN DEALS WITH THE SOVIET UNION. THE FILM ALSO ACCURATELY POINTS UP THE RULING CLASS POTENTIALITY FOR VIOLENT REPRESSION. THE CURRENT REGIME, WITH ITS HORRENDOUS HUMAN RIGHTS RECORD, ITS *DESAPARECIDOS* AND ITS ANTI-SEMITISM, MERELY REAFFIRMS THE CAPACITY FOR VIOLENCE OF AN ELITE THAT HAS "MORE THAN ONCE BATHED THE COUNTRY IN BLOOD."

DESPITE ITS MORE THAN OCCASIONAL AMBIGUITIES, *LA HORA DE LOS HORNOS* REMAINS A SEMINAL CONTRIBUTION TO REVOLUTIONARY CINEMA. TRANSCENDING THE NARCISSISTIC SELF-EXPRESSION OF AUTEURISM, IT VOICES THE CONCERNS OF A MASS MOVEMENT. BY ALLYING ITSELF WITH A CONCRETE MOVEMENT, WHICH HOWEVER "IMPURE" HAS AT LEAST THE VIRTUE OF BEING REAL, IT PRACTICES A CINEMATIC POLITICS OF "DIRTY HANDS." IF ITS POLITICS ARE AT TIMES POPULIST, ITS FILMIC STRATEGIES ARE NOT. IT ASSUMES THAT THE MASS OF PEOPLE ARE QUITE CAPABLE OF GRASPING THE EXACT MEANING OF AN ASSOCIATION OF IMAGES OR OF A SOUND MONTAGE; THAT IT IS READY, IN SHORT, FOR LINGUISTIC EXPERIMENTATION. IT RESPECTS THE PEOPLE BY OFFERING QUALITY, PROPOSING A CINEMA WHICH IS SIMULTANEOUSLY A TOOL FOR CONSCIOUSNESS-RAISING, AN INSTRUMENT FOR ANALYSIS, AND A CATALYST FOR ACTION. *LA HORA* PROVIDES A MODEL FOR AVANT-GARDE POLITICAL FILMMAKING AND A TREASURY OF FORMALIST STRATEGIES. IT IS AN ADVANCED SEMINAR IN THE POLITICS OF ART AND THE ART OF POLITICS, A FOUR-HOUR LAUNCHING PAD FOR EXPERIMENTATION, AN UNDERGROUND GUIDE TO REVOLUTIONARY CINEMATIC PRAXIS.

LA HORA IS ALSO A KEY PIECE IN THE ONGOING DEBATE CONCERNING THE TWO AVANT-GARDES. IT WOULD BE NAIVE AND SENTIMENTAL TO SEE THE TWO AVANT-GARDES AS "NATURALLY" ALLIED. (THE MERE MENTION OF EZRA POUND OR MARINETTI REFUTES SUCH AN IDEA.) THE ALLIANCE OF THE TWO AVANT-GARDES IS NOT NATURAL, IT MUST BE FORGED. THE TWO AVANT-GARDES, YOKED BY A COMMON IMPULSE OF REBELLION, CONCRETELY NEED EACH OTHER. WHILE REVOLUTIONARY AESTHETICS WITHOUT REVOLUTIONARY POLITICS IS OFTEN FUTILE, ("THEY DID AWAY WITH THE GRAMMAR," SAID PERE BRECHT, "BUT THEY FORGOT TO DO AWAY WITH CAPITALISM."), REVOLUTIONARY POLITICS WITH REVOLUTIONARY AESTHETICS IS EQUALLY RETROGRADE, POURING THE NEW WINE OF REVOLUTION INTO THE OLD BOTTLES OF CONVENTIONAL FORMS, REDUCING ART TO A CRUDE INSTRUMENTALITY IN THE SERVICE OF A PREFORMED MESSAGE. *LA HORA*, BY AVOIDING THE TWIN TRAPS OF AN EMPTY ICONOCLASM ON THE ONE HAND, AND

A "CORRECT" BUT FORMALLY NOSTALGIC MILITANCY ON THE OTHER, CONSTITUTES A MAJOR STEP TOWARD THE REALIZATION OF THAT SCANDALOUSLY UTOPIAN AND ONLY APPARENTLY PARADOXICAL IDEA—THAT OF A MAJORITARIAN AVANT-GARDE.

Notes

1. The idea of "Third Cinema" is fully developed in an essay by Solanas and Getino entitled "Toward a Third Cinema" [which is reprinted on pp. 56-80].

2. Solanas and Getino were not historically the first to suggest the combination of film with discussion. In 1933, Bela Balazs proposed that "explanations" be made standard at all screenings: "This does not apply only to our films. We must have critical, satirical analyses of the bourgeois films, expose their reactionary, capitalistic and anti-proletarian ideology, ridicule their philistine narrow-mindedness." Balazs' proposal is, finally, less open than that of Solanas-Getino, since he favors "explanations" rather than "debate," going so far as to suggest that the lecturer record his/her comments on a disc which could accompany the film. More recently, McCall and Tyndall in *Argument* aim to create the preconditions whereby the audience can act on the social situation which the film engages. The film has been shown to small groups followed by discussions with its makers. This experiment too is less audacious than that of Solanas-Getino, since the film is not interrupted, and the debate is only with the filmmakers.

3. Aleatory procedures are, of course, typical of art issues in the sixties. One need think only of "process art" in which chemical, biological or seasonal forces affect the original materials, or of environmental art, or happenings, mixed media, human-machine-interaction systems, street theater and the like. The film formed part of a general tendency to erase the boundaries between art and life, but rarely did this erasure take such a highly politicized form.

4. The Argentine *junta* paid inadvertent tribute to the revolutionary potential of photography when they arrested Che Guevara's mother in 1962, accusing her of having in her possession a "subversive" photograph. The

photograph was of her son Che. See *The New York Times*, May 19, 1980, p. A10.

5. Gerard Chaliand, in *Mythes Revolutionnaires du Tiers Monde* (1976), criticizes what he calls the "macho" attitudes of Latin American guerrillas which led them to expose themselves to combat even when their presence was not required, thus resulting in the death of most of the guerrilla leaders. He contrasts this attitude with the more prudent procedure of the Vietnamese. During fifteen years of war, not one of the fifty members of the central committee of the South Vietnamese National Liberation Front fell into the hands of the enemy.

6. Should there be any doubt about the Peronist allegiances of the film, one need only remember the frequent quotations of Peron, the interviews with Peronist militants, and the critiques of the non-Peronist left. In 1971, Solanas and Getino made a propaganda film for Peron: *Peron: La Revolucion Justicialista (Peron: The Justicialism Revolution)*. The Cine-Liberacion group which made the film, according to Solanas, served as "the cinematic arm of General Peron." During the Campora administration, Getino accepted a post on the national film board. Upon Peron's death, Solanas and Getino made a public declaration supporting the succession of his wife Isabel. Ironically, the repression unleashed after her ouster was levelled as much against Solanas and Getino as against those who had been more consistently on the left.

7. The simplistic view of Peron as a fascist has been revived in many of the reviews of the Broadway production of *Evita*, with a number of critics comparing the play to the kind of spectacle parodied in Mel Brooks' *The Producers*.

THE POLITICS OF MOTHERING [1986]

AN INTERVIEW WITH SUSANA MUÑOZ AND LOURDES PORTILLO ON *LAS MADRES: THE MOTHERS OF THE PLAZA DE MAYO*

COCO FUSCO ᐯᐯᐯᐯᐯᐯᐯᐯᐯᐯᐯᐯᐯᐯᐯᐯᐯᐯᐯᐯᐯᐯ

THE WIDESPREAD EUPHORIA OVER ARGENTINA'S DEMOCRATIZATION STRETCHED ALL THE WAY TO HOLLYWOOD IN 1986, WITH *KISS OF THE SPIDER WOMAN*, *THE OFFICIAL STORY* AND *LAS MADRES: THE MOTHERS OF THE PLAZA DE MAYO* ALL REACHING THE OSCAR NOMINATION LINEUP. OF THE THREE FILMS, *LAS MADRES* IS THE MOST POINTEDLY CRITICAL OF ARGENTINA'S MILITARY ESTABLISHMENT AND THE ATTEMPT TO WHITEWASH THE SORDID DETAILS OF THE COUNTRY'S RECENT PAST. SUSANA MUÑOZ AND LOURDES PORTILLO'S DOCUMENTARY RESORTS NEITHER TO DISPLACED METAPHORS NOR TO TALES OF UPPERCLASS GUILT: THE STORY IS PRESENTED FROM THE POINT OF VIEW OF WOMEN WHO LIVED THE NATIONAL NIGHTMARE.

THE RISE TO POWER OF THE MILITARY GOVERNMENT IN THE 1970S, AND ITS WAR AGAINST LEFT-WING "SUBVERSIVES," RESULTED IN THE DISAPPEARANCES OF 30,000 PEOPLE IN A WAVE OF KIDNAPPING, TORTURES AND MURDERS. IN APRIL 1977, FOURTEEN MOTHERS OF *LOS DESAPARECIDOS* BEGAN MARCHING IN FRONT OF THE PRESIDENTIAL PALACE IN THE PLAZA DE MAYO IN BUENOS AIRES, DEMANDING TO KNOW WHAT HAD BECOME OF THEIR CHILDREN. INTERCUTTING THEIR TESTIMONY WITH STATEMENTS BY GOVERNMENT OFFICIALS AND BACKGROUND SECTIONS ON THE MILITARY, MUNOZ AND PORTILLO TRACE THE DEVELOPMENT OF THIS MOTHERS' MOVEMENT TO 1984, WHEN THE INTERNATIONALLY RECOGNIZED GROUP HAD GROWN TO OVER 2,500 MEMBERS. TODAY, UNDER THE NEW CIVILIAN GOVERNMENT OF PRESIDENT RAUL ALFONSIN, THE MOTHERS CONTINUE TO DEMAND THAT THE PEOPLE RESPONSIBLE FOR THE DISAPPEARANCES BE BROUGHT TO TRIAL. THOUGH MOST RECOGNIZE THAT THEY WILL NEVER LEARN WHAT HAPPENED TO THEIR CHILDREN, THE SENSE OF UNITY THEY HAVE GAINED AMONG THEMSELVES HAS ENABLED THEM TO TURN PERSONAL TRAGEDY INTO A POWERFUL POLITICAL VOICE.

Coco Fusco: Would you tell us about yourselves and how you got involved in filmmaking?

Susana Muñoz: I was born and raised in Argentina. I left when I was eighteen and lived in Israel for seven years. I am Jewish. Then I came to the United States to go to graduate school at the San Francisco Art Institute and just stayed on. That's where Lourdes and I met. The reason for making this film for me was in part, of course, because I am Argentinean. The idea came from a casual conversation that I had with some relatives who were involved in solidarity groups for the *Madres* in New York. They told me that one of the *Madres* was coming to Washington, so we decided to go there, to a Mother's day luncheon on Capitol Hill organized by Ariel Dorfman, Barbara Mikulski and Pat Schroeder. They had invited Renee Epelbaum from Argentina, and three other mothers, one from Chile, one from Guatemala, and one from El Salvador, all mothers of the disappeared. This was May 1983. We taped the event, and out of that we wrote our first proposal.

CF: Did you leave Argentina because of the situation?

SM: No, I left in 1972, just before Peron returned. I have a sister who went into exile for nine years. Through her I became involved in what was really going on. Then I found out that one of my friends from high school, and possibly two or three others, had disappeared and nobody could really give me any clues.

Lourdes Portillo: I am from Mexico. I came here as a teenager. I consider myself Chicana. I started working in film several years ago in Los Angeles. Then I came to San Francisco and started working with Cine Manifest, a group of Marxist filmmakers that produced independent films. I was trained as a camera assistant and then I went to the Art Institute. In 1978 I proposed to make a film for the Sandinistas. We decided to make a dramatic film because we couldn't go to Nicaragua at the time. We wanted to show how the conflict affected people's lives here, so we made *After the Earthquake*.

CF: Both of you had been working in modes other than standard documentary before making *Las Madres*. Was it the subject matter that made you decide to make a stylistic shift?

LP: Absolutely. It had everything to do with the intensity and the power that those mothers gave out. I knew that you couldn't go wrong with this documentary.

CF: How difficult was it to enter the country to film the mothers?

SM: TOWARDS THE END OF 1983, NEAR THE ELECTIONS, THINGS OPENED UP A LOT. IN THOSE FIRST MONTHS OF 1983 A LOT OF INFORMATION STARTED COMING OUT, AND WITH THE POLITICAL PROCESS COMING UP IN MARCH, IT WAS VERY HARD NOT TO ALLOW THESE THINGS.

CF: WHEN YOU ENTERED THE COUNTRY DID YOU IDENTIFY YOURSELF AS INDEPENDENT PRODUCERS?

LP: WE LIED. WE ALWAYS SAID WE WERE FROM PUBLIC TELEVISION.

SM: WE HAD I.D. CARDS FROM AN INDEPENDENT NEW SERVICE. THAT HELPED A LOT. THE ARGENTINE OFFICIALS DIDN'T REALLY UNDERSTAND WHAT THE CARDS SAID.

CF: DID YOU ENCOUNTER ANY DIFFICULTIES WHILE SHOOTING?

LP: NO ONE HARASSED US OR ANYTHING LIKE THAT. BUT WHEN WE WERE IN A PUBLIC DEMONSTRATION, WATCHING THE MOTHERS MARCHING, THERE WERE MANY SECRET SERVICE MEN AROUND WITH CAMERAS AND THEY WOULD STAND IN FRONT OF US AND TAKE PICTURES OF OUR FACES. THAT WAS ABOUT ALL. YOU KNOW, ALFONSIN HAD BEEN IN POWER ONLY ONE HUNDRED DAYS, SO THEY WERE TRYING TO PROVE THERE WAS A DEMOCRACY. THE MILITARY WAS ACTUALLY STILL IN POWER.

CF: DID YOU HAVE ANY TROUBLE GETTING ACCESS TO AREAS YOU WANTED TO FILM?

SM: THERE WERE SOME THINGS WE HAD NO ACCESS TO: CERTAIN DETENTION CAMPS, CERTAIN MILITARY FACILITIES. SOME DETENTION CAMPS COULD BE PHOTOGRAPHED ONLY FROM THE OUTSIDE. I DID TRY DURING A PREPRODUCTION TRIP TO GO TO A PRISON WHERE A FRIEND OF MINE HAD BEEN DETAINED. HE RECOGNIZED IT FROM THE OUTSIDE. WE WENT WITH AN ARGENTINEAN TELEVISION CREW BUT THEY DIDN'T LET US IN EVEN THOUGH WE HAD A LETTER FROM A JUDGE OF THAT DISTRICT.

LP: WE COULD HAVE FOCUSED ON VERY SORDID THINGS IN THE FILM: THE PLACES WHERE PEOPLE HAD BEEN TORTURED, THE POLICE SHOTS. WE JUST MENTIONED IT, AND I THINK THAT WAS BETTER THAN FOCUSING ON IT. IT WOULD HAVE BEEN A DIFFERENT FILM, MORE SENSATIONALISTIC.

CF: WHAT WAS IT LIKE TO WORK ON A COLLABORATIVE PROJECT?

LP: YOU WANT THE TRUTH OR THE ROMANTIC VERSION? IT WAS HORRIBLE, ABSOLUTELY TERRIBLE! IT WAS A PROCESS OF GROWTH, I THINK, OF ACCEPTANCE. WHAT REALLY GOT IN THE WAY FOR SUSANA AND ME WAS THAT OUR ROLES WERE NOT DEFINED. THERE WERE TIMES, THOUGH, WHEN THE COLLABORATION WORKED. WHEN WE WERE SHOOTING, MANY SCENES WERE VERY PAINFUL. ONCE WE HAD TO INTERVIEW A GRANDMOTHER WHO WAS TAKING CARE OF HER FOUR GRANDCHILDREN WHO HAD BEEN ORPHANED. SINCE I HAD THREE CHILDREN, I COULDN'T GO, IT WAS TOO PAINFUL. SO SUSANA WENT TO THAT INTERVIEW. WE GOT VERY CLOSE TO THESE PEOPLE. THEY WOULD REMIND US OF AN AUNT, OR OUR MOTHERS. SEEING THEM IN THIS HORRENDOUS PAIN, WE WOULD TAKE IT ON, AND FILMING WOULD BECOME VERY HARD.

SM: ALSO, WHEN WE INTERVIEWED JUAN JOSE COSSI, THE PARAMILITARY OFFICER, I DID NOT WANT TO DO THE INTERVIEW. I AM FROM ARGENTINA AND WAS APPREHENSIVE. HE SAW ME, BUT I WANTED HIM TO REMEMBER HAVING DONE THE INTERVIEW WITH LOURDES, WHO WOULD NOT BE IN ARGENTINA AGAIN.

CF: How did you get him to talk?

SM: He makes a living nowadays, or used to anyhow, by giving interviews. He retired from the army after the Falklands war. He had a lot of grievances. He had been an infiltrator, and he had been sent by army intelligence to infiltrate a group in 1974. On one occasion the police took him in by mistake and tortured him for thirty-five days, not acknowledging that he was part of the army. He knew exactly who had tortured him.

At no point did he actually say what he really did in the dirty war. He was a pilot and was probably lying to us about his involvement. We think he had probably thrown people out of his plane, but he will never admit it.

CF: So he was being paid to talk?

SM: We paid him forty dollars, which by American standards is peanuts, but by Argentine standards is quite a bit of money. I think that he hoped that by turning to the other side after the regime had changed he could be exonerated. The person who directed us to him was the president of the Madres. He was her neighbor.

CF: What was the mothers' initial response to your filming?

SM: I felt that, if anything, we were accepted because people did not think we were there to exploit their pain. They knew the film would be primarily for them. In fact, they have a copy of the film to use for their own purposes.

CF: In what ways was the film shaped by your interactions with the mothers?

SM: Basically we were trying to respect their point of view. We could have gone into certain things. The mothers claim to be an apolitical group. Even though each of the mothers has very different political ideas, as a group they are nonpartisan. We could have tampered with that frail line, but we respected that.

CF: Were most of the mothers in the film founding members of the group?

SM: No, not really. They had been there from early on, but they weren't all founding members. Rene Epelbaum is on the commission, and so is Hebe, Blandine, Suarez and Galletti. We tried to give a representation of different social classes, of different levels of society—a working class mother, a teacher, the head of a girls' school, a businesswoman, and a grandmother who was very poor.

CF: WHERE DID YOUR FUNDING COME FROM?

LP: FROM PRIVATE FOUNDATIONS, SUCH AS THE MCARTHUR FOUNDATION, AND IN-DIVIDUALS WHO ARE SYMPATHETIC TO HUMAN RIGHTS ISSUES. THE FIRST MONEY WE RECEIVED WAS FROM JOAN BAEZ, AND ANOTHER PERSON WHO HELPED US VERY MUCH WAS MAYA MILLER. THE FILM FUND WAS ALSO VERY HELPFUL. WE COULDN'T GET ANY MONEY FROM THE PUBLIC BROADCASTING SERVICE. WE TRIED THREE TIMES. THE CORPORATION FOR PUBLIC BROADCASTING, THE NATIONAL EN-DOWMENT FOR THE ARTS—ALL THOSE SOURCES WERE CLOSED TO US.

SM: IF YOU LOOK AT THE AFI PROJECTS THAT WERE FUNDED, YOU'LL NOTICE THAT NONE OF THEM WERE ON INTERNATIONAL SUBJECTS. OBVIOUSLY, THE TREND NOW IS TOWARDS SAFE, MILD STUFF. THEY FEEL THAT INDEPENDENTS ARE POINT-OF-VIEW PEOPLE, AND THEY WANT "NON-BIASED" FILMS. ONE OF THE REASONS WE HAD A LOT OF TROUBLE WITH FOUNDATIONS WAS THAT THEY WOULD SAY, "WELL, YOU KNOW, NOW YOUR COUNTRY HAS A DEMOCRACY. SO WHAT'S THE POINT OF MAK-ING A FILM ABOUT THIS?" IT'S A VERY SHORTSIGHTED VIEW OF HISTORY, AND IT'S VERY HARD TO MAKE THEM UNDERSTAND. IN ARGENTINA, AT ANY GIVEN POINT WE ARE ON THE VERGE OF A DICTATORSHIP. YOU CAN'T COUNT ON DEMOCRACY LASTING. AND THE MOTHERS ARE STILL MARCHING. THEY STILL DON'T HAVE ANY ANSWERS.

LP: THE CORPORATION FOR PUBLIC BROADCASTING WANTS TO PROMOTE THE IDEA OF BEING OBJECTIVE. MY OPINION ABOUT THAT IS THAT BY RENDERING EVERYTHING OBJECTIVE, THEY RENDER EVERYTHING MEANINGLESS.

SM: WE TRIED TO INTERVIEW BOTH SIDES. YOU CAN TELL THAT THE BAD SIDE IS REALLY THE BAD SIDE. THERE IS NO WAY OF MAKING IT EVEN—I DON'T BELIEVE THAT THAT KIND OF BALANCE CAN EXIST.

CF: ULTIMATELY, DO YOU THINK THAT YOU CAME UP WITH THE FILM YOU WANTED?

LP: YES, WE DEFINITELY CAME UP WITH THE FILM WE WANTED. THE ONLY OMISSION WAS THE RESULTS OF THE TRIAL. WE'RE THINKING OF ADDING SOMETHING TO THE FILM.

SM: THERE ARE 750 CASES THAT WERE STARTED AGAINST OTHER MILITARY OFFICIALS. THERE'S A LOT AT STAKE RIGHT NOW BECAUSE THE GOVERNMENT IS TRYING TO GET AMNESTY FOR EVERYONE EXCEPT THE NINE WHO WERE ALREADY TRIED. IF THAT HAPPENS, THEN THOSE 750 CASES WILL BE DROPPED. I THINK THE BIGGEST TASK FOR THE MOTHERS AT THIS POINT IS TO PREVENT THE AMNESTY. IT IS HARD FOR THEM TO GO ON AND ON WITHOUT GETTING ANY RESULTS. FOUR OFFICERS WERE ACQUITTED WHO WERE DEFINITELY CRIMINALS. THE WAY THAT THE SENTENCES WERE GIVEN WAS SUCH THAT IN TWO YEARS THE OTHERS WILL BE OUT. PLUS THERE IS THE FACT THAT NO INFORMATION FROM THE MILITARY BECOMES AVAILABLE. THE

MILITARY HAS ALL THE RECORDS, AND THE CIVILIAN GOVERNMENT IS NOT GOING TO INQUIRE ANY FURTHER.

CF: MANY HAVE SPOKEN OF THE CATHARTIC EFFECTS OF ARGENTINA'S ALLEGED DEMOCRATIZATION. WHAT ARE YOUR THOUGHTS ABOUT THIS?

SM: PART OF THE HAPPINESS IN THIS COUNTRY ABOUT THE ALFONSIN GOVERNMENT IS BASICALLY THAT. BUT THE ENTIRE SYSTEM OF DEMOCRACY IN ARGENTINA, AND NOT JUST IN ARGENTINA, IS AT STAKE. IN THE 1970S ALL OF LATIN AMERICA WAS BEING RUN BY DICTATORSHIPS. EVEN COUNTRIES THAT HAD A HISTORY OF DEMOCRACY LIKE URUGUAY, THAT HAD NEVER HAD A DICTATOR, HAD A COUP. CHILE FELL AND WE KNOW VERY WELL THAT THE CIA WAS INVOLVED IN THAT— IT'S NO SECRET TO ANYONE WHO HAS SEEN *MISSING*. AND THE CIA WAS INVOLVED IN ARGENTINA AND BRAZIL AND EVERY COUNTRY WHERE THE U.S. HAS INVESTMENTS. THE SITUATION GOT TO A POINT WHERE, IF THE U.S. DIDN'T GIVE THESE COUNTRIES A LITTLE BREATHING ROOM, THEY WOULD HAVE TO DEAL WITH POPULAR UPRISINGS ONCE AGAIN, IN PROPORTIONS THAT THEY COULDN'T HANDLE, SUCH AS WHAT IS NOW HAPPENING IN EL SALVADOR, GUATEMALA AND NICARAGUA. IN A SENSE, THIS NEW WAVE OF DEMOCRATIZATION IS A WAY OF APPEASING POPULATIONS. IT'S A WAY OF MAKING THINGS LOOK GOOD.

LP: PUTTING A NEW FACE ON CAPITALISM.

CF: MANY CRITICS HAVE POINTED OUT THAT HAVING ELECTIONS IN A COUNTRY WITH A HISTORY OF DICTATORSHIP ISN'T GOING TO CHANGE ANYTHING UNLESS YOU FUNDAMENTALLY CHANGE THE RELATIONSHIP BETWEEN THE MILITARY AND THE GOVERNMENT.

SM: THE DIFFERENCE IS THAT IN A PLACE LIKE GUATEMALA THE WAR IS RAGING RIGHT NOW AND PEOPLE ARE GETTING KILLED DAILY. IN ARGENTINA IT NEVER GOT TO BE QUITE THAT WAY. IT CAN HAPPEN IN GUATEMALA BECAUSE THERE IS NO RESPECT FOR THE INDIAN POPULATION, SO THEY DON'T CARE ABOUT THE DISAPPEARED THAT MUCH. THEY THROW BOMBS AND DESTROY ENTIRE VILLAGES. IN ARGENTINA IT WASN'T LIKE THAT. ONE OF THE REASONS THAT THE GOVERNMENT USED THE SYSTEM, THAT VERY METHODICAL SYSTEM OF MAKING PEOPLE DISAPPEAR IN THE MIDDLE OF THE NIGHT, IS THAT IT'S A MOSTLY WHITE COUNTRY, POPULATED BY EUROPEAN IMMIGRANTS FROM ITALY AND SPAIN. THEY COULDN'T USE THE GUATEMALAN METHOD. IT WOULDN'T HAVE LOOKED GOOD INTERNATIONALLY. THEY COULDN'T JUST RANDOMLY GO INTO NICE NEIGHBORHOODS IN BUENOS AIRES AND TELL ALL THE PEOPLE TO COME OUT SO THEY COULD SHOOT THEM.

CF: DO YOU CONSIDER THIS A FEMINIST FILM?

LP: IT'S A FEMINIST FILM IN THE SENSE THAT IT WAS CONCEPTUALIZED BY WOMEN. IT'S ABOUT WOMEN AND THE POLITICAL EMPOWERMENT OF WOMEN. WE DIDN'T TRY

TO EXCLUDE MEN FROM IT. WE TRIED, THOUGH, TO DEAL WITH THE IDEA THAT WOMEN CAN DO SOMETHING ABOUT THE POLITICAL SITUATION IN THEIR COUNTRY.

SM: I THINK THAT WE WERE TRYING TO SAY THAT THE MOTHERS WERE CONTINUING THE STRUGGLE OF THEIR CHILDREN. THEY WERE ALWAYS SPEAKING ABOUT WHAT THEIR CHILDREN TAUGHT THEM.

CF: IT DOESN'T SOUND AS IF YOU FEEL THERE IS ANYTHING SPECIFICALLY LATIN AMERICAN ABOUT THE SITUATION OR THE RELATIONSHIP BETWEEN THE MOTHERS AND THEIR CHILDREN.

LP: NO, I DON'T THINK IT'S A QUESTION OF NATIONALITY AT ALL. IT'S HAPPENING ALL AROUND THE WORLD, IN MANY THIRD WORLD COUNTRIES.

SM: LOOK AT THE MOTHERS IN IRELAND. YOU CAN SEE THAT THE ISSUES ARE DEFINITELY MORE THAN NATIONAL. HOW WOMEN GO ABOUT IT DEPENDS ON THEIR NATIONALITY, THOUGH.

CF: DO YOU SEE THIS FILM AS A FORM OF ACTIVISM?

LP: THERE ARE MANY PEOPLE IN THE U.S. WHO SEE THIS PROBLEM AS SOMETHING VERY REMOVED FROM THEIR LIVES. WHEN WE SHOW THEM THIS FILM, WE SHOW THEM THAT ARGENTINE MOTHERS ARE LIKE THEIR MOTHERS, AND THEIR SUFFERING IS LIKE THEIR MOTHERS' SUFFERING. THEY CAN IDENTIFY AND FEEL MORE COMPASSION, AND PERHAPS START THINKING ABOUT WHAT THEY CAN DO.

SM: I BELIEVE THAT FILMS CAN DEFINITELY BE A POWERFUL WAY OF BRINGING PEOPLE TOGETHER, OF BRINGING ATTENTION TO SOMETHING. I HOPE THAT THE OSCAR NOMINATION WILL BRING MORE ATTENTION TO THE SUBJECT, AND INTRODUCE PEOPLE TO THE MOTHERS.

The Promised Land

CHILE

FILMMAKERS AND THE POPULAR GOVERNMENT: A POLITICAL MANIFESTO [1970]

A PROCLAMATION ISSUED BY FILMMAKERS WORKING UNDER THE POPULAR UNITY GOVERNMENT OF SALVADOR ALLENDE.

CHILEAN FILMMAKERS, IT IS TIME FOR US ALL TO UNDERTAKE, TOGETHER WITH OUR PEOPLE, THE GREAT TASK OF NATIONAL LIBERATION AND THE CONSTRUCTION OF SOCIALISM.

IT IS TIME FOR US TO BEGIN TO REDEEM OUR OWN VALUES IN ORDER TO AFFIRM OUR CULTURAL AND POLITICAL IDENTITY.

LET US NO LONGER ALLOW THE DOMINANT CLASSES TO UPROOT THE SYMBOLS WHICH THE PEOPLE HAVE PRODUCED IN THE COURSE OF THEIR LONG STRUGGLE FOR LIBERATION.

LET US NO LONGER PERMIT NATIONAL VALUES TO BE USED TO UPHOLD THE CAPITALIST REGIME.

LET US START FROM THE CLASS INSTINCT OF THE PEOPLE AND WITH THIS CONTRIBUTE TO THE MAKING OF A CLASS CONSCIOUSNESS.

LET US NOT LIMIT OURSELVES FROM GOING BEYOND OUR CONTRADICTIONS;

LET US DEVELOP THEM AND OPEN FOR OURSELVES THE WAY WHICH LEADS TO THE CONSTRUCTION OF A LUCID AND LIBERATING CULTURE.

THE LONG STRUGGLE OF OUR PEOPLE FOR THEIR EMANCIPATION HAS LAID DOWN FOR US THE WAY TO BE FOLLOWED. LET US RECOVER THE TRACES OF THOSE GREAT POPULAR STRUGGLES FALSIFIED BY OFFICIAL HISTORY, AND GIVE BACK TO THE PEOPLE THE TRUE VERSION OF THESE STRUGGLES AS A LEGITIMATE AND NECESSARY HERITAGE FOR CONFRONTING THE PRESENT AND ENVISAGING THE FUTURE.

LET US RECOVER THE TREMENDOUS FIGURE OF BALMACEDA, ANTI-OLIGARCHIST AND ANTI-IMPERIALIST.

LET US REAFFIRM THAT RECABARREN BELONGS TO THE PEOPLE, THAT CARRERA, O'HIGGINS, MANUEL RODRIGUEZ, BILBAO, AS WELL AS THE ANONYMOUS MINER WHO FELL ONE MORNING, OR THE PEASANT WHO DIED WITHOUT EVER HAVING UNDERSTOOD THE MEANING OF HIS LIFE OR OF HIS DEATH, CONSTITUTE THE ESSENTIAL FOUNDATIONS FROM WHICH WE EMERGE.

THAT THE CHILEAN FLAG IS A FLAG OF STRUGGLE AND LIBERATION, IT IS THE PATRIMONY OF THE PEOPLE AND THEIR HERITAGE.

AGAINST AN ANEMIC AND NEOCOLONIZED CULTURE, A PASTURE FOR THE CONSUMPTION OF AN ELITE, DECADENT AND STERILE PETITE-BOURGEOISIE, LET US DEVOTE OUR COLLECTIVE WILL, IMMERSED WITHIN THE PEOPLE, TO THE CONSTRUCTION OF AN AUTHENTICALLY NATIONAL AND THEREFORE REVOLUTIONARY CULTURE.

CONSEQUENTLY WE DECLARE:

1. THAT BEFORE BEING FILMMAKERS WE ARE MEN ENGAGED WITHIN THE POLITICAL AND SOCIAL PHENOMENON OF OUR PEOPLE, AND IN THEIR GREAT TASK; THE CONSTRUCTION OF SOCIALISM.

2. THAT THE CINEMA IS ART.

3. THAT THE CHILEAN CINEMA, BECAUSE OF AN HISTORICAL IMPERATIVE, MUST BE A REVOLUTIONARY ART.

4. THAT WE MEAN BY REVOLUTIONARY THAT WHICH IS REALIZED IN CONJUNCTION BETWEEN THE ARTIST AND HIS PEOPLE, UNITED IN A COMMON OBJECTIVE: LIBERATION. THE PEOPLE ARE THE GENERATORS OF ACTION AND FINALLY THE TRUE CREATORS; THE FILMMAKER IS THEIR INSTRUMENT OF COMMUNICATION.

5. THAT THE REVOLUTIONARY CINEMA WILL NOT ASSERT ITSELF THROUGH DECREES. CONSEQUENTLY WE WILL NOT GRANT PRIVILEGE TO ONE PARTICULAR WAY OF MAKING FILM; IT MUST BE THAT THE COURSE OF THE STRUGGLE DETERMINES THIS.

6. THAT, MEANWHILE, WE SHALL REGARD A CINEMA REMOVED FROM THE GREAT

MASSES [WILL] BECOME INEVITABLY A PRODUCT FOR THE CONSUMPTION OF AN ELITE PETIT-BOURGEOISIE WHICH IS INCAPABLE OF CONSTITUTING THE MOTOR OF HISTORY. IN THIS CASE THE FILMMAKER WILL SEE HIS WORK POLITICALLY NULLIFIED.

7. THAT WE REFUSE ALL SECTARIANISM AIMED AT THE MECHANICAL APPLICATION OF THE PRINCIPLES STATED ABOVE, IN THE SAME WAY THAT WE OPPOSE THE IMPOSITION OF OFFICIAL CRITERIA ON THE PRACTICE OF FILMMAKING.

8. THAT WE MAINTAIN THAT THE TRADITIONAL FORMS OF PRODUCTION ARE A VERITABLE RAMPART ENCLOSING YOUNG FILMMAKERS. THEY IMPLY, FINALLY, A CLEAR CULTURAL DEPENDENCY, FOR THESE TECHNIQUES ARE DERIVED FROM AESTHETIC CONCEPTIONS FOREIGN TO THE CULTURE OF OUR PEOPLES.

9. THAT WE MAINTAIN THAT A FILMMAKER WITH THESE OBJECTIVES NECESSARILY IMPLIES A DIFFERENT KIND OF CRITICAL EVALUATION; WE ASSERT THAT THE BEST CRITIC OF A REVOLUTIONARY FILM IS THE PEOPLE TO WHOM IT IS ADDRESSED, WHO HAVE NO NEED OF "MEDIATORS WHO DEFEND AND INTERPRET IT."[1]

10. THAT THERE EXISTS NO SUCH THING AS A FILM THAT IS REVOLUTIONARY IN ITSELF. THAT IT BECOMES SUCH THROUGH THE CONTACT THAT IT ESTABLISHES WITH ITS PUBLIC AND PRINCIPALLY THROUGH ITS INFLUENCE AS A MOBILIZING AGENT FOR REVOLUTIONARY ACTION.

1L. THAT THE CINEMA IS A RIGHT OF THE PEOPLE, AND THAT IT IS NECESSARY TO RESEARCH THOSE FORMS WHICH ARE MOST APPROPRIATE FOR REACHING ALL CHILEANS.

12. THAT THE MEANS OF PRODUCTION MUST BE AVAILABLE TO ALL WORKERS IN THE CINEMA AND THAT, IN THIS SENSE, THERE EXIST NO ACQUIRED RIGHTS; ON THE CONTRARY, UNDER POPULAR GOVERNMENT, EXPRESSION WILL NOT BE THE PRIVILEGE OF SOME, BUT THE INALIENABLE RIGHT OF A PEOPLE MARCHING TOWARDS THEIR FINAL INDEPENDENCE.

13. THAT A PEOPLE WITH A CULTURE ARE A PEOPLE WHO STRUGGLE, WHO RESIST AND WHO FREE THEMSELVES.

CHILEAN FILMMAKERS, WE SHALL OVERCOME!

TRANSLATED BY SYLVIA HARVEY.

Notes
1. Julio Garcia Espinosa, Cuban director.

BRIDGING PAST AND PRESENT: LEGEND AND POLITICS IN *THE PROMISED LAND* [1985]

JULIANNE BURTON

DIRECTOR MIGUEL LITTIN HAS DESCRIBED HIS SECOND FEATURE FILM AS A FRESCO, AN EPIC POEM, A FOLK CANTO. *THE PROMISED LAND* [*LA TIERRA PROMETIDA*, 1973] WAS THE MOST AMBITIOUS FEATURE MADE IN CHILE UNDER THE DEMOCRATICALLY ELECTED SOCIALIST GOVERNMENT OF SALVADOR ALLENDE (1970-1973). ON THE STRENGTH OF LITTIN'S FIRST FEATURE, *EL CHACAL DE NAHUELTORO* [*THE JACKAL OF NAHUELTORO*, 1969], THE NEWLY ELECTED ALLENDE APPOINTED HIM TO HEAD THE FORTY-YEAR-OLD, CHRONICALLY INEFFECTUAL STATE FILM ENTERPRISE, CHILE FILMS. WITHIN THE YEAR, HOWEVER, DESPITE OPTIMISTIC PRONOUNCEMENTS AND ACCORDS, LITTIN HAD RESIGNED IN FRUSTRATION WITH THE BUREAUCRATIC ENCUMBRANCE, INTERNECINE POLITICAL BATTLES, INADEQUATE EQUIPMENT, INSUFFICIENT FUNDING, AND LACK OF A COHERENT NATIONAL CULTURAL POLICY. A NUMBER OF OTHER FILMMAKERS LEFT THE ORGANIZATION WITH LITTIN, PREFERRING TO TRY THEIR LUCK AT GENERATING INDEPENDENT FUNDING.

FILMED IN NORTHERN CHILE, IN LITTIN'S LUSH NATIVE REGION OF COLCHAGUA, UNDER EXTREMELY ADVERSE PHYSICAL CONDITIONS AND WITH CHRONICALLY DEPLETED FUNDS, *THE PROMISED LAND* TOOK EIGHT MONTHS TO SHOOT. NO FILM LAB IN CHILE WAS ABLE TO HANDLE THE PROCESSING WITHIN THE PRODUCTION SCHEDULE, SO THE FILM WAS EDITED AND MIXED IN CUBA IN ORDER TO PREMIERE, BY INVITATION, AT THE BERLIN FILM FESTIVAL IN THE SUMMER OF 1973. LESS THAN A YEAR LATER, THE FILM DEPARTMENT OF THE MUSEUM OF MODERN ART AND THE LINCOLN CENTER FILM SOCIETY SPONSORED THE FILM'S FIRST AMERICAN SHOWING AS PART OF THEIR "NEW DIRECTORS, NEW FILMS" SERIES. THOUGH WIDELY VIEWED ABROAD IN THE AFTERMATH OF THE BLOOD-DRENCHED MILITARY TAKEOVER THAT IT IN MANY WAYS PRESAGES, *THE PROMISED LAND* WAS

NEVER RELEASED IN CHILE BEFORE THE OVERTHROW OF ALLENDE'S GOVERNMENT.

DESPITE THE DIFFICULTIES OF MAINTAINING A FILMMAKING CAREER OUTSIDE HIS OWN COUNTRY, LITTIN MANAGED TO MAKE FOUR FEATURES IN THE DECADE FOLLOWING *THE PROMISED LAND*, TWO OF WHICH RECEIVED ACADEMY AWARD NOMINATIONS FOR BEST FOREIGN-LANGUAGE FILM. *ACTAS DE MARUSIA* (*LETTERS FROM MARUSIA*, 1976) WAS SHOT IN MEXICO, WHERE LITTIN TOOK UP RESIDENCE UPON HIS EXILE FROM CHILE. IN THIS DRAMATIZATION OF TURN-OF-THE-CENTURY COPPER MINERS' STRIKE, LITTIN EXPRESSES HIS OUTRAGE AT THE RUTHLESS BRUTALITY OF THE AUGUSTO PINOCHET UGARTE REGIME (RESPONSIBLE FOR THE ASSASSINA-TION, DETENTION, AND PERMANENT "DISAPPEARANCE" OF TENS OF THOUSANDS OF CHILEANS, AS DOCUMENTED BY A NUMBER OF INTERNATIONAL AGENCIES) THROUGH HIS DEPICTION OF THE FORCES WHICH SUCCESSFULLY REPRESS THE STRIKE. *ALSINO Y EL CONDOR* (*ALSINO AND THE CONDOR, 1983*) IS A MORE LYRIC WORK, SHOT IN NICARAGUA. IN THE INTERIM, LITTIN FILMED TWO INTERNATIONAL COPRODUCTIONS BASED ON THE WORKS OF LEADING LATIN AMERICAN AUTHORS: *RECURSO DEL METODO* (*REASONS OF STATE*, 1978), BASED ON THE NOVEL BY THE CUBAN WRITER ALEJO CARPENTIER, AND *LA VIUDA DE MONTIEL* (*MONTIEL'S WIDOW*, 1979), BASED ON A SHORT STORY BY THE COLOMBIAN WHO WOULD RECEIVE THE 1982 NOBEL PRIZE FOR LITERATURE, GABRIEL GARCIA MARQUEZ. DESPITE THEIR UNMISTAKABLE MATURITY AND POLISH, HOWEVER, NONE OF LIT-TIN'S SUBSEQUENT FILMS HAS RECAPTURED THE DENSITY AND RESONANCE OF HIS TWO EARLIEST FEATURES, SO ENRICHED BY THEIR CONNECTION TO A NATIONAL HISTORY, A CULTURE AND A POLITICAL PROJECT OF WHICH A FILMMAKER IN EXILE IS INEVITABLY DEPRIVED.

SET IN THE EARLY 1930S—A TIME OF SEVERE ECONOMIC CRISIS, SOCIAL TEN-SION, AND POLITICAL TURMOIL—*THE PROMISED LAND* FOLLOWS AN ITINERANT BAND OF UNEMPLOYED WORKERS AND LANDLESS PEASANTS THROUGH THE MAGNIFI-CENT CHILEAN COUNTRYSIDE. CAMPING ON RAILROAD TRACKS AND HILLTOPS, THEIR NUMBERS CONSTANTLY SWELLING, THEY ARE MORE AND MORE BRUSQUELY DRIVEN AWAY FROM THE TOWNS THEY PASS. AS THEY WANDER, ONE WOMAN RECOUNTS A VISITATION FROM THE VIRGIN TO ANOTHER, AND THE VIRGIN (MIREYA KULCHEWSKY) APPEARS TO A YOUNG MAN WHO HAS BEEN LISTENING TO THEIR CONVERSATION. A MAN IN A RAGGED PIN-STRIPED SUIT TALKS DISCONNECTEDLY BUT IN GREAT EARNEST TO ANOTHER ABOUT THE MEXICAN AND RUSSIAN REVOLU-TIONS, ABOUT AUGUSTO CESAR SANDINO IN NICARAGUA, AND THE MINE ORGANIZER RECABARREN IN CHILE. IT IS PIN-STRIPE (MARCELO GAETE) WHO SUG-GESTS THE TAKEOVER OF SOME UNINHABITED GOVERNMENT LANDS, BUT IT IS ANOTHER MAN, JOSE DURAN (NELSON VILLAGRA), WHO LATER BECOMES THE LEADER OF THE GROUP.

THE FOUNDING OF THE PALMILLA SETTLEMENT, THE GROUND CLEARING, PLAN-TING, AND THE FIRST HARVEST FOLLOW IN RAPID AND JOYFUL SUCCESSION; YET THE DISPROPORTIONATE COST OF THE MANUFACTURED GOODS WHICH THE SET-

TLERS MUST BRING IN FROM THE PROVINCIAL CAPITAL OF HUIQUE ALERTS THEM
TO THE LIMITATIONS OF THEIR NEW-FOUND SELF-SUFFICIENCY. ENTER A RED PLANE,
HARBINGER OF A NEW, SOCIALIST GOVERNMENT, SPEWING LEAFLETS. THE PILOT
HOLDS FORTH ON THE VIRTUES OF SOCIALISM. DURAN, FOLLOWING HIS EXHOR-
TATION, LEADS HIS MEN TO HUIQUE TO TAKE OVER THE PROVINCIAL GOVERNMENT.
THE ANDES HAVE MAGICALLY SHIFTED TO THE INTERIOR OF THE COUNTRY, AND
ONLY THROUGH THE INTERCESSION OF THE VIRGIN DEL CARMEN IS DURAN'S BAND
ABLE TO SURMOUNT THE PERILS OF THAT MYTHIC GEOGRAPHY. (THE ARCHAIC QUALI-
TY OF THE LANGUAGE HERE CLARIFIES THE INTENTION; IN FACT, THE SEQUENCE
REENACTS THE LEGENDARY ANDEAN CROSSING OF THE NINETEENTH CENTURY
LIBERATOR BERNARDO O'HIGGINS.)

ONCE HE OCCUPIES THE SEAT OF THE PROVINCIAL GOVERNMENT, JOSE
VACILLATES. THOUGH HE THREATENS AND EXPELS THE EMISSARIES OF THE LAND-
HOLDERS AND SHOP OWNERS, HE GIVES A MORE SYMPATHETIC AUDIENCE TO THEIR
WIVES. THE MEN WHO ARE CLASS ENEMIES MEET AGAIN IN THE LOCAL BROTHEL,
WHERE THE INSURRECTIONISTS LEARN THAT THE SOCIALIST GOVERNMENT WHICH
THEY BELIEVED TO BE IN POWER WAS IN FACT OVERTHROWN A YEAR BEFORE. THE
SERGEANT WHO HAD PREVIOUSLY OFFERED HIS SERVICES TO DURAN IS NOW
ORDERED BY THE MOST POWERFUL OF THE LANDOWNERS, DON FERNANDO (RAFAEL
BENAVENTE), TO ROUT THE INTERLOPERS. IN DEFEAT, DURAN AND HIS MEN RETURN
TO THEIR VALLEY. PROMPTLY SURROUNDED BY THE ARMY AND MEMBERS OF THE

CATHOLIC HIERARCHY, THEY DECIDE TO RESIST TO THE DEATH. SCENES OF SLAUGHTER AND DESTRUCTION ARE INTERCUT WITH VISIONS OF FUTURE VICTORY, AND THE FILM COMES TO AN END WITH THE WORDS OF CHE GUEVARA, "OF THOSE WHO DID NOT UNDERSTAND WELL ENOUGH, OF THOSE WHO FELL WITHOUT SEEING THE DAWN . . . OF BLIND SACRIFICES WITHOUT RETRIBUTION, THE REVOLUTION WAS ALSO MADE."

LITTIN'S FILM CONVEYS THE SAME PROPHETIC CLAIRVOYANCE AS SOME OF CHILEAN POET PABLO NERUDA'S LATER POEMS. "THE ONLY SOLUTION IS IMPLACABLE DICTATORSHIP," INTONES A RIGHT-WING POLITICIAN AT THE RELIGIOUS FESTIVAL WHICH OPENS THE FILM, WHILE A BISHOP ADMONISHES FROM HIS LITTER, "FEED THE HUNGRY LEST THEY DEVOUR YE." MANY OF THE FILM'S PARTICIPANTS LATER LIVED IN A REAL LIFE WHAT THEY HAD ENACTED ON THE SCREEN. LITTIN AND LEAD ACTOR VILLAGRA WENT INTO EXILE, BUT OTHERS WERE NOT SO FORTUNATE. A NUMBER OF THE PEASANTS OF COLCHAGUA FELL VICTIM TO THE NEW MILITARY REGIME. LEAD ACTRESS CARMEN BUENO WAS PICKED UP BY AGENTS OF THE CHILEAN SECRET POLICE IN NOVEMBER, 1974, AND NEVER HEARD FROM AGAIN.

YET TO VIEW THE PROMISED LAND AS SIMPLY AN ACCURATE PREDICTION OF DEFEAT IS TO FAIL TO APPRECIATE THE FILM. THOUGH LITTIN SET HIS FILM BACK FOUR DECADES IN TIME, HIS INTERPRETATION OF THAT HISTORICAL MOMENT CONTAINED CLEAR ECHOES OF THE MOST PRESSING INTERNAL PROBLEMS FACING ALLENDE'S POPULAR UNITY GOVERNMENT. IN ADDITION TO CONJECTURES ABOUT THE ROLE OF THE MILITARY, THESE THEMES ALSO INCLUDE THE ROLE OF ESTABLISHED RELIGION, GENUINELY COLLECTIVE VERSUS OPPORTUNISTIC LEADERSHIP, LAND REFORM, THE DILEMMA OF WHETHER TO ARM THE MASSES, AND THE NEED FOR POPULAR GENERAL AND POLITICAL EDUCATION COMPLICATED BY COMMUNICATIONS DIFFICULTIES AND FALSE CONSCIOUSNESS. ONE OF THE MAJOR STRENGTHS OF THE FILM IS THAT THESE THEMES ARE NOT GRAFTED ONTO THE NARRATIVE BUT EMERGE ORGANICALLY FROM IT. TAKING A POSITION IN LINE WITH THE MOVEMENT OF THE REVOLUTIONARY LEFT (MIR), THE FILM OFFERS A CRITIQUE OF LA VIA CHILENA, THE "CHILEAN ROAD TO SOCIALISM," WITH ITS RELUCTANCE TO DISTURB THE NICETIES OF THE BOURGEOIS ORDER.

ON ANOTHER LEVEL—PERHAPS THE LEAST ACCESSIBLE TO NORTH AMERICAN AUDIENCES—THE FILM CAN BE VIEWED AS BOTH AN APPRECIATION AND A CRITIQUE OF POPULAR CULTURE. NARRATED BY MEANS OF FOLK SONGS, LEGENDARY VERSIONS OF HISTORICAL EVENTS, AND RELIGIOUS AND SECULAR ALLEGORIES, THE PROMISED LAND SETS OUT TO REVEAL THE RESILIENCY AND RESISTANCE AS WELL AS THE DEPRIVATION AND MYSTIFICATION WHICH CHARACTERIZE FOLK CULTURE. VIEWED IN THIS LIGHT, LITTIN'S SELF-CONSCIOUS USE OF MYTHIC MOTIFS AND PIOUS SYMBOLS OF RELIGION AND COUNTRY CANNOT BE SEEN AS OBSCURE, MANIPULATIVE, OR CYNICAL, AS SOME CRITICS HAVE SUGGESTED. SUCH TECHNIQUES ARE CLEARLY PART OF AN EFFORT TO USE THE TRADITIONALLY ELITE MEDIUM OF FILM TO EXPLORE CULTURAL MODES WHICH INFORM THE CONSCIOUSNESS OF THE POPULACE—

HENCE THE SHIFTING USAGE OF CERTAIN SYMBOLS. LA VIRGEN DEL CARMEN [THE VIRGIN OF CARMEN], FOR EXAMPLE, PATRON SAINT OF THE NATION AND OF THE ARMED FORCES, APPEARS ALTERNATELY ON THE SIDE OF THE PRIVILEGED CLASSES AND AMONG THE DISPOSSESSED, BUT IN THE FINAL SEQUENCE, SHE AND HER COURT OF ANGELS STAND FIRMLY BEHIND THE PRIVILEGED OLIGARCHY.

LITTIN'S TECHNIQUES SEEK AUDIENCE PARTICIPATION ON AN INTELLECTUAL AND CRITICAL AS WELL AS EMOTIONAL LEVEL. CHILEAN COMPOSER LUIS ADVIS' MOVING SCORE CANNOT BUT ENLIST THE SPECTATOR'S EMOTIONAL RESPONSE, BUT OTHER ELEMENTS CONSPIRE TO NEUTRALIZE THIS EFFECT. WHAT SOME VIEWERS MAY PERCEIVE AS A VACILLATION, OTHERS WILL PERCEIVE AS A DIALECTIC OF INTENSE EMOTIONAL INVOLVEMENT WITH CRITICAL PERSPECTIVE. PLANES OF HISTORICAL REALITY ARE CONFUSED WITH THE MYSTICAL AND THE LEGENDARY. SEVERAL SCENES ARE REPEATED FROM VARYING ANGLES IN A MANNER REMINISCENT OF THE BRAZILIAN DIRECTOR GLAUBER ROCHA. SEQUENCE TITLES PRODUCE ANOTHER KIND OF DISTANCING EFFECT.

IT IS ON THE AURAL LEVEL, HOWEVER, THAT THESE BRECHTIAN "ALIENATION EFFECTS" ARE THE MOST CONCERTED. THE FILM IS INTERMITTENTLY NARRATED (IN AN AUTHENTIC "COUNTRY" ACCENT AND IDIOM WHICH IS LOST ON THE NON-SPANISH-SPEAKING VIEWER) BY AN OLD MAN, SURVIVOR OF THE EVENTS WHICH HE RELATES, WHO APPEARS ON THE SCREEN AS CHIRIGUA (UNCREDITED), A YOUNG BOY. OFTEN THE EVENTS PORTRAYED ARE SIMULTANEOUSLY NARRATED BY HIM IN VOICE-OVER. SONG LYRICS ARE FREQUENTLY USED TO SPUR THE ACTION FORWARD. LITTIN OFTEN COMBINES THESE TWO AUDITORY DEVICES SO THAT WHAT IS SEEN ON THE SCREEN IS TWICE RECOUNTED—IN PROSE AS WELL AS IN SONG. THERE ARE SCENES, SUCH AS THE CONFRONTATION BETWEEN THE MAJOR AND THE SETTLERS TOWARD THE END OF THE FILM, WHICH OFFER THREE SEPARATE LEVELS OF ORAL INFORMATION: THE VOICE OF THE MAJOR PRESENTING HIS ULTIMATUM, THE NARRATOR'S AGED VOICE RECOUNTING WHAT HAPPENED, AND, OVER THESE, A CHORUS OF VOICES SETTING THE EVENTS TO MUSIC.

THE PROMISED LAND FREQUENTLY TAKES ON A SELF-CONSCIOUSLY ALLEGORICAL DIMENSION, SOMETIMES IN CONTRAST TO, SOMETIMES FUSING WITH, THE REALISTIC STRAIN OF THE NARRATIVE. DURING THEIR MARCH TO THE PROMISED VALLEY, THE MOTLEY BAND COMES UPON A TRAIN, A SYMBOLIC REMNANT OF THE WORLD THEY ARE LEAVING BEHIND. WELL-DRESSED PASSENGERS THROW FOOD AT THEM AND HASTILY CLOSE THEIR WINDOWS IN DISGUST. ONLY THE RIDERS IN AN OPEN BOXCAR (THE PETITE BOURGEOISIE AS OPPOSED TO THE HAUTE BOURGEOISIE OF THE COMPARTMENTS) GREET THEM KINDLY. JUAN DE DIOS (ANIBAL REYNA), THE ENGINEER, EXPLAINS THAT IT IS THE END OF THE LINE AND AS FAR AS THEY WILL GO, AND THE CAMERA REVEALS THAT THE TRACKS STOP SHORT IN OPEN GRASSLAND. THE GREAT LOCOMOTIVE OF THE BOURGEOISIE IS NOT SIMPLY TEMPORARILY STALLED, IT IN FACT HAS NOWHERE TO GO. ONLY THE ENGINEER DESERTS THE DEADENDED VEHICLE TO JOIN THE PILGRIMS.

The film's attempt to portray a mass protagonist is not entirely successful. The female characters are only stereotyped sketches. The ingenuousness of the narrator and his pal, though used as an ironic device, is never rounded into a fuller characterization. What remains is a trio of identifiable males: Jose Duran, Pin-Stripe, and the engineer Juan de Dios. Juan is irresponsible and opportunistic, a disruptive force in the settlement, returning for example from a foray into the surrounding area with a herd of stolen cattle. After the harvest, he solicits orders for store-bought personal goods from each settler, prompting Jose to accuse him of cultivating individual consumer interests at the expense of the needs of the entire group. At the mountain crossing, and again in Huique, Juan is the one who, impatient and uncomprehending, challenges Jose to turn back.

Pin-Stripe is the ideologue. It was he who plants the first seeds of socialism in Jose Duran's mind. Though he successfully organizes neighboring *campesinos* and teaches literacy to the settlers, he is also an incurable drunkard who fails to see the implications of the commercialism promoted by Juan de Dios and who confesses that his claims to an activist past with the great organizer Recabarren are false.

Jose is the true activist, the "natural" leader. Yet because he is indecisive at the crucial moment, because he clings to an unfounded faith in the backing of the army, he also fails. Incapable of initiating the action required by the historical moment, he can only react. Unlike the others, however, he returns as a hero in the popular imagination, galloping back through the final apocalyptic battle scenes. National patriot Arturo Prat is there too, brandishing his sword. In repeated sequences, they hand their weapons to Chirigua, soldier of the future generation.

WITH THE CYCLE OF DEATH AND REBIRTH, DESTRUCTION AND REGENERATION, THE FILM MIXES MYTHIC MOTIFS WITH REVOLUTIONARY IMPERATIVES. "THIS WAR IS STARTING NOW AND IT WILL NEVER END!" CRIES DURAN.

IT IS AT THIS FINAL POINT THAT THE POLITICS OF THE FILM SEEM MOST CONTRADICTORY. ONE OF THE LAST SCENES PRESENTS A SMOKE-FILLED TABLEAU IN WHICH MECHE (CARMEN BUENO) BLOODIED BUT NOW CROWNED, HOLDS JOSE'S BODY. THE OBVIOUS IMPLICATION OF THIS SCENE IS THAT JOSE IS A CHRIST FIGURE MARTYRED TO THE REVOLUTION. YET THE FILM HAS ALSO POSED A CRITIQUE OF JOSE'S INDECISIVE LEADERSHIP, FOR DESPITE HIS POLITICAL PROGRESSION, HE FALTERS AT THE CRUCIAL MOMENT. IT IS TO CRITICIZE JOSE'S FATAL HESITATION THAT CHIRIGUA, HALTING IN HIS NEW LITERACY, READS, "HISTORY DOES NOT FORGIVE THOSE REVOLUTIONARIES WHO VACILLATE JUST AT THE MOMENT WHEN IT IS POSSIBLE TO SEIZE POWER." LITTIN APPARENTLY WANTS BOTH TO FORGIVE JOSE AND TO ADMONISH OTHERS, ON THE VERGE OF MAKING THE SAME ERROR, WITH HIS CHARACTER'S EXAMPLE.

THE ADMONITION NEVER REACHED THE CHILEAN PUBLIC. SINCE *THE PROMISED LAND* NEVER FULFILLED ITS INTENDED FUNCTION AS A "POLITICAL ACTIVATOR" IN THE ARENA FOR WHICH IT WAS INTENDED, BY ITS DIRECTOR'S OWN STANDARDS IT CANNOT BE CONSIDERED A "REVOLUTIONARY" FILM. VIEWED IN CHILE AT THE INTENDED TIME, THE FILM'S TECHNICAL MASTERY (CINEMATOGRAPHER AFONSO BEATO'S SEEPING PANS WHICH UNIFY THE VALLEY OF PALMILLA, HIS LATERAL TRACKING SHOTS OF THE CORRUPT AND HAUGHTY FACES OF THE OLIGARCHY) WOULD HAVE BEEN FUSED WITH THE CONTEXTUAL URGENCY OF THE HISTORICAL MOMENT. VIEWED ELSEWHERE, *THE PROMISED LAND* BECOMES AN EXOTIC AND POTENTIALLY MYSTIFYING CULTURAL ARTIFACT, A COMPELLING CONFIGURATION OF THE POSSIBILITIES AND CONTRADICTIONS OF A HISTORICAL MOMENT WHICH WAS AS PRECARIOUS AS IT WAS PROMISING, SUSPENDED IN TIME.

AN INTERVIEW WITH RAOUL RUIZ [1980]

◊◊◊◊ DON RANVAUD

Don Ranvaud: A CERTAIN NUMBER OF VITAL CONTRADICTIONS BETWEEN THE DIREC-
TORS WHO WORKED WITHIN UNIDAD POPULAR HAVE BECOME A LOT CLEARER NOW
THAT YOU ARE ALL MAKING FILMS IN EXILE. GIVEN THAT EVEN THE LABEL "CINE
OF ALLENDE" IS MISLEADING, IS IT WRONG TO TRY TO SPEAK OF A CHILEAN CINEMA
IN EXILE?

Raoul Ruiz: ALLENDE'S CINE COMPRISED TEN FEATURE FILMS AND SOME EIGHTY SHORTS.
"CHILEAN CINE" IN EXILE HAS ALREADY PRODUCED AT LEAST FIVE TIMES MORE FILMS
THAN THOSE MADE DURING THE ALLENDE PERIOD. TWICE AS MANY FILMS WERE
MADE DURING THE FIRST THREE YEARS OF EXILE THAN DURING THE THREE YEARS
OF THE UNIDAD POPULAR. THIS IS A PARADOXICAL CIRCUMSTANCE WHICH I BELIEVE
IS UNIQUE IN THE HISTORY OF FILMS. IT IS NOT DUE ONLY TO THE FERTILITY OF
CHILEAN PRODUCERS BUT ALSO THE INTEREST WHICH CHILE ROUSED IN THE WHOLE
WORLD AS A SYMBOLIC EXAMPLE OF THE UNIVERSAL POLITICAL CRISIS. THE REASON
WHY CHILEANS ARE PRODUCING VERY DIFFERENT FILMS IS A NATURAL AND DIRECT
CONSEQUENCE OF THE FACT THAT THEY ARE NOW LIVING IN DIFFERENT COUN-
TRIES AND EACH ONE DEPENDS ON THE ECONOMIC MEANS AND SOCIAL
CHARACTERISTICS OF THE COUNTRY THEY ARE LIVING IN. ALTHOUGH LESS IMPOR-
TANT IN THIS RESPECT, POLITICAL DIFFERENCES DO EXIST, AND THESE INDIVIDUAL
DIFFERENCES ARE APPARENT IN THE FILMS PRODUCED AS WELL AS IN THE INTER-
PRETATION OF THE CHILEAN PROCESS. WE ARE TRYING TO UNDERSTAND THE
SIGNIFICANCE OF THE CRISIS OF LENINISM ON THE ONE HAND AND THE CRISIS
OF POLITICAL CINEMA ON THE OTHER; THE DISAPPEARANCE OF THE WHOLE SYM-
BOLIC SYSTEM WHICH WAS THE BASIS OF POLITICAL CINEMA IN THE 60'S IN THE
WHOLE WORLD, NOT ONLY IN CHILE. WE SHOULD NOT ATTRIBUTE TO THE DIREC-
TOR FULL RESPONSIBILITY FOR THE DECISIONS OF THE FILM WHEN WE TALK OF
FILMS GENERALLY; NOT IN ORDER TO AVOID RESPONSIBILITY BUT IN ORDER TO STATE

FACTS. THE HYPOTHESIS OF THE STOLEN PAINTING, THE SUSPENDED VOCATION, DIALOGUE OF EXILES, LA EXPROPIACION, ARE FILMS WHICH ARE COMPLETELY DIFFERENT YET IN ALL OF THEM THERE IS A KIND OF AGREEMENT BETWEEN TWO PARTS: ONE HALF IS ME, COMPLETELY; THE OTHER HALF IS THE SOCIAL MEDIUM IN WHICH THAT FILM WAS MADE POSSIBLE. THE FRENCH SOCIAL MEDIUM IS PARTICULARLY SENSITIVE TO A CERTAIN TYPE OF REFLECTION ON THE NATURE OF FILM AND REVEALING OF AN AESTHETIC SEARCH. THIS ASPECT PREDOMINATES THEREFORE, IN MY LAST FRENCH FILMS. WHEN I WAS IN CHILE I WAS AWARE OF A POLITICAL CONTROVERSY WHICH WAS DEEPLY FELT BY THE PEOPLE AND FELT COMPELLED TO MAKE CERTAIN TYPES OF FILM. LITTIN'S LAST FILM, AND FOR EXAMPLE MY OWN LAST FILM, CAN NO LONGER BE CONSIDERED CHILEAN FILMS. THE THEME ITSELF IS NO LONGER CHILEAN. METAPHORICALLY, IN A VERY GENERAL SENSE, IT COULD BE CHILEAN, SINCE CHILE ITSELF HAS BEEN A METAPHOR FOR OTHER THINGS.

DR: YOU HAVE IN A SENSE BEEN MARGINALIZED WITHIN THE CONTEXT OF UNIDAD POPULAR. CERTAIN DECISIONS LIKE SHOOTING THE PENAL COLONY AWAY FROM CHILE IN '71, WAS CRITICIZED, ALSO YOU DID NOT "FLAUNT" YOUR POSITION OF EXILE AND STARTED WORKING RIGHT AWAY IN VERY DIFFERENT CONTEXTS WITHOUT MANY PROBLEMS.

RR: POLITICAL CINEMA SUFFERED A CRISIS AND SOCIETY STARTED QUESTIONING MANY OF ITS ASPECTS. AT THE CENTER OF THE CRISIS IN THE FIELD OF CINEMA IS THE CRISIS OF THE LEFT, WHICH STARTED TEN YEARS AGO, AND WHICH EXTENDS MUCH FURTHER THAN THE SIMPLE LOSS OF POINTS OF REFERENCE. IT IS NO LONGER SIMPLY LENINISM OR MARXISM WHICH IS BEING QUESTIONED, WE ARE IN A STAGE IN WHICH THIS SEARCH IS GOING TO GENERATE MUCH MORE COMPLEX IDEOLOGY. LIMITING OUR DISCUSSION TO FILM WE CAN SAY THAT WE DON'T EVEN KNOW HOW WE SEE. THERE IS CONTROVERSY BETWEEN THE NATURALIST, NATIVIST, AND EMPIRICAL SCHOOLS AND THEORIES LIKE THOSE OF JACQUES MELER CONSTANTLY QUESTION THE DESCRIPTION OF WHAT IT IS THAT ACTUALLY HAPPENS WHEN WE SEE IT, AS WE DO NOT KNOW EXACTLY, AND THERE IS EVEN CONTROVERSY OVER THE MEANING OF PERSPECTIVE. ABOVE ALL THERE IS CONTROVERSY OVER THE POSSIBLE COMMUNICABILITY OF HUMAN GESTURES WHICH ARE FILMED AND WHICH WE SEE THROUGH FILM. UNDER THESE CONDITIONS THE REEXAMINATION AT ALL LEVELS IS NOT EXACTLY A LABORATORY TASK BUT RATHER, AN INDIVIDUAL SEARCH FOR THE MEANING OF SEEING, OF CINEMA, BY WHICH EXTENSION WE CAN QUESTION EVENTS IN THE POLITICAL FIELD. THE POLITICAL PROBLEM IN GENERAL TERMS, IS A PROBLEM OF REPRESENTATION. WE NEED REFERENCE POINTS, KEY WORDS, IDEAS AND GESTURES, CHARACTERS, FACES AND KEY SITUATIONS TO GUIDE OURSELVES THROUGH THIS LABYRINTH OF MOVEMENT, A LABYRINTH GENERATED BY THESE ENORMOUS MASS MOVEMENTS. TO STUDY THESE GESTURES INDEPENDENTLY FROM THEIR CONTEXT IN ORDER TO UNDERSTAND THEM BETTER INVOLVES DEEP REFLECTION ON ALL THAT IS HAPPENING. WHEN WE TALK OF THIS WE ARE TALKING OF THE

CRISIS TAKING PLACE TODAY AND WE ARE REFERRING TO THE STARTING POINT OF IT ALL WHICH WAS THE ALLENDE COUP. AT THIS MOMENT IT HAS A VERY DIFFERENT KIND OF POLITICAL PROJECTION TO THE ONE IT INITIALLY HAD. ORIGINALLY IT WAS GIVEN A CLASSICAL LENINIST INTERPRETATION: THE CHILEAN PEOPLE COULD NOT ARM THEMSELVES, THEREFORE THEY WERE DEFEATED. TODAY THE INTERPRETATION GIVEN IS INFINITELY MORE COMPLEX AND WORRYING: WE ARE FACING A CONSTANTLY GROWING MILITARIZATION IN ALL FIELDS, WHATEVER THE OFFICIAL IDEOLOGY OF THE COUNTRY. CHILE WAS THE STARTING POINT OF A POPULAR-CIVILIAN REVOLT. ANOTHER CASE WAS NICARAGUA AND NOW WE ARE SEEING A REVOLT IN IRAN. THESE ARE ALL CIVILIAN REVOLTS. WHEN I TALK ABOUT NICARAGUA AND IRAN I REFER TO THE REASONS FOR WHICH THESE REVOLTS TOOK PLACE. IN THEMSELVES THE REVOLTS ARE VERY DIFFERENT BUT IN ALL CASES THEY ARE MASS REVOLTS, EMPTY OF IDEOLOGY OR WITH A TEMPORARY IDEOLOGY, AND THIS IS VERY IMPORTANT. PREVIOUS REVOLTS, BUDAPEST, BERLIN, HAD BEEN OBVIOUSLY MANIPULATED BY THE SUPERPOWERS.

DR: YES, BUT IT IS EXTREMELY DANGEROUS TO MAKE A PARALLEL OF THIS KIND BETWEEN CHILE AND IRAN! THE REFERENCES ARE COMPLETELY DIFFERENT, EVEN BALMACEDA. . . .

RR: NICARAGUA, IRAN, AND HUNGARY ARE TOTALLY DISSIMILAR, BUT THERE IS A COMMON ELEMENT WHICH COMES TO LIGHT AND FORCES US TO REEXAMINE THE CHILEAN PROCESS, AND THAT IS THAT THEY ARE SIMILAR MASSES, ORGANIZED AT A VERY HIGH SPONTANEOUS LEVEL WHICH AT A GIVEN MOMENT OPPOSE ESTABLISHED POWER IN A PARADOXICAL MANNER, LIKE IN CHILE. THE ESSENTIAL ELEMENT IS THAT POWER IS IN THE HANDS NOT OF TECHNOCRATS BUT OF THE MASS AS A WHOLE, WHICH REALIZES THE TOTALITY OF ITS IDENTITY AND THAT OF ITS COUNTRY, AND THIS POWER DOES NOT PASS THROUGH THE HANDS OF MEDIATORS. PERHAPS I EXAGGERATE WHEN I SAY THAT CHILE BEGAN THIS PROCESS, IT'S NOT STRICTLY TRUE. WHAT HAPPENED IN CHILE WAS THAT MANY CONTRADICTIONS ADDED TO THE COMPLEXITY OF THE PROCESS AND THE NOTICEABLE ELEMENT TO EMERGE WAS MASS SPONTANEITY.

DR: WHAT CAN WE SAY WE HAVE LEARNED FROM THE CHILEAN LESSON?

RR: I BELIEVE THAT THE NUMBER OF PARADOXES TAKING PLACE IN THE WORLD TODAY FORCE US TO A MINIMUM OF MODESTY BEFORE ARRIVING AT CONCLUSIONS. IT IS EVIDENT, NONETHELESS, THAT IT WAS NOT THAT ALLENDE DID NOT MANAGE TO ELIMINATE THE CONTRADICTIONS; HE DID NOT WANT TO. THIS GESTURE OF NOT WANTING TO WAS INTERPRETED CRITICALLY TO BEGIN WITH, BUT IT CAN BE REINTERPRETED IN A POSITIVE WAY. ALLENDE ALWAYS WANTED TO GOVERN WITH AN OPPOSITION. HE DID NOT WANT TO ELIMINATE OR EXTERMINATE THE OPPOSITION, EITHER BY PEACEFUL OR VIOLENT MEANS, WHICH IS A DIFFICULT THING TO UNDERSTAND. ALLENDE MIGHT BE DESCRIBED AS A CLASSICAL SOCIAL DEMOCRATIC LEADER

WHO AT THE SAME TIME PUSHED A MASS MOVEMENT. IT IS THE COMBINATION OF THESE TWO FACTS WHICH WE HAVE TO TRY TO UNDERSTAND.

DR: WOULD YOU HAVE MADE THE SAME KINDS OF FILMS WITH THIS KNOWLEDGE?

RR: DIFFERENT, BECAUSE I AM NOW CONDITIONED BY TECHNIQUE. I CAN MAKE FILMS WITH IMPROVED TECHNIQUES HERE BUT AT THE SAME TIME I HAVE ALSO BEEN CONDITIONED. IN ONE SENSE I THINK I WOULD STILL MAKE THE SAME FILMS, I WOULD TRY AT LEAST TO PICK UP THE SAME LEVEL OF IRRESPONSIBILITY.

DR: IRRESPONSIBILITY IS A TERM YOU HAVE USED VERY OFTEN IN THE PAST. WHAT PRECISELY DO YOU MEAN BY THIS?

RR: GENERALLY SPEAKING, RESPONSIBILITY FOR AN ARTIST OR AN INTELLECTUAL FORCES HIM TO BECOME A SPOKESMAN. AS A SPOKESMAN HE BECOMES AUTOMATICALLY A FUNCTIONARY OF THE MINISTER OF DEFENSE. THESE DAYS I FEEL VERY PRO-CIVILIAN, VERY MUCH IN FAVOR OF ASSUMING RESPONSIBILITY FOR THE TOTALITY OF THE REALITY OF A NATION. IN THIS SENSE, IRRESPONSIBILITY MEANS NOT TAKING INTO ACCOUNT THE FINAL CONSEQUENCES, JUST TRYING TO WORK WITH REALITY IN ALL ITS RICHNESS. ONLY IN THIS WAY CAN YOU BECOME IMPREGNATED WITH THE RICHNESS OF REALITY AND NOT IMPOVERISH IT, WHICH IS WHAT WE NORMALLY DO, FILMMAKERS IN PARTICULAR.

DR: THE THEORY OF CULTURAL DEPENDENCY WHICH DOMINATES NOTIONS OF "ARTISTIC" PRODUCTION IN LATIN AMERICA CAN BE APPLIED TO YOUR WORK. IN A SENSE YOU HAVE BEEN (TOO) EASILY ABSORBED INTO THE TEXTURE OF THE CAPITAL OF LATIN AMERICAN CULTURE THAT IS PARIS.

RR: CULTURE IS ALWAYS FALSE. CULTURE IS A WAY OF SEPARATING YOURSELF FROM REALITY. THE GREATER THE DISTANCE FROM REALITY THE MORE RHETORICAL THE CULTURE. FOR EXAMPLE, IF YOU HAVE NOT BEEN BORN INTO AND REARED IN A POPULAR LATIN AMERICAN CULTURE, YOU WILL NEVER BE ABLE TO ASSIMILATE IT. THAT CULTURE IS NOT ACCESSIBLE TO ANYBODY BUT TO THOSE WHO HAVE BEEN BORN INTO IT. I MEAN POPULAR CULTURE IN AN ANTHROPOLOGICAL SENSE. AN OFFICIAL CULTURE, BOURGEOIS, DOMINANT, CULTURE WITH A CAPITAL C, IS HIGHLY RHETORICAL AND CAN BE LEARNED LATER IN LIFE. YOU CAN'T TALK LIKE THE PEOPLE IN MY NEIGHBORHOOD AND NEVER WILL. NEVERTHELESS I CAN, ALMOST AT THE AGE OF FORTY, READ DESCARTES FOR THE FIRST TIME AND UNDERSTAND IT. THIS IS THE ADVANTAGE OF OFFICIAL CULTURE, WHICH IN THIS SENSE I CONSIDER IS MORE DEMOCRATIC THAN POPULAR CULTURE. CULTURAL IMPERIALISM INVOLVES A SERIES OF PHENOMENA WHICH INTEREST ME A LOT. LIKE ALL LATIN AMERICANS I HAVE FEARED IT, LOVED IT, AND SOMETIMES FOUGHT IT IN A MECHANICAL FASHION. IT IS NOT EUROPE WHICH INFLUENCES US, IT IS PRIMARILY THE UNITED STATES. I REMEMBER WELL COMING OUT OF THE CINEMA ON A SUNDAY AFTERNOON WITH THE SENSATION OF FRUSTRATION BECAUSE I WAS NOT GOING OUT INTO AN

AMERICAN CITY, THE FRUSTRATION OF NOT BEING FAIR, OF NOT EATING HAM-BURGERS, OF NOT HAVING BLOND PARENTS. THIS I REMEMBER AS THE MOST FRUSTRATING ASPECT OF CULTURAL IMPERIALISM, A FRUSTRATION SHARED BY ALL OF THE PEOPLE OF THE THIRD WORLD. COMPARED TO IT, EUROPEAN CULTURE WAS ALMOST LIBERATING. THE FIRST IMPACT OF EUROPEAN CULTURE I RECEIVED WAS THROUGH FILMS, SHOCKING FILMS IN BLACK AND WHITE AND WITH UGLY PEOPLE IN THEM. INITIALLY THIS SHOCKED ME, BUT EVENTUALLY THIS BECAME A POSITIVE IMPRESSION. I AM CONVINCED THAT THE CHILEAN LEFT WOULD NOT EXIST HAD IT NOT BEEN FOR DOSTOYEVSKY. I BELIEVE TWO MAJOR FACTORS CREATED THE MEN OF THE LEFT OF MY GENERATION. ONE WAS DOSTOYEVSKY AND THE OTHER THE ANTI-COMMUNIST BOOKS PUBLISHED BY THE AMERICANS AND DISTRIBUTED IN CHILE, IN WHICH THE COMMUNISTS WERE SHOWN TO BE IMMORAL INDIVIDUALS WHO BELIEVED IN FREE-LOVE, WHO LED ADVENTUROUS LIVES, THEY WERE ALL SPIES AND WANTED TO TRANSFORM THE WORLD. THIS DESTRUCTION APPEARED TO BE SUFFICIENTLY TERRIBLE TO THE AMERICANS BUT IT PROVOKED ENOR-MOUS DESIRES IN US TO BE LIKE THE BADDIES OF THE NOVELS. I WOULD NOT LIKE TO GIVE THE IMPRESSION THAT I AM SIMPLY PLAYING RATHER FRIVOLOUS GAMES, ON THE CONTRARY I HAVE THOUGHT ABOUT THIS A LOT. AT ONE STAGE I WANTED TO CREATE A SERIES OF CHARACTERS WHICH WOULD TYPIFY THE LATIN AMERICAN INTELLECTUAL IN RELATION TO THE POWER OF CULTURE. IN THIS CONTEXT I SEE AT LEAST THREE TYPIFICATIONS OF THE LATIN AMERICAN INTELLECTUAL. IN THE FIRST PLACE LAUTARO, A CHILEAN INDIAN WHO FIGHTS AGAINST THE INVASION OF FOREIGNERS AND UNDERSTANDING THAT HE DOESN'T HAVE THE NECESSARY WEAPONS COPIES THE STYLE OF FIGHTING OF THE INVADER. HE RAISES HIS PEOPLE IN REVOLT AND WINS, BUT IN A DEEPER SENSE THE INVASION WAS SUCCESSFUL BECAUSE THE INDIAN CULTURE WAS PENETRATED BY THE FOREIGNER. THE SECOND SYMBOLIC CHARACTER IS JIMMY BUTTON, WHOM CAPTAIN FITZROY KIDNAPPED IN SOUTHERN CHILE. JIMMY BUTTON BELONGED TO ONE OF THE MOST PRIMITIVE TRIBES IN THE WORLD, WHOSE VOCABULARY CONSISTED OF SIXTY WORDS, WHO WERE CANNIBALS AND WHOSE CULTURE WAS REDUCED TO A MINIMUM. HE IS KID-NAPPED BY FITZROY AND IN A PERIOD OF TWO MONTHS LEARNS ENGLISH PERFECTLY AS WELL AS OTHER LANGUAGES, BECOMES CONSCIOUS OF HIS IDENTITY WHEN HE IS GIVEN A MIRROR AND IN ENGLAND INTEGRATES WITH THE PURITAN WORLD, BECOMING A PROTESTANT. HE ACHIEVES MUCH MORE THAN HAD BEEN EXPECTED OF HIM. HE IS THEN TAKEN BACK TO CHILE AND THE SIMPLE CONTACT WITH HIS PEOPLE MAKES HIM FORGET ALL THAT HE HAS LEARNED IN A VERY SHORT TIME. THAT IS, HE COULD COMMUNICATE WITH HIS PEOPLE ONLY IF HE FORGOT ALL THAT HE HAD LEARNED. THE THIRD IS VALDEROMAR, THE OSCAR WILDE OF THE IN-DIAN, WHOSE RELATIONSHIP WITH THE CIVILIZED WORLD IS MUCH MORE USUAL IN OUR INTELLECTUALS. HE IS THE MAN USED BY THE CIVILIZED WORLD IN ORDER TO EMPHASIZE THEIR FEELINGS OF SUPERIORITY. HE IS THE MAN WHO IS INVITED TO BANQUETS SO THAT THE SOCIETY OF LIMA, PERU, CAN LAUGH.

DR: What you said earlier made me think of "Notes on or from the (New York) Underground" . . . but seriously, your French films seem to bridge a gap between the popular and cultural traditions not only of Chile but of larger Latin American issues . . . similar perhaps to Borges (especially *Hypothesis*) and Vargas Llosa.

RR: I don't know if Borges is a typical example of an intellectual. He is rather a model. His political stance is an exemplary case: he utilizes paradox as a way of evading commitment to political tyranny suffered by his generation.

DR: And Vargas Llosa?

RR: Vargas Llosa is not among my saints. I do not see him as typical. As far as I know he's never been a political exile, he simply lives abroad in order to write about his country from a distance.

DR: There has been another form of dependency established in recent years for Latin American and especially Chilean filmmakers. Cuba and Mexico with their vast differences are practically shaping the "new" cinema.

RR: They were the only ones who could help, and their action was very positive. Cuba is a very monolithic country, where everything is produced in an organic way and it is not surprising that films made in Cuba always correspond to the general Cuban political line. Mexico does not impose an ideology so directly, but it does impose one of the fundamental aspects of all State cinema, which is that films must be impressive and monumental. Films made in Cuba and Mexico are different, but I think they are two aspects of what I describe as State cinema, which shows the official face of a country. With regards to the Third World you often find the best artists collaborating with the State to produce official art. Some time ago I believed this to be an excellent thing, but today I think it's terrible, although I haven't worked out my argument sufficiently to propound a thesis on the subject.

DR: Would you like to work in Cuba?

RR: I don't like to close any doors but I don't see it happening in the immediate future, although things do change so quickly.

DR: You have often talked of the relationship between actor and camera. In *Hypothesis* we find an inversion of technique from your previous work. The actor seems to be almost in complete control. Could you relate this to the linguistic frame of reference you made through *El Realismo Socialista* and then *Dialogue of Exiles*?

RR: THE SUBJECT MATTER OF THE FILMS IS ABSOLUTELY DIFFERENT. IN ONE I WAS MAK-
ING A CINEMA OF FOUNDATION, TRYING TO FORMALIZE GESTURES WHICH HAVE
NOT YET BEEN SEEN ON FILM, TRYING TO INVENT THE COUNTRY THROUGH FILM.
THE ENRICHMENT OF THE RELATIONSHIP CAMERA-ACTOR SEEMED TO ME TO BE VERY
IMPORTANT. LATER ON I MADE *DIALOGUE OF EXILES* TRYING TO PRODUCE A
POLITICAL FILM IN THE MOST ELEMENTARY SENSE OF THE WORD. SUBSEQUENT
CRITICISM LED ME TO QUESTION THE SIGNIFICANCE OF VISUAL REPRESENTATION,
HOW THIS KIND OF SYMBOLIC REPRESENTATION SHOULD BE SEEN AND BECAME IN-
TERESTED IN SOCIALIST REALISM, WHICH HAS ITS ROOTS IN OFFICIAL PAINTINGS IN
ART GALLERIES OF THE 19TH CENTURY. THIS IN TURN LED ME TO STUDY EVERYTHING
RELATED TO COMMITTED, OFFICIAL ART, ART AS AN EXPRESSION OF THE STATE. IN
THE SUSPENDED VOCATION I WORKED ON ALL THESE ASPECTS, SEARCHING FOR
A MEANING IN A CORRECT LINE. THE FILM IS BASICALLY TWO FILMS IN ONE, TWO
VERSIONS IN ONE FILM, AND THE MONTAGE ATTEMPTS TO GIVE THE CORRECT
UNITARIAN VERSION OF THE CHURCH. MY INTEREST IN THE CHURCH DATES FROM
THIS PERIOD, WHEN I WAS TRYING TO GAIN PERSPECTIVE ON MY POLITICAL MILITANCY.
THE GOALS OF THESE FILMS IS THEREFORE VERY DIFFERENT. IN ONE FILM, AN IMAGE
OF A COUNTRY WAS BEING CREATED, FOUNDED ON BLOCKS OF REALITY, MUCH
LIKE THE NEOREALISTS DID. IN THE OTHER I WAS QUESTIONING THE SYMBOLISM
OF SPONTANEOUS MATTER.

I TALKED ELSEWHERE ABOUT TWO TYPES OF SPECTATORS, THOSE WHO ALLOW
THEMSELVES TO BE CARRIED ALONG AND THOSE WHOSE PLEASURE LIES IN FINDING
FAULT.

*. . . (AT THIS POINT THE DIRECTOR STANDS UP, WORDS BECOME INAUDIBLE,
THE INTERVIEWER WALKS IN THE OPPOSITE DIRECTION GATHERING SOME PAPERS.
THE TAPE RUNS ON FILLING THE GAP OF THE STOLEN CONVERSATION. WHAT FOLLOWS
IS AN UNEDITED RECORDING, BUT AS SUCH IT IS ONLY A HYPOTHESIS OF WHAT
MAY NOT HAVE BEEN SAID. YET.)*

I DON'T BELIEVE, EVEN IF THERE IS A CLASSIC MARXIST-LENINIST ATTITUDE IN
CHILE, THAT ANY OF US KNEW EXACTLY WHAT IT MEANT. I DON'T BELIEVE THAT
ANY OF US HAD AN IMPORTANT BASIC UNDERSTANDING OF MARXISM-LENINISM
AND THIS IS APPARENT IN OUR SUBSEQUENT INTERPRETATIONS, WHICH HAVE BEEN
INTUITIVE AND MARKED BY FRAGMENTED THEORIZATION. I DON'T BELIEVE WE HAVE
TRIED TO RE-EVALUATE INTELLECTUAL ACTIVITY AT A PRACTICAL THEORETICAL LEVEL.
WHAT THEORETICAL WORK I HAVE DONE MYSELF HAS BEEN AT A VERY FUNDAMEN-
TALIST LEVEL. I KNOW THAT THERE ARE MANY PITFALLS THAT I MUST WATCH OUT
FOR, BUT FOR THE TIME BEING I'M PREPARED TO CONTINUE WITH THIS APPROACH.

I WOULD LIKE TO SAY THAT MOST OF US, AT LEAST THOSE OF US WHO ARE IN EUROPE, HAVE SUFFERED AN EXPERIENCE OF SHOCK WHICH IS VERY IMPORTANT. WE HAVE FOUND OURSELVES IN A POSITION OF INVISIBLE MEN WITH REGARDS TO CLASS. WE ALL BELONGED, MORE OR LESS, TO A CHILEAN PROGRESSIVE PETIT-BOURGEOISIE WHICH HAD PRODUCED ITS OWN INTELLECTUALS, A PHENOMENON ENCOUNTERED ONLY IN CHILE, ARGENTINA, AND URUGUAY. WE KNEW WE BELONGED, WE WERE FAMILIAR WITH THE ROLES WE HAD TO PLAY. SUDDENLY WE WERE IN EUROPE, SUBMERGED IN THE NOTION THAT WE WERE FOREIGNERS, PEOPLE WHO DIDN'T SPEAK THE LANGUAGE PROPERLY, AND THIS GAVE US THE STRANGE SENSATION OF BEING INVISIBLE MEN, OF NOT BELONGING TO ANY SOCIAL CLASS. THIS HAS PARTICULARLY AFFECTED MEMBERS OF THE CHILEAN LEFT WHO BELONGED TO A HIGHER SOCIAL CLASS, WHO SUDDENLY FOUND THEY WERE BEING CONFUSED WITH WORKERS AND MEMBERS OF THE PETIT-BOURGEOISIE. TO A FRENCHMAN OUR ACCENTS ARE ALL THE SAME. BUT WE HAVE ALL LOST THE CAPACITY TO COMMUNICATE FULLY, TO TRANSMIT SUBTLETY. AT THE SAME TIME WE GAINED CLASS MOBILITY AND SOME OF US, FROM A LOWER SOCIAL CLASS, FIND OURSELVES OCCUPYING IMPORTANT POSITIONS. THIS HAS PRODUCED STRONG REACTIONS AND SOME RATHER HYSTERICAL THEORIES, BUT THERE IS NO DOUBT THAT IT IS A PHENOMENON WHICH HAS AFFECTED ALL CHILEANS GREATLY. I WOULD SAY THAT ALL THIS HAS BEEN DUE EXCLUSIVELY TO LANGUAGE, IT IS NOT RELATED TO BEHAVIOR OR HABITS AND IT INTRIGUES ME VERY MUCH.

TRANSLATED BY CHRISTINA WELLER

IMAGES OF EXILE: TWO FILMS BY RAOUL RUIZ [1987]

RICHARD PEÑA

IT'S REFRESHING TO HAVE A CHANCE TO BEGIN THINKING ABOUT THE WORK OF FILMMAKER RAOUL RUIZ WITHIN THE CONTEXT OF "LATIN AMERICAN CINEMA," NOW THAT HIS WORK HAS BEEN SUITABLY SCRUTINIZED, IN OTHER STUDIES FROM VANTAGE POINTS RANGING FROM SURREALISM TO POST-MODERN AESTHETICS. THE WORK OF RUIZ, TO MY MIND, RE-ADDRESSED A NUMBER OF IMPORTANT ISSUES WHICH HAD BEGUN TO BE EXPLORED IN THE SIXTIES AND EARLY SEVENTIES BY A NUMBER OF LATIN AMERICAN FILMMAKERS, BUT TO WHICH CHANGING POLITICAL TIDES IN THE SEVENTIES PUT A PREMATURE HALT. IT'S A FAMILIAR IRONY, PERHAPS, THAT THE MOST VITAL LATIN AMERICAN CINEMA BEING CREATED TODAY IS EMERGING FROM EUROPE.

TO BEGIN WITH, WE CAN ASK, "WHO IS RAOUL RUIZ?" ANYONE WITH EVEN A PASSING FAMILIARITY WITH CONTEMPORARY FILM LITERATURE WOULD HAVE SEEN HIS NAME A DOZEN TIMES OVER THE PAST DECADE, A RISING NOTORIETY WHICH CULMINATED IN A SPECIAL ISSUE OF *CAHIERS DU CINEMA* DEVOTED TO RUIZ'S WORK IN 1983. YET FOR AN AUTHOR TO BE INVISIBLE, TO BE UNDER WRAPS, SO TO SPEAK, IS VERY MUCH PART OF THE RUIZIAN AESTHETIC. BORN IN PUNTO MONTT, CHILE, IN 1941, RUIZ GREW UP IN A MIDDLE-CLASS FAMILY; HIS FATHER FOR MOST OF HIS YOUTH WAS EMPLOYED AS A SHIP CAPTAIN, A FACT THAT WILL COME AS NO SURPRISE TO THOSE FAMILIAR WITH HIS FILMS. AFTER STUDIES IN THEOLOGY AND LAW AT THE UNIVERSITY OF SANTIAGO, RUIZ LEFT SCHOOL TO DEVOTE HIMSELF FULL TIME TO WRITING, THANKS TO A FORD FOUNDATION GRANT RECEIVED IN 1962. HIS FIRST LITERARY EFFORTS WERE IN THEATER, AND BY HIS OWN ESTIMATE HE'D WRITTEN WELL OVER ONE HUNDRED PLAYS BEFORE MOVING INTO CINEMA.

IN 1964, RUIZ WENT TO FILM SCHOOL IN SANTA FE, ARGENTINA, AT THE PROGRAM RUN BY FERNANDO BIRRI, AN ARGENTINE DOCUMENTARIST AND ONE OF THE MOST IMPORTANT IDEOLOGUES OF THE "NEW LATIN AMERICAN CINEMA." RUIZ LEFT AFTER A YEAR, CLAIMING THAT HE "HAD TO FORGET EVERYTHING THEY TAUGHT ME," AND RETURNED TO CHILE. SHORTLY AFTER HIS RETURN, HE FELL IN WITH A GROUP OF INTELLECTUALS AND CINEPHILES WHO WOULD FORM THE

NUCLEUS OF THE "NEW CHILEAN CINEMA" OF THE LATE SIXTIES—FUTURE DIREC-
TORS SUCH AS MIGUEL LITTIN, PEDRO CHASKELL, ALDO FRANCIA AND OTHERS,
WHO WERE HOPING TO CREATE A CINEMA IN THE SPIRIT OF THE BRAZILIAN CINEMA
NOVO OF THE SAME PERIOD. HIS FIRST FEATURE, *TRES TIGRES TRISTES*—NO RELA-
TION TO THE GUILLERMO CABRERA INFANTE NOVEL OF THE SAME NAME—WAS
COMPLETED IN 1967; RUIZ RECALLS THAT THE SAME CAMERA USED FOR THAT FILM
WAS USED SIMULTANEOUSLY FOR LITTIN'S *THE JACKAL OF NAHUERLTERO* AND FRAN-
CIA'S *VALPARAISO, VALPARAISO*. POLITICALLY, RUIZ JOINED THE SOCIALIST PARTY,
THEN ALLIED WITH ALLENDE'S POPULAR FRONT. DURING THE ALLENDE YEARS,
HE WORKED CLOSELY WITH CHILE FILMS, THE STATE FILM AGENCY, ON A NUMBER
OF FILMS AND TELEVISION PROGRAMS, ALTHOUGH SEVERAL OF HIS FILMS WERE
ATTACKED AT THE SAME TIME FOR BEING "DIVISIVE" AND "OBSCURE."

FOLLOWING ALLENDE'S OVERTHROW, RUIZ FLED TO EUROPE, EVENTUALLY SET-
TLING IN FRANCE. THE SHEER QUANTITY OF HIS OUTPUT SINCE 1974 IS SIMPLY
STAGGERING; TO DATE, RUIZ HAS COMPLETED WELL OVER SEVENTY FEATURE FILMS,
SHORTS AND VIDEOS SINCE HIS ARRIVAL IN EUROPE. IN 1985, FOR EXAMPLE, HE
COMPLETED FOUR FEATURE FILMS, THREE ONE-HOUR CHILDREN'S FILMS, TWO
CHAPTERS, EACH AN HOUR LONG, OF A SERIAL, PLUS SEVERAL SHORTS. TO COM-
PLICATE MATTERS, IN AUGUST, 1985, RUIZ BECAME DIRECTOR OF THE MAISON
DE CULTURE IN LE HAVRE, FRANCE, WHERE HE HOPES TO PRODUCE FILM, VIDEO
AND STAGE PROJECTS FOR FIGURES SUCH AS MANOEL DE OLIVEIRA AND SERGEI
PARAJANOV.

TO BEGIN ASSESSING RUIZ'S WORK SINCE HIS DEPARTURE FROM CHILE, ONE
MUST PLACE IT WITHIN PERHAPS ITS MOST IMPORTANT CONTEXT: THAT OF THE
CHILEAN "CINEMA IN EXILE." SINCE 1973, IF WE INCLUDE BOTH FEATURE FILMS
AND SHORTS MADE BY CHILEAN FILMMAKERS ACTIVE BEFORE AND DURING ALLENDE'S
REGIME, AND THOSE WHO STARTED WORK ONLY AFTER ENTERING EXILE, THE TOTAL
OUTPUT OF FILMS BY EXILED CHILEANS WOULD TOTAL OVER 250—FAR MORE FILMS,
IN FACT, THAN WERE PRODUCED IN CHILE FROM 1896 TO 1973. THIS REPRESENTS,
PERHAPS, A UNIQUE PHENOMENON IN FILM HISTORY: A NATIONAL CINEMA PRO-
DUCED, FOR THE MOST PART, OUTSIDE OF NATIONAL BOUNDARIES, A NATIONAL
CINEMA CHARACTERIZED OR DEFINED BY THE CONDITIONS OF EXILE. ALTHOUGH
WE CAN SPEAK OF OTHER EXILE EXPERIENCES IN FILM HISTORY—SUCH AS THAT OF
THE RUSSIAN EXPATRIATES OF THE TWENTIES, OR WITH REGARDS TO THE WORK
OF SEVERAL CONTEMPORARY POLISH FILMMAKERS—FOR NO OTHER NATIONAL
CINEMA HAS THE CONDITION OF EXILE BEEN SO DECISIVE AN EXPERIENCE.

THE FILMS OF THE CHILEAN CINEMA IN EXILE HAVE BEEN MADE IN MANY DIF-
FERENT COUNTRIES AND IN MANY DIFFERENT LANGUAGES—IN CUBA, MEXICO,
THE U.S., CANADA, FRANCE, HOLLAND, BULGARIA, THE SOVIET UNION, AND
OTHER UNLIKELY SPOTS—YET THERE ARE CERTAIN GENERAL TENDENCIES TO BE FOUND
IN THESE DIVERSE WORKS BY AS MANY AS PERHAPS FORTY DIFFERENT FILMMAKERS.
THE EARLIEST FILMS TENDED TO BE PREOCCUPIED WITH THE SPECIFICS OF THE CHILEAN

NATIONAL EXPERIENCE, OFTEN BEING CHRONICLES OF THE ALLENDE YEARS OR THEIR IMMEDIATE AFTERMATH; RUIZ'S CONTROVERSIAL *DIALOGUE OF EXILES*, PRODUCED IN FRANCE IN 1974, IS PERHAPS HIS ONLY WORK ILLUSTRATIVE OF THIS TENDENCY; OTHER EXAMPLES MIGHT BE HELVIO SOTO'S *IT'S RAINING IN SANTIAGO* OR PATRICIO GUZMAN'S *THE BATTLE OF CHILE*.

A SECOND TENDENCY WOULD BE THE ADOPTION OF A KIND OF CRITICAL ATTITUDE TOWARDS ONE'S HOST COUNTRY, WITH A CONSTANT EMPHASIS ON THE FILMMAKER'S POSITION AS AN OUTSIDER. CERTAINLY RUIZ'S TELEVISION WORK, INCLUDING *HYPOTHESIS OF THE STOLEN PAINTING* AND *OF GREAT EVENTS AND ORDINARY PEOPLE*, IS EXEMPLARY OF THIS, AS ARE DOCUMENTARIES BY MARILU MALLET, JAIME BARRIOS AND VALERIA SARMIENTO.

FINALLY, A THIRD TENDENCY COULD BE DEFINED AS A PREOCCUPATION WITH A SEARCH FOR PERSONAL IDENTITY, WITH ESTABLISHING THE CONDITIONS FOR INDIVIDUALITY. WORKS BY LEONARDO DE LA BARRA AND SERGIO CASTILLA POWERFULLY ILLUSTRATE THIS MOST RECENT TENDENCY, AS WELL AS DO THE MAJOR FEATURE FILMS RUIZ HAS DIRECTED SINCE 1981, FILMS SUCH AS *THE TOP OF THE WHALE*, *THE THREE CROWNS OF THE SAILOR*, *CITY OF PIRATES* AND *THE SLEEPWALKERS OF THE PONT D'ALMA*.

BEGINNING IN 1977, RUIZ WORKED ALMOST EXCLUSIVELY FOR THE FRENCH INSTITUT NATIONAL DE LA COMMUNICATION AUDIOVISUELLE, OR INA, UNTIL THE SUCCESS OF *THE THREE CROWNS OF THE SAILOR* (1983, ALSO PRODUCED BY INA), ENABLED HIM TO DEVOTE HIMSELF FULL TIME TO FEATURE FILMS. DURING THESE YEARS WORKING FOR INA, RUIZ PRODUCED A LARGE NUMBER OF WORKS IN BOTH FILM AND VIDEO IN A VARIETY OF FORMATS, WORKS RAGING FROM 3 MINUTE EXPERIMENTAL *TELETESTS* TO FEATURE-LENGTH WORKS SUCH AS *THE SUSPENDED VOCATION*. FAR AND AWAY HIS TWO BEST KNOWN PRODUCTIONS FROM THIS "INA PERIOD," EXCLUDING *THE THREE CROWNS OF THE SAILOR*, WERE THE 1978 *THE HYPOTHESIS OF THE STOLEN PAINTING* AND THE 1979 *OF GREAT EVENTS AND ORDINARY PEOPLE*. BOTH WORKS ARE INCISIVE CRITIQUES OF TELEVISION FORMS AND NARRATIVE STRUCTURES, AS WELL AS DEEPLY AFFECTING MEDITATIONS ON THE EXILE EXPERIENCE.

MADE FOR THE FRENCH TELEVISION SERIES *CAMERA JE*, *HYPOTHESIS* BEGAN AS A PROPOSAL BY RUIZ TO MAKE A FILM ON THE AESTHETIC THEORIES OF FRENCH THEORIST AND NOVELIST PIERRE KLOSSOWSKI; ACCORDING TO RUIZ, SOON AFTER AGREEING TO WORK ON THE FILM, KLOSSOWSKI SOMEWHAT MYSTERIOUSLY DECIDED TO LEAVE PARIS AND GO ON VACATION. LEFT WITH A CREW AND A BUDGET, YET NO CLEAR SCRIPT, RUIZ HASTILY ASSEMBLED WHAT HE WOULD LATER TERM "A FICTION ABOUT THEORY," IN WHICH SEVERAL OF KLOSSOWSKI'S IDEAS, ESPECIALLY THOSE RELATING TO THE EFFECT OF THE USE OF *TABLEAUX VIVANT* IN NINETEENTH CENTURY PAINTING, COULD BE EXPLICATED.

AS A VOICE-OVER NARRATION READS VARIOUS CONFLICTING COMMENTARIES ON THE WORK OF AN OBSCURE PAINTER, TONNERE, THE CAMERA GLIDES OVER

A GROUP OF SIX RATHER UNREMARKABLE GENRE PAINTINGS, RANDOMLY DISPLAYED IN A LARGE HALL. AT POINTS IN THE NARRATION, A MAN, SEEN MOVING BETWEEN THE PAINTINGS, ANNOUNCES THE SOURCES OF THE COMMENTARIES BEING CITED; HE IS THE COLLECTOR, A DAPPER, SIXTY-ISH LOOKING GENTLEMAN. AFTER HAVING BRIEFLY VIEWED THE WORKS, WE ARE TOLD BY THE COLLECTOR WHAT IS MOST REMARKABLE ABOUT THEM: WHEN FIRST EXHIBITED, THEY SEEMED TO HAVE TOUCHED OFF AN ENORMOUS SCANDAL, WHICH EVENTUALLY BROUGHT IN THE POLICE AND FORCED TONNERE TO FLEE FRANCE FOR ITALY. HOW COULD SUCH WORKS, SEEM-INGLY BANAL, ACADEMIC PAINTINGS, CAUSE SUCH EVENTS TO TRANSPIRE? THE COL-LECTOR THEN PROCEEDS TO EXPLAIN HOW THE MEANING OF THE PAINTINGS CAN ONLY BE UNDERSTOOD THROUGH THE EXISTENCE OF A SEVENTH PAINTING, ONCE AN INTEGRAL PART OF THE SERIES BUT NOW LOST. RE-CREATING THE VARIOUS SCENES DEPICTED IN THE PAINTINGS THROUGH THE USE OF ACTUAL FIGURES IN *TABLEAUX VIVANT*, THE COLLECTOR ATTEMPTS TO UNRAVEL THE VARIOUS MYSTERIES IN THE WORKS—THE BIZARRE LIGHTING SCHEMA, THE GROUPINGS OF FIGURES, THE THEOLOGICAL REFERENCES—YET ALL HIS EXPLANATIONS HINGE ON THE ACCEPTANCE OF THE MISSING SEVENTH PAINTING, WHOSE EXISTENCE THE COLLECTOR CAN'T PROVE.

Hypothesis of the Stolen Painting

Stills from *Hypothesis of the Stolen Painting*

With the casual but supremely well-informed manner of the Collector, and frequent interruptions by the off-screen narrator often disputing the logic of the Collector's observations, *Hypothesis* is an often hilarious parody of the kind of "sophisticated" art documentaries typified on American television by the work of Kenneth Clark or Robert Hughes. Yet Ruiz's construction of the mystery of Tonnere evokes the most basic process of cinematic reception: how images are ordered and their meaning derived. Without a knowledge of the codes present in the paintings, codes apparently well understood by nineteenth century Parisians who found the works scandalous, the paintings remain simply repositories of dead symbols. After announcing his final conclusion—that the paintings represent various stages of a forbidden pagan ritual—even the Collector admits that it's not really convincing. The power of the images remains not in their meaning, but the elusiveness of that meaning.

Ruiz's final sequence has an almost nightmarish quality to it; as the courteous Collector leads us out of his home, the camera glides past all the figures, still motionless, from the *tableaux vivant*, implying that the Collector will forever be trapped in a world full of symbols whose meaning can't be deciphered. That realization, especially after the remarkably ingenious, even if unsuccessful, historical detective work witnessed in the previous hour, gives *Hypothesis* a haunting, poignant quality that allows it to transcend the limits of a mere formal exercise. As an exile, Ruiz, like the Collector, had been thrust into a world full of symbols he can't fully comprehend, as his knowledge of the codes for those symbols is imperfect or incomplete. "Meaning," as such, becomes seen as a jealously and vigorously guarded institution, visualized in *Hypothesis* through the military-looking figures who seem to be patrolling the corridors filled with *tableaux vivant*.

British critic Ian Christie has claimed that the approach found in Ruiz's television work of this period alternates between parody and literalism; if *Hypothesis* succinctly exemplifies the former, *Of Great Events And Ordinary People* is illustrative of the later approach. Conceived (by INA) as a part of a series of films on the 1978 French presidential elections—with this Ruiz contribution meant to represent a foreigner's perspective on the process—*Of Great Events* becomes instead a meditation on the creation of political documentaries, and the implications of the form itself. It is in the "standardness" of the assignment, in the existence of a clear set of precedents for the kind of film which INA imagined Ruiz would make, that the underlying assumptions of ideology burst through; not through a deconstruction, but simply through attempting to follow the premises of the form itself to their logical conclusion.

THE FILM BEGINS WITH A VOICE-OVER ANNOUNCEMENT ABOUT THE ASSIGN-MENT TO MAKE A FILM ON THE UPCOMING FRENCH ELECTIONS BASED AROUND THE ATTITUDES AND RESPONSES OF THOSE WITHIN RUIZ'S OWN NEIGHBORHOOD. QUESTIONS, USUALLY PUT FORTH BY AN ON-SCREEN NARRATOR (A CHILEAN FRIEND OF RUIZ), ELICIT INFORMATION ABOUT PEOPLE'S LIVING ARRANGEMENTS, THEIR OCCUPATIONS, AND GRADUALLY THEIR POLITICAL PREFERENCES. GRADUALLY, QUES-TIONS BEGIN TO EMERGE: IS WHAT THE NEWSPAPER VENDOR IS REVEALING MORE INTERESTING THAN WHAT HE MIGHT BE CONCEALING? SINCE THE NEIGHBORHOOD BAR REFUSES TO ALLOW RUIZ TO FILM THERE, WILL ANY OTHER BAR DO JUST AS WELL? IS IT THE INFORMATION RECEIVED, OR MERELY THE MOTIF, "INTERVIEW IN A LOCAL BAR," THAT IS REALLY IMPORTANT?

THE PROCESS OF INTERROGATION BECOMES WEDDED INTO THE VERY STRUC-TURE OF THE FILM ITSELF, AS RUIZ DIVIDES IT INTO CHAPTERS, EACH ONE REPRESEN-TING THE WORK OF A DIFFERENT DAY; THE OBJECTIVITY OF THE NEWS DOCUMENTARY IS THUS REPLACED BY THE SUBJECTIVITY OF THE DIARY FORM. THE QUESTIONS POS-ED BY THE OFF-SCREEN NARRATION BECOME INCREASINGLY AUTOBIOGRAPHICAL: DO THOSE QUESTIONED REALIZE THAT THE FILMMAKER IS NOT FRENCH? THE FILM-ING OF ACTUAL POLLING PLACES AND ELECTION BOOTHS TAKES ON A SPECIAL EMO-TIONAL RELEVANCE WHEN ONE CONSIDERS THE IRONY OF A FILMMAKER DRIVEN OUT OF HIS OWN COUNTRY BY AN ANTI-DEMOCRATIC MILITARY JUNTA BEING ASK-ED TO COMMENT UPON ELECTIONS WHICH ARE STAGED AND REPORTED LIKE SPOR-TING EVENTS. THE INTERVIEW FORMAT ITSELF BEGINS TO SEEM REMARKABLE; THE EASE WITH WHICH PEOPLE RESPOND TO THE QUESTIONS PERHAPS IMPLIES THE RELATIVE UNIMPORTANCE OF WHATEVER THEY SAY, WHEREAS THOSE SAME QUES-TIONS, IF HONESTLY ANSWERED IN SANTIAGO OR CHILE, COULD LEAD TO ONE'S DEATH.

FOR RUIZ, WHAT'S REVEALED BY THE FILMMAKING PROCESS IS NOT THE DEMOCRATIC, ELECTORAL PROCESS BUT THE SPECTACLE OF THAT PROCESS. THE FRE-QUENT, INCREASINGLY RAPID REPETITION OF PREVIOUS SEQUENCES SERVES NOT ONLY TO NULLIFY THE CONTENT OF THOSE SEQUENCES BUT ALSO TO REVEAL THE WORK-INGS OF THE NEWS DOCUMENTARY FORMAT; ONE ALMOST FEELS THAT THE VIEWER COULD FILL IN ALL THE APPROPRIATE DIALOGUE. THE FORMAT ITSELF, WITH ITS "CAN-DID" OPINIONS, AND CONTRASTING VIEWS, IS THE ACTUAL MESSAGE; THE FILMMAKER—HIM OR HERSELF—SIMPLY BECOMES AN EMPLOYEE OF AN INSTITUTION. RUIZ GOES FURTHER TO QUESTION THE ENTIRE ANCESTRY OF THE DOCUMENTARY (HIS OWN FILM SUGGESTS A RE-WORKING OF CHRIS MARKER'S *LE JOLI MAI*), LINKING IT IMPLICITLY WITH IMPERIALISM (IN ITS FREQUENT TASTE FOR EXOTICISM) AND WITH SUBTLE FORMS OF SOCIAL CONTROL THROUGH ITS PRESENTATION OF A SOCIAL COHESION THAT ACTUALLY MASKS THE DEEP DIVISIONS IN SOCIETY.

BOTH *HYPOTHESIS* AND *OF GREAT EVENTS* EVOKE A NOTION OF THE DISAP-PEARANCE OF THE "ARTIST/CREATOR"; THE FORMER THROUGH ITS FOCUS ON THE LOSS OF MEANING IN TONNERE'S PAINTINGS, THE LATTER THROUGH ITS DETAILING

OF THE WORKINGS OF A PARTICULAR FORMAT. THIS NOTION CAN ACTUALLY BE SEEN TO RUN THROUGHOUT RUIZ'S WORK. IN SEVERAL FILMS, IT IS EVOKED THROUGH THE IMAGE OF A DISMEMBERED, DISPERSED CORPSE, AS IN HIS SHORT *DOGS' DIALOGUE*, HIS SERIAL *THE ONE-EYED MAN*, OR HIS EARLY FEATURE *THE SCATTERED BODY OR THE WORLD UPSIDE DOWN*. THE DISAPPEARANCE OR ABSENCE OF THE ARTIST ALSO FORMS THE CENTRAL THEME OF HIS ADAPTATION OF PIERRE KLOSSOWSKI'S *THE SUSPENDED VOCATION*, RUIZ'S FIRST INA PROJECT, IN WHICH A CONTEMPORARY FILMMAKER ATTEMPTS TO PIECE TOGETHER A FILM ON THE PRIESTHOOD USING FOOTAGE SHOT IN TWO EARLIER PERIODS, A PROCESS WHICH UNLEASHES A BARRAGE OF NEW MEANINGS IN THE FOOTAGE.

THIS PROBLEM OF THE ROLE OR NATURE OF THE CINEMATIC AUTEUR WAS FREQUENTLY DEBATED IN THE NEW LATIN AMERICAN CINEMA OF THE SIXTIES. ON ONE EXTREME, THERE WAS BRAZILIAN GLAUBER ROCHA'S RADICAL RE-READING OF THE *CAHIERS DU CINEMA* POLITIQUE DES AUTEURS, SEEN ESPECIALLY IN HIS 1963 *CRITICAL REVIEW OF THE BRAZILIAN CINEMA*, IN WHICH THE CREATION OF A PERSONAL CINEMATIC STYLE OR VISION WITHIN AT LEAST THE CONTEXT OF BRAZILIAN CINEMA, WAS SEEN AS AN INHERENTLY PROGRESSIVE STANCE AGAINST THE TYRANNY OF THE COMMERCIAL CINEMA. ANOTHER, LATER MEDITATION ON THE AUTEURIST QUESTION CAN BE SEEN IN THE FAMOUS ESSAY "TOWARD A THIRD CINEMA" BY ARGENTINE DIRECTORS OCTAVIO GETINO AND FERNANDO SOLANAS. IN IT, SOLANAS AND GETINO CRITICIZED ROCHA'S POSITION AS ESSENTIALLY REFORMIST. "THE THIRD CINEMA," ACCORDING TO THEM, WOULD TRANSFORM THE FILM-OBJECT INTO THE FILM-ACT; RATHER THAN THE FILM AS AN EXAMPLE OF PERSONAL EXPRESSION, THE FILM WITHIN THE THIRD CINEMA WOULD ESSENTIALLY PROVIDE A PROVOCATION FOR MEMBERS OF THE VIEWING AUDIENCE TO DISCUSS THE ISSUES PRESENTED. "THE FILM ACT," ACCORDING TO SOLANAS AND GETINO, "MEANS AN OPEN-ENDED FILM; IT IS ESSENTIALLY A WAY OF LEARNING."

THE "FILM ACT," IN A SENSE, WOULD PROVIDE, THROUGH DISCUSSION, THE CODE FOR INTERPRETING WHAT WAS SEEN ON SCREEN; SOLANAS AND GETINO, OF COURSE, WERE WRITING AT A MOMENT IN WHICH THE DREAM OR IMAGINATION OF A COMMUNITY IN LATIN AMERICA FOR SUCH "FILM ACTS" WAS BECOMING A REALITY, WITH THE RADICALIZATION OF THE ARGENTINE LEFT AND THE VICTORY OF THE POPULAR FRONT IN CHILE. RUIZ, HOWEVER, AT LEAST DURING HIS MATURE, POST-CHILE PERIOD, WOULD FIND HIMSELF BEREFT OF THAT COMMUNITY. LIKE SO MANY OF HIS PROTAGONISTS—THINK OF THE COLLECTOR IN *HYPOTHESIS*—RUIZ, AS AN EXILE, FINDS HIMSELF ADRIFT IN A WORLD IN WHICH OBJECTS AND EVENTS APPEAR TO BE MEANINGFUL, YET WITHOUT A KNOWLEDGE OF THE PROPER CODES, THERE IS NO WAY TO DERIVE THEIR SIGNIFICANCE. RUIZ'S DEPICTION OF A WORLD IN WHICH THERE EXISTS AN UNBRIDGEABLE CHASM BETWEEN REFERENT AND SIGNIFIED, BETWEEN OBJECTS AND THEIR MEANING, BRINGS HIM VERY CLOSE TO THE WORK OF FRENCH THEORIST JEAN BAUDRILLARD (*FOR A POLITICAL ECONOMY OF THE SIGN*, *THE MIRROR OF PRODUCTION*, ETC.). THE

ARTIST-SELF OF RUIZ, OFTEN EMBODIED IN HIS PROTAGONISTS, BECOMES, IN BAUDRILLARDIAN TERMS, "ONLY A PURE SCREEN, A SWITCHING CENTER FOR ALL THE NETWORKS OF INFLUENCE." THIS CONDITION, WHICH BAUDRILLARD SPECIFICALLY LIKENS TO "A NEW FORM OF SCHIZOPHRENIA," IS SPECIFICALLY THE CONDITION OF EXILE, BUT PERHAPS MORE GENERALLY IT IS THE "LATIN AMERICAN CONDITION" ITSELF, THE FATE OF THOSE FOR WHOM, TO PARAPHRASE THE BRAZILIAN CRITIC PAULO EMILIO SALLES GOMES, EVERYTHING IS FOREIGN, AND YET NOTHING IS.

Long Distance Filmmaking: An Interview with the Cine-Ojo Collective

[1986]

Coco Fusco

A GROUP OF CHILEAN FILMMAKERS IN AND OUTSIDE THE COUNTRY FORMED A WORKING GROUP IN 1983, WHEN POPULAR PROTEST AGAINST THE GOVERNMENT OF AUGUSTO PINOCHET BECAME MORE WIDESPREAD AND PUBLIC THAN IT HAD BEEN IN THE 10 YEARS SINCE THE U.S.-BACKED COUP TERMINATED THE PRESIDENCY OF SALVATOR ALLENDE, ALSO RESULTING IN HIS DEATH. THEIR FIRST FILM, *CHILE, I DON'T TAKE YOUR NAME IN VAIN*, WAS AMONG THE FIRST DOCUMENTARY WORK DONE BY CHILEANS INSIDE CHILE UNDER THE DICTATORSHIP. SINCE THEN, THE COLLECTIVE HAS ALSO PRODUCED *MEMORIES OF AN EVERYDAY WAR* (1986).

IN THE FOLLOWING INTERVIEW, A NORTH AMERICAN-BASED COLLECTIVE MEMBER RECOUNTS THE DIFFICULTIES OF FILMMAKING CLANDESTINELY IN CHILE.

Coco Fusco: HOW DID THIS PROJECT COME ABOUT?

Cine-Ojo Collective: NO FILM WITH AN OVERALL VIEW OF CHILE HAD BEEN MADE SINCE THE COUP IN 1973. OUR FILM IS ABOUT THE BEGINNING OF A THAW, A BREAKTHROUGH. IT WAS DONE AS A COLLABORATION BETWEEN PEOPLE INSIDE AND OUTSIDE, BUT THE IDEA CAME FROM OUTSIDE. WE SENSED THAT THIS WAS THE MOMENT TO MAKE A FILM ABOUT CHILE.

A GROUP OF PEOPLE WORKING IN CHILE, A TEAM OF CAMERAMAN, PRODUCTION MANAGER, SOUND TECHNICIANS, ETC., HAD BEEN PRODUCING VIDEO REPORTS. SOME HAD WORKED AS CREWS FOR FOREIGN TELEVISION. THE MEMBERS OF OUR GROUP IN PARIS WERE ABLE TO FORMALIZE THOSE ACTIVITIES INTO A RELA-

TIONSHIP WITH FRENCH TELEVISION. OUR GROUP BEGAN TO SELL SHORT REPORTS OF SPECIFIC EVENTS TO FRENCH TELEVISION, ON THE THINGS THAT WE PROPOSED. BECAUSE THAT IMPLIED MONEY, AND FORMALIZED THE RELATIONSHIP WITH FRENCH TELEVISION IT TENDED TO FORMALIZE THE GROUP'S RELATIONSHIP TO A CERTAIN DEGREE.

CF: HOW DID THE INVOLVEMENT EXTEND FROM CHILE TO FRANCE, CANADA, AND THE U.S.?

CO: CANADA CAME MUCH LATER. FIRST THERE WAS FRANCE AND CHILE. MANY FILM PEOPLE IN CHILE AT THE MOMENT ARE VERY YOUNG. FOR EXAMPLE, THE SOUND MAN FOR THE FILM WAS 28 AT THE TIME, MEANING THAT HE WAS 18 AT THE COUP. HE HAD NEVER BEEN OUTSIDE OF CHILE. SO HIS PERSPECTIVE ON CHILE, AND HIS SENSE OF HOW CHILE IS PERCEIVED FROM ABROAD IS VERY NARROW. HE HAS A VERY GOOD UNDERSTANDING OF CHILE BUT NOT A VERY GOOD UNDERSTANDING OF HOW CHILE WAS SEEN FROM OUTSIDE. IT WAS HARD FOR THEM TO DETERMINE WHAT ABOUT THE EVENTS HAPPENING IN CHILE WAS IMPORTANT FOR THE OUTSIDE WORLD TO SEE. THAT'S WHY THE TEAM OUTSIDE BEGAN TO SAY THAT THIS WAS IMPORTANT OUTSIDE. SOMETIMES THEY AGREED, BUT SOMETIMES THEY DISAGREED VEHEMENTLY.

CF: HOW DID YOU COMMUNICATE AT THE TIME?

CO: TELEPHONE. THIS WAS DURING THE THAW OF '83, AND PEOPLE WERE VERY PARANOID—AND RIGHTLY SO. THIS HAD NEVER BEEN DONE SYSTEMATICALLY, CALLING AND PLANNING EVERY WEEK. FIRST WE HAD TO AGREE ON WHAT TO SHOOT AND TO DISCUSS IT OVER THE PHONE. ALL OF THIS WAS GOING ON THROUGH TRANSNATIONAL PHONE CALLS AT ENORMOUS COST. THERE WERE MAYBE FIFTY TELEPHONE CONVERSATIONS IN THE PROCESS OF MAKING THE FILM, ANYWHERE FROM THREE TO TEN MINUTES EACH. USUALLY THEY WOULD CALL FROM A PHONE BOOTH COLLECT, USING A KIND OF CODE SO AS NOT TO SPEAK DIRECTLY ABOUT THE FILM. AND WE HAD ARRANGED IT SO THAT WE WOULD ONLY SELL THE TELEVISION RIGHTS TO WHAT WAS AIRED. SOON WE HAD AN ARCHIVE OF MATERIAL, AND THEN CAME THE IDEA THAT SINCE TELEVISION COULD AFFORD TO DO IT WE SHOULD RECORD ADDITIONAL FOOTAGE TO MAKE A FILM.

AT THE BEGINNING THE CREW REALLY WANTED TO FILM DEMONSTRATIONS ALL THE TIME. WE HAD TO SAY—YOU CAN'T JUST HAVE DEMONSTRATIONS, YOU NEED TO TALK TO PEOPLE, TO GET INTO PEOPLE'S LIVES. THEY WOULDN'T UNDERSTAND OUR REQUESTS AND WOULD SAY TO US, "WHAT'S THE BIG DEAL IF A WOMAN GETS ARRESTED, THAT HAPPENS EVERY DAY AND THERE ARE PEOPLE GETTING KILLED." AND WE WOULD ASK FOR INTERVIEWS WITH LEADERS TO PUT THINGS INTO PERSPECTIVE AND THEY WOULDN'T UNDERSTAND WHY THERE WAS ANY NEED TO DO SO. FOR PEOPLE IN CHILE EVERYTHING IS SO CLEAR. IT WAS OFTEN VERY FUNNY AND VERY FRUSTRATING ON THE OUTSIDE AND I'M SURE IT WAS INSIDE AS WELL.

Chile, I Don't Take Your Name In Vain

I THINK IT WAS VERY HARD FOR THEM TO HAVE AN OVERALL SENSE OF HOW KEY PEOPLE AND ACTIONS WERE RELATED. PEOPLE IN CHILE ARE SO ISOLATED FROM ONE ANOTHER. THE FILM PEOPLE KNEW MANY OF THE PEOPLE INVOLVED IN STREET ACTIONS, BUT DIDN'T ALWAYS KNOW THE PEOPLE BACKSTAGE, WHO WERE DOING THE ORCHESTRATING AND DISCUSSING POLICY. AND THEY WERE DISTRUSTFUL OF POLITICIANS AND POLITICAL ANALYSTS IN GENERAL—VERY DISTRUSTFUL OF THEM. ON THE OTHER HAND WE ON THE OUTSIDE WERE MORE IN TOUCH WITH THE PEOPLE IN THE POLITICAL AND HUMAN RIGHTS MOVEMENTS. INSIDE CHILE, THERE ARE NO NEWSPAPER, TELEVISION OR RADIO REPORTS OF WHAT THESE PEOPLE ARE DOING, MAKING IT VERY HARD FOR A YOUNG CAMERAMAN TO KNOW WHAT, FOR EXAMPLE, THE COMMISSION OF HUMAN RIGHTS WAS WORKING ON. ONLY FROM THE OUTSIDE COULD THE CONNECTIONS BE MADE BETWEEN A STREET DEMONSTRA-TION, PEOPLE BEING ARRESTED AND THE WORK BEING DONE THREE BLOCKS AWAY BY THE HUMAN RIGHTS COMMISSION. EVEN THE APPOINTMENTS TO INTERVIEW PEOPLE WERE DONE SOMETIMES FROM THE OUTSIDE, BECAUSE THE COMMISSION MEMBERS DIDN'T KNOW WHO THE CREW WAS.

CF: BECAUSE OF THE WAY THE FILM IS ORGANIZED THEN, YOU DON'T HAVE A VERY CLEAR SENSE THAT PEOPLE ARE ISOLATED FROM EACH OTHER. CAN YOU TALK ABOUT THIS?

CO: EVERYBODY LIVES IN LITTLE WORLDS. THE PEOPLE WHO DEAL WITH HUMAN RIGHTS—THE LAWYERS—ARE TOTALLY IMMERSED IN THEIR WORK. BUT THEY HAVE NO CONNECTION, EXCEPT IF THEY WENT OUT OF THEIR WAY, TO WHAT THE PEOPLE IN THE ARTS ARE DOING. THIS IS BECAUSE THERE IS NO COMMON MEDIA OR FORUM AND THERE'S NO PAPER THAT COVERS THESE ISSUES. THE OPPOSITION PRESS COVERS SOME OF THESE THINGS, BUT USUALLY THEY FOCUS ON THE DAY-TO-DAY THINGS, THE MAJOR POLITICAL EVENTS. AND MOST OF THE FILM PEOPLE ARE NOT CONNECTED TO JOURNALISM, THEY MAKE THEIR LIVING WORKING ON COMMERCIALS AND INDUSTRIALS. SO THEY ARE CUT OFF FROM THE POLITICAL SUPERSTRUCTURE.

CF: WHAT DREW THEM INTO MAKING A FILM ABOUT THESE THINGS THEN?

CO: THEY WERE VERY CLEAR ABOUT THINGS THAT WERE SELF EVIDENT, SUCH AS THE STREET DEMONSTRATIONS, AND THEY WERE HELPING PEOPLE RECORDING THOSE EVENTS. BUT TO GO FROM THERE TO THE LARGER PICTURE—IT WAS VERY HARD, BECAUSE THEY WEREN'T NATURALLY CONNECTED. WE THOUGHT THAT IT WASN'T AS IMPORTANT TO DEAL WITH THESE SORTS OF ISSUES IN THE FILM, BUT RATHER THAT WE SHOULD MAKE A FILM THAT WOULD SUPPORT THE ERUPTION OF A POPULAR MOVEMENT AGAIN AND TO DOCUMENT THAT IN ALL ITS FACETS AND NOT TO TRY TO DEAL WITH THE SUBTLETIES LIKE THE LACK OF COMMUNICATION.

CF: DID THE CREW HAVE PROBLEMS DURING THE SHOOT?

CO: THEY RAN INTO PROBLEMS ALL THE TIME, BUT THEY HAD CREDENTIALS FROM FOREIGN TELEVISION TO FILM. THEY GOT IN HASSLES WITH THE POLICE MANY TIMES AND ONE OF THE PEOPLE WAS PUT IN JAIL, BUT NOTHING VERY TERRIBLE HAPPENED.

CF: TO WHAT EXTENT DO YOU SEE IT AS AN ACCURATE DOCUMENTATION OF WHAT WAS FELT AND EXPERIENCED AT THAT MOMENT?

CO: I THINK WE CAUGHT THAT VERY WELL. NINETEEN EIGHTY-THREE WAS A MOMENT OF ELATION, A MOMENT OF BEGINNING, OF DEFIANCE. AND I THINK THAT THE EFFERVESCENCE WAS WIDESPREAD. THERE WAS AN EXTRAORDINARY SENSE OF POWER, OF MASS MOVEMENT THAT WOULD BE ABLE TO CONFRONT THE GOVERNMENT.

CF: SOME YOUNGER LATIN AMERICAN DIRECTORS HAVE SAID THAT THEY THINK THE OLDER GENERATION OF FILMMAKERS MAKE LATIN AMERICA AND LATIN AMERICANS SEEM TOO VIOLENTLY POLITICIZED. ONE YOUNGER CHILEAN DIRECTOR I RECENTLY SPOKE TO SAID HE FELT THAT HE HAD TO DEAL WITH WHAT HE PERCEIVED TO BE A REALITY IN CHILE—THAT THERE WERE MANY PEOPLE WHO WERE JUST INDIFFERENT, WHO DIDN'T WANT TO DO ANYTHING, AND JUST LIVE THEIR LIVES. WHAT IS YOUR OPINION ABOUT THIS?

CO: I THINK THERE IS A GREAT DEGREE OF IDEALIZATION OF THE POLITICAL PROCESS IN LATIN AMERICA AND OF CHILE AS WELL. MANY PEOPLE IN CHILE AND CHILEANS

ABROAD THOUGHT THAT WHEN THE PROTEST BEGAN IN '83 THAT THAT WAS IT, PINOCHET WOULD FALL. WE NEVER THOUGHT THAT THIS PROTEST MOVEMENT ALONE WOULD CHANGE THINGS. WE KNEW THAT MUCH MORE WAS NEEDED. BUT IT WAS THE FIRST TIME IN TEN YEARS THAT YOU SAW A HUNDRED THOUSAND PEOPLE MARCHING DOWN THE STREET. THAT GAVE A LOT OF PEOPLE A LOT OF HOPE. EVEN THOUGH THERE WERE MANY WHO SAID THEY DIDN'T WANT TO KNOW ABOUT IT, THEY DIDN'T WANT TO DEAL WITH IT, THAT THE COST WAS TOO HIGH. AND THERE WERE MANY PEOPLE KILLED THAT YEAR. THE REACTION OF THE CHILEAN GOVERNMENT WAS VERY VIOLENT. THOUSANDS OF PEOPLE WERE ARRESTED AND TORTURED. I THINK THAT MANY PEOPLE WERE SKEPTICAL ABOUT WHAT WAS HAPPENING. I THINK MANY WERE AFRAID—THINKING WHAT IS GOING TO HAPPEN, FEARING THAT IT WOULD ALL END WITH A CIVIL WAR. WE'RE GOING TO HAVE CHAOS AGAIN, THEY WOULD SAY. BUT FOR THE OPPOSITION IT WAS A MOMENT OF CATHARSIS. TO BE ABLE TO SCREAM, TO YELL, TO DO THINGS, IT JUST HADN'T HAPPENED IN TEN YEARS.

CF: I HAD THE OPPORTUNITY TO LOOK AT SOME OF THE OPPOSITION MAGAZINES, AND WAS SURPRISED TO SEE HOW MODERATE THEY WERE. IN GENERAL THE TONE AND STYLE WAS VERY MUCH LIKE THE FRENCH *LE NOUVEL OBSERVATEUR*.

CO: THEY HAVE TO PLAY A VERY CAREFUL GAME JUST TO STAY OPEN. NOW THEY ARE ALL CLOSED (DUE TO THE STATE OF SEIGE IMPOSED BY PINOCHET AFTER THE ASSASSINATION ATTEMPT IN SEPTEMBER, 1986). GIVEN THE COMBINATION OF SELF CENSORSHIP AND IMPOSED CENSORSHIP THEY'RE DOING AS MUCH AS THEY CAN. THEY CAN'T GO ANY FURTHER.

CF: ON THE ONE HAND IT SEEMED LIKE A SAD INDICATION OF HOW LITTLE IT TAKES TO BE CONSIDERED OPPOSITIONAL, BUT ON THE OTHER HAND HOW GOOD IT WAS THAT THEY COULD SAY THESE THINGS IN SPITE OF THE DEGREE OF CENSORSHIP.

CO: IN FACT, SOME OF THE MAGAZINES HAVE SAID VERY HARSH THINGS. EVEN AS MILD AS THEY MIGHT BE, THEY'VE BEEN A VERY IMPORTANT VOICE.

CF: HOW WOULD YOU DISTINGUISH THE FILM'S VIEW OF THINGS FROM THE MAGAZINES?

CO: THE MAGAZINES ARE PUT OUT BY JOURNALISTS, ANALYZING THE SITUATION FROM INSIDE CHILE. THE FILM WAS NOT CONCEIVED OF AS SOMETHING TO BE SEEN INSIDE CHILE, BUT OUTSIDE. AND ALSO THE PEOPLE AT THE MAGAZINES ARE DEALING WITH THE CRITICAL MOMENTS WEEK TO WEEK. THE FILM SHOULD HAVE, AND COULD NOT HAVE, DEALT WITH THE MOMENT. FINALLY, I THINK THAT A LOT OF MATERIAL WAS LEFT OUT OF THE FINAL VERSION BECAUSE WE THOUGHT IT CONVEYED TOO MUCH WISHFUL THINKING—THAT IT WASN'T TRULY REPRESENTATIVE. WE TRIED TO INCLUDE SOME OF THE HESITATIONS PEOPLE HAD AS WELL. THE FILM CONVEYS A WISH TO GO FORWARD, BUT I HOPE THAT IT'S NOT A TRIUMPHAL FILM THAT SAYS, WELL FROM HERE WE ARE ALL SET.

CF: WAS IT SEEN IN CHILE?

CO: YES, IN VIDEO. PEOPLE IN CHILE, HOWEVER, SPEND A LOT OF TIME TRYING TO FIGURE OUT WHAT THE POINT OF VIEW OF THE FILM IS. WE WERE TRYING TO BE VERY ECUMENICAL AND NOT LET ONE POLITICAL VIEW OVERSHADOW THE OTHERS. EVERYONE FROM THE OPPOSITION SAYS WHAT THEY WANT TO SAY. EVERYBODY FELT THAT THEIR POINT OF VIEW WAS BEING PROPERLY REPRESENTED, FROM THE CHRISTIAN DEMOCRATS TO THE COMMUNISTS. THERE IS NOTHING IN THE FILM THAT IS ANTI-CHRISTIAN DEMOCRAT, ANTI-SOCIALIST, ANTI-COMMUNIST, ANTI-CHRISTIAN, LEFT OR ANTI-CHURCH. BUT WE TRIED TO FIND THE POINTS THAT EVERYONE AGREED ON, AND TO PORTRAY THEM AS OPPOSED TO SHOWING INTERNAL DISCORD BETWEEN THE DIFFERENT GROUPS—WHICH IS WHAT A GREAT DEAL OF THE INTERNAL DEBATE WITHIN THE OPPOSITION IN CHILE IS ABOUT. WE WOULDN'T CONTRIBUTE ANYTHING BY PUTTING A VERY COMPLEX, VERY QUICKLY CHANGING SITUATION IN THE FILM—NO ONE WOULD UNDERSTAND IT. MANY PEOPLE SAW IT AS A RECORD. BUT IN CHILE IT'S NOT A BIG DEAL TO SEE A DEMONSTRATION, A CONFRONTATION, BECAUSE IT HAPPENS ALL THE TIME.

CF: DID YOU FEEL THAT YOU WERE FOLLOWING SOME SORT OF DOCUMENTARY STRUCTURE?

CO: WE TRIED NOT TO WORRY ABOUT THAT TOO MUCH. THE FOOTAGE WAS WHAT IT WAS. THE RATIO WAS VERY LIMITED—MAYBE 2 OR 3 TO 1 AT MOST. AND WE HAD CERTAIN NEEDS TO COVER CERTAIN EVENTS. WE HAD TO SHOW IT TO AN AUDIENCE WHO WOULD NOT NECESSARILY KNOW ABOUT CHILE.

CF: WAS THERE EVER ANY GOVERNMENT REACTION TO THE FILM?

CO: THE GOVERNMENT DOESN'T CARE A GREAT DEAL ABOUT FILMS LIKE THIS. OF COURSE IT WAS NEVER OFFICIALLY APPROVED—THEY WOULD NEVER ALLOW THE FILM TO BE SHOWN. BUT THEY DIDN'T GO OUT OF THEIR WAY TO FIND OUT WHO THE CREW WAS. I'M SURE THAT SOMEONE TOOK NOTE OF IT; THEY COULD HAVE MADE A FUSS, BUT THEY DECIDED NOT TO.

OUR ORIGINAL IDEA WAS TO MAKE A GROUP OF FILMS TO RECORD THE PROCESS, THE ONGOING PROCESS, OF CREATING A VISUAL MEMORY OF THESE TIMES. THE ONLY VISUAL RECORD HAD BEEN PRODUCED BY STATE CONTROLLED TELEVISION. BUT OURS WAS AN ATTEMPT TO RECORD COLLECTIVE MEMORY—THE THINGS THAT WOULD OTHERWISE BE LOST. IT'S THE HISTORY OF CHILE IN THESE TIMES. FOR THIS REASON WE'VE BEEN VERY CAREFUL TO KEEP EVEN THE MATERIAL WE DON'T USE.

CF: WHAT HAS HAPPENED TO THE COLLECTIVE SINCE THE MAKING OF THE FILM?

CO: NOW THE TIMES HAVE CHANGED ENOUGH SO THAT WE DON'T HAVE TO MAKE FILMS THE WAY WE DID THE FIRST TIME, AND DUE TO THAT NEW SITUATION AND

A COPRODUCTION RELATIONSHIP WITH THE NATIONAL FILM BOARD OF CANADA, WE DECIDED THAT SOMEONE FROM THE OUTSIDE HAD TO GO IN. WE DIDN'T HAVE TO FILM IN SUCH A CLANDESTINE FASHION AS WE HAD BEFORE. WE COULD PUT OUR NAMES ON THE FILM WHICH LENT IT MORE CREDIBILITY. EVERYTHING WAS GOING ON MORE IN THE OPEN, IN KEEPING WITH THE CHANGING REALITY OF CHILE. THREE OF US TOOK RESPONSIBILITY FOR THE SECOND FILM—GASTON ANCELOUICI, JAIME BARRIOS, AND RENE DAVILA. GASTON WAS THE ONLY ONE WHO COULD GO BACK TO CHILE SO WE DECIDED THAT HE SHOULD GO. THE EDITING HAD TO BE DONE OUTSIDE . . . SOME PEOPLE WHO WORKED ON IT USED PSEUDONYMS IN THE FILM—THEY WANTED TO MAKE SURE THAT THEY WERE MENTIONED EVEN UNDER A PSEUDONYM SO THAT LATER THEY COULD SAY "THAT WAS ME".[1]

CF: WHAT IS THE CINEMATECA CHILENA?

CO: IT BEGAN AS A REPOSITORY OF THE FILMS MADE IN EXILE. THEN IT BECAME THE UMBRELLA FOR MANY ACTIVITIES. IT WAS BASED IN PARIS AND NOW IT IS BASED IN NEW YORK CITY AND IN CANADA. NOW IT SERVES AS A PRODUCTION UNIT AND HELPS TO DISTRIBUTE OTHER FILMS COMING FROM CHILE. THERE ARE MANY FILMS—ABOUT 50 OR 60—MADE BY CHILEANS ABOUT THE EXPERIENCE OF EXILE.

CF: HOW DO THE FIRST AND THE SECOND FILM FIT INTO THE SITUATION IN RELATION TO THINGS NOW?

CO: I THINK THAT THE FIRST ONE REFLECTED A MOMENT VERY WELL. THEN WE THOUGHT WE SHOULD GO FROM THE VERY GENERAL TO THE PARTICULAR WITH THIS FILM— TO THE INDIVIDUALS. AND I THINK THAT IF ANYTHING IT WOULD HAVE BEEN BETTER TO HAVE WORKED THAT ELEMENT INTO THE FIRST FILM—THE ELEMENT OF THE INDIVIDUAL IN THE MIDDLE OF THE VASTNESS OF THE MOVEMENT. WE JUDGED THAT IT COULDN'T BE DONE AT THE MOMENT. THE TWO FILMS COMPLEMENT EACH OTHER BECAUSE THEY ARE PART OF THE SAME REALITY. THE SAME PEOPLE WHO GO OUT AND DEMONSTRATE ARE THE ONES WHO HAVE EXTRAORDINARY STORIES OF THEIR OWN. THESE PEOPLE ARE NOT NECESSARILY GUIDED BY MILITANCY. THEY ARE JUST VERY ANTI-DICTATORSHIP, AND THEY ARE GUIDED BY ETHICS, MORE THAN BY POLITICS.

CF: TO WHAT EXTENT IS IT POSSIBLE FOR A POLITICAL CHANGE TO TAKE PLACE THERE IF THE OPPOSITION DOESN'T HAVE A CLEAR POLITICAL STAND?

CO: THE OPPOSITION DOES HAVE A POLITICAL STAND THAT HAS BEEN FAIRLY WELL DOCUMENTED. WE DIDN'T WANT TO DEAL WITH THE POLITICAL QUESTIONS, BECAUSE THE POLITICAL SITUATION IS CHANGING SO FAST THAT ANY FILM THAT WE COULD MAKE WOULD BE DATED.

CF: THERE IS NO SENSE IN THE FILMS OF THERE BEING AN ARMED OPPOSITION. WHY ISN'T THIS DEALT WITH IN THE FILM?

CO: AT THE TIME WE FILMED THE MANUEL RODRIGUEZ PATRIOTIC FRONT (FPMR) WASN'T AS IMPORTANT AS IT IS NOW. THEY'VE OBVIOUSLY BECOME AN IMPORTANT FACTOR SINCE THEY TRIED TO KILL PIONCHET. BUT EVEN SO, THEIR IMPORTANCE IS TRANSITORY, BECAUSE POLITICAL CHANGE IN CHILE IS REALLY BEING CARRIED OUT BY THE NON-ARMED OPPOSITION—THESE PEOPLE ARE THE PRIME ACTORS. THEY WOULD BE TREMENDOUSLY EFFECTED IF THE FPMR TERMINATED PINOCHET. THEY MIGHT LIKE A GREAT DEAL OF WHAT THE FPMR IS DOING, BUT THAT DOESN'T MEAN THAT THE FPMR WILL BECOME THE MAIN FORCE IN CHILEAN POLITICS. NOW IS THE TIME TO DO SOMETHING ON THE IMPORTANCE OF THE FPMR. WE CANNOT DO THAT, BUT SOMEONE ELSE SHOULD.

Notes
1. The film is *Memoirs from an Everyday War*, a film by G. Ancelouici, J. Barrios, and R. Davila. A production of Cinemateco Chilena. English version: 29:10 min. Distributed by Icarus Films, 200 Park Avenue South, N.Y., N.Y. 10003.

Stills from *Blood of the Condor*

BOLIVIA

LANGUAGE AND POPULAR CULTURE
[1970]

JORGE SANJINES

We invent a new language through popular culture

THE CONCEPT OF UTILITY IS FUNDAMENTAL TO OUR WORK IN CINEMA, SINCE WE AIM TO ASSIST LIBERATION STRUGGLES IN LATIN AMERICA.[1]

WE HAVE COME A LONG WAY SINCE MAKING OUR FIRST POLITICAL FILM IN 1962. WE HAVE SPENT MOST OF THIS TIME SEARCHING FOR THE NECESSARY MEANS TO DEVELOP A CINEMA WHICH IS BOTH COMMITTED AND POLITICAL. WE HAVE HAD TO "BURN OUR BRIDGES" ON MORE THAN ONE OCCASION IN ORDER TO REMAIN TRUE TO OUR PRINCIPLES.

EXILE FROM BOLIVIA HAS DEPRIVED US OF ONE OF THE MAIN SOURCES OF INSPIRATION AND PREVENTED US FROM WORKING ON FILMS IN COLLABORATION WITH THE PEOPLE, AS WE HAD DONE IN *THE COURAGE OF THE PEOPLE*.

HOWEVER, WE KNEW WHEN WE LEFT BOLIVIA THAT THE ENEMY WAS THE SAME IN NEIGHBORING COUNTRIES, THE CONTRADICTIONS WERE IDENTICAL AND THE STRUGGLE EQUALLY URGENT . . . WE THEREFORE WENT TO PERU, EQUADOR AND COLUMBIA, WHICH ARE CLOSE TO US GEOGRAPHICALLY AND CULTURALLY. IN THOSE COUNTRIES WE MADE *EL ENEMIGO PRINCIPAL* AND *FUERA DE AQUI*: THESE FILMS IN ANY CASE WILL EVENTUALLY BE SEEN IN BOLIVIA WHEN BANZER FALLS AND OUR PEOPLE RECOGNIZE THEMSELVES FULLY.

THE CONFRONTATION WITH AN AUDIENCE HAS SLOWLY MODIFIED OUR CINEMA: THE LANGUAGE AND OBJECTIVES HAVE BECOME MORE DEFINED. THE SPECTATORS IN TURN HAVE BECOME CREATORS OF OUR WORK. OUR FIRST FILMS DEALT WITH LIBERATION THEMES, BUT WE NOW CONSIDER THAT WHILE THESE FILMS WERE VALID AT THE LEVEL OF CONTENT, THEY WERE NOT SO AT THE LEVEL OF FORM, WHICH GREATLY CURTAILED THEIR EFFECTIVENESS.

We find a new language

BLOOD OF THE CONDOR HAD A SIGNIFICANT IMPACT AMONG THE PETTY BOURGEOIS CIRCLES IN BOLIVIA AND SUCCEEDED IN MOBILIZING THEM TO A CERTAIN EXTENT. FOR INSTANCE, TWO COMMISSIONS OF ENQUIRY WERE SET UP AT THE UNIVERSITY OF LA PAZ AND IN THE SENATE, TO INVESTIGATE THE ACTIVITIES

OF THE U.S. "PEACE CORPS" WITH RESPECT TO BIRTH CONTROL AND THE STERILIZATION OF INDIAN WOMEN WITHOUT THEIR CONSENT. THE RESULT WAS THAT THE AMERICANS DISMANTLED THEIR THREE CENTERS, DENYING THAT THEY HAD EVER EXISTED IN THE FIRST PLACE AND THEY WERE FINALLY EXPELLED BY GENERAL TORRES WHO BACKED THE FINDINGS OF THESE COMMISSIONS. EVIDENTLY THE FILM HAD CONTRIBUTED TO THIS DECISION AND HAD THEREFORE PLAYED ITS PART. HOWEVER, WHEN WE SHOWED IT IN THE COUNTRYSIDE TO THE INDIANS THEMSELVES, WE REALIZED THAT IT DID NOT COMMUNICATE A GREAT DEAL. IT WAS NOT ENOUGH THAT THE FILM WAS SPOKEN IN QUECHUA, THAT ALL THE ACTORS WERE PEASANTS AND THAT IT TOOK THEIR SIDE. IN OTHER WORDS, *BLOOD OF THE CONDOR* WORKED FOR A SECTOR OF THE COUNTRY FORMED BY WESTERN CULTURE, BUT IT DID NOT WORK—AT THE LEVEL OF LANGUAGE AND CULTURAL STRUCTURES—FOR THE MAJORITY OF OUR POPULATION WHO ARE IMBUED IN AN ANDEAN INDIGENOUS CULTURE: QUECHUA AYMARA. FOR THIS REASON WE STARTED TO LOOK FOR A CINEMATIC LANGUAGE SUITABLE FOR THIS CULTURE. IN THIS DIFFICULT OPERATION WE HAD TO START WITHIN OURSELVES, SINCE WE HAD BEEN FORMED WITHIN THE PARAMETERS OF THE DOMINANT, COLONIZING CULTURE. THIS IS THE LESSON THAT WE TOOK AWAY FROM INNUMERABLE SHOWINGS TO THE INDIAN. IT WAS NOT THAT THEY COULD NOT UNDERSTAND WHAT WAS BEING SAID, IT WAS RATHER A FORMAL CONFLICT AT THE LEVEL OF THE MEDIUM ITSELF WHICH DID NOT CORRESPOND TO THE INTERNAL RHYTHMS OF OUR PEOPLE OR THEIR PROFOUND CONCEPTION OF REALITY. THANKS TO LIVING WITH THESE PEOPLE, AND OUR DESIRE TO KEEP IN CONTACT WITH THEIR DAILY CULTURE, WE MANAGED TO EVOLVE A DIFFERENT LANGUAGE TO THAT WHICH WE HAD USED IN *UKAMU* AND *BLOOD OF THE CONDOR*. IT WAS WITH THE FILM *CAMINOS DE LA MUERTE* (WHICH WAS LOST THROUGH AN ACCIDENT OR SABOTAGE IN A EUROPEAN LABORATORY) THAT WE BEGAN TO BREAK WITH THE TRADITIONAL FORMS OF LANGUAGE. IT WAS NOT YET A TOTAL CHANGE (A POINT WHICH WE STILL HAVE NOT REACHED IN OUR LATEST FILM) BUT THE BEGINNINGS OF A CHANGE WITHIN OURSELVES. AT FIRST WE NOTICED THAT THE SUBSTANTIAL DIFFERENCE LAY IN THE WAY IN WHICH THE QUECHUA-AYMARA PEOPLE CONCEIVE OF THEMSELVES COLLECTIVELY, IN THE NON-INDIVIDUALISTIC FORM OF THEIR CULTURE. THE ORGANIZING PRINCIPLE IN THIS SOCIETY IS NOT THE ISOLATED INDIVIDUAL BUT SOCIETY IN ITS TOTALITY: IT IS THIS SOCIETY THAT MUST BE FORMED COLLECTIVELY. THEY DO NOT CONCEIVE OF AN INDIVIDUAL LIVING ABOVE OR ON THE MARGINS OF SOCIETY. THIS DOES NOT MEAN THE NEGATION OF THE INDIVIDUAL; QUITE THE REVERSE: THE EQUILIBRIUM OF COLLECTIVITY PROTECTS HIM, IMMUNIZING HIM AGAINST NEUROSES. FOR THIS REASON HISTORY IS LIVED COLLECTIVELY, WHAT AFFECTS A MEMBER OF THE COMMUNITY AFFECTS THE WHOLE COMMUNITY BOTH IN LIFE AND DEATH.

A collective protagonist

WE HAD CONCLUDED THAT WE HAD TO PORTRAY A COLLECTIVE AND NOT

AN INDIVIDUAL PROTAGONIST, AND THAT THAT WAS THE BEST WAY TO EXPRESS ANY FACT. SIMILARLY, IN *LOS CAMINOS DE LA MUERTE* WE HAD BEGUN TO CREATE THIS COLLECTIVE PROTAGONIST, WHILST PRESERVING THE PRINCIPLE OF "INDIVIDUATION" IN CERTAIN CHARACTERS, WHO SERVE AS GUIDES IN THE FILM. WHEN WE FILMED *COURAGE OF THE PEOPLE* WE WORKED IN THE SAME WAY AND THE SAME ELEMENTS RECUR: THE RESTORATION OF HISTORICAL FACTS BY THOSE WHO WERE THE ACTORS IN REAL LIFE, AND THE CRITICAL PARTICIPATION OF WHAT CAN BE CALLED THE "PEOPLE-ACTOR." SUCH A CHOICE LEADS TO A HORIZONTAL RELATIONSHIP BETWEEN THE FILM CREW AND THE PEOPLE. THE WOMEN OF THE SIGLO XX MINING CAMP KNEW BETTER THAN THE RESEARCHERS THE PLACE WHERE THE MASSACRE OF SAINT-JEAN HAD TAKEN PLACE, AND WHAT HAD HAPPENED, AND THEY WERE THEREFORE IN A BETTER POSITION TO RECALL FACTS, DIALOGUES AND EMOTIONS.

IN THIS WAY WE OURSELVES BECAME PART OF THIS COLLECTIVE PHENOMENON AS ITS INSTRUMENT OF EXPRESSION, ALLOWING THE COMMUNITY TO TALK ABOUT ITSELF THROUGH US.

IN *COURAGE OF THE PEOPLE* THE STRUCTURE AND DIVISION OF SCENES CORRESPONDS TO CERTAIN VISUAL CONCEPTS IN WESTERN ART WHICH HAVE BEEN INTRODUCED TO THE CINEMA, THOUGH THE FILM ITSELF HAS NO INTEREST IN AESTHETIC RESEARCH FOR ITS OWN SAKE. IN *COURAGE OF THE PEOPLE*, SUSPENSE IS CONCEIVED IN A VERY TRADITIONAL MANNER, THOUGH IT IS TREATED WITH GREAT MODERATION.

CONTINUING OUR OBSTINATE SEARCH FOR A SUITABLE LANGUAGE, WE MADE *EL ENEMIGO PRINCIPAL*, A FILM WHICH IN OUR OPINION SYNTHESIZES OUR EARLIER EXPERIENCES AND GREATLY CLARIFIES OUR IDEAS. WE INTRODUCED THE SEQUENCE SHOT AS ESSENTIAL TO THE COHERENCE OF THE FILM. THE NARRATOR WHO PRESENTS THE FACTS INTERVENES DURING THE FILM, BREAKING UP THE FLOW OF THE PLOT TO GIVE THE AUDIENCE GREATER POSSIBILITY FOR REFLECTION. THIS DOES NOT OCCUR JUST SO THAT THE AUDIENCE CAN REFLECT ON THE FACTS THEMSELVES, FOR IT IS A CULTURAL PRODUCT LINKED TO THE QUECHUA-AYMARA ORAL TRADITION OF NARRATORS WHOSE FUNCTION WAS PRECISELY TO ANTICIPATE HISTORY SO THAT THEY COULD ANALYZE IT DURING THE NARRATION.

The function of the sequence-shot

THE SEQUENCE-SHOT [LONG SHOT] IN *EL ENEMIGO PRINCIPAL*, WHICH IS NOT VERY LONG FOR PURELY TECHNICAL REASONS (ARRIFLEX 35MM, WITH AN INDEPENDENT BLIMP), ALLOWS US TO ATTEMPT A MORE DEMOCRATIC STRUCTURE, FOR IT DOES NOT IMPOSE ITSELF IN THE SAME WAY AS A CLOSE-UP OR A SHORT SEQUENCE: BECAUSE OF ITS BREADTH IT OFFERS THE VIEWPOINT OF THE PARTICIPATING AUDIENCE WHO CAN MOVE INSIDE THE SCENE, ATTRACTED BY THE MOST INTERESTING POINTS. IF IN THE SCENE THE CAMERA MOVES TO WHAT IS ALMOST A CLOSE-UP, THE CHOICE OF CHARACTER WILL BE DETERMINED BY THE COLLECTIVE INTEREST AND THE CAMERA

SHOT WILL IN ANY CASE KEEP THE SAME DISTANCE AS ANY REAL SPECTATOR.

THE CIRCULATION OF *EL ENEMIGO PRINCIPAL* AMONG ECUADORIAN WORKERS AND PEASANTS, WHO ALL SPEAK QUECHUA, REASSURED US, SINCE THIS FILM REALLY ESTABLISHES CONNECTIONS, COMMUNICATION AND PARTICIPATION TO AN OPTIMUM DEGREE. SOMETIMES THE PEASANTS TOOK THE INITIATIVE OF PROJECTING THE FILM TO OTHER PEASANTS SO AS TO PROVOKE DISCUSSION ON MATTERS THAT CONCERNED THEM GREATLY. DURING THESE SHOWINGS, WE EXPERIENCED THE PHENOMENON OF CULTURAL IDENTITY. THE FILM REALLY WAS APPROPRIATED BY THEM; IT WAS NO LONGER A TECHNICAL PRODUCT MADE FOR THEM WHICH THEY MISTRUSTED OR CONSIDERED STRANGE AND INTRUSIVE. THE OLD NARRATOR DOES NOT TALK IN AN ABSTRACT WAY, HE ADDRESSES THE PEASANTS CONCRETELY AND TALKS TO THEM IN THEIR OWN LANGUAGE; HE IS ONE OF THEM. THE PROTAGONIST IS THE PEOPLE, THAT IS TO SAY, THE PEASANTS WHO WERE ABUSED AND EXPLOITED BY CARILLES. THE USE OF THE SEQUENCE-SHOT AND THE HAND-HELD CAMERA MAKES THEM FEEL THAT THEY ARE PARTICIPATING IN THE SCENES AND IN THE EVENTS THEMSELVES. THERE ARE NO BRUTAL CUTS TO THROW THEM OFF BALANCE, OR LIE TO THEM.

BUT THIS WORK DOES NOT CONTRADICT BEAUTY AND ART. QUITE THE REVERSE! WE ARE ANXIOUS TO TRANSMIT THE CULTURAL VIEW OF OUR PEOPLE AND THE FILM, LOCATED WITHIN THE RHYTHMS OF OUR ANDEAN CULTURE, TRANSMITS ITS BEAUTY. THAT IS WHY IT IS NOT A POLITICAL TRACT, FOR IT COMMUNICATES A SENSE OF IDENTITY AND CREATIVITY. IT EXPRESSES NOT JUST A SUBJECT BUT A WHOLE CULTURAL UNIVERSE. THIS PROCESS IS DIALECTICAL AND FOR THIS REASON GREATLY FACILITATES COMMUNICATION.

The role of film-as-weapon

WHEN WE MADE *FUERA DI AQUI* WE WANTED THE FILM TO CONTRIBUTE MORE DIRECTLY TO THE CONJUNCTURE IN WHICH IT WAS MADE. WE REALIZED MORE CLEARLY THAN EVER BEFORE THE ROLE OF THE FILM-AS-WEAPON, AS AN INSTRUMENT FOR STRUGGLE. *FUERA DE AQUI* MET WITH GREAT PRODUCTION PROBLEMS. THE FILMING HAD TO BE INTERRUPTED FOR 8 MONTHS THROUGH LACK OF APPROPRIATE MATERIAL, WHICH RAISED THE COST OF PRODUCTION. FILMED IN ONE COUNTRY, IT WAS PROCESSED IN TWO OTHERS, AND AN AIRCRAFT COMPANY LOST THE FIRST CUTTING COPY, TOGETHER WITH THE SYNCED-TAPES. THAT WAS TWO MONTHS OF HARD WORK LOST. WE HAD BEEN FORCED TO USE OUT OF DATE STOCK BECAUSE A COMRADE TRAVELLING FROM BOLIVIA, WHERE WE HAD LEFT HER AFTER THE FALL OF GENERAL TORRES, WHO WAS GOING TO BUY NEW MATERIAL IN PERU, WAS PURSUED BY BOLIVIAN POLICE AND FORCED TO LEAVE BEHIND HER PAPERS AND A COPY OF *COURAGE OF THE PEOPLE*. ANTONIO EGUINO, WHO HAD BEEN THE DIRECTOR OF PHOTOGRAPHY, WAS IMPRISONED FOR THAT REASON.

BUT THIS WAS THE PRICE WE HAD TO PAY FOR AN ANONYMOUS PRODUCTION. IT WAS THE PRICE OF EXILE AND OUR COMMITMENT. IN A STRUGGLE ONE

CANNOT HOPE TO FIND A PATH OPENING UP CALMLY AND HOSPITABLY, VERY OFTEN THOSE WHO FIGHT HAVE TO HACK OUT A PATH WITH MACHETE BLOWS, LEAVING BEHIND IN THEIR HURRIED JOURNEY, BITS OF CLOTHES OR THEIR OWN FLESH.

THIS DELAY IN FILMING ALLOWED US TO GET TO KNOW THE PEOPLE BETTER AND A NUMBER OF NEW ELEMENTS WERE INCORPORATED INTO THE FILM. TAKE FOR EXAMPLE ONE OF THE FINAL SCENES: THE PEASANTS MEETING TO DISCUSS THE SITUATION AFTER THE ARMY MASSACRE. TWO OPPOSING FACTIONS EMERGED: ON THE ONE HAND THERE WERE THE SUPPORTERS OF "INDIANISM," WHO ARE QUITE STRONG IN ECUADOR, AND ON THE OTHER THE SUPPORTERS OF A MATERIALIST ANALYSIS BASED ON THE CLASS STRUGGLE. THIS FUNDAMENTAL SCENE IN THE FILM REVEALS THE DEGREE OF MATURITY OF THESE PEASANT LEADERS WHO USE THEIR OWN VOCABULARY AND PRODUCE THEIR OWN IDEAS. WE HAD NOT LAID DOWN A PRECISE SCENARIO OR IMPOSED SCRIPTED DIALOGUE BUT WE AGREED TO WRITE THE SCENE ON THE BASIS OF ARGUMENTS THAT EACH GROUP COULD USE IN FAVOR OF ITS CONNECTION TO THE PROBLEMS. THE CAMERA PLAYED AN IMPORTANT ROLE AND IN LONG SHOTS WAS CAREFUL TO FOCUS ON THOSE WHO WERE TALKING, BUT WITHOUT IMPRISONING THEM IN A CLOSE-UP WHICH COULD HAVE PREVENTED THE OTHER COMRADES FROM EXPRESSING THEMSELVES; IT REMAINED SUFFICIENTLY DISTANT TO ALLOW A SPONTANEOUS AND DEMOCRATIC PARTICIPATION WITHIN THE FRAME. WE HAVE SAID ON OCCASIONS THAT THE PEOPLE DO NOT RECOGNIZE THEMSELVES IN CLOSE-UP AND THAT THEIR FORCE AND VITALITY IS ADEQUATELY EXPRESSED IN LONG SHOT AND IN SHOTS OF THE COLLECTIVE PROTAGONIST OF THE WHOLE WORK.

THE POLITICAL PROPOSALS OF THESE ECUADORIAN PEASANTS ARE REAL AND CONTEMPORARY. THEY ARE NOT THE RESULT OF AN ARBITRARY AND "VERTICAL" WILL OF THE FILMMAKERS WHO, IN FACT, ARE NOT AS WELL PLACED AS THE PEASANTS TO SAY WHAT THEY THINK. ONE CAN AGREE OR NOT AGREE WITH THE PRINCIPLE OF ORGANIZING THE UNION OF PEASANTS AND WORKERS—IN THE REVOLUTIONARY PARTY—BUT THAT IS ANOTHER QUESTION, WHICH CANNOT BE DECREED THROUGH A FILM. THE AIM OF *FUERA DE AQUI* IS TO BRING OUT THE SINISTER MECHANISM USED BY THE IMPERIALIST ENEMY TO DESTROY OR WEAKEN OUR COUNTRY. FROM THIS PERSPECTIVE THE FILM CANNOT BE MISTAKEN, IT MUST BE OF SOME USE. IT CAN REALLY BECOME AN INSTRUMENT FOR THE STRUGGLE AND WORK.

We are not concerned with an imperialist cinema

THAT IS WHY WE EXPECT CRITICISM OF THIS FILM, WHICH IS PUT FORWARD AS A WEAPON, TO BE DIFFERENT. IF CRITICISM UNDERSTANDS THE FUNCTION OF SUCH A CINEMA, THEN IT WILL CONTRIBUTE TO THE FILM BY ANALYZING ITS EFFEC-TIVENESS. IT IS ESSENTIAL ALSO THAT CRITICISM COMES FROM THOSE FOR WHOM THE FILM IS MADE, SINCE IT IS THEY WHO ARE FACING UP TO AND KNOW THE ENEMY WHICH IS BEING DENOUNCED.

THIS CINEMA IS SIMILAR TO THE POPULAR AND DIDACTIC POLITICAL BOOK AND CANNOT THEREFORE BE JUDGED BY CRITERIA SUCH AS "I LIKE IT" OR "I DON'T LIKE IT." ONE CAN SAY IF ONE AGREES OR NOT, BUT FOR US ANY CRITICISM MUST TAKE AS ITS CENTRAL PREMISE THE "EFFECTIVENESS" OF THE FILM AND SUBORDINATE OTHER VALUES. THAT IS TO SAY THAT THE CINEMA WILL BEGIN TO DEMAND A CRITICAL REACTION BASED NOT SO MUCH ON ITS FORM, BUT RATHER ON ITS CONTENT: THOSE WHO JUDGE IT WILL REVEAL THEIR OWN COMMITMENT TO THE REALITY IN QUESTION.

IN *FUERA DE AQUI* WE WERE CAREFUL TO POPULARIZE THE FEELINGS OF LOVE AND SOLIDARITY AMONG THE PEASANTS. IN THEIR CONFLICT WITH THE AMERICAN MISSIONARIES, AND THEN WITH THE MULTINATIONALS AND THE "HARKIS" (NATIONALS WHO "SELL OUT" TO FOREIGN CAPITAL) THE PEASANTS APPEAR AS LIVING AND HUMANLY RICH PEOPLE, THEIR SINCERE AND OFTEN NAIVE ACTIONS RESPOND TO A NON-CONTAMINATED CULTURE IN WHICH HUMAN VALUES ARE DOMINANT. THIS NAIVETY IS PURITY, AS CAN BE SEEN IN THE QUESTION WHICH THE PEASANT ASKS ABOUT THE FUTURE OF HIS ANIMALS AND HIS SMALL PLOT OF LAND. THIS QUESTION IS SEEN AS NAIVE BY THE "WOLVES" OF THE MULTINATIONALS BUT FOR THE PEASANTS IT IS VITAL: THIS LAND AND THESE ANIMALS ARE THE WHOLE MEANING OF HIS LIFE.

WE THINK WITH THIS FILM WE ARE CLOSE TO WHAT AN EXTRAORDINARY PEASANT LEADER SAID IN A SEMINAR ON AGRARIAN REFORM ATTENDED BY TECHNOCRATS FROM DIFFERENT COUNTRIES: "WE PEASANTS KNOW VERY WELL HOW TO IMPLEMENT THE AGRARIAN REFORM. IT IS NOT YOU THAT WILL TEACH US." WHAT IS IMPORTANT, ON THE OTHER HAND, IS TO KNOW HOW THE ENEMY WORKS, WHAT METHODS THEY USE, AND WHAT MECHANISMS ARE SUPPORTING THEM. THAT IS WHAT INTERESTS US, FOR IF WE THE PEASANTS CANNOT DISCOVER THESE FACTS, WE WILL NEVER BE ABLE TO SHAKE OFF OUR OPPRESSORS.

THE FOREIGNERS WHO, IN THE FILM, STERILIZE AND EXPLOIT OUR PEOPLE, COULD NOT BE SHOWN IN A FAVORABLE LIGHT. IT WAS NECESSARY FOR THEIR EVIL TO EMERGE UNEQUIVOCALLY ON THE SCREEN. THE IMAGE ON THE SCREEN IS A VERY "DETATCHED" ONE THAT THE COMMUNITY ITSELF HAD OF FOREIGNERS AS INHUMAN BEINGS, LACKING IN SINCERITY, REPEATING RELIGIOUS DISCOURSES WHICH THEY CLEARLY DID NOT BELIEVE. THAT IS WHY WE HAVE BEEN SO DRACONIAN WITH THEM, FOR WE COULD NOT ALLOW ANY CONCESSIONS TO BE MADE. WHY SHOULD WE SHOW JUST ONE OF THEM AS SYMPATHETIC, SINCE THEY CONSISTENTLY HARMED THE PEASANT COMMUNITY. IT IS TRUE THAT AMONG THOSE WHO CAME TO THE VILLAGES, THERE WAS THE OCCASIONAL HONEST MAN, BUT SUCH MEN ARE USED AND ARE THEREFORE NOT REPRESENTATIVE IN ANY MEANINGFUL WAY. WE ARE NOT INTERESTED IN A PSYCHOLOGICAL OR IMPARTIAL CINEMA: OUR CINEMA IS THAT OF STRUGGLE, WE ARE AT WAR, AND WHEN THE ENEMY FIRES AT US FROM THE TRENCHES WE DO NOT HAVE THE TIME TO WORK OUT IF HE'S REALLY A NICE GUY, IF HE HAS A MOTHER. WE HAVE ONLY THE TIME TO REPLY IN DEFENSE OF OUR COUNTRY. THOSE YANKEES CAME TO KALAKALA TO DECIMATE OUR POPULA-

TION, TO STERILIZE, DISSOLVE AND DEVIDE IT. THEY HAD BEGUN TO BE SUCCESSFUL IN THIS TASK AND THEIR WORK HAS NOT ENDED SINCE OTHER STERILIZING TEAMS CARRY ON THIS FILTHY BUSINESS. OUR DUTY, THEREFORE, IS TO WARN, DENOUNCE AND REVEAL THE TRUE NATURE OF THEIR ACTIONS.

THE PEASANTS HAVE THEIR OWN CAPACITY FOR EXPRESSION AND CREATION AND TRANSMIT THROUGH THE FORCE OF THEIR COLLECTIVE PRESENCE, THEIR IMMENSE HUMANITY. THESE ARE THE REAL HUMAN BEINGS. THEY DO NOT "PLAY." BY RE-CREATING THE SITUATIONS IN WHICH THEY ARE STILL LIVING, THEY EXPRESS THEIR LIVES AND THEIR EXPERIENCES. THAT IS WHAT MAKES THIS FILM AN EXTENSION OF THEIR REAL LIVES, THE CONTINUATION OF THEIR DAILY STRUGGLE, WHICH IS MADE UP OF SUFFERING, BUT ALSO OF AWARENESS.

TRANSLATED BY JOHN KING.

1. Sanjines worked as part of a collective called the Ukamu Film Group.

One Way Or Another

CUBA

FOR AN IMPERFECT CINEMA [1969]

^^^^^^^^^^^^^^^^^^^^^^^ JULIO GARCIA ESPINOSA

NOWADAYS PERFECT CINEMA—TECHNICALLY AND ARTISTICALLY MASTERFUL—IS ALMOST ALWAYS REACTIONARY CINEMA. THE MAJOR TEMPTATION FACING CUBAN CINEMA AT THIS TIME—WHEN IT IS ACHIEVING ITS OBJECTIVE OF BECOMING A CINEMA OF QUALITY, ONE WHICH IS CULTURALLY MEANINGFUL WITHIN THE REVOLUTIONARY PROCESS—IS PRECISELY THAT OF TRANSFORMING ITSELF INTO A PERFECT CINEMA.

THE "BOOM" OF LATIN AMERICAN CINEMA—WITH BRAZIL AND CUBA IN THE FOREFRONT, ACCORDING TO THE APPLAUSE AND APPROVAL OF THE EUROPEAN INTELLIGENTSIA—IS SIMILAR, IN THE PRESENT MOMENT, TO THE ONE WHICH THE LATIN AMERICAN NOVEL HAD PREVIOUSLY BEEN THE EXCLUSIVE BENEFACTOR. WHY DO THEY APPLAUD US? THERE IS NO DOUBT THAT A CERTAIN STANDARD OF QUALITY HAS BEEN REACHED. DOUBTLESS, THERE IS A CERTAIN POLITICAL OPPORTUNISM, A CERTAIN MUTUAL INSTRUMENTALITY. BUT WITHOUT DOUBT THERE IS ALSO SOMETHING MORE. WHY SHOULD WE WORRY ABOUT THEIR ACCOLADES? ISN'T THE GOAL OF PUBLIC RECOGNITION A PART OF THE RULES OF THE ARTISTIC NAME? WHEN IT COMES TO ARTISTIC CULTURE, ISN'T EUROPEAN RECOGNITION EQUIVALENT TO WORLDWIDE RECOGNITION? DOESN'T IT SERVE ART AND OUR PEOPLES AS WELL WHEN WORKS PRODUCED BY UNDERDEVELOPED NATIONS OBTAIN SUCH RECOGNITION?

ALTHOUGH IT MAY SEEM CURIOUS, IT IS NECESSARY TO CLARIFY THE FACT THAT THIS DISQUIET IS NOT SOLELY MOTIVATED BY ETHICAL CONCERNS. AS A MATTER OF FACT, THE MOTIVATION IS FOR THE MOST PART AESTHETIC, IF INDEED IT IS POSSIBLE TO DRAW SUCH AN ARBITRARY DIVIDING LINE BETWEEN BOTH TERMS. WHEN WE ASK OURSELVES WHY IT IS WE WHO ARE THE FILM DIRECTORS AND NOT THE OTHERS, THAT IS TO SAY, THE SPECTATORS, THE QUESTION DOES NOT STEM FROM AN EXCLUSIVELY ETHICAL CONCERN. WE KNOW THAT WE ARE FILMMAKERS BECAUSE WE HAVE BEEN PART OF A MINORITY WHICH HAS HAD THE TIME AND THE CIRCUMSTANCES NEEDED TO DEVELOP, WITHIN ITSELF, AN ARTISTIC CULTURE, AND BECAUSE THE MATERIAL RESOURCES OF FILM TECHNOLOGY ARE LIMITED AND THEREFORE AVAILABLE TO SOME, NOT TO ALL. BUT WHAT HAPPENS IF THE FUTURE HOLDS THE UNIVERSALIZATION OF COLLEGE-LEVEL INSTRUCTION, IF ECONOMIC AND SOCIAL DEVELOPMENT REDUCE THE HOURS IN THE WORK DAY, IF THE EVOLUTION

OF FILM TECHNOLOGY (THERE ARE ALREADY SIGNS IN EVIDENCE) MAKES IT POSSI-
BLE THAT THIS TECHNOLOGY CEASES BEING THE PRIVILEGE OF A SMALL FEW? WHAT
HAPPENS IF THE DEVELOPMENT OF VIDEOTAPE SOLVES THE PROBLEM OF INEVITABLY
LIMITED LABORATORY CAPACITY, IF TELEVISION SYSTEMS WITH THEIR POTENTIAL FOR
"PROJECTING" INDEPENDENTLY OF THE CENTRAL STUDIO RENDERS THE *AD INFINITUM*
CONSTRUCTION OF MOVIE THEATERS SUDDENLY SUPERFLUOUS?

 WHAT HAPPENS THEN IS NOT ONLY AN ACT OF SOCIAL JUSTICE— THE POSSIBILI-
TY FOR EVERYONE TO MAKE FILMS—BUT ALSO A FACT OF EXTREME IMPORTANCE
FOR ARTISTIC CULTURE: THE POSSIBILITY OF RECOVERING, WITHOUT ANY KINDS
OF COMPLEXES OR GUILT FEELINGS, THE TRUE MEANING OF ARTISTIC ACTIVITY. THEN
WE WILL BE ABLE TO UNDERSTAND THAT ART IS ONE OF MANKIND'S "IMPARTIAL"
OR "UNCOMMITTED" ACTIVITIES [*UNA ACTIVIDAD DESINTERESADA*]. THAT ART IS
NOT WORK, AND THAT THE ARTIST IS NOT IN THE STRICT SENSE A WORKER. THE
FEELING THAT THIS IS SO, AND THE IMPOSSIBILITY OF TRANSLATING IT INTO PRAC-
TICE, CONSTITUTES THE AGONY AND AT THE SAME TIME THE "PHARISEE-ISM" OF
ALL CONTEMPORARY ART. IN FACT, THE TWO TENDENCIES EXIST: THOSE WHO PRE-
TEND TO PRODUCE CINEMA AS AN "UNCOMMITTED" ACTIVITY AND THOSE WHO
PRETEND TO JUSTIFY IT AS A "COMMITTED" ACTIVITY. BOTH FIND THEMSELVES IN
A BLIND ALLEY.

 ANYONE ENGAGED IN AN ARTISTIC ACTIVITY ASKS HIMSELF AT A GIVEN MO-
MENT WHAT IS THE MEANING OF WHATEVER HE IS DOING. THE SIMPLE FACT THAT
THIS ANXIETY ARISES DEMONSTRATES THAT FACTORS EXIST TO MOTIVATE IT—FACTORS,
WHICH, IN TURN, INDICATE THAT ART DOES NOT DEVELOP FREELY. THOSE WHO
PERSIST IN DENYING ART A SPECIFIC MEANING FEEL THE MORAL WEIGHT OF THEIR
EGOISM. THOSE WHO, ON THE OTHER HAND, PRETEND TO ATTRIBUTE ONE TO IT,
BUY OFF THEIR BAD CONSCIENCE WITH SOCIAL GENEROSITY. IT MAKES NO DIF-
FERENCE THAT THE MEDIATORS (CRITICS, THEORETICIANS, ETC.) TRY TO JUSTIFY CERTAIN
CASES. FOR THE CONTEMPORARY ARTIST, THE MEDIATOR IS LIKE AN ASPIRIN, A TRAN-
QUILIZER. AS WITH A PILL, THE ARTIST ONLY TEMPORARILY GETS RID OF THE
HEADACHE. THE SURE THING, HOWEVER, IS THAT ART, LIKE A CAPRICIOUS LITTLE
DEVIL, CONTINUES TO SHOW ITS FACE SPORADICALLY IN NO MATTER WHICH
TENDENCY.

 NO DOUBT IT IS EASIER TO DEFINE ART BY WHAT IT IS NOT THAN BY WHAT
IT IS, ASSUMING THAT ONE CAN TALK ABOUT CLOSED DEFINITIONS NOT JUST FOR
ART BUT FOR ANY OF LIFE'S ACTIVITIES. THE SPIRIT OF CONTRADICTION PERMEATES
EVERYTHING NOW. NOTHING, AND NOBODY LETS HIMSELF BE IMPRISONED IN A
PICTURE FRAME, NO MATTER HOW GILDED. IT IS POSSIBLE THAT ART GIVES US A
VISION OF SOCIETY OR OF HUMAN NATURE AND THAT, AT THAT SAME TIME, IT
CANNOT BE DEFINED AS A VISION OF SOCIETY OR OF HUMAN NATURE. IT IS POSSI-
BLE THAT A CERTAIN NARCISSISM OF CONSCIOUSNESS—IN RECOGNIZING IN ONESELF
A LITTLE HISTORICAL, SOCIOLOGICAL, PSYCHOLOGICAL, PHILOSOPHICAL
CONSCIOUSNESS—IS IMPLICIT IN AESTHETIC PLEASURE, AND AT THE SAME TIME THAT

THIS SENSATION IS NOT SUFFICIENT IN ITSELF TO EXPLAIN AESTHETIC PLEASURE.

IS IT NOT MUCH CLOSER TO THE NATURE OF ART TO CONCEIVE OF IT AS HAV- ING ITS OWN COGNITIVE POWER? IN OTHER WORDS, BY SAYING THAT ART IS NOT THE "ILLUSTRATION" OF IDEAS WHICH CAN ALSO BE EXPRESSED THROUGH PHILOSOPHY, SOCIOLOGY, PSYCHOLOGY. EVERY ARTIST'S DESIRE TO EXPRESS THE INEXPRESSIBLE IS NOTHING MORE THAN THE DESIRE TO EXPRESS THE VISION OF A THEME IN TERMS THAT ARE INEXPRESSIBLE THROUGH OTHER THAN ARTISTIC MEANS. PERHAPS THE COGNITIVE POWER OF ART IS LIKE THE POWER OF A GAME FOR A CHILD. PERHAPS AESTHETIC PLEASURE LIES IN SENSING THE FUNCTIONALITY (WITHOUT A SPECIFIC GOAL) OF OUR INTELLIGENCE AND OUR OWN SENSITIVITY. ART CAN STIMULATE, IN GENERAL, THE CREATIVE FUNCTION OF MAN. IT CAN FUNCTION AS A CONSTANT STIMULUS TOWARD ADOPTING AN ATTITUDE OF CHANGE WITH REGARD TO LIFE. BUT, AS OPPOSED TO SCIENCE, IT ENRICHES US IN SUCH A WAY THAT ITS RESULTS ARE NOT SPECIFIC AND CANNOT BE APPLIED TO ANYTHING IN PARTICULAR. IT IS FOR THIS REASON THAT WE CAN CALL IT AN "IMPARTIAL" OR "UNCOMMIT- TED" ACTIVITY, AND CAN SAY THAT ART IS NOT STRICTLY SPEAKING A "JOB," AND THAT THE ARTIST IS PERHAPS THE LEAST INTELLECTUAL OF ALL INTELLECTUALS.

WHY THEN DOES THE ARTIST FEEL THE NEED TO JUSTIFY HIMSELF AS A "WORKER," AS AN "INTELLECTUAL," AS A "PROFESSIONAL," AS A DISCIPLINED AND ORGANIZED MAN, LIKE ANY OTHER INDIVIDUAL WHO PERFORMS A PRODUCTIVE TASK? WHY DOES HE FEEL THE NEED TO EXAGGERATE THE IMPORTANCE OF HIS AC- TIVITY? WHY DOES HE FEEL THE NEED TO HAVE CRITICS (MEDIATORS) TO JUSTIFY HIM, TO DEFEND HIM, TO INTERPRET HIM? WHY DOES HE SPEAK PROUDLY OF "MY CRITICS"? WHY DOES HE FIND IT NECESSARY TO MAKE TRANSCENDENTAL DECLARA- TIONS, AS IF HE WERE THE TRUE INTERPRETER OF SOCIETY AND OF MANKIND? WHY DOES HE PRETEND TO CONSIDER HIMSELF CRITIC AND CONSCIENCE OF SOCIETY WHEN (ALTHOUGH THESE OBJECTIVES CAN BE IMPLICIT OR EVEN EXPLICIT IN CER- TAIN CIRCUMSTANCES) IN A TRULY REVOLUTIONARY SOCIETY ALL OF US—THAT IS TO SAY, THE PEOPLE AS A WHOLE—SHOULD EXERCISE THOSE FUNCTIONS? AND WHY, ON THE OTHER HAND, DOES THE ARTIST SEE HIMSELF FORCED TO LIMIT THESE OBJECTIVES, THESE ATTITUDES, THESE CHARACTERISTICS? WHY DOES HE AT THE SAME TIME SET UP THESE LIMITATIONS AS NECESSARY TO PREVENT HIS WORK FROM BEING TRANSFORMED INTO A "TRACT" OR A SOCIOLOGICAL ESSAY? WHAT IS BEHIND SUCH PHARISEE-ISM? WHY PROTECT ONESELF AND SEEK RECOGNITION AS A (REVOLU- TIONARY, IT MUST BE UNDERSTOOD) POLITICAL AND SCIENTIFIC WORKER, YET NOT BE PREPARED TO RUN THE SAME RISKS?

THE PROBLEM IS A COMPLEX ONE. BASICALLY, IT IS NEITHER A MATTER OF OP- PORTUNISM OR COWARDICE. A TRUE ARTIST IS PREPARED TO RUN ANY RISK AS LONG AS HE IS CERTAIN THAT HIS WORK WILL NOT CEASE TO BE AN ARTISTIC EX- PRESSION. THE ONLY RISK WHICH HE WILL NOT ACCEPT IS THAT OF ENDANGERING THE ARTISTIC QUALITY OF HIS WORK.

THERE ARE THOSE WHO ACCEPT AND DEFEND THE "IMPARTIAL" FUNCTION

OF ART. THESE PEOPLE CLAIM TO BE MORE CONSISTENT. THEY OPT FOR THE BIT-
TERNESS OF A CLOSED WORLD IN THE HOPE THAT TOMORROW HISTORY WILL JUSTIFY
THEM. BUT THE FACT IS THAT EVEN TODAY NOT EVERYONE CAN ENJOY THE MONA
LISA. THESE PEOPLE SHOULD HAVE FEWER CONTRADICTIONS; THEY SHOULD BE
LESS ALIENATED, BUT IN FACT IT IS NOT SO, EVEN THOUGH SUCH AN ATTITUDE
GIVES THEM THE POSSIBILITY OF AN ALIBI WHICH IS MORE PRODUCTIVE ON A PER-
SONAL LEVEL. IN GENERAL THEY SENSE THE STERILITY OF THEIR "PURITY" OR THEY
DEDICATE THEMSELVES TO WAGING CORROSIVE BATTLES, BUT ALWAYS ON THE DEFEN-
SIVE. THEY CAN EVEN, IN A REVERSE OPERATION, REJECT THEIR INTEREST IN FIN-
DING TRANQUILITY, HARMONY, A CERTAIN COMPENSATION IN THE WORK OF ART,
EXPRESSING INSTEAD DISEQUILIBRIUM, CHAOS, AND UNCERTAINTY WHICH ALSO
BECOMES THE OBJECTIVE OF "IMPARTIAL" ART.

WHAT IS IT, THEN, WHICH MAKES IT IMPOSSIBLE TO PRACTICE ART AS AN "IM-
PARTIAL" ACTIVITY? WHY IS THIS PARTICULAR SITUATION TODAY MORE SENSITIVE
THAN EVER? FROM THE BEGINNING OF THE WORLD AS WE KNOW IT, THAT IS TO
SAY, SINCE THE WORLD WAS DIVIDED INTO CLASSES, THIS SITUATION HAS BEEN LA-
TENT. IF IT HAS GROWN SHARPER TODAY IT IS PRECISELY BECAUSE TODAY THE POSSIBILI-
TY OF TRANSCENDING IT IS COMING INTO VIEW. NOT THROUGH A *PRISE DE
CONSCIENCE*, NOT THROUGH THE EXPRESSED DETERMINATION OF ANY PARTICULAR
ARTIST, BUT BECAUSE REALITY ITSELF HAS BEGUN TO REVEAL SYMPTOMS (NOT AT
ALL UTOPIAN) WHICH INDICATES THAT "IN THE FUTURE THERE WILL NO LONGER
BE PAINTERS, BUT RATHER MEN WHO, AMONG OTHER THINGS, DEDICATE THEMSELVES
TO PAINTING" (MARX).

THERE CAN BE NO "IMPARTIAL" OR "UNCOMMITTED" ART, THERE CAN BE NO
NEW AND GENUINE QUALITATIVE JUMP IN ART, UNLESS THE CONCEPT AND THE
REALITY OF THE "ELITE" IS DONE AWAY WITH ONCE AND FOR ALL. THREE FACTORS
INCLINE US TOWARD OPTIMISM: THE DEVELOPMENT OF SCIENCE, THE SOCIAL
PRESENCE OF THE MASSES, AND THE REVOLUTIONARY POTENTIAL IN THE CONTEM-
PORARY WORLD. ALL THREE ARE WITHOUT HIERARCHIAL ORDER, ALL THREE ARE
INTERRELATED.

WHY IS SCIENCE FEARED? WHY ARE PEOPLE AFRAID THAT ART MIGHT BE CRUSH-
ED UNDER OBVIOUS PRODUCTIVITY AND UTILITY OF SCIENCE? WHY THIS INFERIORITY
COMPLEX? IT IS TRUE THAT TODAY WE READ A GOOD ESSAY WITH MUCH GREATER
PLEASURE THAN A NOVEL. WHY DO WE KEEP REPEATING THEN, HORRIFIED, THAT
THE WORLD IS BECOMING MORE MERCENARY, MORE UTILITARIAN, MORE
MATERIALISTIC? IS IT NOT REALLY MARVELOUS THAT THE DEVELOPMENT OF SCIENCE,
SOCIOLOGY, ANTHROPOLOGY, PSYCHOLOGY, IS CONTRIBUTING TO THE "PURIFICA-
TION" OF ART? THE APPEARANCE, THANKS TO SCIENCE, OF EXPRESSIVE MEDIA LIKE
PHOTOGRAPHY AND FILM MADE A GREATER "PURIFICATION" OF PAINTING AND
THE THEATER POSSIBLE (WITHOUT INVALIDATING THEM ARTISTICALLY IN THE LEAST).
DOESN'T MODERN DAY SCIENCE RENDER ANACHRONISTIC SO MUCH "ARTISTIC"
ANALYSIS OF THE HUMAN SOUL? DOESN'T CONTEMPORARY SCIENCE ALLOW US

TO FREE OURSELVES FROM SO MANY FRAUDULENT FILMS, CONCEALED BEHIND WHAT HAS BEEN CALLED THE WORLD OF POETRY? WITH THE ADVANCE OF SCIENCE, ART HAS NOTHING TO LOSE; ON THE CONTRARY, IT HAS A WHOLE WORLD TO GAIN. WHAT, THEN, ARE WE SO AFRAID OF? SCIENCE STRIPS ART BARE AND IT SEEMS THAT IT IS NOT EASY TO GO NAKED THROUGH THE STREETS.

THE REAL TRAGEDY OF THE CONTEMPORARY ARTIST LIES IN THE IMPOSSIBILITY OF PRACTICING ART AS A MINORITY ACTIVITY. IT IS SAID—AND CORRECTLY—THAT ART CANNOT EXERCISE ITS ATTRACTION WITHOUT THE COOPERATION OF THE SUBJECT. BUT WHAT CAN BE DONE SO THAT THE AUDIENCE STOPS BEING AN OBJECT AND TRANSFORMS ITSELF INTO THE SUBJECT?

THE DEVELOPMENT OF SCIENCE, OF TECHNOLOGY, OF THE MOST ADVANCED SOCIAL THEORY AND PRACTICE, HAS MADE POSSIBLE AS NEVER BEFORE THE ACTIVE PRESENCE OF THE MASSES IN THE SOCIAL LIFE. IN THE REALM OF ARTISTIC LIFE, THERE ARE MORE SPECTATORS NOW THAN AT ANY OTHER MOMENT IN HISTORY. THIS IS THE FIRST STAGE IN THE ABOLITION OF "ELITES." THE TASK CURRENTLY AT HAND IS TO FIND OUT IF THE CONDITIONS WHICH WILL ENABLE SPECTATORS TO TRANSFORM THEMSELVES INTO AGENTS—NOT MERELY MORE ACTIVE SPECTATORS, BUT GENUINE CO-AUTHORS—ARE BEGINNING TO EXIST. THE TASK AT HAND IS TO ASK OURSELVES WHETHER ART IS REALLY AN ACTIVITY RESTRICTED TO SPECIALISTS, WHETHER IT IS, THROUGH EXTRA-HUMAN DESIGN, THE OPTION OF A CHOSEN FEW OR A POSSIBILITY FOR EVERYONE.

HOW CAN WE TRUST THE PERSPECTIVES AND POSSIBILITIES OF ART SIMPLY TO THE EDUCATION OF THE PEOPLE AS A MASS OF SPECTATORS? TASTE AS DEFINED BY "HIGH CULTURE," ONCE IT IS "OVERDONE," IS NORMALLY PASSED ON TO THE REST OF SOCIETY AS LEFTOVERS TO BE DEVOURED AND RUMINATED OVER BY THOSE WHO WERE NOT INVITED TO THE FEAST. THIS ETERNAL SPIRAL HAS TODAY BECOME A VICIOUS CIRCLE AS WELL. "CAMP" AND ITS ATTITUDE TOWARD EVERYTHING OUTDATED IS AN ATTEMPT TO RESCUE THESE LEFTOVERS AND TO LESSEN THE DISTANCE BETWEEN HIGH CULTURE AND THE PEOPLE. BUT THE DIFFERENCE LIES IN THE FACT THAT CAMP RESCUES IT AS AN AESTHETIC VALUE, WHILE FOR THE PEOPLE THE VALUES INVOLVED CONTINUE TO BE ETHICAL ONES.

MUST THE REVOLUTIONARY PRESENT AND THE REVOLUTIONARY FUTURE INEVITABLY HAVE "ITS" ARTISTS AND "ITS" INTELLECTUALS, JUST AS THE BOURGEOISIE HAD "THEIRS"? SURELY THE TRULY REVOLUTIONARY POSITION, FROM NOW ON, IS TO CONTRIBUTE TO OVERCOMING THESE ELITIST CONCEPTS AND PRACTICES, RATHER THAN PURSUING AD ETERNUM THE "ARTISTIC QUALITY" OF THE WORK. THE NEW OUTLOOK FOR ARTISTIC CULTURE IS NO LONGER THAT EVERYONE MUST SHARE THE TASTE OF A FEW, BUT THAT ALL CAN BE CREATORS OF THAT CULTURE. ART HAS ALWAYS BEEN A UNIVERSAL NECESSITY; THAT IT HAS NOT BEEN IS AN OPTION FOR ALL UNDER EQUAL CONDITIONS. PARALLEL TO REFINED ART, POPULAR ART HAS HAD A SIMULTANEOUS BUT INDEPENDENT EXISTENCE.

POPULAR ART HAS ABSOLUTELY NOTHING TO DO WITH WHAT IS CALLED MASS

ART. POPULAR ART NEEDS AND CONSEQUENTLY TENDS TO DEVELOP THE PERSONAL, INDIVIDUAL TASTE OF A PEOPLE. ON THE OTHER HAND, MASS ART (OR ART FOR THE MASSES) REQUIRES THE PEOPLE TO HAVE NO TASTE. IT WILL ONLY BE GENUINE WHEN IT IS ACTUALLY THE MASSES WHO CREATE IT, SINCE AT PRESENT IT IS ART PRODUCED BY A FEW FOR MASSES. GROTOWSKI SAYS THAT TODAY'S THEATER SHOULD BE MINORITY ART FORM BECAUSE MASS ART CAN BE ACHIEVED THROUGH CINEMA. THIS IS NOT TRUE. PERHAPS FILM IS THE MOST ELITIST OF ALL THE CONTEMPORARY ARTS. FILM TODAY, NO MATTER WHERE, IS MADE BY A SMALL MINORITY FOR THE MASSES. PERHAPS FILM WILL BE THE ART FORM WHICH TAKES THE LONGEST TIME TO REACH THE HAND OF THE MASS ART AS *POPULAR* ART, ART CREATED BY THE MASSES. CURRENTLY, AS HAUSER POINTS OUT, MASS ART IS ART PRODUCED BY A MINORITY IN ORDER TO SATISFY THE DEMAND OF A PUBLIC REDUCED TO THE SOLE ROLE OF SPECTATOR AND CONSUMER.

POPULAR ART HAS ALWAYS BEEN CREATED BY THE LEAST LEARNED SECTOR OF SOCIETY, YET THIS "UNCULTURED" SECTOR HAS MANAGED TO CONSERVE PROFOUND-LY CULTURED CHARACTERISTICS OF ART. ONE OF THE MOST IMPORTANT OF THESE IS THE FACT THAT THE CREATORS ARE AT THE SAME TIME THE SPECTATORS AND VICE VERSA. BETWEEN THOSE WHO PRODUCE AND THOSE WHO CONSUME, NO SHARP LINE OF DEMARCATION EXISTS. CULTIVATED ART, IN OUR ERA, HAS ALSO ATTAINED THIS SITUATION. MODERN ART'S GREAT DOSE OF FREEDOM IS NOTHING MORE THAN THE CONQUEST OF A NEW INTERLOCUTOR: THE ARTIST HIMSELF. FOR THIS REASON IT IS USELESS TO STRAIN ONESELF STRUGGLING FOR THE SUBSTITUTION OF THE MASSES AS A NEW AND POTENTIAL SPECTATOR FOR THE BOURGEOISIE. THIS SITUATION, MAIN-TAINED BY POPULAR ART, ADOPTED BY CULTIVATED ART, MUST BE DISSOLVED AND BECOME THE HERITAGE OF ALL. THIS AND NO OTHER MUST BE THE GREAT OBJEC-TIVE OF AN AUTHENTICALLY REVOLUTIONARY ARTISTIC CULTURE.

POPULAR ART PRESERVED ANOTHER EVEN MORE IMPORTANT CULTURAL CHARACTERISTIC: IT IS CARRIED OUT AS BUT ANOTHER LIFE ACTIVITY. WITH CULTIVATED ART, THE REVERSE IS TRUE; IT IS PURSUED AS A UNIQUE, SPECIFIC AC-TIVITY, AS A PERSONAL ACHIEVEMENT. THIS IS THE CRUEL PRICE OF HAVING HAD TO MAINTAIN ARTISTIC ACTIVITY AT THE EXPENSE OF ITS INEXISTENCE AMONG THE PEOPLE. HASN'T THE ATTEMPT TO REALIZE HIMSELF ON THE EDGE OF SOCIETY PRO-VED TO BE TOO PAINFUL A RESTRICTION FOR THE ARTIST AND FOR ART ITSELF? TO POSIT ART AS A SECT, AS A SOCIETY WITHIN SOCIETY, AS THE PROMISED LAND WHERE WE CAN FLEETINGLY FULFILL OURSELVES FOR A BRIEF INSTANT— DOESN'T THIS CREATE THE ILLUSION THAT SELF-REALIZATION ON THE LEVEL OF CONSCIOUSNESS ALSO IMPLIES SELF-REALIZATION ON THE LEVEL OF EXISTENCE? ISN'T THIS PATENTLY OBVIOUS IN CONTEMPORARY CIRCUMSTANCES? THE ESSENTIAL LESSON OF POPULAR ART IS THAT IT IS CARRIED OUT AS A LIFE ACTIVITY; MAN MUST NOT FULFILL HIMSELF AS AN ARTIST BUT FULLY; THE ARTIST MUST NOT SEEK FULFILLMENT AS AN ARTIST BUT AS A HUMAN BEING.

IN THE MODERN WORLD, PRINCIPALLY IN DEVELOPED CAPITALIST NATIONS AND

IN THOSE COUNTRIES ENGAGED IN A REVOLUTIONARY PROCESS, THERE ARE ALARMING SYMPTOMS, OBVIOUS SIGNS OF AN IMMINENT CHANGE. THE POSSIBILITIES FOR OVERCOMING THIS TRADITIONAL DISASSOCIATION ARE BEGINNING TO ARISE. THESE SYMPTOMS ARE NOT A PRODUCT OF CONSCIOUSNESS BUT OF REALITY ITSELF. A LARGE PART OF THE STRUGGLE WAGED IN MODERN ART HAS BEEN, IN FACT, TO "DEMOCRATIZE" ART. WHAT OTHER GOAL IS ENTAILED IN COMBATTING THE LIMITATIONS OF TASTE, MUSEUM ART, AND THE DEMARCATION LINES BETWEEN THE CREATOR AND THE PUBLIC? WHAT IS CONSIDERED BEAUTY TODAY, AND WHERE IS IT FOUND? ON CAMPBELL'S SOUP LABELS, IN A GARBAGE CAN LID, IN GADGETS? EVEN THE ETERNAL VALUE OF A WORK OF ART IS TODAY BEING QUESTIONED. WHAT ELSE COULD BE THE MEANING OF THOSE SCULPTURES, SEEN IN RECENT EXHIBITIONS, MADE OF BLOCKS OF ICE WHICH MELT AWAY WHILE THE PUBLIC LOOKS AT THEM? ISN'T THIS—MORE THAN THE DISAPPEARANCE OF ART—THE ATTEMPT TO MAKE THE SPECTATOR DISAPPEAR? DON'T THOSE PAINTERS WHO ENTRUST A PORTION OF THE EXECUTION OF THEIR WORK TO JUST ANYONE, RATHER THAN TO THEIR DISCIPLES, EXHIBIT AN EAGERNESS TO JUMP OVER THE BARRICADE OF "ELITIST" ART? DOESN'T THE SAME ATTITUDE EXIST AMONG COMPOSERS WHOSE WORKS ALLOW THEIR PERFORMERS AMPLE LIBERTY?

THERE'S A WIDESPREAD TENDENCY IN MODERN ART TO MAKE THE SPECTATOR PARTICIPATE EVER MORE FULLY. IF HE PARTICIPATES TO A GREATER AND GREATER DEGREE, WHERE WILL THE PROCESS END UP? ISN'T THE LOGICAL OUTCOME—OR SHOULDN'T IT IN FACT BE—THAT HE WILL CEASE BEING A SPECTATOR ALTOGETHER? THIS SIMULTANEOUSLY REPRESENTS A TENDENCY TOWARD COLLECTIVISM AND TOWARD INDIVIDUALISM. ONCE WE ADMIT THE POSSIBILITY OF UNIVERSAL PARTICIPATION, AREN'T WE ALSO ADMITTING THE INDIVIDUAL CREATIVE POTENTIAL WHICH WE ALL HAVE? ISN'T GROTOWSKI MISTAKEN WHEN HE ASSERTS THAT TODAY'S THEATER SHOULD BE DEDICATED TO AN ELITE? ISN'T IT RATHER THE REVERSE: THAT THE THEATER OF POVERTY IN FACT REQUIRES THE HIGHEST REFINEMENT? IT IS THE THEATER WHICH HAS NO NEED FOR SECONDARY VALUES: COSTUMES, SCENERY, MAKE-UP, EVEN A STAGE. ISN'T THIS AN INDICATION THAT MATERIAL CONDITIONS ARE REDUCED TO A MINIMUM AND THAT, FROM THIS POINT OF VIEW, THE POSSIBILITY OF MAKING THEATER IS WITHIN EVERYONE'S REACH? AND DOESN'T THE FACT THAT THE THEATER HAS AN INCREASINGLY SMALLER PUBLIC MEAN THAT CONDITIONS ARE BEGINNING TO RIPEN FOR IT TO TRANSFORM ITSELF INTO A TRUE MASS THEATER? PERHAPS THE TRAGEDY OF THE THEATER LIES IN THE FACT THAT IT HAS REACHED THIS POINT IN ITS EVOLUTION TOO SOON.

WHEN WE LOOK TOWARD EUROPE, WE WRING OUR HANDS. WE SEE THAT THE OLD CULTURE IS TOTALLY INCAPABLE OF PROVIDING ANSWERS TO THE PROBLEMS OF ART, THE FACT IS THAT EUROPE CAN NO LONGER RESPOND IN A TRADITIONAL MANNER BUT AT THE SAME TIME FINDS IT EQUALLY DIFFICULT TO RESPOND IN A MANNER THAT IS RADICALLY NEW. EUROPE IS NO LONGER CAPABLE OF GIVING THE WORLD A NEW "ISM"; NEITHER IS IT IN A POSITION TO PUT AN END TO

"ISMS" ONCE AND FOR ALL. SO WE THINK THAT OUR MOMENT HAS COME, THAT AT LAST THE UNDERDEVELOPED CAN DECK THEMSELVES OUT AS "MEN OF CULTURE." HERE LIES OUR GREATEST DANGER AND OUR GREATEST TEMPTATION. THIS ACCOUNTS FOR THE OPPORTUNISM OF SOME ON OUR CONTINENT. FOR, GIVEN OUR TECHNICAL AND SCIENTIFIC BACKWARDNESS AND GIVEN THE SCANTY PRESENCE OF THE MASSES IN SOCIAL LIFE, OUR CONTINENT IS STILL CAPABLE OF RESPONDING IN A TRADITIONAL MANNER, BY REAFFIRMING THE CONCEPT AND THE PRACTICE OF ELITE ART. PERHAPS IN THIS CASE THE REAL MOTIVE FOR THE EUROPEAN APPLAUSE WHICH SOME OF OUR LITERARY AND CINEMATIC WORKS HAVE WON IS NONE OTHER THAN A CERTAIN NOSTALGIA WHICH WE INSPIRE. AFTER ALL, THE EUROPEAN HAS NO OTHER EUROPE TO WHICH TO TURN.

THE THIRD FACTOR, THE REVOLUTION—WHICH IS THE MOST IMPORTANT OF ALL—IS PERHAPS PRESENT IN OUR COUNTRY AS NOWHERE ELSE. THIS IS OUR ONLY TRUE CHANCE. THE REVOLUTION IS WHAT PROVIDES ALL OTHER ALTERNATIVES, WHAT CAN SUPPLY AN ENTIRELY NEW RESPONSE, WHAT ENABLES US TO DO AWAY ONCE AND FOR ALL WITH ELITIST CONCEPTS AND PRACTICES IN ART. THE REVOLUTION AND THE ONGOING REVOLUTIONARY PROCESS ARE THE ONLY FACTORS WHICH MAKE THE TOTAL AND FREE PRESENCE OF THE MASSES POSSIBLE—AND THIS WILL MEAN THE DEFINITIVE DISAPPEARANCE OF THE RIGID DIVISION OF LABOR AND OF A SOCIETY DIVIDED INTO SECTORS AND CLASSES. FOR US, THEN, THE REVOLUTION IS THE HIGHEST EXPRESSION OF CULTURE BECAUSE IT WILL ABOLISH ARTISTIC CULTURE AS FRAGMENTARY HUMAN ACTIVITY.

CURRENT RESPONSES TO THIS INEVITABLE FUTURE, THIS UNCONTESTABLE PROSPECT, CAN BE AS NUMEROUS AS THE COUNTRIES ON OUR CONTINENT. BECAUSE CHARACTERISTICS AND ACHIEVED LABELS ARE NOT THE SAME, EACH ART FORM, EVERY ARTISTIC MANIFESTATION, MUST FIND ITS OWN EXPRESSION. WHAT SHOULD BE THE RESPONSE OF THE CUBAN CINEMA IN PARTICULAR? PARADOXICALLY, WE THINK IT WILL BE A NEW POETICS, NOT A NEW CULTURAL POLICY. A POETICS WHOSE TRUE GOAL WILL BE TO COMMIT SUICIDE, TO DISAPPEAR AS SUCH. WE KNOW HOWEVER, THAT IN FACT OTHER ARTISTIC CONCEPTIONS WILL CONTINUE TO EXIST AMONG US, JUST LIKE SMALL RURAL LANDHOLDINGS AND RELIGION CONTINUE TO EXIST.

ON THE LEVEL OF CULTURAL POLICY WE ARE FACED WITH A SERIOUS PROBLEM: THE FILM SCHOOL. IS IT RIGHT TO CONTINUE DEVELOPING A HANDFUL OF FILM SPECIALISTS? IT SEEMS INEVITABLE FOR THE PRESENT, BUT WHAT WILL BE THE ETERNAL QUARRY THAT WE CONTINUE TO MINE: THE STUDENTS IN ARTS AND LETTERS AT THE UNIVERSITY? BUT SHOULDN'T WE BEGIN TO CONSIDER RIGHT NOW WHETHER THAT SCHOOL SHOULD HAVE A LIMITED LIFESPAN? WHAT END DO WE PURSUE THERE—A RESERVE CORPS OF FUTURE ARTISTS? OR A SPECIALIZED FUTURE PUBLIC? WE SHOULD BE ASKING OURSELVES WHETHER WE CAN DO SOMETHING NOW TO ABOLISH THIS DIVISION BETWEEN ARTISTIC AND SCIENTIFIC CULTURE.

WHAT CONSTITUTES IN FACT THE TRUE PRESTIGE OF ARTISTIC CULTURE, AND

HOW DID IT COME ABOUT THAT THIS PRESTIGE WAS ALLOWED TO APPROPRIATE THE WHOLE CONCEPT OF CULTURE? PERHAPS IT IS BASED ON THE ENORMOUS PRESTIGE WHICH THE SPIRIT HAS ALWAYS ENJOYED AT THE EXPENSE OF THE BODY. HASN'T ARTISTIC CULTURE ALWAYS BEEN SEEN AS THE SPIRITUAL PART OF SOCIETY WHILE SCIENTIFIC CULTURE IS SEEN AS ITS BODY? THE TRADITIONAL REJECTION OF THE BODY, OF MATERIAL LIFE, IS DUE IN PART TO THE CONCEPT THAT THINGS OF THE SPIRIT ARE MORE ELEVATED, MORE ELEGANT, SERIOUS AND PROFOUND. CAN'T WE, HERE AND NOW, BEGIN DOING SOMETHING TO PUT AN END TO THIS ARTIFICIAL DISTINCTION? WE SHOULD UNDERSTAND FROM HERE ON IN THAT THE BODY AND THE THINGS OF THE BODY ARE ALSO ELEGANT, AND THAT MATERIAL LIFE IS BEAUTIFUL AS WELL. WE SHOULD UNDERSTAND THAT, IN FACT THE SOUL IS CONTAINED IN THE BODY JUST AS THE SPIRIT IS CONTAINED IN MATERIAL LIFE, JUST AS— TO SPEAK IN STRICTLY ARTISTIC TERMS—THE ESSENCE IS CONTAINED IN THE SURFACE AND THE CONTENT IN THE FORM.

WE SHOULD ENDEAVOR TO SEE THAT OUR FUTURE STUDENTS, AND THEREFORE OUR FUTURE FILMMAKERS, WILL THEMSELVES BE SCIENTISTS, SOCIOLOGISTS, PHYSICIANS, ECONOMISTS, AGRICULTURAL ENGINEERS, ETC., WITHOUT OF COURSE CEASING TO BE FILMMAKERS. AND, AT THE SAME TIME, WE SHOULD HAVE THE SAME AIM FOR OUR MOST OUTSTANDING WORKERS, THE WORKERS WHO ACHIEVE THE BEST RESULTS IN TERMS OF POLITICAL AND INTELLECTUAL FORMATION. WE CANNOT DEVELOP THE TASTE OF THE MASSES AS LONG AS THE DIVISION BETWEEN THE TWO CULTURES CONTINUES TO EXIST, NOR AS LONG AS THE MASSES ARE NOT THE REAL MASTERS OF THE MEANS OF ARTISTIC PRODUCTION. THE REVOLUTION HAS LIBERATED US AS AN ARTISTIC SECTOR. IT IS ONLY LOGICAL THAT WE CONTRIBUTE TO THE LIBERATION OF THE PRIVATE MEANS OF ARTISTIC PRODUCTION.

A NEW POETICS FOR THE CINEMA WILL, ABOVE ALL, BE A "PARTISAN" AND "COMMITTED" ART, A CONSCIOUSLY AND RESOLUTELY "COMMITTED" CINEMA— THAT IS TO SAY, AN "IMPERFECT" CINEMA. AN "IMPARTIAL" OR "UNCOMMITTED" (CINEMA), AS A COMPLETE AESTHETIC ACTIVITY, WILL ONLY BE POSSIBLE WHEN IT IS THE PEOPLE WHO MAKE ART. BUT TODAY ART MUST ASSIMILATE ITS QUOTA OF WORK SO THAT WORK CAN ASSIMILATE ITS QUOTA OF ART.

THE MOTTO OF THIS IMPERFECT CINEMA (WHICH THERE'S NO NEED TO INVENT, SINCE IT ALREADY EXISTS) IS, AS GLAUBER ROCHA WOULD SAY, "WE ARE NOT INTERESTED IN THE PROBLEMS OF NEUROSIS; WE ARE INTERESTED IN THE PROBLEM OF LUCIDITY." ART NO LONGER HAS USE FOR THE NEUROTIC AND HIS PROBLEMS, ALTHOUGH THE NEUROTIC CONTINUES TO NEED ART—AS A CONCERNED OBJECT, A RELIEF, AN ALIBI OR, AS FREUD WOULD SAY AS A SUBLIMATION OF HIS PROBLEMS. A NEUROTIC CAN PRODUCE ART, BUT ART HAS NO REASON TO PRODUCE NEUROTICS. IT HAS BEEN TRADITIONALLY BELIEVED THAT THE CONCERNS OF ART WERE NOT TO BE FOUND IN THE SANE BUT IN THE SICK, NOT IN THE NORMAL BUT IN THE ABNORMAL, NOT IN THOSE WHO STRUGGLE BUT IN THOSE WHO WEEP, NOT IN LUCID MINDS BUT IN NEUROTIC ONES. IMPERFECT CINEMA IS CHANGING

THIS WAY OF SEEING THE QUESTION. WE HAVE MORE FAITH IN THE SICK MAN THAN IN THE HEALTHY ONE BECAUSE HIS TRUTH IS PURGED BY SUFFERING. HOWEVER, THERE IS NO NEED FOR SUFFERING TO BE SYNONYMOUS WITH ARTISTIC ELEGANCE. THERE IS STILL A TREND IN MODERN ART—UNDOUBTEDLY RELATED TO CHRISTIAN TRADITION—WHICH IDENTIFIES SERIOUSNESS WITH SUFFERING. THE SPECTER OF MARGUERITE GAUTIER STILL HAUNTS ARTISTIC ENDEAVOR IN OUR DAY. ONLY IN THE PERSON WHO SUFFERS DO WE PERCEIVE ELEGANCE, GRAVITY, EVEN BEAUTY; ONLY IN HIM DO WE RECOGNIZE THE POSSIBILITY OF AUTHENTICITY, SERIOUSNESS, SINCERITY. IMPERFECT CINEMA MUST PUT AN END TO THIS TRADITION.

IMPERFECT CINEMA FINDS A NEW AUDIENCE IN THOSE WHO STRUGGLE, AND IT FINDS ITS THEMES IN THEIR PROBLEMS. FOR IMPERFECT CINEMA, "LUCID" PEOPLE ARE THE ONES WHO THINK AND FEEL AND EXIST IN A WORLD WHICH THEY CAN CHANGE; IN SPITE OF ALL THE PROBLEMS AND DIFFICULTIES, THEY ARE CONVINCED THAT THEY CAN TRANSFORM IT IN A REVOLUTIONARY WAY. IMPERFECT CINEMA THEREFORE HAS NO NEED TO STRUGGLE TO CREATE AN "AUDIENCE." ON THE CONTRARY, IT CAN BE SAID THAT AT PRESENT A GREATER AUDIENCE EXISTS FOR THIS KIND OF CINEMA THAN THERE ARE FILMMAKERS ABLE TO SUPPLY THAT AUDIENCE.

WHAT DOES THIS NEW INTERLOCUTOR REQUIRE OF US—AN ART FULL OF MORAL EXAMPLES WORTHY OF IMITATION? NO. MAN IS MORE OF A CREATOR THAN AN INNOVATOR. BESIDES, HE SHOULD BE THE ONE TO GIVE *US* MORAL EXAMPLES. HE MIGHT ASK US FOR A FULLER, MORE COMPLETE WORK, AIMED—IN A SEPARATE OR COORDINATED FASHION—AT THE INTELLIGENCE, THE EMOTIONS, THE POWERS OF INTUITION.

SHOULD HE ASK US FOR A CINEMA OF DENUNCIATION? YES AND NO. NO, IF THE DENUNCIATION IS DIRECTED TOWARD THE OTHERS, IF IT IS CONCEIVED THAT THOSE WHO ARE NOT STRUGGLING MIGHT SYMPATHIZE WITH US AND INCREASE THEIR AWARENESS. YES, IF THE DENUNCIATION ACTS AS INFORMATION, AS TESTIMONY, AS ANOTHER COMBAT WEAPON FOR THOSE ENGAGED IN THE STRUGGLE. WHY DENOUNCE IMPERIALISM TO SHOW ONE MORE TIME THAT IT IS EVIL? WHAT'S THE USE IF THOSE NOW FIGHTING ARE FIGHTING PRIMARILY AGAINST IMPERIALISM? WE CAN DENOUNCE IMPERIALISM BUT SHOULD STRIVE TO DO IT AS A WAY OF PROPOSING CONCRETE BATTLES. A FILM WHICH DENOUNCES THOSE WHO STRUGGLE AGAINST THE EVIL DEEDS OF AN OFFICIAL WHO MUST BE EXECUTED WOULD BE AN EXCELLENT EXAMPLE OF THIS KIND OF FILM-DENUNCIATION.

WE MAINTAIN THAT IMPERFECT CINEMA MUST ABOVE ALL SHOW THE PROCESS WHICH GENERATES THE PROBLEMS. IT IS THUS THE OPPOSITE OF A CINEMA PRINCIPALLY DEDICATED TO CELEBRATING RESULTS, THE OPPOSITE OF A SELF-SUFFICIENT AND CONTEMPLATIVE CINEMA, THE OPPOSITE OF A CINEMA WHICH "BEAUTIFULLY ILLUSTRATES" IDEAS OR CONCEPTS WHICH WE ALREADY POSSESS. (THE NARCISSISTIC POSTURE HAS NOTHING TO DO WITH THOSE WHO STRUGGLE.) TO SHOW A PROCESS IS NOT EXACTLY EQUIVALENT TO ANALYZING IT. TO ANALYZE, IN THE TRADITIONAL SENSE OF THE WORD, ALWAYS IMPLIES A CLOSED PRIOR JUDGEMENT. TO

ANALYZE A PROBLEM IS TO SHOW THE PROBLEM (NOT THE PROCESS) PERMEATED WITH JUDGMENTS WHICH THE ANALYSIS ITSELF GENERATES A PRIORI. TO ANALYZE IS TO BLOCK OFF FROM THE OUTSET ANY POSSIBILITY FOR ANALYSIS ON THE PART OF THE INTERLOCUTOR.

TO SHOW THE PROCESS OF A PROBLEM, ON THE OTHER HAND, IS TO SUBMIT IT TO JUDGEMENT WITHOUT PRONOUNCING THE VERDICT. THERE IS A STYLE OF NEWS REPORTING WHICH PUTS MORE EMPHASIS ON THE COMMENTARY THAN ON THE NEWS ITEM. THERE IS ANOTHER KIND OF REPORTING WHICH PRESENTS THE NEWS AND EVALUATES IT THROUGH THE ARRANGEMENT OF THE ITEM ON THE PAGE OR BY ITS POSITION IN THE PAPER. TO SHOW THE PROCESS OF A PROBLEM IS LIKE SHOWING THE VERY DEVELOPMENT OF THE NEWS ITEM, WITHOUT COMMENTARY; IT IS LIKE SHOWING THE MULTIFACED EVOLUTION OF A PIECE OF INFORMATION WITHOUT EVALUATING IT. THE SUBJECTIVE ELEMENT IS THE SELECTION OF THE PROBLEM, CONDITIONED AS IT IS BY THE INTEREST OF THE AUDIENCE—WHICH IS THE SUBJECT. THE OBJECTIVE ELEMENT IS SHOWING THE PROCESS—WHICH IS THE OBJECT.

IMPERFECT CINEMA IS AN ANSWER, BUT IT IS ALSO A QUESTION WHICH WILL DISCOVER ITS OWN ANSWERS IN THE COURSE OF ITS DEVELOPMENT. IMPERFECT CINEMA CAN MAKE USE OF THE DOCUMENTARY OR THE FICTIONAL MODE, OR BOTH. IT CAN USE WHATEVER GENRE, OR ALL GENRES. IT CAN USE CINEMA AS A PLURALISTIC ART FORM OR AS A SPECIALIZED FORM OF EXPRESSION. THESE QUESTIONS ARE INDIFFERENT TO IT, SINCE THEY DO NOT REPRESENT ITS REAL ALTERNATIVES OR PROBLEMS, AND MUCH LESS ITS REAL GOALS. THESE ARE NOT THE BATTLES OR POLEMICS IT IS INTERESTED IN SPARKING.

IMPERFECT CINEMA CAN ALSO BE ENJOYABLE, BOTH FOR THE MAKER AND ITS NEW AUDIENCE. THOSE WHO STRUGGLE DO NOT STRUGGLE ON THE EDGE OF LIFE, BUT IN THE MIDST OF IT. STRUGGLE IS LIFE AND VICE VERSA. ONE DOES NOT STRUGGLE IN ORDER TO LIVE "LATER ON." THE STRUGGLE REQUIRES ORGANIZATION— THE ORGANIZATION OF LIFE. EVEN IN THE MOST EXTREME PHASE, THAT OF TOTAL AND DIRECT WAR, THE ORGANIZATION OF LIFE IS EQUIVALENT TO THE ORGANIZATION OF THE STRUGGLE. AND IN LIFE, AS IN THE STRUGGLE, THERE IS EVERYTHING, INCLUDING ENJOYMENT. IMPERFECT CINEMA CAN ENJOY ITSELF DESPITE EVERYTHING WHICH CONSPIRES TO NEGATE ENJOYMENT.

IMPERFECT CINEMA REJECTS EXHIBITIONISM IN BOTH (LITERAL) SENSES OF THE WORD, THE NARCISSISTIC AND THE COMMERCIAL (GETTING SHOWN IN ESTABLISHED THEATERS AND CIRCUITS). IT SHOULD BE REMEMBERED THAT THE DEATH OF THE STAR-SYSTEM TURNED OUT TO BE A POSITIVE THING FOR ART. THERE IS NO REASON TO DOUBT THAT THE DISAPPEARANCE OF THE DIRECTOR AS STAR WILL FAIL TO OFFER SIMILAR PROSPECTS. IMPERFECT CINEMA MUST START WORK NOW, IN COOPERATION WITH SOCIOLOGISTS, REVOLUTIONARY LEADERS, PSYCHOLOGISTS, ECONOMISTS, ETC. FURTHERMORE, IMPERFECT CINEMA REJECTS WHATEVER SERVICES CRITICISM HAS TO OFFER AND CONSIDERS THE FUNCTION OF MEDIATORS AND INTERMEDIARIES ANACHRONISTIC.

IMPERFECT CINEMA IS NO LONGER INTERESTED IN QUALITY OR TECHNIQUE. IT CAN BE CREATED EQUALLY WELL WITH A MITCHELL OR WITH AN 8MM CAMERA, IN A STUDIO OR IN A GUERRILLA CAMP IN THE MIDDLE OF A JUNGLE. IMPERFECT CINEMA IS NO LONGER INTERESTED IN PREDETERMINED TASTE, AND MUCH LESS IN "GOOD TASTE." IT IS NOT QUALITY WHICH IT SEEKS IN AN ARTIST'S WORK. THE ONLY THING IT IS INTERESTED IN IS HOW AN ARTIST RESPONDS TO THE FOLLOWING QUESTION: WHAT ARE YOU DOING IN ORDER TO OVERCOME THE BARRIER OF THE "CULTURED" ELITE AUDIENCE WHICH UP TO NOW HAS CONDITIONED THE FORM OF YOUR WORK?

THE FILMMAKER WHO SUBSCRIBES TO THIS NEW POETICS SHOULD NOT HAVE PERSONAL SELF-REALIZATION AS HIS OBJECT. FROM NOW ON HE SHOULD ALSO HAVE ANOTHER ACTIVITY. HE SHOULD PLACE HIS ROLE AS REVOLUTIONARY OR ASPIRING REVOLUTIONARY ABOVE ALL ELSE. IN A WORD, HE SHOULD TRY TO FULFILL HIMSELF AS A MAN AND NOT JUST AS AN ARTIST. IMPERFECT CINEMA CANNOT LOSE SIGHT OF THE FACT THAT ITS ESSENTIAL GOAL AS A NEW POETICS IS TO DISAPPEAR. IT IS NO LONGER A MATTER OF REPLACING ONE SCHOOL WITH ANOTHER, ONE "ISM" WITH ANOTHER, POETRY WITH ANTI-POETRY, BUT OF TRULY LETTING A THOUSAND DIFFERENT FLOWERS BLOOM. THE FUTURE LIES WITH FOLK ART. BUT LET US NO LONGER DISPLAY FOLK ART WITH DEMAGOGIC PRIDE, WITH A CELEBRATIVE AIR. LET US EXHIBIT IT INSTEAD AS A CRUEL DENUNCIATION, AS A PAINFUL TESTIMONY TO THE LEVEL AT WHICH THE PEOPLES OF THE WORLD HAVE BEEN FORCED TO LIMIT THEIR ARTISTIC CREATIVITY. THE FUTURE, WITHOUT DOUBT, WILL BE WITH FOLK ART, BUT THEN THERE WILL BE NO NEED TO CALL IT THAT, BECAUSE NOBODY AND NOTHING WILL ANY LONGER BE ABLE TO AGAIN PARALYZE THE CREATIVE SPIRIT OF THE PEOPLE.

ART WILL NOT DISAPPEAR INTO NOTHINGNESS; IT WILL DISAPPEAR INTO EVERYTHING.

TRANSLATED BY JULIANNE BURTON.

The Viewer's Dialectic [1984]

Tomas Gutierrez Alea

"The work of art, and similarly any other product, creates a public that's sensitive to art and able to enjoy beauty. Thus producing it doesn't just create an object for a subject, rather it also creates a subject for that object."

—From Marx, "Introduction" to
Critique of Political Economy

Introduction

Twenty years after taking power, the revolution has left behind its most spectacular moments. Our shaken land offered then unique, one-time only images, such as that incredible caravan which accompanied Fidel Castro in his entrance to Havana, the bearded men, the palm fronds, and the vertigo of all the transformations that were happening. We saw the traitors and timorous ones leave, the jailors judged, and the enemy's immediate response. On our part, we saw nationalizations and a more radicalized process day after day. Later came the armed confrontations, sabotages, counterrevolution in Escambray, the Bay of Pigs, and the [Missile] Crisis of October.

Those deeds—by themselves and on their very surface— revealed profound changes occurring at a rhythm that could not have been foreseen. For cinema, it was almost sufficient just to record deeds, seize some fragment directly from reality, and give witness to what was going on in the streets. This image projected on the screen turned out to be interesting, revealing and spectacular.[1]

In that conjuncture, and stimulated, or rather pressured by, ever-changing reality, Cuban cinema emerged as one more facet of reality within the revolution. Directors learned to make films on the march and played their instruments by ear, like old-time musicians. They interested viewers more by what they showed than through how they showed it. In those first years our filmmaking emphasized documentary. Little by little, through constant practice, it acquired its own physiognomy and dynamism, which has let it stand with renewed force next to older

FILM STYLES THAT ARE MORE DEVELOPED BUT ALSO TIRED.

ALL THAT SHAPES OUR HISTORY. OUR SUBSEQUENT REVOLUTIONARY DEVELOPMENT CARRIES US INEVITABLY TOWARD A PROCESS OF MATURATION, OF REFLECTION ON AND ANALYSIS OF OUR ACCUMULATED EXPERIENCES.

OUR CURRENT STAGE OF INSTITUTIONALIZATION IS POSSIBLE ONLY BECAUSE IT'S BASED ON A HIGH DEGREE OF POLITICAL AWARENESS WHICH OUR PEOPLE HAVE REACHED THROUGH YEARS OF INCESSANT FIGHTING. BUT THIS STAGE ALSO DEMANDS THE MASSES' ACTIVE, INCREASED PARTICIPATION IN BUILDING A NEW SOCIETY. INCREASINGLY, A GREATER AND GREATER RESPONSIBILITY FALLS ON THE MASSES. FOR THAT REASON, WE CAN NO LONGER HAVE THE PUBLIC MERELY CLING ENTHUSIASTICALLY AND SPONTANEOUSLY TO THE REVOLUTION AND ITS LEADERS. TO THE DEGREE THAT THE GOVERNMENT PASSES ON ITS TASKS TO THE PEOPLE, THE MASSES HAVE TO DEVELOP WAYS OF UNDERSTANDING PROBLEMS, STRENGTHENING IDEOLOGICAL COHERENCE, AND REAFFIRMING DAILY THE REVOLUTION'S ANIMATING PRINCIPLES. IT'S THAT PROCESS WHICH GIVES THE REVOLUTION LIFE.

EVERYDAY EVENTS PROCEED NOW IN ANOTHER WAY. THE IMAGE OF REVOLUTION HAS BECOME ORDINARY, FAMILIAR. IN SOME WAYS WE'RE ACHIEVING TRANSFORMATIONS EVEN MORE PROFOUND THAN EARLIER ONES, BUT ONES THAT AREN'T SO "APPARENT" NOW, NOT IMMEDIATELY VISIBLE TO THE OBSERVER. AND THESE CHANGES OR TRANSFORMATIONS ARE NOT SO SURPRISING, NOR DO PEOPLE RESPOND TO THEM WITH APPLAUSE OR THE SAME OPEN EXPRESSION OF SUPPORT. WE JUST DON'T HAVE THOSE KIND OF SPECTACULAR TRANSFORMATIONS WE DID 15 OR 20 YEARS AGO. CUBAN CINEMA CONFRONTS THAT NEW AND DIFFERENT WAY OF THINKING ABOUT WHAT SOCIAL PROCESSES ARE GOING TO HOLD FOR US BECAUSE OUR FILM DRAWS ITS STRENGTH FROM CUBAN REALITY AND ASSUMES, AMONG OTHER THINGS, TO EXPRESS IT. THUS WE FIND IT NO LONGER SUFFICIENT JUST TO TAKE CAMERAS OUT IN THE STREET AND CAPTURE FRAGMENTS OF THAT REALITY. THIS CAN ALWAYS BE A LEGITIMATE WAY OF FILMMAKING, BUT ONLY WHEN AND IF THE FILMMAKER KNOWS HOW TO SELECT THOSE ASPECTS WHICH, IN CLOSE INTERRELATION, OFFER A *SIGNIFICANT* IMAGE OF REALITY, WHICH SERVES THE FILM AS BOTH A POINT OF DEPARTURE AND ARRIVAL. THE FILMMAKER IS IMMERSED IN A COMPLEX MILIEU, THE PROFOUND SIGNIFICANCE OF WHICH DOES NOT LIE ON THE SURFACE. IF FILMMAKERS WANT TO EXPRESS THEIR WORLD COHERENTLY AND AT THE SAME TIME RESPOND TO THE DEMANDS THEIR WORLD PLACES ON THEM, THEY SHOULD NOT GO OUT ARMED WITH JUST A CAMERA AND THEIR SENSIBILITY BUT ALSO WITH SOLID THEORETICAL CRITERIA. THEY NEED TO BE ABLE TO INTERPRET AND TRANSMIT REALITY'S IMAGE RICHLY AND AUTHENTICALLY.

ON THE OTHER HAND, IN MOMENTS OF RELATIVE EXPANSION, CAPITALISM AND SOCIALISM AIR THEIR STRUGGLE ABOVE ALL IDEOLOGICALLY. AND ON THAT LEVEL, FILM PLAYS A RELEVANT ROLE BOTH AS A MASS MEDIUM, IN TERMS OF DIFFUSION, AND AS A MEDIUM OF ARTISTIC EXPRESSION. THE LEVEL OF COMPLEXITY AT WHICH THE IDEOLOGICAL STRUGGLE DEVELOPS DEMANDS THAT FILMMAKERS COMPLETELY

OVERCOME NOT ONLY THE SPONTANEITY OF THE FIRST YEARS AFTER THE REVOLU-
TIONARY TRIUMPH, BUT ALSO THE DANGERS CONTAINED WITHIN A TENDENCY TO
SCHEMATIZE. PEOPLE ARE IN THE HABIT OF FALLING INTO SCHEMATIZATION WHEN
THEY HAVEN'T ORGANICALLY ASSIMILATED THE MOST ADVANCED TECHNOLOGIES,
THE MOST REVOLUTIONARY ONES, THE MOST IN VOGUE, ESPECIALLY THOSE WHICH
SPEAK TO THE SOCIAL FUNCTION WHICH THE CINEMATIC SPECTACLE SHOULD FULFILL.
FOR FILMMAKERS CREATE CULTURAL PRODUCTS WHICH AIM AT MASS DIFFUSION,
WHICH MANIPULATE EXPRESSIVE RESOURCES THAT HAVE A CERTAIN EFFICACY. FILM
NOT ONLY DIVERTS AND INFORMS, IT ALSO SHAPES TASTE, INTELLECTUAL CRITERIA,
AND STATES OF CONSCIOUSNESS. IF FILMMAKERS FULLY ASSUME THEIR OWN SOCIAL
AND HISTORICAL RESPONSIBILITY, THEY FIND THEMSELVES CONFRONTING THE IN-
EVITABLE NECESSITY OF PROMOTING THE THEORETICAL DEVELOPMENT OF THEIR AR-
TISTIC PRACTICE.

WE UNDERSTAND WHAT CINEMA'S SOCIAL FUNCTION SHOULD BE IN CUBA
IN THESE TIMES. IT SHOULD CONTRIBUTE IN THE MOST EFFICIENT WAY POSSIBLE
TO ELEVATING VIEWER'S REVOLUTIONARY CONSCIOUSNESS AND ARMING THEM FOR
ALL THE IDEOLOGICAL STRUGGLES WHICH WE HAVE TO CARRY ON AGAINST ALL
KINDS OF REACTIONARY TENDENCIES. IT SHOULD CONTRIBUTE TO THE BEST EN-
JOYMENT THAT CAN BE GOTTEN OUT OF LIFE. WE WANT TO ESTABLISH WHAT MIGHT
BE THE HIGHEST LEVEL WHICH FILM—AS SPECTACLE—COULD REACH IN FULFILLING
THIS FUNCTION. THUS WE ASK OURSELVES TO WHAT DEGREE A CERTAIN TYPE OF
SPECTACLE CAN PROVOKE PEOPLE'S COMING TO CONSCIOUSNESS AND THEIR CON-
SEQUENT ACTIVITY. WE ALSO WONDER WHAT THAT COMING TO CONSCIOUSNESS
CONSISTS OF AND WHAT ACTIVITY OUGHT TO BE GENERATED IN SPECTATORS ONCE
THEY HAVE STOPPED BEING SUCH. THAT IS, PEOPLE LEAVE THE MOVIE THEATER AND
ENCOUNTER ONCE AGAIN THAT OTHER REALITY, THEIR SOCIAL AND INDIVIDUAL
LIFE, DAILY LIFE.

CAPITALIST CINEMA, REDUCED TO THE CONDITION OF MERCHANDISE, RARELY
TRIES TO ANSWER THESE QUESTIONS. ON THE OTHER HAND (AND FOR OTHER
REASONS) SOCIALIST CINEMA HAS NOT ORDINARILY FULLY SATISFIED THAT DEMAND.
NEVERTHELESS, FINDING OURSELVES IN THE MIDST OF REVOLUTION AT THIS PAR-
TICULAR STAGE OF CONSTRUCTING SOCIALISM, WE SHOULD BE ABLE TO ESTABLISH
THE PREMISE OF A CINEMA WHICH WOULD BE GENUINELY AND INTEGRALLY REVOLU-
TIONARY, ACTIVE, MOBILIZING, STIMULATING, AND EFFECTIVELY POPULAR.

THE EXPRESSIVE POSSIBILITIES OF THE FILM SPECTACLE ARE INEXHAUSTIBLE. TO
CREATE WITH THEM AND FULLY REALIZE THEM IS A POET'S TASK. BUT ON THAT
POINT, FOR THE TIME BEING, THIS ANALYSIS CAN GO NO FURTHER, FOR I AM NOT
FOCUSING ON FILM'S PURELY AESTHETIC ASPECTS BUT RATHER TRYING TO DISCOVER
IN THE RELATION WHICH THE FILM ESTABLISHES OVER AND OVER AGAIN BETWEEN
SPECTACLE AND SPECTATOR, THE LAWS WHICH GOVERN THIS RELATION AND THE
POSSIBILITIES WITHIN THOSE LAWS FOR DEVELOPING A SOCIALLY PRODUCTIVE
SPECTACLE.

WE WANT TO EXPRESS OUR GRATITUDE TO PROFESSOR ZAIRA RODRIGUEZ AND JORGE DE LA FUENTE FOR THEIR HELP AND STIMULATING IDEAS OFFERED WHILE WRITING THIS WORK.

"Popular" Film and People's Film

AMONG ALL THE ARTS FILM IS HELD TO BE THE MOST POPULAR. IT WASN'T ALWAYS. FOR A LONG TIME, CONFUSION REIGNED AS TO WHETHER FILM WAS AN ART OR NOT. THAT CONFUSION CONTINUES BECAUSE OF FILM'S POPULAR CHARACTER.

CINEMA TODAY IS STILL MARKED BY ITS CLASS ORIGIN. DURING ITS SHORT HISTORY, IT HAS HAD MOMENTS OF REBELLION, INVESTIGATION, AND AUTHENTIC ACHIEVEMENT IN EXPRESSING THE MOST REVOLUTIONARY TENDENCIES. NEVERTHELESS, TO A LARGE DEGREE, CINEMA KEEPS ON BEING THE MOST NATURAL INCARNATION OF THE PETIT BOURGEOIS SPIRIT WHICH GAVE IT LIFE AT ITS BIRTH ALMOST EIGHTY YEARS AGO.

CAPITALISM WAS GOING INTO ITS IMPERIALIST PHASE. IN PRINCIPLE, THE MODEST INVENTION OF AN APPARATUS FOR THE CAPTURING AND REPRODUCING OF MOVING IMAGES FROM REALITY WAS NO MORE THAN AN INGENIOUS TOY FOR FAIRS. BY MEANS OF THAT TOY, SPECTATORS COULD FEEL THEMSELVES CARRIED OFF TO THE FARTHEST REACHES OF THE WORLD WITHOUT MOVING FROM THEIR SEATS. VERY SOON THE TOY LEFT THE FAIR GROUND. THAT DOES NOT MEAN TO SAY THAT IT ACHIEVED A MORE DIGNIFIED AND RESPECTABLE *STATUS*: IT WENT ON TO BE DEVELOPED AS A REAL INDUSTRY FOR SPECTACLE. THAT INDUSTRY BEGAN MASS PRODUCTION OF A KIND OF MERCHANDISE ABLE TO SATISFY THE TASTES AND ENCOURAGE THE ASPIRATIONS OF A SOCIETY DOMINATED BY A BOURGEOISIE WHICH EXTENDED ITS POWER INTO EVERY CORNER OF THE WORLD. FROM ITS VERY FIRST MOMENT, TWO PARALLEL PATHS WERE OPENED UP IN FILM: IT OFFERED A "TRUE" DOCUMENT OF CERTAIN ASPECTS OF REALITY AND, ON THE OTHER HAND, IT HAD THIS FASCINATION FOR MAGIC. BETWEEN THESE TWO POLES—DOCUMENTARY AND FICTION—FILM HAS ALWAYS MOVED. VERY SOON IT BECAME "POPULAR," NOT IN THE SENSE THAT IT WAS AN EXPRESSION OF THE *PEOPLE*, OF THE SECTORS MOST OPPRESSED AND MOST EXPLOITED BY AN ALIENATING SYSTEM OF PRODUCTION. RATHER, IT COULD ATTRACT AN UNDIFFERENTIATED PUBLIC, A MAJORITY AVID FOR ILLUSIONS.

PERHAPS MORE RADICALLY THAN ANY OTHER MEDIUM OF ARTISTIC EXPRESSION, CINEMA CAN NEVER LEAVE BEHIND ITS CONDITION AS MERCHANDISE. THE COMMERCIAL SUCCESS IT ACHIEVED PUSHED IT ON TO VERTIGINOUS DEVELOPMENT. IT WAS CONVERTED INTO A COMPLEX AND COSTLY INDUSTRY. IT HAD TO INVENT ALL KINDS OF FORMULAE AND RECIPES SO THAT THE SPECTACLE WHICH IT OFFERED WOULD GAIN FAVOR WITH THE BROADEST PUBLIC. NUMBERS OF VIEWERS ARE WHAT CINEMA DEPENDS ON FOR ITS VERY SUBSISTENCE. SURELY IT WAS A MEDIUM WHICH STILL COULD EXPRESS ITSELF ONLY IN BABY TALK. BUT MORE THAN THAT, IT'S CINEMA'S CONDITION AS MERCHANDISE AND ITS "POPULAR" CHARACTER THAT PROVOKE THE RESISTANCE WHICH EXISTED IN CIRCLES THAT PAID UNCONDITIONAL REVERENCE

TO "HIGH" ART; THEY DID NOT WANT TO ELEVATE CINEMA TO THE CATEGORY OF TRUE ART. ART AND THE PEOPLE DIDN'T GET ALONG.

THEN SOME FOLKS THOUGHT THAT CINEMA, TO BE ART, SHOULD TRANSLATE THE MASTER WORKS FROM UNIVERSAL CULTURE; THUS WERE FILMED A LOT OF PRETENTIOUS, GILDED WORKS, HEAVY AND THEORETICAL ONES WHICH HAD NOTHING TO DO WITH THE EMERGING FILM LANGUAGE. BEYOND THOSE DETOURS, SURELY CINEMA CONSTITUTED A HUMAN ACTIVITY WHICH WAS FULFILLING BETTER THAN OTHERS A FUNDAMENTAL NECESSITY FOR ENJOYMENT. IN FILM PRACTICE, AS IT DIRECTED ITSELF FUNDAMENTALLY TOWARD THAT OBJECTIVE, FILM LANGUAGE BEGAN TO MATURE AND DISCOVER EXPRESSIVE POSSIBILITIES, WHICH LET CINEMA ACHIEVE AN AESTHETIC HEIGHT, ALTHOUGH WITHOUT PROPOSING THAT AS ITS GOAL.

U.S. CINEMA, WITH ITS PRAGMATIC SENSE, WAS HERE THE MOST ADVANCED. IT WAS THE MOST VITAL AND THE RICHEST IN TECHNICAL AND EXPRESSIVE DISCOVERIES. FROM THE FIRST YEARS OF THIS CENTURY, IT WAS BUILDING DISTINCT GENRES—COMEDIES, WESTERNS, GANGSTER FILMS, HISTORICAL SUPER-PRODUCTIONS, MELODRAMAS—WHICH RAPIDLY BECAME CONVERTED INTO "CLASSICS." THAT IS TO SAY, THE GENRES CONSOLIDATED THEMSELVES INTO FORMAL MODELS AND REACHED A HIGH LEVEL OF DEVELOPMENT; AT THE SAME TIME, THEY WERE CONVERTED INTO EMPTY STEREOTYPES. THEY OFFERED THE MOST EFFECTIVE EXPRESSION OF A CULTURE OF THE MASSES, WHO FUNCTIONED AS PASSIVE CONSUMERS, AS CONTEMPLATING SPECTATORS, AS SHAMELESS IN TERMS OF LETTING REALITY NOT DEMAND ACTION FROM THEM. THE GENRES CLOSED DOWN POSSIBILITIES FOR ACTION.

CINEMA CAN CREATE GENUINE GHOSTS, IMAGES OF LIGHTS AND SHADOWS WHICH CAN'T BE CAPTURED. IT'S LIKE A SHARED DREAM. IT HAS BEEN THE MAJOR VEHICLE TO ENCOURAGE VIEWER'S FALSE ILLUSIONS AND SERVE THEM AS A REFUGE. IT ACTS AS A SUBSTITUTE FOR THAT REALITY WHICH THE SPECTATORS ARE KEPT FROM DEVELOPING HUMANLY, AND WHICH, AS A SORT OF COMPENSATION, IT LETS THEM DREAM ABOUT WHILE AWAKE.

FILM EQUIPMENT AND THE MEANS OF FILM PRODUCTION WERE INVENTED AND CREATED IN TERMS OF BOURGEOIS TASTES AND NEEDS. FILM RAPIDLY BECAME THE MOST CONCRETE MANIFESTATION OF THE BOURGEOIS SPIRIT, IN OBJECTIFYING ITS DREAMS. CLEARLY, FOR THE BOURGEOISIE, FILM DID NOT REPRESENT AN EXTENSION OF WORK, NOR OF SCHOOL, NOR OF DAILY LIFE WITH ITS MANY TENSIONS; IT WAS NEITHER A FORMAL CEREMONY NOR A POLITICAL DISCOURSE. THE FIRST THING BURDENED SPECTATORS WERE LOOKING FOR IN IT WAS GRATIFICATION AND RELAXATION TO FILL UP THEIR FREE TIME. SURELY MOST CINEMATIC PRODUCTION RARELY WENT BEYOND THE MOST VULGAR LEVELS OF COMMUNICATING WITH ITS PUBLIC. THE IMPORTANT THING WAS HOW MUCH MONEY COULD BE OBTAINED WITH ANY PRODUCT, NOT THE HIGHEST ARTISTIC QUALITY.

IN THE 20S THE EUROPEAN AVANT-GARDE ALSO MADE ITS INCURSION INTO FILMMAKING AND LEFT A FEW WORKS IN WHICH IT EXPLORED A VAST RANGE OF EXPRESSIVE POSSIBILITIES. BUT THAT WAS A VAIN ATTEMPT TO RESCUE FILM FROM

THE VULGARITY TO WHICH COMMERCIALISM HAS CONDEMNED IT. IT COULDN'T PUT DOWN ROOTS. HOWEVER, THANKS TO A FEW EXCEPTIONAL WORKS, THE MOVEMENT WAS NOT COMPLETELY STERILE.

BUT IT WASN'T UNTIL THE CREATION OF SOVIET FILM THAT THE ART WORLD BEGAN TO OFFICIALLY ACCEPT THE EVIDENCE THAT NOT JUST A NEW LANGUAGE HAD BEEN BORN, BUT ALSO A NEW *ART*. THIS WAS BECAUSE OF THE THEORETICAL PREOCCUPATION OF THE SOVIET DIRECTORS AND THE PRACTICAL SUPPORT GIVEN TO THE NEW MEDIUM. "COLLECTIVE ART *PAR EXCELLENCE*, DESTINED FOR THE MASSES," IT WAS CALLED THEN. SOVIET CINEMA ATTAINED A REAL CLOSENESS TO THE MOVEMENT OF RADICAL SOCIAL TRANSFORMATION IN WHICH IT WAS OPERATING. IT WAS A COLLECTIVE ART BECAUSE IT COMBINED DIVERSE INDIVIDUALS' EXPERIENCE, AND IT DREW NOURISHMENT FROM ARTISTIC PRACTICE IN OTHER MEDIA ABOUT HOW TO BE A NEW ART, A SPECIFICALLY DIFFERENT ART, ABOUT WHICH FILM WAS DEFINITELY SELF-CONSCIOUS. IT WAS DESTINED FOR THE MASSES AND POPULAR BECAUSE IT EXPRESSED THE INTERESTS, ASPIRATIONS, AND VALUES OF NUMEROUS SECTORS OF THE POPULATION WHO AT THAT MOMENT WERE ADVANCING HISTORY. THAT FIRST MOMENT OF SOVIET FILMMAKING LEFT PROFOUND TRACES ON ALL FILMMAKING THAT FOLLOWED, AND TODAY THE MOST MODERN FILMMAKING CONTINUES TO DRINK FROM ITS FOUNTAINS AND NOURISH ITSELF FROM THAT CINEMA'S EXPLORATIONS, EXPERIMENTS, AND THEORETICAL ACHIEVEMENTS, WHICH STILL HAVEN'T BEEN COMPLETELY MINED.

IN THE CAPITALIST WORLD, THE FIRST YEARS OF SOUND FILMMAKING COINCIDED WITH THE ECONOMIC CRISIS OF 1929. CINEMA CONSOLIDATED ITSELF AS AN AUDIO-VISUAL LANGUAGE AND CONSTRUCTED SO COMPLICATED A PRODUCTION APPARATUS THAT FOR A LONG TIME IT WAS NOT POSSIBLE TO MAKE FILMS ON THE MARGIN OF THIS GREAT INDUSTRY, NOR BYPASS ITS INTERESTS. IN SPITE OF THAT, IN THE 30S, THE U.S. INDUSTRY BECAME MOTIVATED TO PRODUCE A FEW FILMS WITH A CRITICAL VISION ABOUT SOCIETY AND ABOUT THE SOCIAL MOVEMENT IN WHICH PEOPLE WERE LIVING. THESE FILMS MAINTAINED ALL THE CONVENTIONS OF AN ESTABLISHED AND FILTERED LANGUAGE, BUT THEY ALSO DEMONSTRATED AN AUTHENTIC REALISM IN DEALING WITH IMPORTANT CONTEMPORARY THEMES. THIS CINEMA, WHICH SPOKE ABOUT SOCIAL CONFLICTS AFFLICTING EVERYONE, AROSE AT A FAVORABLE CONJUNCTURE, BUT VERY SOON DETOURED TOWARDS COMPLACENT REFORMISM. THOSE WERE THE YEARS OF THE HAYS CODE, ALSO KNOWN AS THE CODE OF PROPRIETY, AN INSTRUMENT FOR CENSORSHIP AND PROPAGANDA WHICH RESPONDED TO THE INTERESTS OF FINANCE CAPITAL AND WHICH INDICATED THE NARROW IDEOLOGICAL STRAITS WHICH U.S. CINEMA WOULD TRAVERSE FOR A LONG TIME.[2]

TOWARD THE END OF WORLD WAR II, WITH WOUNDS STILL OPEN AND UNDER POLITICALLY FAVORABLE CIRCUMSTANCES, ITALIAN NEOREALIST CINEMA SURGED FORWARD. WITH ALL ITS POLITICAL AND IDEOLOGICAL LIMITATIONS, IT WAS A LIVING, FECUND MOVEMENT INSOFAR AS IT WENT THE ROUTE OF AUTHENTICALLY

POPULAR CINEMA.

IN THE HEAT OF POST-WAR FRANCE, A "NEW WAVE" OF YOUNG DIRECTORS APPEARED WHO THREW THEMSELVES IMPETUOUSLY INTO REVOLUTIONIZING FILM-MAKING WITHOUT UNDERSTANDING THE LIMITS OF THE PETIT BOURGEOIS WORLD. AMONG THEM, GODARD STANDS OUT AS THE GREAT DESTROYER OF BOURGEOIS CINEMA. TAKING BRECHT AS HIS POINT OF DEPARTURE—AND THE NEW LEFT AS HIS POINT OF ARRIVAL—HE TRIED TO MAKE REVOLUTION FROM THE SCREEN. HIS GENIUS, INVENTIVENESS, IMAGINATION, AND CLUMSY AGGRESSIVENESS GIVE HIM A PRIVILEGED PLACE AMONG THE "DOOMED" FILMMAKERS. HE ACHIEVED MAKING ANTI-BOURGEOIS CINEMA BUT HE COULDN'T MAKE PEOPLE'S CINEMA. NOTEWOR-THY DRONES LIKE JEAN-MARIE STRAUB, ADMIRABLE FOR HIS ALMOST RELIGIOUS ASCETICISM, HAVE ALREADY INSTITUTIONALIZED THAT POSITION; SOME THINK THEY ARE MAKING A REVOLUTION IN THE SUPERSTRUCTURE WITHOUT NEEDING TO MOVE THE BASE.

ANOTHER PHENOMENON INSCRIBED IN THOSE SEARCHES FOR REVOLUTIONARY FILMMAKING PRACTICE IS THE CINEMA CALLED "PARALLEL" OR "MARGINAL" OR "ALTERNATIVE." THIS HAS ARISEN IN THE LAST FEW YEARS DUE TO THE DEVELOP-MENT OF TECHNOLOGY AND EQUIPMENT WHICH PERMIT THE PRODUCTION OF RELATIVELY CHEAP FILMS. IT'S WITHIN THE REACH OF SMALL, INDEPENDENT GROUPS AND OF REVOLUTIONARY MILITANTS. IN THIS CINEMA REVOLUTIONARY IDEOLOGY IS OPENLY PUT FORTH. IT'S A POLITICAL CINEMA WHICH CAN SERVE TO MOBILIZE THE MASSES AND CHANNEL THEM TOWARD REVOLUTION. AS A REVOLUTIONARY PRACTICE IT HAS BEEN EFFICIENT WITHIN THE NARROW LIMITS IN WHICH IT OPERATES. BUT IT CANNOT REACH LARGE NUMBERS, NOT ONLY BECAUSE OF THE POLITICAL OBSTACLES IT ENCOUNTERS WITHIN THE DISTRIBUTION AND EXHIBITION SYSTEM, BUT ALSO FOR HOW IT'S MADE. MOST PEOPLE CONTINUE TO PREFER THE MOST POLISHED PRODUCT WHICH THE GREAT SPECTACLE INDUSTRY OFFERS THEM.

IN THE CAPITALIST WORLD—AND IN A GOOD PART OF THE SOCIALIST WORLD—THE PUBLIC IS CONDITIONED BY SPECIFIC CONVENTIONS OF FILM LANGUAGE, BY FORMULAE AND GENRES WHICH ARE THOSE OF BOURGEOIS COMMERCIAL FILM-MAKING. THIS OCCURS SO MUCH THAT WE CAN SAY THAT CINEMA, AS A PRODUCT ORIGINATING FROM THE BOURGEOISIE, ALMOST ALWAYS HAS RESPONDED BETTER TO CAPITALISM'S INTERESTS THAN TO SOCIALISM'S, TO BOURGEOIS INTERESTS MORE THAN TO PROLETARIAN ONES, TO A CONSUMER SOCIETY'S INTERESTS MORE THAN TO A REVOLUTIONARY SOCIETY'S INTERESTS, TO ALIENATION MORE THAN TO NON-ALIENATION, TO HYPOCRISY AND LIES MORE THAN TO THE PROFOUND TRUTH.

PEOPLE'S CINEMA, IN SPITE OF ITS MANY NOTABLE EXPONENTS AND FEW EX-CEPTIONAL PHENOMENA, HAS NOT ALWAYS BEEN ABLE FULLY TO COMBINE REVOLU-TIONARY IDEOLOGY WITH MASS APPEAL. ON OUR PART, WE CANNOT ACCEPT SIMPLE NUMERICAL CRITERIA TO DETERMINE THE ESSENCE OF A PEOPLE'S CINEMA. CLEAR-LY, FINALLY WHEN WE SPEAK ABOUT THE GREAT MASSES OF PEOPLE, WE HAVE TO REFER TO THE WHOLE COMMUNITY. BUT SUCH A CRITERION IS SO BROAD AND

SO VAGUE THAT IT BECOMES IMPOSSIBLE TO INTRODUCE ANY KIND OF VALUE JUDGMENT INTO IT. THE NUMBER OF PEOPLE IN A COUNTRY OR IN A CERTAIN SECTION OF A COUNTRY IS NO MORE THAN THE COINCIDENCE OF PEOPLE WHO, LOOKED AT LIKE THAT, ABSTRACTLY, LACK ANY KIND OF SIGNIFICANCE. IF WE WANT TO SET UP SOME KIND OF CONCRETE CRITERION ABOUT WHAT *POPULAR* MEANS, IT'S NECESSARY TO KNOW WHAT THOSE PEOPLE SITUATED IN THAT PLACE REPRESENT, NOT JUST IN TERMS OF GEOGRAPHICAL LOCATION, BUT RATHER IN TERMS OF THEIR HISTORICAL MOMENT AND AS A SPECIFIC CLASS. IT'S NECESSARY TO DISTINGUISH IN THAT BROAD CONFLUENCE WHICH GROUPS—THE GREAT MASSES—BEST INCARNATE, CONSCIOUSLY OR UNCONSCIOUSLY, THE LINES OF FORCE WHICH WILL BE THOSE OF HISTORICAL DEVELOPMENT. THAT IS TO SAY, WHICH ARE MOVING TOWARD THE *INCESSANT BETTERMENT OF LIVING CONDITIONS ON THIS PLANET*? AND IF THE CRITERION FOR DETERMINING "POPULAR" ACCEPTS AS ITS BASE LINE THAT DISTINCTION, WE CAN SAY THAT ITS ESSENCE RESIDES IN WHAT WOULD BE THE *BEST* THING FOR *THOSE* GRAND MASSES, THAT WHICH BEST RESPONDS TO THEIR MOST VITAL INTERESTS.

SURELY, IMMEDIATE INTERESTS SOMETIMES OBLITERATE THE MID-RANGE ONES, AND YOU MAY OFTEN LOSE VIEW OF YOUR FINAL OBJECTIVES. TO BE MORE PRECISE: THE POPULAR OUGHT TO RESPOND NOT ONLY TO IMMEDIATE INTERESTS (EXPRESSED IN THE NEED TO ENJOY YOURSELF, TO PLAY, TO ABANDON YOURSELF TO THE MOMENT OR ILLUSION, TO GET OUT OF YOUR OWN SKIN) BUT ALSO BASIC NEEDS AND THE FINAL OBJECTIVE: TRANSFORMING REALITY AND BETTERING HUMANKIND. FROM THIS POINT ON, WHEN I SPEAK ABOUT POPULAR FILM, I AM NOT REFERRING TO CINEMA WHICH IS SIMPLY ACCEPTED BY THE COMMUNITY, BUT RATHER TO A CINEMA WHICH *ALSO* EXPRESSES THE PEOPLE'S MOST PROFOUND AND AUTHENTIC INTERESTS AND RESPONDS TO THOSE INTERESTS. IN ACCORDANCE WITH THIS CRITERION (AND WE MUST KEEP IN MIND THAT IN A CLASS SOCIETY, CINEMA CAN'T STOP BEING AN INSTRUMENT OF THE DOMINANT CLASS), AN AUTHENTICALLY POPULAR CINEMA CAN BE FULLY DEVELOPED ONLY IN A SOCIETY WHERE THE PEOPLE'S INTERESTS COINCIDE WITH THE STATE'S INTERESTS. THAT IS, IN A SOCIALIST SOCIETY.

DURING THE CONSTRUCTION OF SOCIALISM THE PROLETARIAT HAS NOT DISAPPEARED AS A CLASS WHICH EXERCISES ITS POWER THROUGH A COMPLEX STATE APPARATUS. DIFFERENCES CONTINUE BETWEEN CITY AND COUNTRY LIFE, AND BETWEEN INTELLECTUAL AND PHYSICAL WORK. MERCANTILE RELATIONS HAVE NOT YET DISAPPEARED, AND ALONG WITH THEM CERTAIN MANIFESTATIONS—CONSCIOUS OR UNCONSCIOUS—OF BOURGEOIS IDEOLOGY (OR WHAT IS EVEN WORSE, PETIT BOURGEOIS IDEOLOGY). STILL WE HAVE ONLY AN INSUFFICIENT MATERIAL BASE TO DEPEND ON. ABOVE ALL, IMPERIALISM CONTINUES TO EXIST IN THE WORLD. DURING THIS TIME, ART'S SOCIAL FUNCTION ACQUIRES VERY SPECIFIC SHADINGS IN ACCORDANCE WITH OUR MOST URGENT NEEDS AND OBJECTIVES. IT RESPONDS TO THE MOST IMMEDIATE TASKS PEOPLE SET FOR THEMSELVES WHEN THEY ARE FEELING

OWNERS OF THEIR DESTINY AND ARE WORKING TO ACCOMPLISH IT.[3] HERE ART'S FUNCTION IS TO CONTRIBUTE TO THE BEST ENJOYMENT OF LIFE, AT THE AESTHETIC LEVEL, AND IT DOES THIS NOT BY OFFERING A LUDICROUS PARENTHESIS IN THE MIDDLE OF EVERYDAY REALITY BUT BY ENRICHING THAT VERY REALITY. AT THE COGNITIVE LEVEL, IT CONTRIBUTES TO A MORE PROFOUND COMPREHENSION OF THE WORLD. THIS HELPS VIEWERS DEVELOP CRITERIA CONGRUENT WITH THE PATH THAT SOCIETY HAS TRAVERSED. AT THE IDEOLOGICAL LEVEL, FINALLY, ART ALSO CONTRIBUTES TO REAFFIRMING THE NEW SOCIETY'S VALUES AND THUS TO FIGHT FOR ITS PRESERVATION AND DEVELOPMENT. GIVEN THAT AT THIS STAGE, THE IDEOLOGICAL LEVEL HAS PRIMACY, ART'S EFFICACY HERE STANDS IN DIRECT RELATION TO ITS AESTHETIC AND COGNITIVE EFFICACY.

I WILL TRY TO ESTABLISH WHICH APPROACHES MIGHT BE MOST APPROPRIATE FOR CINEMA, AS ONE OF ART'S SPECIFIC MANIFESTATIONS, SO THAT IT CAN MOVE TOWARD THOSE OBJECTIVES.

From Spectacle in its Purest Sense to the "Cinema of Ideas"

AS WITH LITERATURE, FILM HAS PROCEEDED TO ESTABLISH CERTAIN BASIC GENRES ACCORDING TO THE EXPRESSIVE NEEDS OF EACH SPECIFIC MATERIAL. IN THE SAME WAY THAT WE HAVE JOURNALISM—MAGAZINES AND NEWSPAPERS—FICTIONAL LITERATURE AND ESSAYS, WITH ALL THEIR VARIETY AND SHADINGS, ALL THEIR OWN RESOURCES AND CHARACTERISTICS, IN FILM WE HAVE NEWSCASTS, SHORT FILMS, AND FEATURE FILMS. SUPERFICIALLY WE CAN POINT OUT AFFINITIES BETWEEN NEWSCASTS AND DAILY JOURNALISM, BETWEEN SHORT FILMS AND CERTAIN KINDS OF ARTICLES AND REPORTS, WHICH USUALLY APPEAR IN MAGAZINES; AND BETWEEN FEATURE FILMS AND FICTIONAL LITERATURE, ESPECIALLY NOVELS, OR, AND WE SEE THIS MORE AND MORE, THE LONG ESSAY. BUT THESE SIMILARITIES ARE PRETTY OBVIOUS AT FIRST GLANCE. OF MORE INTEREST IS TO DEFINE SOME BASIC CINEMATIC GENERIC PECULIARITIES AND TO UNDERLINE THE FACT THAT, AS ALSO HAPPENS IN LITERATURE, THIS DIVISION IS CONVENTIONAL; AND THE FRONTIERS WHICH SEPARATE GENRES DO NOT HINDER THE INTERCHANGE OF EXPRESSIVE RESOURCES AND EVEN OF SPECIFIC ELEMENTS BETWEEN GENRES.

NEWSCASTS OFFER PRIMARILY DIRECT REPORTAGE ON CONTEMPORARY EVENTS. CERTAIN EVENTS WITH A SPECIFIC SIGNIFICANCE ARE SELECTED BY THE CAMERA AND PROJECTED ON THE SCREEN TO INFORM US ABOUT WHAT'S HAPPENING IN THE WORLD. YOU USUALLY DO NOT RECEIVE A PROFOUND ANALYSIS OF THESE EVENTS' SIGNIFICANCE, BUT BECAUSE OF THEIR VERY SELECTION AND FORM OF PRESENTATION, POLITICAL CRITERIA ARE MANIFEST AND, OBVIOUSLY, IDEOLOGY. FIRST OF ALL, BECAUSE OF THE EMPHASIS ON INFORMATION, THE NEWSCAST OPERATES WITH MATERIAL VERY LIMITED IN TIME SPAN. NEVERTHELESS, AND AT A SECOND GLANCE, THESE NEWSCASTS CONSTITUTE A BODY OF MATERIAL THAT IS TESTIMONY TO AN EPOCH, AND THE IMPORTANCE OF WHICH IS NOT ALWAYS PREDICTABLE. THAT IS, THESE NEWSCASTS CAN ACQUIRE A GROWING HISTORICAL VALUE AND CONSTITUTE

THE PRIME MATERIALS FOR LATER ANALYTIC RE-ELABORATION. SUCH A DOUBLE FUNC-
TION TURNS THE NEWSREEL INTO A MOST IMPORTANT POLITICAL INSTRUMENT. THE
EMPHASIS HERE LIES IN ITS POLITICAL (IDEOLOGICAL) AND COGNITIVE ASPECTS. THE
AESTHETIC ASPECT IS SUBORDINATE TO THEM, WHICH ISN'T TO SAY THAT IT DOESN'T
EXIST OR CAN'T—OR SHOULDN'T—PLAY A DECISIVE ROLE IN DECIDING THE GREATER
OR LESSER EFFICACY OF THE OTHER TWO ASPECTS.

THE SHORT SUBJECT OFFERS MORE VARIANTS. IT CAN BE A PRIMARILY INFOR-
MATIVE REPORT. IT CAN BE DOCUMENTARY WHERE THE DEEDS BROUGHT TO THE
SCREEN—EITHER IN IMAGE OR SOUND—WERE NOT CAPTURED DIRECTLY FROM A
REAL-LIFE EVENT BUT RATHER WHICH WERE CREATIVELY ELABORATED BY THE DIREC-
TOR; THE INTENT WOULD BE TO SELECT OUT FROM AN UNDIFFERENTIATED SUR-
FACE THOSE ACTIONS THAT HAD A MORE PROFOUND SIGNIFICANCE, WHICH WOULD
BE MANIPULATED IN THE FILM IN TERMS OF ANALYTIC OBJECTIVE. HERE THE
COGNITIVE ASPECT TAKES PRIMACY. ALSO, THE SHORT FILM INCLUDES FICTIONAL
WORKS—LITTLE CINEMATIC POEMS, THE NARRATION OF A SHORT STORY, ETC. IT'S
GENERALLY 20-40 MINUTES LONG; THAT LENGTH PRESUPPOSES A MORE ELABORATED
STRUCTURE THAN THE NEWSREEL HAS AND MORE COMPLEXITY IN TREATING A THEME.
CONSEQUENTLY THE FORM ALLOWS THE FILMMAKER TO GO INTO GREATER DEPTH—
BOTH IN TERMS OF INFORMATION AND ANALYSIS. THUS, ITS OPERATION—ITS
TRANSCENDENCY—IS BROADER, AND THE AESTHETIC ASPECT HERE USUALLY PLAYS
A CERTAIN DETERMINANT AND RELEVANT ROLE.

THE FEATURE FILM IS GENERALLY FICTION. THE PLOTS ARE COMPLETELY
FABRICATED, ACCORDING TO A PRECONCEIVED IDEA, AND DEVELOPED ON THE BASIS
OF DRAMATIC PRINCIPLES. ALL THIS CORRESPONDS TO AN ESTABLISHED CONVEN-
TION, WHICH CAN BE EITHER A SUPPORT OR HINDRANCE FOR THE BEST AND MOST
COHERENT CONCRETIZING OF THAT IDEA WHICH WAS THE POINT OF DEPARTURE.
ON THE OTHER HAND, IN CUBA WE HAVE EXTENSIVELY DEVELOPED A TYPE OF
FEATURE-LENGTH DOCUMENTARY IN WHICH EVENTS ARE RECREATED OR SHOWN
AS THEY COULD HAVE BEEN HAD THE CAMERA CAPTURED THEM DIRECTLY AT THE
MOMENT OF THEIR OCCURRENCE. THEN THESE ACTIONS ARE ARRANGED IN SUCH
A WAY THAT THEY FUNCTION AS ELEMENTS OF A COMPLEX STRUCTURE, THROUGH
WHICH THE FILM CAN OFFER A MORE PROFOUND ANALYSIS OF SOME ASPECT OF
REALITY. IN ADDITION, NEWS REPORTAGE CAN GET TO BE FEATURE LENGTH, BUT
THAT STRUCTURE IS USED INFREQUENTLY. GENERALLY THEN CERTAIN EXCEPTIONALLY
IMPORTANT EVENTS ARE REGISTERED ON FILM AND ORDERED IN CHRONOLOGICAL
ORDER OR SOME OTHER WAY SO AS TO FACILITATE VIEWERS' BETTER UNDERSTAND-
ING OF THEM.

NORMAL THEATRICAL PROGRAMMING IN GENERAL IS COMPOSED OF A
NEWSREEL, A DOCUMENTARY OR SHORT, AND A FICTION FEATURE. THUS THE BASIC
GENRES, DISTINCT BUT COMPLEMENTARY, GET SEEN AT ONE SITTING. HERE VIEWERS
CAN EXPERIENCE *DISTINCT LEVELS OF MEDIATION WHICH BRING THEM CLOSER TO
OR FARTHER AWAY FROM REALITY* AND WHICH CAN OFFER THEM A BETTER

UNDERSTANDING OF THOSE LEVELS OF MEDIATION. THIS PLAY OF APPROXIMATIONS, PRODUCED THROUGH SEEING DISTINCT GENRES AT ONE SCREENING, DOESN'T ALWAYS HAVE THE GREATEST COHERENCE OR REACH THE GREATEST LEVEL OF "PRODUCTIVI-TY," BECAUSE VIEWERS THEN USUALLY ARE SEEING WORKS MADE INDEPENDENTLY OF EACH OTHER WHICH EXHIBITIONISTS FOUND A WAY TO TIE TOGETHER ONLY LATER ON. NEVERTHELESS, THIS POSSIBILITY OF MUTUAL RELATIONS THROWS LIGHT ON WHAT COULD BE ACHIEVED HERE, EVEN IF WE ARE CONSIDERING JUST *THE FRAMEWORK OF A SINGLE FILM*, IN THE ELABORATION OF WHICH THE FILMMAKER HAS KEPT IN MIND THIS WHOLE BROAD RANGE OF *LEVELS OF APPROXIMATING REALITY*.

I WANT TO FOCUS ON THAT GENRE WHICH BEST CORRESPONDS TO THE CON-CEPT OF "SPECTACLE" AND WHICH CONSTITUTES THE BASIC PRODUCT IN ANY CINEMA: THE FEATURE FICTION FILM.

FIRST, I WANT TO CONSIDER AND PUT ASIDE A VERY SPECIFIC GENRE: EDUCA-TIONAL FILM. HERE, EVEN WHEN IT'S OPERATING WITH THE SAME ELEMENTS AND RESOURCES AS FILM-SPECTACLES, THESE FILMS ARE ORGANIZED IN TERMS OF A SPECIAL FUNCTION: TO COMPLEMENT, AMPLIFY, OR ILLUSTRATE IN A DIRECT MANNER CLASSROOM TEACHING. IT'S LIKE A TEXTBOOK BUT DOESN'T SUBSTITUTE FOR IT. A STUDENT'S ATTITUDE VIS-A-VIS EDUCATIONAL FILM IS RADICALLY DIFFERENT FROM THE SPECTATOR CONFRONTING SPECTACLE-FILM. DEMAND OF STUDENTS IS A CON-SCIOUS EFFORT, ONE DIRECTED TOWARD ACQUIRING A SPECIFIC UNDERSTANDING. IN CONTRAST, SPECTATORS GO TO SPECTACLE SO AS TO FILL UP THEIR FREE TIME— TO RELAX, SEEK DIVERSION AND ENTERTAINMENT, AND GET PLEASURE. AND IF THESE VIEWERS DO GET OUT OF IT SOME KIND OF CONSCIOUS UNDERSTANDING, IT'S OF ANOTHER ORDER. THAT ISN'T THE SPECTATOR'S PRIMARY MOTIVATION.

WITHOUT GOING BEYOND THE FRAMEWORK OF SPECTACLE FILM, AND MORE SPECIFICALLY FICTIONAL FILM, WE CAN FIND DISTINCT POSSIBILITIES IN THE EMPHASIS, ACCORDING TO THE FILM'S CONDITION AS A SPECTACLE OR AS A VEHICLE OF IDEAS. WE MUST HAVE IN MIND, OF COURSE, THAT ALWAYS, TO SOME DEGREE, SPECTACLE REMAINS A BEARER OF IDEOLOGY.

THERE'S A SUPERFICIAL INTERPRETATION OF HOW FILM (OR ART IN GENERAL) SHOULD FUNCTION IN OUR SOCIETY. THIS NOTION PROPOSES DOLING OUT AESTHETIC ENJOYMENT WHILE YOU ARE AT THE SAME TIME "RAISING THE PEOPLE'S CULTURAL LEVEL." OVER AND OVER, SUCH A VULGAR STAND HAS LED SOME TO PROMOTE ADDITIVE FORMULAE IN WHICH "SOCIAL" *CONTENT* (UNDERSTOOD AS AN EDUCATIONAL ASPECT, FORMING REVOLUTIONARY CONSCIOUSNESS BUT ALSO SOMETIMES JUST DIFFUSING POLITICAL SLOGANS) SHOULD BE INTRODUCED IN AN ATTRACTIVE *FORM*. THAT IS, THE "MESSAGE" OUGHT TO BE DECKED OUT AND CON-FECTIONED IN SUCH A WAY THAT IT'S AGREEABLE TO THE CONSUMER PALATE. SOMETHING LIKE THAT WOULD PRODUCE A SORT OF IDEOLOGICAL PAP FOR EASY DIGESTION.

OBVIOUSLY, IT'S ONLY A SIMPLISTIC SOLUTION TO CONSIDER FORM AND CON-

TENT AS TWO SEPARATE INGREDIENTS WHICH YOU CAN MIX IN APT PROPORTION, ACCORDING TO SOME IDEAL RECIPE. FURTHERMORE, THIS ATTITUDE CONSIDERS THE SPECTATOR AS A PASSIVE ENTITY. SUCH A PERSPECTIVE CAN ONLY LEAD TO BUREAUCRATIZING ARTISTIC ACTIVITY. IT DOES NOT HAVE ANYTHING TO DO WITH A DIALECTICAL UNDERSTANDING OF THE PROCESS OF AN ORGANIC INTEGRATION OF FORM AND CONTENT, IN WHICH BOTH ASPECTS ARE SEEN TO BE INDISSOLUBLY UNITED AT THE SAME TIME THAT THEY WORK OFF OF AND INTERPENETRATE EACH OTHER, EVEN TO THE POINT WHERE THEY TAKE OVER EACH OTHER'S FUNCTIONS IN THAT RECIPROCAL INTERPLAY. THAT IS, WE'RE DEALING WITH A COMPLEX AND RICH PROCESS OF CONTRADICTIONS AND POSSIBILITIES FOR DEVELOPMENT, IN WHICH THE FORMAL, AESTHETIC, AND EMOTIONAL ASPECTS, ON THE ONE HAND, AND THE THEMATIC, EDUCATIONAL AND RATIONAL ASPECTS, ON THE OTHER, REVEAL CERTAIN AFFINITIES BUT ALSO THEIR OWN PECULIARITIES. THE DIVERSE MODALITIES OF THEIR MUTUAL INTERACTION (TO THE DEGREE TO WHICH THE INTERACTION IS ORGANIC, FOLLOWING UPON THE PREMISES WHICH GENERATE THE TEXT) GIVE RISE TO VARIOUS LEVELS OF "PRODUCTIVITY" (IN TERMS OF FUNCTIONALITY, EFFECTIVENESS, AND FULFILLMENT OF ASSIGNED FUNCTIONS) IN THE WORK'S RELATION TO THE SPECTATOR.

LATER I WILL OFFER SOME CONSIDERATIONS ABOUT THE RELATION BETWEEN THE CINEMATIC SPECTACLE AND ITS SPECTATOR, AND TRY TO TRACE OUT CERTAIN MECHANISMS WHICH THAT RELATION RESTS ON. FOR NOW I ONLY WISH TO POINT OUT THAT THOSE DISTINCT LEVELS OF PRODUCTIVITY—OR LEVELS OF POTENTIAL FUNCTIONALITY, WHICH DERIVE PRIMARILY FROM THE MANNER IN WHICH THE EMPHASIS IS DISTRIBUTED AMONG AESTHETIC, COGNITIVE, AND IDEOLOGICAL ASPECTS—*ARE NOT EXCLUSIVE LEVELS*. THAT IS TO SAY, FICTION FILM *IS* BASICALLY SPECTACLE. ITS FUNCTION AS SPECTACLE, IN THE PUREST SENSE, IS TO ENTERTAIN, DISTRACT, AND OFFER AN ENJOYMENT THAT COMES FROM REPRESENTATION. REPRESENTED ARE ACTIONS, SITUATIONS AND DIVERSE THINGS WHICH HAVE AS THEIR POINT OF DEPARTURE REALITY—IN ITS BROADEST SENSE. THESE THINGS CONSTITUTE A FICTION, ANOTHER DISTINCTLY NEW REALITY. AND THAT CAN ENRICH OR IMPOVERISH THE REALITY WHICH HAS BEEN ALREADY ESTABLISHED OR KNOWN UP TO THIS POINT.

A SIMPLE SPECTACLE IS HEALTHY TO THE DEGREE THAT IT DOES NOT OBSTRUCT VIEWERS' SPIRITUAL DEVELOPMENT. HOWEVER, A CLASS-SOCIETY SPECTACLE'S SPIRIT OF RECREATION MUST SOMEHOW REINFORCE ESTABLISHED VALUES, WHATEVER THOSE MIGHT BE, BECAUSE THESE VALUES BROADLY FUNCTION AS AN ESCAPE VALVE TO LET PEOPLE AVOID CONFRONTING THOSE PROBLEMS AND TENSIONS WHICH REAL SOCIAL CONFLICTS ARE GENERATING. AT THIS LEVEL, THE SOCIAL AND MORAL ACCENT ALWAYS FALLS BACK ON EMOTION IN GENERAL. THUS SPECTACLE, IN ITS PUREST SENSE, JUST SEEKS TO GENERATE EMOTIONS IN THE SPECTATOR AND TO DOLE OUT A SENSORY PLEASURE, AS, LET'S SAY, A SPORTS EVENT DOES. WE SHOULD NOT MISTRUST THIS PLEASURE, EXCEPT WHEN LIGHTNESS GOES BEYOND THAT INTO STUPIDITY, WHEN HAPPINESS BECOMES FRIVOLITY, WHEN HEALTHY EROTICISM BECOMES

PORNOGRAPHY—AND WHEN, UNDER THE GUISE OF SIMPLE ENTERTAINMENT, SPEC-
TACLE BECOMES CONVERTED INTO A VEHICLE FOR AFFIRMING ALL BOURGEOIS
CULTURAL TRAITS. THEN—CONSCIOUSLY OR UNCONSCIOUSLY—IT INCARNATES
BOURGEOIS IDEOLOGY. THAT IS, EVEN "ENTERTAINMENT" FILMS WHICH APPARENT-
LY "SAY NOTHING" AND ARE SEEMINGLY SIMPLE OBJECTS OF CONSUMPTION, THOSE
FILMS COULD ALSO FULFILL THE ELEMENTAL FUNCTION OF SPIRITUALLY ENRICHING
THE SPECTATOR IF THEY DID NOT, TO USE A COINED EXPRESSION, PROMOTE
"IDEOLOGICAL DEVIATIONISM." CONSUMPTION DOES NOT—AND SHOULD NOT—
HAVE THE SAME MEANING IN A CAPITALIST SOCIETY THAT IT WOULD HAVE IN A
SOCIALIST ONE.

BUT IF WE WANT TO GO FARTHER, IF WE WANT FILM TO SERVE SOMETHING
HIGHER (OR DO THE SAME THING, BUT DO IT MORE PROFOUNDLY), IF WE WANT
IT TO FULFILL ITS FUNCTION MORE PERFECTLY (AESTHETIC, SOCIAL, ETHICAL, AND
REVOLUTIONARY), WE OUGHT TO GUARANTEE THAT IT CONSTITUTES A *FACTOR IN
SPECTATORS' DEVELOPMENT*. FILM WILL BE MORE FRUITFUL TO THE DEGREE THAT
IT PUSHES SPECTATORS TOWARD A MORE PROFOUND UNDERSTANDING OF REALITY
AND, CONSEQUENTLY, TO THE DEGREE THAT IT HELPS VIEWERS LIVE MORE ACTIVELY
AND INCITES THEM TO STOP BEING MERE SPECTATORS IN THE FACE OF REALITY. TO
DO THIS, FILM OUGHT TO APPEAL NOT ONLY TO EMOTION AND FEELING BUT ALSO
TO REASON AND INTELLECT. IN THIS CASE, BOTH INSTANCES OUGHT TO EXIST IN-
DISSOLUBLY UNITED, IN SUCH A WAY THAT THEY COME TO PROVOKE, AS PASCAL
SAID, AUTHENTIC "SHUDDERINGS AND TREMBLINGS OF THE MIND."

THUS, WE DON'T HAVE A CASE OF ANY OLD EMOTION TO WHICH YOU CAN
ADD A DOSE OF REASON, IDEAS, OR "CONTENT." RATHER IT'S EMOTION TIED TO
THE *DISCOVERY* OF SOMETHING, TO THE RATIONAL COMPREHENSION OF SOME
ASPECT OF REALITY. SUCH EMOTION IS QUANTITATIVELY DISTINCT FROM THAT WHICH
A SIMPLE SPECTACLE WILL ELICIT (*SUSPENSE*, THE CHASES, TERROR, SENTIMENTAL
SITUATIONS, ETC.) ALTHOUGH IT MIGHT WELL BE REINFORCED OR IMPEDED BY THOSE.

ON THE OTHER HAND, IT'S GOOD TO REMEMBER THAT CINEMA, IN THE WELL-
INTENTIONED PROCESS OF SHAPING ITS OBJECTIVES TO APTLY FULFILL ITS SOCIAL
FUNCTION, CAN NEGLECT ITS FUNCTION AS SPECTACLE. IF IT APPEALS EXCLUSIVELY
TO REASON OR TO THE VIEWERS' INTELLECTUAL EFFORTS, IT NOTICEABLY REDUCES
ITS EFFICACY BECAUSE IT IS FORGETTING ONE OF ITS ESSENTIAL ASPECTS, PLEASURE.

ART EXPRESSES ITS DEVELOPMENT NOT ONLY IN A SUCCESSIVE CHANGE IN FUNC-
TION, ACCORDING TO THE DISTINCT SOCIAL FORMATIONS WHICH GENERATE ART
ACROSS HISTORY. RATHER WE ALSO SEE AN ENRICHMENT AND GREATER COMPLEXI-
TY OF RESOURCES WHICH ART HAS AT ITS DISPOSAL. FROM THE MAGICIAN CAVE
ARTIST TO THE ARTIST OF THE SCIENTIFIC ERA, THE ART OBJECT HAS TAKEN ON DIVERSE
FUNCTIONS. SUCCESSIVELY, IT HAS HAD THE FUNCTION OF BEING AN INSTRUMENT
TO DOMINATE NATURAL FORCES, OF ONE CLASS DOMINATING ANOTHER, OF AF-
FIRMING AN IDEA, OF COMMUNICATING, OF KNOWING ONE'S SELF, OF DEVELOP-
ING A CRITICAL CONSCIOUSNESS, OF CELEBRATION, OF EVADING REALITY, OF

COMPENSATING, OR OF SIMPLE AESTHETIC PLEASURE. EVERY HISTORICAL MOMENT PLACES AN ACCENT ON ONE OR ANOTHER OF THESE FUNCTIONS AND DENIES OTHERS. NEVERTHELESS, WE MUST NOT FORGET THAT ALL OF THESE FUNCTIONS FORM ONE BODY OF ACCUMULATED EXPERIENCE, AND OUT OF ALL OF THEM, SOME VALUABLE ELEMENT ENDURES WHICH WILL ENRICH THE OTHERS. THE VARIOUS LEVELS OF COMPREHENSION (OR OF INTERPRETATION) OF AN ARTISTIC WORK BECOME JUXTAPOSED AND EXPRESS ART'S ACCUMULATION OF MULTIPLE FUNCTIONS ACROSS HISTORY. THUS, THE CAVE ARTIST PERSISTS IN ALL REAL ART, AND IF HE WAS NEVER EFFECTIVE ENOUGH TO ATTRACT REAL BISON, CERTAINLY HE WAS ABLE TO MOBILIZE THE HUNTERS. SUGGESTION CONTINUES TO OPERATE WITH GREATER OR LESSER SUCCESS, ACCORDING TO THE SPECIFIC CIRCUMSTANCES OF EACH PARTICULAR WORK. THAT'S HOW SO MANY ARTISTIC WORKS OPERATE WHEN THEY PREFIGURE VICTORY OVER AN ENEMY OR EXALT A WARRIOR'S HEROISM. BUT THE COURSE OF HISTORY HAS GIVEN US ANOTHER TYPE OF ARTIST WHO WORKS WELL THROUGH REASON, THROUGH UNDERSTANDING AND WHO, IN SPECIFIC CIRCUMSTANCES, FULLY ATTAINS HIS OR HER OBJECTIVE. THE VARIOUS FUNCTIONS WHICH ART HAS FULFILLED HAVE ENRICHED ARTISTIC ACTIVITY WITH NEW EXPRESSIVE RESOURCES. THE MAGNIFICENT ARSENAL OF RESOURCES ACCUMULATED ACROSS HISTORY WHICH CONTEMPORARY ART HAS AT ITS DISPOSITION PERMITS IT TO EXERCISE ITS FUNCTIONS AT ALL LEVELS OF COMPREHENSION, SUGGESTION AND ENJOYMENT.

Spectacle and Reality: The Extraordinary and the Everyday

THERE ARE SOME FILMS WHICH YOU CAN USUALLY SEE ON TV WHICH MATURE SPECTATORS MAY FEEL UNCOMFORTABLE WITH AND FIND MEANINGLESS BECAUSE THEY CANNOT COHERENTLY RELATE THE FILMS TO THE COMPLEX IMAGES OF THE WORLD WHICH THEY HAVE FORMED DURING THEIR LIFE. SUCH PEOPLE MAY WELL ASK, "WHAT DOES THIS HAVE TO DO WITH REALITY?" TO WHICH A CHILD MIGHT ANSWER WITH ANOTHER QUESTION, "WELL, ISN'T IT JUST A MOVIE?" THE QUESTIONS STAY IN PURE AIR, OF COURSE. IT WOULD BE A HARD TASK TO EXPLAIN TO A CHILD HOW, FOR MATURE PEOPLE, THE SPHERE OF REALITY IS CONSTANTLY ARTICULATED IN MORE DETAIL IN ONE'S MIND, AND HOW SOME THINGS ARE LEFT BEHIND. IT HAPPENS IN SUCH A WAY THAT AN ADULT'S IMAGE OF THE WORLD COMES TO BE VERY DIFFERENT FROM WHAT A CHILD CAN IMAGINE. MATURE ADULTS KEEP SEPARATING OUT MORE OR LESS APPARENT LAYERS OF REALITY, SO THAT THEY DRAW CLOSER AND CLOSER TO ITS ESSENCE. THEY DISCRIMINATE AND VALORIZE REALITY'S DISTINCT ASPECTS AS A CONSEQUENCE OF HUMAN UNDERSTANDING, WHICH BECOMES MORE AND MORE PROFOUND ABOUT REALITY ITSELF. THAT'S WHY A MATURE PERSON PROBABLY FEELS DISSATISFIED CONFRONTING SOME MOVIES. BUT IT'S ALSO WHY THE CHILD'S QUESTION DOESN'T ALLOW FOR A QUICK, SUPERFICIAL RESPONSE. CERTAINLY A FILM IS ONE THING AND REALITY IS ANOTHER. WE CAN'T FORGET THAT THOSE ARE THE RULES OF THE GAME. OF COURSE, FILM AND REALITY ARE NOT—CANNOT BE—COMPLETELY DIVORCED FROM EACH OTHER. A FILM

FORMS PART OF REALITY. LIKE ALL WORKS WHICH PEOPLE INSCRIBE IN ART, FILM IS A MANIFESTATION OF SOCIAL CONSCIOUSNESS AND ALSO CONSTITUTES A REFLECTION OF REALITY.

IN RELATION TO CINEMA, ONE CIRCUMSTANCE OF ITS PRODUCTION CAN BE DECEPTIVE. THE SIGNS WHICH CINEMATIC LANGUAGE EMPLOYS ARE NO MORE THAN IMAGES OF SEPARATE ASPECTS OF REALITY ITSELF. IT'S NOT JUST A QUESTION OF COLORS, LINES, SOUNDS, TEXTURES AND FORMS, BUT ALSO OF OBJECTS, PERSONS, SITUATIONS, GESTURES, AND WAYS OF SPEAKING. IN THIS WAY, FREED FROM THEIR HABITUAL CONNOTATIONS AND DAILY USE, THEY ARE CHARGED WITH A NEW SIGNIFICANCE WITHIN THE CONTEXT OF THE FICTION. FILM THUS CAPTURES IMAGES OF ISOLATED ASPECTS OF REALITY. IT'S NOT A SIMPLE, MECHANICAL COPY. IT DOES NOT CAPTURE REALITY ITSELF, IN ALL ITS BREADTH AND DEPTH. BUT CINEMA CAN REACH A HIGHER DEGREE OF PROFUNDITY AND GENERALIZATION, BECAUSE OF THE POSSIBILITY OF FINDING NEW RELATIONS AMONG THOSE IMAGES OF ISOLATED ASPECTS. THOSE ASPECTS THUS TAKE ON NEW MEANING, A MEANING NOT COMPLETELY ALIEN TO THEM, YET ONE THAT CAN BE MORE PROFOUND AND MORE REVEALING. FILM CAN RELATE ASPECTS OF REALITY TO OTHER ASPECTS AND PRODUCE SURPRISES OR KINDS OF ASSOCIATIONS WHICH IN DAILY REALITY WERE DILUTE AND OPAQUE BECAUSE OF THEIR HIGH DEGREE OF COMPLEXITY AND BECAUSE PEOPLE WERE SATURATED WITH SEEING SUCH THINGS IN THEIR DAILY LIFE. THUS WE FIND THE POTENTIAL FOR A REVEALING OPERATION DESTINED TO RAISE THE LEVEL OF FILM'S COMPLEXITY AND RICHNESS BUT WHICH IS A POTENTIAL STILL IN GROWTH. IT'S A POTENTIAL SPECIFIC TO FILM, BECAUSE WE'RE TALKING ABOUT A FILM LANGUAGE WHICH IS NOURISHED BY REALITY AND REFLECTS IT ON THE BASIS OF IMAGES OF OBJECTS WHICH ARE OFFERED UP TO SIGHT AND SOUND, AS IF WE WERE DEALING WITH A HUGE ORDERING AND SELECTING MIRROR. SUCH A WAY OF LOOKING AT REALITY *THROUGH* FICTION OFFERS SPECTATORS THE POSSIBILITY OF APPRECIATING, ENJOYING, AND UNDERSTANDING REALITY BETTER.

BUT THAT SHOULD NOT CONFUSE US. CINEMATIC REALISM, IN ITS PRESENT CAPACITY, CANNOT CAPTURE REALITY "JUST LIKE IT IS" (WHICH BECOMES ONLY "JUST LIKE IT *APPEARS* TO BE"). RATHER IT DOES HAVE THE CAPACITY TO REVEAL, THROUGH ASSOCIATIONS AND THROUGH RELATING DIVERSE ASPECTS PULLED OUT FROM DAILY REALITY—THAT IS TO SAY, THROUGH CREATING A "NEW REALITY." IN THIS WAY, IT CAN REVEAL DEEPER, MORE ESSENTIAL LAYERS OF REALITY ITSELF. IT CAN DO IT IN A WAY THAT LETS US ESTABLISH A DIFFERENCE BETWEEN THAT OBJECTIVE REALITY WHICH THE WORLD OFFERS US—LIFE IN ITS BROADEST SENSE—AND THE IMAGE OF REALITY WHICH CINEMA OFFERS US WITHIN THE NARROW FRAME OF THE SCREEN. ONE WOULD BE GENUINE *REALITY*; THE OTHER, *FICTION*.

NOW I'D LIKE TO ELABORATE HOW THE CINEMATIC SPECTACLE OFFERS VIEWERS AN IMAGE OF REALITY WHICH BELONGS TO THE SPHERE OF FICTION, THE IMAGINARY, THE UNREAL. IN THIS SENSE IT STANDS IN RELATIVE OPPOSITION TO THE VERY REALITY WITHIN WHICH IT IS INSERTED. CLEARLY, THE SPHERE OF THE REAL, IN ITS BROADEST

SENSE, INCLUDES SOCIAL LIFE AND ALL CULTURAL MANIFESTATIONS. IT ALSO EN-
COMPASSES THE SPHERE OF FICTION, OF SPECTACLE—AS CULTURAL OBJECTS. BUT
TO BE RIGOROUS, IT'S REALLY A QUESTION OF TWO DIVERSE SPHERES, EACH WITH
ITS OWN PECULIARITIES, DESCRIBABLE NOT JUST AS TWO ASPECTS OF REALITY, BUT
AS TWO *MOMENTS* IN THE PROCESS OF APPROXIMATING REALITY'S ESSENCE. SPEC-
TACLE THUS CAN BE CONCEIVED AS A MEDIATION IN THE PROCESS OF PENETRATING
INTO REALITY. THE MOMENT OF THE SPECTACLE CORRESPONDS TO THE MOMENT
OF ABSTRACTION IN THE PROCESS OF UNDERSTANDING.

THE ARTISTIC SPECTACLE BECOMES INSERTED INTO THE SPHERE OF *EVERYDAY*
REALITY (THE SPHERE OF WHAT IS CONTINUOUSLY STABLE AND RELATIVELY CALM)
AS AN *EXTRAORDINARY* MOMENT, AS A RUPTURE. IT'S OPPOSED TO DAILY LIFE AS
AN UNREALITY, AN OTHER-REALITY, INSOFAR AS IT MOVES AND RELATES TO THE
SPECTATOR ON AN IDEAL PLANE. (IN THIS BEING *IDEAL*—STRANGE AS OPPOSED TO
THE DAILY OR THE NORMATIVE—IT EXPRESSES ITS UNUSUAL AND EXTRAORDINARY
CHARACTER. IT'S NOT THAT SPECTACLE IS OPPOSED TO THE TYPICAL, BUT RATHER
IT CAN INCARNATE THE TYPICAL IN THAT IT IS A SELECTIVE PROCESS WHICH EX-
ACERBATES RELEVANT—SIGNIFYING—TRAITS FROM REALITY). WE CAN'T SAY,
HOWEVER, THAT IT'S AN EXTENSION OF (DAILY) REALITY BUT RATHER IS ALWAYS
AN EXTENSION OF (THE ARTISTS' AND THE VIEWERS') SUBJECTIVE REALITY TO THE
DEGREE THAT IT OBJECTIFIES PEOPLE'S IDEOLOGICAL AND EMOTIONAL PROCESS.

CINEMA CAN DRAW VIEWERS CLOSER TO REALITY WITHOUT GIVING UP ITS
CONDITION OF UNREALITY, FICTION, AND OTHER-REALITY. THIS HAPPENS WHEN
AND IF IT LAYS DOWN A BRIDGE TO REALITY SO THAT VIEWERS CAN RETURN LADEN
WITH EXPERIENCES AND STIMULATION. ALL THE EXPERIENCES, INFORMATION, AND
LIVELINESS WHICH VIEWERS GAIN ON THE BASIS OF THIS RELATION MAY REMAIN
JUST ON THAT LEVEL— ONE WHICH MAY BE MORE OR LESS ACTIVE IN TERMS OF
REFLECTION, THE SENSORY LEVEL. BUT FILM CAN ALSO INITIATE IN VIEWERS, ONCE
THEY'VE STOPPED BEING VIEWERS AND ARE FACING THAT OTHER ASPECT OF REALI-
TY (THE VIEWERS' OWN LIFE, THEIR DAILY REALITY), A SERIES OF THINKING PRO-
CESSES, REASONINGS, JUDGMENTS, IDEAS AND THUS A BETTER COMPREHENSION
OF REALITY ITSELF AND A MORE ADEQUATE WAY OF CONDUCTING THEMSELVES,
OF ACTING PRACTICALLY. THE SPECTATOR'S RESPONSE WHICH FOLLOWS THE MO-
MENT OF THE SPECTACLE IS AN EFFECT OF THE SPECTACLE.[4]

THE MOST SOCIALLY PRODUCTIVE SPECTACLE SURELY CANNOT BE ONE WHICH
LIMITS ITSELF TO A MORE OR LESS PRECISE ("HONEST," SERVILE) REFLECTION OF REALITY
JUST AS REALITY OFFERS ITSELF IN ITS IMMEDIACY. THAT WOULD DO NO MORE THAN
DUPLICATE THE IMAGE WE ALREADY HAVE OF REALITY. IT'D BE REDUNDANT, A KIND
OF SUMMING UP LACKING MEANING. WE COULD HARDLY TELL THAT IT WAS A
SPECTACLE. THE SPECTACLE PROPER (THAT IS, THE ONE THAT MANIFESTS ITSELF
THROUGH WHAT WE CALL *FICTION*) ASSERTS ITSELF AS A MOMENT OF RUPTURE
AND AS A KIND OF STRONG EMOTION IN THE MIDST OF DAILY REALITY, AND IN
THIS SENSE OPPOSED TO IT AND NEGATING IT. WE MUST ESTABLISH VERY CLEARLY

WHAT THIS *NEGATION* OF REALITY OUGHT TO CONSIST OF SO THAT IT BECOMES SOCIALLY PRODUCTIVE.

THERE'S A STORY OF A PAINTER, A CHINESE PAINTER FOR ALL WE KNOW, WHO ONCE PAINTED A BEAUTIFUL LANDSCAPE IN WHICH YOU COULD SEE MOUNTAINS, RIVERS, TREES. THEY WERE EXECUTED WITH SO MUCH ELEGANCE, SO CONGRUENT WITH THE IMAGINATION WHICH DICTATED THEM, THAT ALL A VIEWER NEEDED WAS TO HEAR THE BIRDS' SONGS AND FEEL THE WIND PASS BETWEEN THE TREES TO COMPLETE THE ILLUSION OF STANDING IN FRONT OF A REAL LANDSCAPE AND NOT A PICTURE. THE PAINTER, ONCE FINISHED, STOOD THERE CONTEMPLATING THE LANDSCAPE WHICH HAD SPRUNG FROM HIS HEAD AND HANDS. HE WAS IN SUCH ECSTASY THAT HE BEGAN TO WALK TOWARD THE PICTURE AND FEEL COMPLETELY SURROUNDED BY THE LANDSCAPE. HE WALKED AMONG THE TREES. FOLLOWED THE COURSE OF THE RIVER, AND WITHDREW MORE AND MORE IN THE MOUNTAINS UNTIL HE DISAPPEARED TOWARD THE HORIZON.

A GREAT EXIT FOR AN ARTIST PROBABLY. BUT SIMILAR EXPERIENCES OF AESTHETIC ECSTACY FOR ANY VIEWERS OUGHT TO BE CONDITIONED SO THAT THEY DO NOT LOSE THEIR WAY BACK, AND SO THAT THEY CAN RETURN TO REALITY SPIRITUALLY ENRICHED AND STIMULATED TO LIVE BETTER IN IT. FOR THAT REASON, WHATEVER THE LANDSCAPE OF THE CHINESE PAINTER OFFERS WITH ALL OF ITS MYSTERIOUS CHARM, IT REPRESENTS THE ABSOLUTE NEGATION OF REALITY AND THUS (MAINTAINING OURSELVES ON THE PLANE OF METAPHOR) DEATH OR INSANITY.

A SPECTACLE WHICH EXERCISES THIS KIND OF FASCINATION FOR THE SPECTATOR CAN BE CHARACTERIZED AS A "METAPHYSICAL NEGATION" OF REALITY. THAT IS, IT'S A NEGATION WHICH TRIES TO ABOLISH REALITY THROUGH THE ACT OF EVADING IT. OF COURSE, THAT WOULD NOT BE THE MOST SOCIALLY PRODUCTIVE KIND OF SPECTACLE.

BUT FOR A LONG TIME THAT'S BEEN THE IDEAL OF SPECTACLE FOR A CLASS WHICH IS ESSENTIALLY HYPOCRITICAL AND IMPOTENT, BUT WHICH HAS BEEN CAPABLE OF INVENTING THE MOST SOPHISTICATED MECHANISMS FOR JUSTIFYING ITSELF. IT TRIES TO HIDE FROM ITSELF THE MOST PROFOUND LEVELS OF REALITY WHICH IT CANNOT—OR DOES NOT—WANT TO CHANGE. BUT THAT'S NOT THE CASE IN A SOCIETY WHICH IS CONSTRUCTING ITSELF ON A NEW BASIS, WHICH PROPOSES TO ELIMINATE ALL VESTIGES OF HUMAN EXPLOITATION, WHICH DEMANDS ALL ITS MEMBERS' ACTIVE PARTICIPATION AND THUS EACH PERSON'S DEVELOPING A SOCIAL CONSCIENCE. HERE METAPHYSICAL NEGATION, WHICH TRIES TO ABOLISH REALITY THROUGH AN ACT OF NEGATION, IS PRECISELY OPPOSED TO DIALECTICAL NEGATION, WHICH AIMS TO TRANSFORM REALITY THROUGH REVOLUTIONARY PRACTICE. AS ENGELS SAID, "TO NEGATE, IN DIALECTICS, DOESN'T CONSIST JUST OF CALMLY AND SMOOTHLY SAYING, 'NO,' IN SAYING THAT A THING DOESN'T EXIST, OR IN CAPRICIOUSLY DESTROYING IT." FURTHER ON HE SAYS, "EVERY CLASS OF THINGS HAS, THEREFORE, ITS OWN PARTICULAR MODE OF BEING NEGATED, IN SUCH A WAY THAT IT ENGENDERS A PROCESS OF DEVELOPMENT. AND THE SAME OCCURS WITH

IDEAS AND CONCEPTS." (*ANTI-DUHRING*) IN THIS WAY A *SPECTACLE WHICH IS SOCIALLY PRODUCTIVE* WILL BE THAT WHICH NEGATES DAILY REALITY (THE FALSE VALUES CRYSTALLIZED IN DAILY OR ORDINARY THOUGHT) AND AT THE SAME TIME FEELS THE PREMISE OF ITS OWN NEGATION. THAT IS, IT NEGATES BEING A SUBSTITUTE FOR REALITY OR AN OBJECT OF CONTEMPLATION. IT CAN'T JUST OFFER ITSELF AS A SIMPLE WAY OUT OR CONSOLATION FOR A BURDENED SPECTATOR. RATHER IT MUST AID THE VIEWERS' RETURN FROM THE OTHER REALITY—THE ONE WHICH PUSH-ED THEM MOMENTARILY TO RELATE THEMSELVES TO THE SPECTACLE, TO DISTRACT THEMSELVES, TO PLAY. THEY SHOULD NOT RETURN COMPLACENT, TRANQUIL, EMP-TY, WORN OUT, AND INERT. RATHER THE VIEWER SHOULD BE STIMULATED AND ARMED FOR PRACTICAL ACTION. THIS MEANS SPECTACLE MUST CONSTITUTE A FAC-TOR IN THE DEVELOPMENT, THROUGH ENJOYMENT, OF THE SPECTATORS' CON-SCIOUSNESS. IN DOING THAT, IT MOVES THEM TO STOP BEING SIMPLE, PASSIVE (CONTEMPLATIVE) SPECTATORS IN THE FACE OF REALITY.

TRANSLATED BY JULIA LESAGE.

Notes

1. Patricio Guzman, in notes he wrote before making *The Battle of Chile,* said at that time—the months preceding the fascist coup—he'd never have made a fictional film with actors reciting a text, because reality itself, which was developing before their very eyes, was changing tremendously. At those moments of social convulsion, reality lost its "daily" character, and everything which happened was "extraordinary," new, unique. The dynamics of the change, the tendencies of that development, the very essence of it, were manifested most directly and clearly in moments of relative quiet. For that reason, it captured our attention, and in that sense we can say it is spectacular. Surely the most effective thing at that time was to try to cap-ture those moments in their purest state: documentary. Leave for re-elaboration elements from those moments in which reality seems to be proceeding without any apparent alteration or change. Then fiction becomes a fit instrument for penetrating into reality's essence.

2. This famous code demanded, amongst other things, that film ought to "shape characters, develop an ideal and inculate just principles, by using attractive incidents and offering to the spectators' admiration fine examples of good conduct." Independently of any discrepancy from "ideal" and "just" principles which this revealing document was trying to promote, it is interesting for us to see how it resorts to the most puerile mechanism—posing that spectators admire "fine examples of good conduct." Without a doubt, that mechanism best hides reactionary attitudes, because it only aims at creating an idealized image complacent about reality.

3. In the thesis about artistic and literary culture contained in the *Platform and Program of the Cuban Communist Party*, we can read, "Socialist society demands an art and literature which, at the same time that it provides aesthetic enjoyment, contributes to raising the whole people's cultural level. It ought to create a climate which is extremely creative, which impels art and literature's progress as the legitimate aspiration of working people. Art and literature will promote the highest human values, enrich our people's lives, and participate actively in forming the communist person."

4. Certainly t.v. has brought into homes the most spectacular images of reality; for example, I think about the middle class American drinking beer while seeing on television how the chief of police in Saigon opened a hole in a prisoner's head in full public view; all of that was presented in color. Already the *representation* of those moments has to adjust itself to new circumstances. But the most important thing is that an act is so potent, so unusual, so bloodthirsty, once it's presented as spectacle—that is to say once it is offered up to the spectator's contemplation—it's found to have notably reduced potency as a generator of a consequent reaction on the practical plane. Probably, surprise would make the viewer jump from his or her chair, but following that, they'd go to the refrigerator to open up another beer, which would make them sleep tranquilly. After all, those deeds have passed little by little into the plane of every-dayness. What would we have to do to move this viewer? It's not enough that the spectacle be real—and that it might be happening at the very moment that one looks at it—so as to generate a productive reaction in the spectator. For that it will be necessary, possibly, to acquire more sophisticated mechanisms.

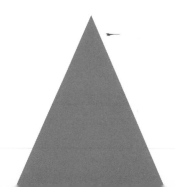

The Perspective of the Present: Cuban History, Cuban Filmmaking
[1986]

The Last Supper

Osvaldo Sanchez Crespo ∿∿∿∿∿∿∿∿∿∿∿∿∿∿∿∿∿∿

> His excellency, Senor Conde de Casa Bayona, in an act of profound Christian fervor, decided to humiliate himself before his slaves. One Holy Thursday, imitating Christ, he washed the feet of the twelve negroes, sat them at his table and served them from his plates. But it was there that these slaves, whose theological knowledge was not very profound, instead of behaving like apostles, rose in rebellion. Taking advantage of the prestige they had acquired before other members of the group, they ended by burning the sugar mill. This most Christian act was finished by the runaway slave hunters, who pursued the runaway negro slaves and speared twelve heads, the same twelve before whom his excellency Senor Conde de Casa Bayona had humiliated himself.[1]

(An extended description written by Don Miguel de Moya and signed by almost all the sugar mill owners of the territory on January 19, 1790.)

WITH THE BRILLIANCE OF *MEMORIES OF UNDERDEVELOPMENT* (1968) AS ITS PRECEDENT, *THE LAST SUPPER* (1976) MARKS TOMAS GUTIERREZ ALEA'S ARTISTIC MATURITY. IT IS ALSO ONE OF THE ONLY CUBAN FILMS OF THE '70'S THAT OVER-CAME THE PREDOMINANT TENDENCY TOWARD HISTORICISM. MAKING HISTORICAL EPICS MIGHT SEEM FROM A DISTANCE TO BE AN ELEGANT WAY TO AVOID TAKING A POLITICAL STAND IN RELATION TO CONTEMPORARY CUBAN REALITY. I DO NOT THINK THAT THESE FILMS OR THIS KIND OF FILMMAKING CAN BE UNDERSTOOD WITHOUT ALSO TAKING INTO ACCOUNT CHANGES THAT WERE TAKING PLACE IN CUBAN CULTURAL INSTITUTIONS IN 1975 AND THEREAFTER. THE ESTABLISHMENT OF THE MINISTRY OF CULTURE, TOGETHER WITH LARGER POLITICAL DEVELOPMENTS OF THE PERIOD LED TO A REVITALIZATION OF CULTURAL OBJECTIVES. INCLUDED IN THIS WAS THE DEVELOPMENT OF A MORE COHERENT, MORE LUCID HISTORICAL VISION, WHICH UP TO THAT POINT HAD BEEN NEITHER AS PROFOUND NOR AS COMPREHENSIVE. BECAUSE OF THOSE TRANSFORMATIONS AND THE WORKS THAT CAME OUT OF THEM, IT IS NOW POSSIBLE TO SPEAK OF THE AVANT-GARDE OF THE PRESENT DECADE, THE FIRST TO BE PRODUCED ENTIRELY WITHIN THE REVOLUTION.

WORKING AMID THESE CHANGES IN THE '70'S, GUTIERREZ ALEA PERCEIVED THAT THE DESIRE FOR HISTORICAL DRAMA "CANNOT BE REDUCED TO A DESIRE TO RECONSTRUCT PARTICULAR MOMENTS OF THE PAST," BUT RATHER IS TRIGGERED BY THE DEGREE TO WHICH THOSE HISTORIES COMPREHEND THE TENDENCIES OF THE

PRESENT.[2] ALTHOUGH CUBAN CINEMA IN GENERAL DID NOT AND STILL HAS NOT REACHED THE LEVEL OF ACHIEVEMENTS OF THE EARLY AND MID-1970'S, GUTIER-REZ ALEA'S FILM, WITH ITS CRITICAL APPROACH TO HISTORICAL REPRESENTATION, BOTH DEPICTS AND TRANSCENDS THE SPIRIT AND LIMITS OF ITS TIME.

WHILE USING THE BIBLICAL THEME OF CHRIST'S PASSION COULD HAVE LED TO SIMPLISTIC DEMYSTIFICATION AND SARDONIC BLASPHEMY, FOR GUTIERREZ ALEA IT WAS ONE INROAD INTO COMPLEX HISTORICAL DRAMA. THE STORY IS BASED ON AN OLD FORGOTTEN TEXT FROM ABOUT 1790, ABOUT A SLAVE UPRISING THAT BEGAN WITH A COUNT'S CHRISTIAN EXTRAVAGANCES, AND ITS SUGGESTIVENESS WAS TOO TEMPTING FOR THIS DIRECTOR TO PASS OVER. EVEN THE TIME PERIOD IS KEY TO UNDERSTANDING WHAT CUBA IS TODAY: PART OF THE THIRD WORLD.

BETWEEN THE ENGLISH TAKEOVER OF HAVANNA IN 1762, AND THE HAITIAN REVOLUTION WHICH DESTROYED THAT COUNTRY'S SUGAR INDUSTRY IN 1793, CUBA BECAME THE BASE OF THE WORLD'S SUGAR INDUSTRY. THE SUGAR MILL WOULD BECOME THE COLONIAL SYSTEM'S FULCRUM, AND THE SYMBOL OF ALL COLONIAL SOCIETY. IT IS TO THIS DAY THE CRUCIBLE OF CUBA'S NATIONAL IDENTITY.

THE COUNT OF CASA BAYONA'S BLACK LAST SUPPER IS NOT SIMPLY A JOKE BASED ON THE 20TH CHAPTER OF ST. MATTHEW. BENEATH THE COUNT'S SINCERELY CHRISTIAN IMPULSE ARE THE CONTRADICTIONS THAT PLANTATION OWNERS LIVED AT THE BEGINNING OF THE 19TH CENTURY, ASCRIBING AS THEY DID TO THE

ENLIGHTENMENT BELIEFS OF THE EMERGING BOURGEOISIE AND OWNING SLAVES. BY THEATRICALIZING A HOLY THURSDAY, THE COUNT WAS ABLE TO FICTIONALIZE A STATE OF HARMONY, USING THE DIDACTIC POTENTIAL OF THE LITURGY AND THE WEIGHT OF THE ENLIGHTENMENT TO REPRESENT THE "FRATERNAL" DEPENDENCY BETWEEN CHRIST AND THE DISCIPLES. THIS SYMBOLIC OPPOSITION, THE CLASSIC DUALITY OF MASTER AND SLAVE, IS ONE OF CLASS, IDEOLOGY AND CULTURE. REVEALED THROUGHOUT THE FILM IS HOW THE TWO VERY DIFFERENT WORLD VIEWS ADDRESS THE SINGULAR REALITY OF COLONIZATION.

SOME MIGHT SEE THE FINAL ESCAPE OF THE SEBASTIAN/CHRIST FIGURE AS A DIDACTIC IMPOSITION FROM THE PRESENT ONTO THE PAST. IN MY OPINION, HOWEVER, THE RUNAWAY SLAVES' CAPACITY TO TRANSFORM THEIR SITUATION DID NOT GO BEYOND PARODY OF THE BIBLE, EVEN IN THEIR RUNNING AWAY. CLEARLY, THEY ARE NOT THE ONES WHO WERE TO PARTICIPATE IN THE INDEPENDENCE WAR SEVENTY YEARS LATER. THE SLAVES AT THIS SUPPER ARE NOT ONLY THE COUNT'S VICTIMS, BUT THE VICTIMS OF THEIR OWN IDEOLOGICAL LIMITATIONS. IT IS A PRINCIPLE THAT TRIUMPHS AT THE END OF THE FILM, NOT THE ESCAPIST SOLUTIONS REPRESENTED BY THE ACTUAL SLAVES, EITHER AS INDIVIDUALS OR AS A CLASS.

THE LAST SUPPER'S STRENGTH LIES IN ITS PLAY ON THIS PARABLE. THE DEBATE BETWEEN CHRIST, JUDAS AND HIS BLACK DISCIPLES, CALL UPON THE SPECTATOR ULTIMATELY TO DETERMINE THE SOCIO-POLITICAL CAST OF THIS PARTICULAR PASSION. MAKING THE SPECTATOR THINK ABOUT HISTORY IN IDEOLOGICAL TERMS HAS REPEATEDLY BEEN GUTIERREZ ALEA'S INTENT, AND PROOF OF HIS INTELLECTUAL VITALITY. *THE LAST SUPPER* WAS A CLASSIC FROM THE NIGHT OF ITS FIRST SCREENING. THOUGH IT HAS RECEIVED MANY AWARDS INTERNATIONALLY, IT HAS NOT WON THE PUBLIC, OR THE CRITICAL SPACE IT DESERVES IN ITS OWN COUNTRY.

TRANSLATED AND EDITED BY COCO FUSCO.

Notes
1. Moreno Fraginals, Manuel. *El Ingenio*. T.I. p. 117 Ed. C. Sociales. L. Habana, 1977.
2. T.G. Alea, interview, *Cine Cubano*, no. 93, 1978.

The Perspective of the Present: Cuban History, Cuban Filmmaking

[1986]

One Way or Another

Osvaldo Sanchez Crespo

> *Today is different, though there are still many people who are mistaken, who don't understand the revolution; yes, people in the ghettos who don't understand, who don't want to leave the environment, some because they don't want to, others because they don't know how. They lived in ghettos before the revolution, where the poor lived, the poorest, both blacks and whites.*
>
> Eva Menendez, age 59

> *The ghetto is a product of exploitation. The people who lived there endured very much, didn't have the opportunity to work, to be educated and to learn. I think that the new buildings should be given to people who have integrated themselves—even if that leaves me out, they deserve them. I also think that people have to be very strong not to let themselves be taken, not to be dragged down by the environment that we ourselves create.*
>
> Barbara Belran, age 26

(These testimonies are from people in the ghetto of Las Yaguas, which no longer exists, and on which the drama is based. They are part of a sociological study done by Lazara Menendez and Raquel Mendieta of the University of Havana.)

Defining the popular has been a constant source of controversy in debates on Cuban film and filmmaking. In some instances it has been synonymous with authenticity, in others, with mediocrity and cultural insignificance. Rarely has the making of socially productive films in Cuba incorporated a serious questioning of Cuban popular culture. This, above all, is Sara Gomez's lasting contribution to Cuban cinema.

Being a black woman from the Third World, with all that implies, Sara Gomez decided to use the camera as a means of ideological engagement. She "didn't just want to be a nice middle-class girl who played the piano."[1] *One Way Or Another* is her first and last feature. She died a few days before finishing the filming. But this tragic event is not the only reason that *One Way Or Another* is a truncated project. Gomez initiated a way of making films that unfortunately has not been taken up by other Cuban filmmakers.

Among the directors who emerged in the 1980's there are some who have also attempted to address the question of the popular. Perhaps this is due to their learning filmmaking by making documentaries, as Sara Gomez did. Yet none of their films have attained *One Way Or Another's* conceptual rigor, its unpatronizing lucidity, or its insight into Cuban culture's basic problems. Only Gutierrez Alea, in dedicating his most recent film, *Up To A Certain Point* (1983) to Sara Gomez, recognized her way of filmmaking as a path to follow and as a challenge for the younger generation of directors just making their debuts. Few of them took notice of this.

Thus, Sara Gomez's work continues to be an island unto itself in our film history. Refusing affectation, she dispensed with that pretentious sense of beauty other filmmakers try to overwhelm us with. She chose to film in black and white, and in 16mm. She insisted on avoiding all technical excesses that would inhibit communication. It is enough for her to be in a lively place with living people. Is this Neorealism, cinema verite, or something completely different?

Marginality for Sara Gomez was an endless source of melodrama. Rather than seeing it as something to be pitied, Gomez recognized its social and cultural importance, integral to the lives of vast sectors of the population in a neocolonial country—as Cuba was, and as many Third World countries continue to be. Her story takes place among marginals, a sector where delinquency runs high. They are being moved to a recently constructed residential area with the promise of a higher

STANDARD OF LIVING AND STEADY EMPLOYMENT. BUT FAR FROM PRESENTING THIS PROCESS AS A GLORIFIED IMAGE OF REVOLUTIONARY PROGRESS, GOMEZ PRESENTS THE SITUATION FROM THE PERSPECTIVE OF THE "OUTSIDER," WHOSE TOTAL INTEGRATION, BOTH ECONOMIC AND SPIRITUAL, IS THE GREATEST CHALLENGE TO ANY PROJECT OF SOCIAL TRANSFORMATION.

ONE WAY OR ANOTHER IS THE STORY OF A TRANSITION, OF A PAINFUL PROCESS BY WHICH PEOPLE RECOGNIZE THEIR ABILITY TO BREAK WITH OUTDATED COLONIAL ETHICS, WITH THEIR RESISTANCE TO CHANGE AND WITH THEIR INDIVIDUALISM. SEEKING A DIALOGUE WITHIN THEIR MARGINAL WORLD. SARA GOMEZ EXPLORED THE REASONS FOR THEIR RESISTANCE, AND ITS RELATION TO THE DEFENSE OF CUBAN POPULAR TRADITIONS AND POPULAR CULTURE.

IT MIGHT SEEM ODD AND PERHAPS EVEN SYMPTOMATIC THAT THE FIRST WOMAN TO DIRECT FEATURE FILMS IN CUBA WOULD NOT HAVE TAKEN UP THE THEME OF MACHISMO, OR SEXISM AS HER LEITMOTIF. BUT SARA GOMEZ'S BROADER STUDY OF CUBAN CULTURAL ROOTS ALLOWS US TO SEE WHAT UNDERLIES OUR CONTEMPORARY PATRIARCHAL MENTALITY. GOMEZ ENTERED THE ANTECHAMBERS OF CUBA'S SYNCRETIC CULTS, TOUCHING ON ONE OF MACHISMO'S STRONGEST UNDERPINNINGS—THE ABAKUA CULT, A SECRET SOCIETY THAT EXCLUDES WOMEN FROM ALL BROTHERHOOD ACTIVITIES, AND REGULATES MASCULINE BEHAVIOR AND SEXUALITY IN AN EXPLICITLY DISCRIMINATORY MANNER.

SINCE *ONE WAY OR ANOTHER*, OTHER FILMS HAVE DEALT WITH WOMEN'S RIGHTS (TAKE, FOR EXAMPLE, *PORTRAIT OF THERESA*), BUT FEW HAVE ADDRESSED THIS ISSUE IN ALL ITS COMPLEXITY, BEING LIMITED INSTEAD TO OUTLINING THE PROBLEMS OF MARRIED COUPLES AND THEIR DOMESTIC LIVES. GOMEZ'S FILM APPROACHES THE QUESTION OF MARRIAGE THROUGH A COUPLE'S SELF-QUESTIONING. WHILE THIS HETEROSEXUAL COUPLE'S CENTRALITY MIGHT APPEAR TO ACQUIESCE TO CONVENTION, IN THE HISTORY OF CULTURAL AND RELIGIOUS MINORITIES IN CUBA, THE FAMILY AND THE MARRIED COUPLE HAVE FUNCTIONED AS A SITE OF RESISTANCE AGAINST THE IMPOSITION OF CULTURAL AND ETHICAL STANDARDS. IN ADDITION, THOUGH IN AFRO-CUBAN CULTURE THE FAMILY AND THE "COUPLE" TOOK ON CHARACTERISTICS FROM THE SPANISH, TO A CERTAIN EXTENT THEY COMPENSATE FOR THE TRAUMATIC PERIOD OF SLAVERY DURING WHICH AFRICAN KINSHIP STRUCTURES WERE DESTROYED. ONLY AFTER 1880 WAS IT POSSIBLE FOR CUBA'S BLACK POPULATION TO SPEAK OF A FAMILY AS A SOCIAL UNIT.

HAVING STUDIED WITH DIRECTORS SUCH AS AGNES VARDA AND GUTIERREZ ALEA, GOMEZ ACQUIRED A KEEN SENSE OF HOW TO FIND HER OWN CINEMATIC LANGUAGE FOR THE REALITIES SHE CHOSE TO FILM. DISPENSING WITH ANY SORT OF "MISE EN SCENE" THAT ROMANTICIZES MARGINALITY AND SURVIVAL, GOMEZ OPTED FOR A STYLE SIMILAR TO THAT OF INVESTIGATIVE REPORTAGE, TAKING ADVANTAGE OF THE CAMERA'S POWER OF DISCOVERY, ITS BLUNTNESS AND ITS VIOLENCE. *ONE WAY OR ANOTHER* ALSO DERIVES ITS EXPRESSIVE VITALITY FROM ITS WONDERFULLY RESONANT DIALOGUES, WHICH ARE MORE AUTHENTICALLY POPULAR THAN ANY ARGOT. RECENT CUBAN FILMS HAVE NOT YET MATCHED GOMEZ'S EXPRESSIVE POWER, TAKING RECOURSE INSTEAD TO OVERLY SUGGESTIVE BACKGROUND MUSIC IN ORDER TO COMPENSATE FOR THE DIALOGUE'S LIMITATIONS.

ONE WAY OR ANOTHER'S MUSICAL SOUNDTRACK SUBTLY REINFORCES THE FILM'S DRAMATIC CONFLICTS, COUNTERPOSING *FEELING* AND *GUAGUANCO* MUSICAL STYLES, BOTH OF WHICH ARE ASSOCIATED WITH CHARACTERS, MOMENTS AND ATTITUDES IN THE STORY. *FEELING* SONGS ARE "SAD," THEIR LYRICS ARE INTIMATE AND MEDITATIVE, ALWAYS REFERRING TO THE SINGER'S EMOTIONS. IN *ONE WAY OR ANOTHER* THE ETHICAL IMPERATIVE TO ABANDON MARGINALITY AND INTEGRATE ONESELF SOCIALLY IS CONVEYED THROUGH *FEELING*. THE *GUAGUANCO'S* AFRICAN-BASED RHYTHMS AND DANCE STEPS EVOKE CONFRONTATION AND CHALLENGE, AND SURFACE AT POINTS IN THE FILM THAT FOCUS ON MARGINAL TRADITIONS. CONTRARY TO *FEELING'S* SINCERE REFLEXIVE TONE, THE *GUAGUANCO* SPEAKS OF MALE-FEMALE RELATIONS IN TERMS OF OPPOSITION.

IN KEEPING WITH HER IMPROVISATIONAL SENSE OF FILMMAKING, GOMEZ WORK-

ED WITH AN OPEN SCRIPT, CONSTANTLY CHANGING MODES OF EXPRESSION, CREATING A RICH, EXPRESSIVE MOSAIC THAT INCORPORATES EVERYTHING FRON CINE-SURVEY TO THE POSSIBILITIES OF PSYCHODRAMA. LATIN AMERICAN CINEMA, ESPECIALLY CUBAN FILM, OWES MUCH TO SARA GOMEZ.

TRANSLATED AND EDITED BY COCO FUSCO.

Notes
1. Sara Gomez studied piano at the Havana Conservatory of music.

RECONSTRUCTING NICARAGUA: CREATING NATIONAL CINEMA [1986]

COMBINED INTERVIEWS WITH JORGE DENTI, ARGENTINE DIRECTOR, AND FRANK PINEDA, NICARAGUAN CINEMATOGRAPHER AND INCINE CO-FOUNDER, ABOUT *CULTURAL INSURRECTION*

∿∿∿∿∿∿∿∿∿∿∿∿∿∿∿∿∿∿ *COCO FUSCO*

BY THE TIME OF THE NICARAGUAN INSURRECTION, CINEMA WAS PERCEIVED AS AN INTEGRAL PART OF THE REVOLUTIONARY EFFORT. ARGENTINE FILMMAKER JORGE DENTI AND NICARAGUAN CINEMATOGRAPHER FRANK PINEDA WERE INVOLVED WITH THE DEVELOPMENT OF NICARAGUAN CINEMA AT ITS EARLY STAGES. THEY WORKED TOGETHER ON *CULTURAL INSURRECTION*, AN "INTERNATIONALIST" CO-PRODUCTION ABOUT THE LITERACY CAMPAIGN, THAT HAS NEVER BEFORE BEEN DISTRIBUTED IN THE U.S. IN THE FOLLOWING INTERVIEWS THEY DISCUSS ITS MAKING AND THE BIRTH OF CINEMA IN NICARAGUA.

Coco Fusco: HOW DID YOUR INVOLVEMENT WITH FILMMAKING IN NICARAGUA BEGIN?

Jorge Denti: IN MAY OF 1979, A GROUP OF LATIN AMERICAN FILMMAKERS TRAVELLED THROUGH NICARAGUA TO RECORD THE NICARAGUAN PEOPLE'S STRUGGLE AGAINST THE SOMOZA DICTATORSHIP. WE GOT TO KNOW NICARAGUAN PEOPLE, FROM THE OLD VETERANS WHO FOUGHT WITH GENERAL SANDINO TO THEIR CHILDREN AND GRANDCHILDREN WHO FOUGHT IN THAT "CRAZY LITTLE ARMY" WHICH, ON THE 16TH OF JULY AFTER THE FALL OF ESTELI SAW HOW THE DICTATOR AND HIS SUPPORTERS FLED THE COUNTRY. FROM ESTELI, WE WENT TO MATAGALA AND FROM THERE TO GUACO. THEN WE ACCOMPANIED A COLUMN OF 800 FSLN SOLDIERS UNTIL MIDDAY ON THE 19TH, WHEN WE ARRIVED IN MANAGUA. WE FILMED THE COMBATS, THE LIBERATED ZONES AND THE CELEBRATIONS OF THESE PEOPLE WHO HAD LIBERATED THEMSELVES FROM THE SOMOZA DYNASTY AFTER MORE THAN FOUR DECADES.

Frank Pineda: NICARAGUAN CINEMA WAS BORN OUT OF THE NECESSITY TO DOCUMENT THE WAR OF LIBERATION. WE WANTED TO CREATE AN ARCHIVE OF THESE IMAGES. IN THE WAR'S FINAL STAGES, AN INTERNATIONAL GROUP OF ACTIVIST FILMMAKERS JOINED US, ENTERING THE GUERRILLA-CONTROLLED ZONES. AT THAT TIME, I WAS IN MEXICO IN EXILE. THE FSLN HAD PROPOSED THAT FILM TEAMS BE ORGANIZED THAT INCLUDED NICARAGUANS WHO COULD BE TRUSTED TO ENTER THE GUERRILLA CAMPS AND FILM THE LEADERS AND THEIR ACTIVITIES. A GROUP OF US RECEIVED SIX MONTHS OF TRAINING, SOME WENT TO THE SOUTHERN FRONT. I WORKED FROM MEXICO AS A PRODUCER. WHEN THE TRIUMPH CAME, I WENT TO NICARAGUA, AND TOGETHER WITH SIX OTHERS WE TOOK OVER SOMOZA'S PROPAGANDA FILM OFFICES. THE MOST IMPORTANT THING IN THEM WAS THE ARCHIVE, WHICH WE PRESERVED.

THE FIRST THREE OR FOUR MONTHS WERE SPENT TRYING TO FIGURE OUT WHAT TO DO. OUR PRIORITIES AT THE TIME WERE TO FILM ALL THE DESTRUCTION THAT THE WAR HAD CAUSED. WE WANTED TO FILM ALL OVER NICARAGUA, TO RECORD ALL THOSE VIVID IMAGES. THEN, WITH THE HELP OF THE OTHER LATIN AMERICAN FILMMAKERS WHO WERE WORKING WITH US, WE STARTED TO GIVE SHAPE TO OUR NATIONAL CINEMA. WE WANTED TO BEGIN WITH CO-PRODUCTIONS, TO COLLABORATE WITH ALL THE FILMMAKERS WHO WERE COMING HERE. *CULTURAL INSURRECTION* WAS ONE OF THE FIRST PROJECTS WE UNDERTOOK.

JD: I WAS TOLD DURING THE CELEBRATIONS RIGHT AFTER THE TRIUMPH THAT THE NATIONAL RECONSTRUCTION GOVERNMENT WOULD ENGAGE IN A "WAR AGAINST IGNORANCE." IN JANUARY OF 1980 I PROPOSED THE FILM TO RAMIRO LACAYO, THE DIRECTOR OF INCINE. WE STARTED TO RAISE MONEY, LOOK FOR EQUIPMENT AND MATERIALS FROM DIFFERENT COUNTRIES AND ORGANIZATIONS AND SIGNED AN AGREEMENT.

CF: HOW DID YOU ORGANIZE THE PRODUCTION?

FP: It was logical for Nicaraguan cinema to record the process. We began to work with a plan that would enable us to document the event in all its detail. We travelled to the Atlantic Coast by boat and helicopter, joining a literacy brigade. Wrapping our equipment in plastic to protect it from the constant rain, we started to record the phenomenon in different communities. We saw the interaction between the brigadistas and the communities. Some of the brigadistas were experiencing incredible culture shock. One of them might mention a traffic light and his or her student wouldn't know what it was. They had to adjust the materials to the reality of their students. Now there are texts that are adjusted to these situations.

The brigadistas' return home was also amazing to film. The welcome of the mothers, the celebration in the Plaza of the Revolution. And the people who did not see their children return. Some of the literacy workers were assassinated by the contras.

CF: What made you incorporate past Nicaraguan history into the story of the campaign? How did you do this?

JD: The literacy crusade confirmed that "achieving literacy is a political act with pedagogical implications." In the first testimony in the documentary, an old man about 80 years old, who is learning to read and write, and who fought with Sandino tells us that "we are learning how to read, which is the most important thing we should know so that we men can no longer be exploited by other men," and that that happened in Nicaragua with Yankee interventionism. There was a need to analyze contemporary history, which had been suppressed by the dictatorship. The literacy campaign primers returned to the past, starting with Sandino's struggle and covering Nicaraguan history up to the present. All these factors influenced me, making me not want to separate Nicaraguan history from the history of the literacy campaign, so I incorporated it as another narrative line. For the music, I discussed my ideas with Luis Enrique Mejia Godoy about how to use it as another narrative form parallel to those of the classes and the different testimonies. I wanted the music to be like a voice from the land, from history.

CF: What was working in collaboration like for you?

FP: IT WAS A HARMONIC RELATIONSHIP. THERE WERE COLLECTIVE DISCUSSIONS. IN-CINE MADE SUGGESTIONS TO IMPROVE THE DOCUMENTARY AND OFFERED AR-CHIVAL MATERIALS.

ESSENTIALLY, WE HAD THE CHANCE TO LEARN WITH PEOPLE WHO HAD MORE EXPERIENCE, WHICH WAS LIKE HAVING A SCHOOL. THE FUNDAMENTAL THING WAS THIS EXCHANGE, SO WE COULD ABSORB THEIR KNOWLEDGE AND SET UP COPRODUC-TIONS AS A WAY OF TRAINING OURSELVES.

THIS FIRST STAGE OF THE REVOLUTION WAS IMPORTANT NOT JUST IN TERMS OF FILM BUT ALSO IN TERMS OF THE POLITICAL POSITION THAT I ADOPTED AS A RESULT. I SPEAK OF MY PERSONAL EXPERIENCE BUT I THINK THAT THOSE FIRST YEARS DEEPLY INFLUENCED ALL THE PEOPLE WHO WERE HERE. YOU HAD TO KNOW WHERE YOU STOOD POLITICALLY BEFORE YOU COULD FILM, SO THAT YOU COULD HAVE A SENSE OF WHAT WAS HAPPENING TO KNOW WHAT TO FILM. MANY IMPORTANT THINGS WERE HAPPENING—THE LITERACY CAMPAIGN, THE AGRICULTURE REFORMS, THE FORMATION OF THE ARMY, HEALTH PROGRAMS. THE BUILDING OF A NEW STATE APPARATUS. WE HAD TO TAKE THE OLD STRUCTURES APART AND BUILD NEW ONES. WE HAD TO DESTROY AN ENTIRE CONCEPT OF CULTURE AND MAKE A NEW ONE.

CF: DID THE FOREIGN COLLABORATORS UNDERSTAND THIS?

FP: WE HAD PROBLEMS WITH SOME OF THEM. THEY HAD THE TECHNICAL KNOWLEDGE, BUT WE, AS NICARAGUANS WHO HAD LIVED THE REVOLUTION, HAD A CLEAR CON-CEPT OF WHAT HAD TO BE RECORDED. THEY HAD A TECHNICAL AND AESTHETIC SENSE OF MAKING FILMS, HOW TO FRAME THINGS, HOW TO PLAN THINGS. FOR US THOSE THINGS WEREN'T AS IMPORTANT. IT WAS MORE IMPORTANT TO DOCU-MENT A MOMENT THAN TO WORRY ABOUT WHETHER THE SHOT WAS IN FOCUS. WE JUST MADE A LIST OF IMAGES WE NEEDED AT THE BEGINNING, OF ALL THE DESTRUCTION, THE DIFFICULTIES EVERYONE WAS HAVING WITH TRANSPORT, WITH GETTING FOOD, ETC. WE WERE BUILDING AN ARCHIVE SO THAT WHEN WE HAD BETTER RESOURCES WE COULD GO ON TO MAKE DOCUMENTARIES. SOMETIMES THEY WOULD LOOK AT US AND NOT UNDERSTAND. THEY HAD A CONCEPT OF CINEMA AS PERFECT CINEMA, SO TO SPEAK. NOT THAT WE KNEW ABOUT JULIO GARCIA ESPINOSA'S "IMPERFECT CINEMA" AT THE TIME, BUT WE WERE INTERESTED IN THE NEEDS OF THE MOMENT.

CF: WHEN YOU WERE MAKING *CULTURAL INSURRECTION* WHAT KIND OF AUDIENCES WERE YOU THINKING OF? WAS THIS IMPORTANT TO YOU THEN?

FP: WHEN WE WERE WORKING ON IT WE WEREN'T THINKING ABOUT WHO THE AUDIENCE WAS. WE JUST KNEW THAT IF WE DIDN'T RECORD THE FIRST MOMENTS OF THE REVOLUTION THEY WOULD BE LOST. IT WAS ONLY THE FIRST YEAR OF THE REVOLUTION AND WE DIDN'T EVEN KNOW WHAT LINE OF WORK WOULD BE STRESSED AT INCINE.

BUT WE DID HAVE TO LEARN TO THINK ABOUT WHAT KIND OF FILMMAKING WE HAD TO ENGAGE IN, AND HOW TO TAKE INTO ACCOUNT WHO THE SPECTATORS WOULD BE. WE LIVE IN A STATE OF WAR, A TENSE SITUATION FULL OF LIMITATIONS. AS A RESULT, WE BECOME MORE RADICAL. WE KNOW THAT THE U.S. IS ATTACKING US THROUGH THE CONTRAS AND THAT HONDURAS IS BEING USED. WE KNOW THAT WE HAVE MANY PROBLEMS IN OUR COUNTRY, AND WE KNOW WE HAVE TO DEFEND IT. IN OUR DOCUMENTARIES, WE SHOW THE VIOLENCE THAT IS SO MUCH A PART OF OUR LIVES NOW. FOR A WHILE WE LOST THE SENSE OF PERSPECTIVE WE NEED TO REALIZE THAT IF WE ARE MAKING FILMS FOR THE OUTSIDE WORLD, THEY CANNOT BE SO VIOLENT, OR SO DIDACTIC. THEY HAVE TO BE BETTER SUITED TO THE VISIONS OF OTHER PEOPLE. WE WERE MAKING FILMS THAT WERE REALLY FOR INTERNAL CONSUMPTION.

NOW INCINE IS MAKING FILMS THAT ARE LESS AGIT PROP FOR FOREIGN DISTRIBUTION, TAKING INTO ACCOUNT FOREIGN PUBLIC OPINION. WE ARE SURVIVING AS A RESULT OF INTERNATIONAL SOLIDARITY. NICARAGUA COULD NOT SURVIVE WITHOUT INTERNATIONAL AID, NOT EVEN ONE DAY OF WAR. IN FILM, WE HAVE TO USE OUR LIMITED RESOURCES RATIONALLY, AND THINK ABOUT APPROPRIATE THEMES. WE HAVE TO THINK ABOUT WHAT KIND OF FILMS WILL CREATE THE IMAGE OF NICARAGUA THAT WE WANT TO CREATE.

TRANSLATED AND EDITED BY COCO FUSCO.

Central America: A Defiant Volcano

Public Access Media and the Information War
[1986]

An interview with the Radio Veneceremos Collective (Sistema Radio Veneceremos).

〜〜〜〜〜〜〜〜〜〜〜〜〜〜〜〜〜〜〜〜〜〜〜 *Coco Fusco*

In 1979, public opposition to the Salvadoran government and its human-rights abuses grew too contentious to be officially tolerated and was severely suppressed. Opposition continued in the form of an armed guerrilla movement led by the Farabundo Marti National Liberation Front (FMLN) in the mountains and countryside. The different factions of the FMLN united in 1985 with the non-military opposition group, the Democratic Revolutionary Front (FDR), to form what is now referred to as "The Unity." The Sistema Radio Venceremos (Radio Venceremos Collective) or SRV has been part of the FMLN since 1981. While the Film Institute of Revolutionary El Salvador works in conjunction with the FMLN in the rebel-controlled Chalatenango area, the SRV Collective, which is an integral part of the FMLN, operates in Morazan, another rebel-controlled area. Since 1986, SRV and the Film Institute have worked together as a single production unit.

The SRV produces radio broadcasts, photo and print information, and films and videos, which are distributed internationally. Since 1981, they have produced 12 films for export and several others for inter-

NAL CONSUMPTION: *CENTROAMERICA: UN VOLCAN DESAFIANTE* (*CENTRAL AMERICA: A DEFIANT VOLCANO*, 1985), IS AN ANALYSIS OF THE SALVADORAN WAR IN THE CONTEXT OF REGIONAL PROBLEMS, U.S. POLICY IN CENTRAL AMERICA, AND WESTERN MASS MEDIA'S REPRESENTATIONS OF THEIR COUNTRY AND THEIR CONFLICT.

THE FOLLOWING IS A COMPILATION OF INTERVIEWS WITH FOUR COLLECTIVE MEMBERS, WHICH WAS ORIGINALLY PUBLISHED IN *AFTERIMAGE* (ROCHESTER, N.Y.) IN MARCH, 1987, AND APPEARS HERE IN A SLIGHTLY ABRIDGED VERSION.

Coco Fusco: WHY DON'T WE START WITH A LITTLE BACKGROUND ON THE COLLECTIVE?

Sistema Radio Venceremos: BEFORE THAT, MAYBE WE SHOULD TALK ABOUT HOW WE DEAL WITH OUR WORK. FILM IS A NECESSITY FOR US. IT'S NOT AS IF THE MAJORITY OF THE COLLECTIVE STUDIED FILMMAKING BUT RATHER THERE WAS A NEED TO LEARN ABOUT FILM AS A MEDIUM. WITH A CERTAIN SENSIBILITY, OF COURSE. FUNDAMENTALLY THE OBJECTIVE IS TO RECOVER HISTORY, AND AT THE SAME TIME TO CREATE A NEW MOVEMENT, WHICH OUR PEOPLE NEED. THEY NEED A CINEMA. WE ARE WORKING AGAINST THE POLITICS OF THE GOVERNMENT WHICH DOES NOT PROMOTE A NATIONAL CINEMA. IN EL SALVADOR, LATIN AMERICA AND IN THE THIRD WORLD IN GENERAL CINEMA IS SEEN AS SOMETHING SEPARATE, AS SOMETHING EXTREMELY SPECIALIZED, THAT PEOPLE CAN ONLY LOOK AT AND ADMIRE ONCE IT IS ALREADY PRODUCED. TO DISPEL THE IDEA THAT CINEMA IS SOMETHING UNREACHABLE, WE WANTED TO SHOW THAT CINEMA IS WITHIN OUR REACH. AND THAT IT COULD BE DONE WITH RUDIMENTARY MATERIALS. THE CONCEPT THAT BEGAN TO MATURE WITHIN THE COLLECTIVE WAS THAT WHAT WAS IMPORTANT ISN'T THE MACHINES, WHETHER THE CAMERA IS AN ATON, OR SOME OTHER GOOD CAMERA, BUT THE FACT THAT YOU'RE FILMING AND WHAT YOU'RE FILMING. AND THE RELATION YOU HAVE WITH WHAT OR WHO YOU'RE FILMING. IN ONE WAY OR ANOTHER IT COMES OUT IN THE FILM. AND WE ALSO WANT TO PREPARE FOR WHAT OUR CINEMA COULD BE.

THE PEOPLE WHO SUPPORT US GUARANTEE THAT WE CAN DO WHAT WE'RE DOING, THAT WE CAN, FOR EXAMPLE, SHOOT SIXTY HOURS OF FILM. EVERYONE PARTICIPATES IN ONE WAY OR ANOTHER—HOW DO YOU, FOR EXAMPLE, GET SIXTY CANS OF FILM OUT OF AN AREA? YOU HIDE THEM FROM THE ARMY AND THEN RECOVER THEM AFTERWARDS. THERE ARE SOME BEAUTIFUL STORIES ABOUT THAT. THERE WAS A COMPANERO WHO WAS TRYING TO GET A BUNCH OF CANS ACROSS TO THE OTHER SIDE AFTER HAVING FILMED. THE ARMY WAS COMING, AND HE REALIZED THAT HE COULDN'T TAKE IT ALL HIMSELF. A GROUP OF CAMPESINOS CAME ALONG AND HE DECIDED TO DIVIDE THE CANS UP BETWEEN THEM. SO ABOUT SIXTY PEOPLE EACH TAKE ONE AND THAT WAS HOW THEY MANAGED TO SAVE ALL THE FILM.

ALL THOSE CIRCUMSTANCES MAKE IT SUCH THAT PEOPLE SENSE THEY ARE PARTICIPATING IN THE MAKING OF THEIR CINEMA. THERE ARE PEOPLE WHO ASK US TO TAKE A PICTURE OF THEM WHO DON'T ALWAYS UNDERSTAND EXACTLY WHAT WE ARE DOING. THEY SAY, "TAKE ONE OF ME WITH MY CHILD, MY GRANDMOTHER, MY AUNT. HERE'S A PICTURE, WHY DON'T YOU TAKE A PICTURE OF THAT PICTURE? THAT'S MY DAUGHTER, WHO DIED IN A BOMBING." THEY DO HAVE A SENSE THAT A PIECE OF HISTORY WILL BE PHOTOGRAPHED. SOME PEOPLE SEE IT ALL AS A BIT OF CRAZINESS, AS A BIT OF MAGIC BECAUSE THEY ARE NOT USED TO SEEING THIS SORT OF THING. THE FIRST TIME WE SHOWED A FILM THERE WAS AN OLD MAN IN THE AUDIENCE WHO HAD NEVER SEEN A FILM IN HIS ENTIRE LIFE.

CF: HOW LONG HAVE YOU BEEN WORKING?

SRV: FIVE YEARS. WHEN PEOPLE STARTED SUGGESTING TO US IN THE SEVENTIES THAT WE MAKE FILMS, WE WOULD SAY, HOW ARE WE GOING TO MAKE FILMS? FILMS FOR US ONLY EXISTED WHEN WE SAW THEM IN THE MOVIE THEATERS. AND WHAT'S MORE, WHAT WE HAD SEEN WAS FOR THE MOST PART VERY COMMERCIAL.

SO WE HAD TO THINK ABOUT HOW WE WERE GOING TO MAKE THE KIND OF FILMS WE WANTED TO MAKE. WE HAD SOME IDEA OF WHAT WE WANTED TO DO, BUT WE HAD BEEN STRONGLY INFLUENCED BY ALL THE ACTION FILMS, THE KARATE AND JUDO MOVIES WE HAD SEEN ALL OUR LIVES. WE HAD A SENSE THAT WE COULD MAKE FILMS ABOUT OTHER THINGS. THAT WE COULD, FOR EXAMPLE, FILM A WOMAN IN THE MARKET. THAT'S A DIFFERENT CINEMA. A DOCUMENTARY CINEMA THAT RESPONDS TO NECESSITY.

CF: WHAT SENSE OF EDITING DID YOU HAVE WITH SUCH LITTLE EXPOSURE AND EXPERIENCE WITH DOCUMENTARY FILM?

SRV: THE REALITY OF OUR SITUATION IS SUCH THAT WE MUST FILM IN A WAY THAT OTHER PEOPLE IN OTHER COUNTRIES WHO DON'T EVEN KNOW WHERE OUR COUNTRY IS WILL UNDERSTAND. WE WANTED TO DO TWO THINGS: SHOW PEOPLE OUTSIDE THE COUNTRY WHAT THE REALITY WE WERE EXPERIENCING WAS AND WE ALSO WANTED OUR OWN PEOPLE TO SEE THEMSELVES ON FILM. WE DIDN'T HAVE TO LOOK FOR THEMES. THE THEMES ARE THERE. IT'S THE REALITY WE LIVE IN. WE JUST HAVE TO KNOW HOW TO FILM IT. IN TERMS OF THE ORGANIZATION OF IMAGES, THAT IS SOMETHING WE'RE WORKING ON.

CF: HOW DO YOU CHOOSE A THEME WHEN MAKING A FILM?

SRV: THERE ARE DIFFERENT WAYS, DEPENDING ON THE CREW. EACH CREW HAS ITS OWN DYNAMIC. TAKE, FOR EXAMPLE, OUR CAPACITY TO MOBILIZE OURSELVES. AT A GIVEN MOMENT THERE MIGHT BE A CONCENTRATED FORCE. WHEN THE ENEMY CONCENTRATES ON A CERTAIN AREA, WE DISPERSE. WHILE DISPERSED THERE ARE THEMES THAT CAN'T BE DEVELOPED THAT WELL. SUDDENLY THEN THE ARMY DISPERSES AND WE COME BACK TOGETHER. WITHIN THAT DYNAMIC WE HAVE TO DEFINE OUR

THEMES. THE THEME WE MIGHT WANT TO DO MIGHT CALL FOR PEOPLE BEING TOGETHER AND, CONSEQUENTLY, WE WOULDN'T BE ABLE TO WORK ON IT, SO WE'D GO ON TO ANOTHER ONE. THERE ARE MANY THEMES WE LOSE BECAUSE OF THE REALITY WE LIVE IN AND BECAUSE OF WHAT WE DON'T WANT TO SAY OUTSIDE THE COUNTRY. CERTAIN FILMS WE MAKE ARE ONLY FOR INTERNAL CONSUMPTION. FOR THE OUTSIDE WORLD WE WANT TO DEAL WITH OUR DEVELOPMENT AND HOW IT IS PERCEIVED. HOW HAVE WE PROGRESSED, AND WHAT ARE OUR NEEDS. TRYING TO GIVE A REAL VISION OF WHAT REALITY IS. OF COURSE THERE ARE INTERNAL FACTORS THAT ALSO DETERMINE THINGS.

CF: CAN YOU TALK ABOUT FILM'S ROLE IN THE LIBERATION STRUGGLE?

SRV: I THINK THAT FUNDAMENTALLY IT IS TO WRITE OUR HISTORY WITH IMAGES. IT HAS TO BE SEEN IN RELATION TO HOW LIBERATION MOVEMENTS HAVE DEVELOPED IN THE THIRD WORLD IN GENERAL. WE HAVE TO BE EVEN MORE PREPARED THAN WE ARE BECAUSE THE ATTACKS ON US ARE STRONGER. EVERY INTERVENTION MARKS OUT FOR US WHAT OUR TASKS ARE. WITH FILM WE REACH FURTHER AND THAT IS OUR NEED. IF WE COULD DO IT WITH COMPUTERS WE'D LEARN HOW TO USE COMPUTERS AS WELL. AND FIFTY OTHER TECHNICAL MEANS—THOSE ARE THE NECESSITIES OF THIS WAR.

WE SEE THAT WE ARE SHAPING HISTORY. RECOVERY AND STUDY OF OUR CULTURAL HISTORY HELPS US TO DELINEATE THE CHANGES THAT HAVE TAKEN PLACE AND HOW WE HAVE ADVANCED. WE REALIZED THAT WE HAD TO PUT ASIDE MAKING DOCUMENTARIES PURELY ABOUT THE WAR, AND MOVE ONTO THE OTHER SOCIAL FUNCTIONS OF CINEMA. WE'RE ALSO CONCERNED WITH OUR PEOPLE'S ROOTS, CULTURAL AND ANCESTRAL. WE ARE MODIFYING OUR IMAGES SLOWLY. WE'RE MAKING MORE IMAGES THAT HAVE AESTHETIC AND NATURAL ELEMENTS. THE CUBAN REVOLUTION WAS A SURPRISE. THE NICARAGUAN REVOLUTION WAS A SURPRISE. OUR REVOLUTION ISN'T. WE HAVE TO CONTEND WITH THE FACT THAT WE HAVE A FEROCIOUS ENEMY, THAT HAS POWERFUL TECHNOLOGY. IF WE HAVE TO PREPARE OURSELVES WITH THERMONUCLEAR ENERGY WE WILL. WE ALWAYS TRY ON PRINCIPLE TO REVIVE OUR CULTURAL VALUES BECAUSE SALVADORAN CULTURE HAS BEEN TRAMPLED ON. IN NICARAGUA THERE IS A VAST AND RICH CULTURE. MAYBE THERE ISN'T SUCH A VAST CULTURE IN EL SALVADOR, BUT IT EXISTS. VERY FEW PEOPLE HAVE BEEN ABLE TO LEARN ABOUT IT. SO IN OUR CINEMA WE ARE TRYING TO DEMONSTRATE THIS, TO SHOW IT IN EVERY WAY WE CAN. WE ARE ALL INDIGENOUS TO SOME EXTENT. WE KNOW WE ARE GOOD AT FIGHTING, WE'VE ALREADY SHOWN IT SO MANY TIMES. WE HAVE OTHER THINGS NOW. WE HAVE TO RECOVER OUR CULTURE. IF WE DON'T, NOBODY WILL. SO, IN ADDITION TO MAKING AN OVERTLY POLITICAL CINEMA, WE WANT AND HAVE TO MAKE FILMS WHICH, THROUGH THEIR IMAGES, SYMBOLS AND OTHER SIGNALS EXPRESS WHAT OUR CULTURE IS.

CF: WHO IS YOUR AUDIENCE? WHAT STRATEGIES DO YOU USE TO ADDRESS YOUR

PUBLIC(S) BOTH INSIDE AND OUTSIDE EL SALVADOR?

SRV: THAT IS A DIFFICULT QUESTION IN THE SENSE THAT WE'RE STILL IN THE PROCESS OF LOOKING FOR AN AUDIENCE. IT WAS IMPORTANT AT THE BEGINNING TO SAY THAT WE WERE A POPULAR ARMY AT WAR. THAT WAS A MESSAGE THAT WAS FIRST OF ALL IMPORTANT TO TRANSMIT TO PEOPLE WITHIN THE COUNTRY AND TO GROUPS OUTSIDE. WE STARTED JUST AFTER THE NICARAGUAN INSURRECTION, AND PEOPLE SAW IT AS ANOTHER REVOLUTION NEXT DOOR. BUT IT WASN'T LIKE THAT. THINGS ARE MORE COMPLICATED THAN THAT. NOW WE MAKE FILMS IN ACCORDANCE WITH THE PUBLIC WE WANT TO REACH. FOR EXAMPLE, THE NORTH AMERICAN PUBLIC. WE THINK THEY CAN HELP TO STOP NORTH AMERICAN INTERVENTION. IN TERMS OF INSIDE THE COUNTRY, IN ACCORDANCE WITH OUR POSITION IN FAVOR OF PARTICIPATORY GOVERNMENT, WE ARE INTERESTED IN APPROACHING PEOPLE WITH INFORMATION SO THAT THEY MIGHT BE ABLE TO SEE THE ALTERNATIVE WE OFFER AS ONE THAT COULD SOLVE SOME OF THE ECONOMIC AND SOCIAL PROBLEMS IN THE COUNTRY.

CF: WHEN YOU SPEAK OF THE NORTH AMERICAN PUBLIC WHAT AUDIENCE THERE ARE YOU THINKING OF?

SRV: UP TO THIS POINT WE HAVE BEEN CONCENTRATING ON THE MORE LIMITED PUBLIC FROM THE SOLIDARITY MOVEMENT. BUT WE WOULD LIKE TO BROADEN OUR AUDIENCE, AS WE HAVE BROADENED THE SCOPE OF OUR WORK. MAYBE NO ONE WILL FINALLY BE ABLE TO MAKE REAL CINEMA AND ENTER A NEW STAGE. ALTHOUGH WE HAVE DECIDED NOT TO DO IT NOW, WE WERE THINKING OF MAKING A FICTION FILM AND HAVEN'T ELIMINATED THE POSSIBILITY. WE DON'T KNOW IF WE CAN; AT THIS POINT WE KNOW THAT IT IS THE NEXT STAGE.

THERE IS ALSO THE PROBLEM OF PERSPECTIVE. THERE HAVE BEEN MANY FILMS MADE ABOUT EL SALVADOR BY EUROPEANS AND NORTH AMERICANS. BUT WHAT WE SEE IN THOSE DOCUMENTARIES IS THAT THEY DO NOT REFLECT OUR SPIRIT, WHICH IS SOMETHING WE CAN CAPTURE IN OUR FILMS. IT SEEMS AS THOUGH THE FOREIGNERS SAW OUR REALITY AS IF IT WERE A SCREEN IN FRONT OF THEM. WE LIKE TO LEARN ABOUT WHAT OTHERS ARE SAYING ABOUT EL SALVADOR. WE SEE HOW THEY SEE IT FROM THE POINT OF VIEW OF THEIR CULTURE. IT'S NOT THE SAME FOR A DUTCH FILMMAKER TO SEE A WOMAN WITH A WOUNDED CHILD AS IT IS FOR A SALVADORAN, AND THE WAY OF FILMING CHANGES.

CF: WHICH FILMMAKER'S WORKS HAVE INFLUENCED YOU?

SRV: WE'VE BEEN INFLUENCED BY LATIN AMERICAN CINEMA, BY BRAZILIAN CINEMA. THE NEW LATIN AMERICAN CINEMA. CUBAN CINEMA AND THEIR TREATMENT OF CERTAIN ISSUES. NORTH AMERICAN CINEMA, OF COURSE. EVEN MEXICAN CINEMA. BASICALLY WHATEVER WE CAN GET OUR HANDS ON. EDUCATIONAL FILMS. THERE WAS A PROJECT SPONSORED BY THE GOVERNMENT DURING THE PERIOD OF REFORMS AFTER '79. IT INCLUDED AN ATTEMPT TO USE TELEVISION FOR EDUCATIONAL PUR-

POSES. OF COURSE, THERE WAS ALSO A POLITICAL AIM, WHICH WAS TO STOP THE TEACHERS FROM DOING TOO MUCH TALKING.

WHEN MEMBERS OF THE FMLN HAVE THE CHANCE TO SEE THE WORK PRODUCED IN LATIN AMERICA IT GIVES THEM A BROADER VISION OF THE CONFLICT THEY ARE IN. *CENTRAL AMERICA: A DEFIANT VOLCANO* ATTEMPTS TO DO PRECISELY THIS—TO PUT EL SALVADOR IN THE CONTEXT OF WHAT IS GOING ON THROUGHOUT LATIN AMERICA. IN THAT SENSE I THINK THAT NEW LATIN AMERICAN CINEMA HELPS TO ENRICH OUR VISION. WE LEARN ABOUT THE PROBLEMS GENERATED BY THE FOREIGN DEBT, ABOUT THE DISAPPEARED IN ARGENTINA, ABOUT THE STRUGGLES THAT ARE TAKING PLACE IN LATIN AMERICA.

CF: WHAT POSSIBILITIES EXIST IN EL SALVADOR AT THIS TIME TO HAVE ACCESS TO THIS SORT OF INFORMATION?

SRV: THERE HAS ALWAYS BEEN A FORM OF CENSORSHIP OF INFORMATION IN EL SALVADOR. YOU WILL FIND THEATERS FULL OF NORTH AMERICAN PRODUCTIONS, COMMERCIAL CINEMA. UNFORTUNATELY, THERE HAS BEEN LITTLE POSSIBILITY OF SHOWING THE WORKS OF THE NEW LATIN AMERICAN CINEMA THERE. FOR EXAMPLE, IT'S RARE THAT YOU WOULD SEE A CUBAN, OR NICARAGUAN FILM THAT MAY NOT NECESSARILY BE POLITICAL, BUT MIGHT HAVE TO DO WITH PROBLEMS LIKE MACHISMO. SOMETIMES PEOPLE IN THE CITIES SHOW THESE SORTS OF FILMS CLANDESTINELY, BUT THE DUARTE GOVERNMENT WILL NOT ALLOW THIS MATERIAL TO BE SHOWN PUBLICLY.

CF: WHAT ARE THE LIMITS? HOW DO YOU KNOW WHAT CAN AND CANNOT BE SHOWN?

SRV: IT'S A QUESTION OF WHETHER THE MATERIAL CAN BE CONSIDERED TO BE OPENLY AGAINST THE SYSTEM OF POWER. THE SO-CALLED DEMOCRACY THAT THE GOVERNMENT REPRESENTS HAS CREATED A SPACE WITHIN WHICH CERTAIN FILMS CAN BE INTRODUCED. THESE ARE FILMS WHICH THEY CONSIDER WILL NOT INTRODUCE ANY SORT OF PROBLEMS IN EL SALVADOR. IT ALSO HAS A GREAT DEAL TO DO WITH THE GOVERNMENT STRUCTURE. IF AT A GIVEN MOMENT IT IS IN THE INTEREST OF

Central America: A Defiant Volcano

THE GOVERNMENT TO MAINTAIN A CERTAIN KIND OF UNDERSTANDING OF THINGS AMONG PEOPLE, THEY WILL, TO PREVENT THEM FROM BEING ABLE TO ENVISION A REALITY OTHER THAN THE ONE PRESENTED IN THESE FILMS IN GENERAL. AT NO POINT ARE THEY GOING TO GO AGAINST WHAT IS IN THE INTEREST OF THEIR MARKET. WHAT IS THE THREAT TO THEM—COULD IT BE THE EXAMPLE OF CUBA AND NICARAGUA, WHERE THAT KIND OF ALIENATING CINEMA CAN NO LONGER EXERT THE INFLUENCE IT ONCE HAD? EL SALVADOR AND COUNTRIES LIKE IT REPRESENT MARKETS FOR THEM. THEY PROBABLY BELIEVE THAT IF THE REVOLUTION TRIUMPH-ED THEIR ACCESS TO THOSE MARKETS WOULD BE CUT OFF. ON THE OTHER HAND, IF AT SOME MOMENT FOR SOME REASON THEY WANTED TO SHOW A FILM THAT WENT AGAINST GOVERNMENT INTERESTS THEY WOULD HAVE PROBLEMS. THEY WOULD BE TOLD THAT IT WOULD HAVE BAD POLITICAL REPERCUSSIONS IN THE COUNTRY, ESPECIALLY AMONG PEOPLE IN POWER, WHO, IN GENERAL, ARE ALSO THE PEOPLE WHO GO TO THE MOVIES MOST OFTEN. SO DIRECTLY OR INDIRECTLY THE TRANSITIONALS AND THE GOVERNMENT FORM A KIND OF CULTURAL OVERSEER—THEIR INTERESTS COINCIDE.

CF: HOW DOES THE FACT THAT YOU WORK COLLECTIVELY AFFECT YOUR WORK?

SRV: WHEN YOU HAVE COLLECTIVITY, YOU HAVE STRENGTH. WHEN YOU HAVE A COL-LECTIVE YOU HAVE STRENGTH. WHEN YOU WORK INDIVIDUALLY IT DIMINISHES. WE HAVE TO JOIN TOGETHER TO BE STRONG, AND TO RESOLVE PROBLEMS THAT WE FACE. YOUR IDEAS BECOME COLLECTIVE ALSO. FOR EXAMPLE, I MIGHT HAVE AN IDEA AND I TELL THE COLLECTIVE. FROM THAT MOMENT ON IT ISN'T MY IDEA. IN THE END IT'S A COLLECTIVE IDEA. THEN THERE IS THE QUESTION OF HOW WE RESOLVE PROBLEMS COLLECTIVELY. ONCE THERE WAS A WOUNDED GIRL WE WANTED TO FILM. THE GIRL WAS HYSTERICAL—SHE HAD JUST SEEN HER MOTHER DIE. AND ALL HER BROTHERS HAD JUST DIED IN A BOMBING. ONLY SHE AND HER FATHER WERE LEFT. EVERY TIME WE'D ASK HER A QUESTION SHE WOULD START TO CRY. SO WE OFFERED HER CANDY AND SHE STILL SAID NO. THEN WE OFFERED HER WATER AND SHE SAID NO. FOOD—NO. SHE WOULD CRY AND CRY. WE HAD THE CAMERA GOING AND WE HAD TO SHUT IT OFF. SHE WAS ONLY EIGHT YEARS OLD. SKIN AND BONES. WE ASKED HER WHAT SHE WANTED. AND SHE SAID, "I WANT A JACOTE." SO WE SAID, IF WE GIVE YOU ONE WILL YOU STOP CRYING WILL YOU STOP CRYING AND TALK TO US? YES, SHE SAYS. THE PRODUCER THEN CRIES OUT, "A JACOTE!" AND ALL OF US START LOOKING FOR ONE LIKE CRAZY. WE CLIMBED TREES UNTIL WE FOUND ONE AND COULD START FILMING.

CF: I SAW YOUR LAST DOCUMENTARY, *CENTRAL AMERICA: A DEFIANT VOLCANO* AS A RESPONSE TO THE ISSUE OF DEMOCRATIZATION, ALMOST AS A CRITIQUE OF THE PROJECT.

SRV: ONE OF OUR AIMS IS TO SHOW THE LACK OF VALIDITY AND UNREALITY OF THIS PROJECT. WE ALSO WANT TO SHOW THE NEED FOR PEACE WHICH IS REAL AND

CONCRETE, AND THE FMLN'S DESIRE FOR DIALOGUE. AND THAT OUR ARMY IS A LIBERATING ARMY AND NO ONE CAN NEGATE THAT. AND THAT THERE IS A POLITICAL WAY OUT OF INTERVENTION. THOSE ARE OUR TERMS. THE FILM GIVES YOU A CONCRETE IDEA OF THE REGION AND SHOWS HOW INVALID THIS PROJECT IS. WE KNOW WHAT OUR OBJECTIVES ARE, THE QUESTION IS HOW CAN WE REACH THE NORTH AMERICAN PUBLIC, WHO CAN HELP TO STOP THE INTERVENTION. WE DON'T WANT WAR, WE WANT PEACE. TELL THEM THAT WE DON'T WANT ANY MORE BOMBS. AFTER VIETNAM, ONE OF THE LARGEST DEMONSTRATIONS THAT HAS TAKEN PLACE OUTSIDE THE WHITE HOUSE WAS FOR EL SALVADOR. THIS IS NOT ENOUGH.

TRANSLATED AND EDITED BY COCO FUSCO.

Photo Credits

PHOTOGRAPHS ON PP. 8-9, 31, 35, 40, 43, 99, 102, 105, 116-117, 123, 126-127, 158-159 (GUNS), AND 162 COURTESY OF JULIANNE BURTON; PP. 54-55, AND 114 COURTESY OF FIRST RUN FEATURES; P. 50 COURTESY OF ROBERT STAM; PP. 103, 198, AND 199 COURTESY OF THE MUSEUM OF MODERN ART FILM STILL ARCHIVES; PP. 139, 140-141 COURTESY OF ZANZIBAR PRODUCTIONS; P. 148 COURTESY OF ICARUS FILMS; PP. 164-165, AND 204 COURTESY OF *CINEASTE;* PP. 109, 110, 205, 208, 209, 211, 217, 219 COURTESY OF COCO FUSCO. ALL OTHER PHOTOS COURTESY OF HALLWALLS (THANKS TO BARBARA LATTANZI).

CONTRIBUTORS

Ariel Dorfman, AUTHOR OF SIXTEEN BOOKS—INCLUDING *HOW TO READ DONALD DUCK* (WITH ARMAND MATTELART)—IS CURRENTLY IN EXILE FROM HIS NATIVE CHILE, LIVING IN WASHINGTON, D.C., WHERE HE TEACHES AT THE CENTER FOR INTERNATIONAL STUDIES/DUKE UNIVERSITY. HE FREQUENTLY CONTRIBUTES ARTICLES ON THIRD WORLD AFFAIRS TO MAJOR NEWSPAPERS IN BOTH LATIN AMERICAN AND THE UNITED STATES.

Coco Fusco LIVES AND WORKS IN NEW YORK CITY AS A FREE LANCE JOURNALIST, SPECIALIZING IN FILM—PARTICULARLY THIRD WORLD CINEMA—AND THE ARTS. SHE FREQUENTLY CONTRIBUTES ARTICLES AND INTERVIEWS TO *AFTERIMAGE*, *CINEASTE*, *CONNOISSEUR MAGAZINE*, AND *THE INDEPENDENT*.

Glauber Rocha WAS ONE OF THE FOUNDERS OF CINE NOVO, AND ITS LEADING POLEMICIST. HIS FILMS INCLUDE *BARRAVENTO* (1962), *BLACK GOD, WHITE DEVIL* (1964), *LAND IN ANGUISH* (1967), AND *ANTONIO DAS MORTES* (1968). WHILE IN EXILE HE ALSO MADE *DER LEONE HAVE SEPT CABECAS* (ZAIRE, 1969), *CABEZAS CORTADAS* (SPAIN, 1970), AND *CLARO!* (FRANCE, 1976).

Fernando Solanas, ARGENTINE FILMMAKER WHOSE WORKS INCLUDE *THE HOUR OF THE FURNACES* (CO-DIRECTED WITH OCTAVIO GETINO), *THE SONS OF IRON*, *THE LOOK OF OTHERS* AND *TANGOES: THE EXILE OF GARDEL* (1985).

Octavio Getino, FILMMAKER AND MEDIA CRITIC, IS CURRENTLY THE DIRECTOR OF THE CENTER FOR STUDIES IN POPULAR CULTURE IN BUENOS AIRES. HE CO-DIRECTED *THE HOUR OF THE FURNACES* WITH FERNANDO SOLANAS.

Robert Stam IS PROFESSOR OF CINEMA STUDIES AT NEW YORK UNIVERSITY, AND CO-AUTHOR WITH RANDALL JOHNSON OF *BRAZILIAN CINEMA*.

Julio Garcia Espinosa, FILMMAKER AND WRITER, IS THE DIRECTOR OF THE CUBAN FILM INSTITUTE.

Tomas Gutierrez Alea, FILMMAKER AND WRITER, WHOSE FILMS INCLUDE *MEMORIES OF UNDERDEVELOPMENT* (1968), *DEATH OF A BUREAUCRAT* (1966), *THE LAST SUPPER* (1977), AND *UP TO A CERTAIN POINT* (1983).

Osvaldo Sanchez IS A POET, SCRIPTWRITER AND ART CRITIC, WHO TEACHES ART HISTORY AT THE SAN ALEJANDRO ART ACADEMY IN HAVANA.

Julianne Burton IS ASSOCIATE PROFESSOR OF LITERATURE AT THE UNIVERSITY OF CALIFORNIA AT SANTA CRUZ, AND THE AUTHOR OF NUMEROUS ARTICLES ON NEW LATIN AMERICAN CINEMA.

Richard Peña IS THE DIRECTOR OF THE FILM CENTER AT THE CHICAGO ART IN-STITUTE AND WRITES FREQUENTLY ON LATIN AMERICAN FILM.

Jorge Sanjines IS A FILMMAKER WHOSE WORKS INCLUDE *BLOOD OF THE CONDOR* (1968) AND *COURAGE OF THE PEOPLE* (1971).

FILM CREDITS

Antonio Das Mortes.
DIRECTED BY GLAUBER ROCHA.
BRAZIL, 1968, 100 MIN. COLOR

Barren Lives (VIDAS SECAS).
DIRECTED BY NELSON PEREIRA DOS
  SANTOS.
BRAZIL, 1963, 115 MIN. B&W.

Blood of the Condor
  (YAWAR MALLKU)
DIRECTED BY JORGE SANJINES.
BOLIVIA, 1979, 72 MIN. B&W.

**Central America:
A Defiant Volcano.**
  (CENTROAMERICA: UN VOLCAN
  DESAFIANTE)
DIRECTED BY COLLECTIVA RADIO
  VENCEREMOS.
EL SALVADOR, 1985, 60 MIN. COLOR.

**Chile, I Don't Take Your
Name in Vain.**
DIRECTED BY COLECTIVO CINE-OJO.
CHILE, 1984, 55 MIN. COLOR

Cultural Insurrection
  (LA INSURRECCION CULTURAL).
DIRECTED BY JORGE DENTI. NICARAGUA.
1981, 57 MIN. COLOR

The Hour of the Furnaces
  (LA HORA DE LOS HORNOS).
DIRECTED BY FERNANDO SOLANAS
  AND OCTAVIO GETINO.
ARGENTINA, 1968, 260 MIN. B&W.

Hypothesis of the Stolen Painting
  (L'HYPOTHESE DU TABLEAU VOLE).
DIRECTED BY RAOUL RUIZ.
FRANCE, 1978, 67 MIN. B&W.

The Last Supper (LA ULTIMA CENA).
DIRECTED BY TOMAS GUTIERREZ ALEA.
CUBA, 1977, 110 MIN. COLOR.

**Las Madres: The Mothers of the
Plaza de Mayo.**
DIRECTED BY SUSANA MUÑOZ
  AND LOURDES PORTILLO.
ARGENTINA/USA, 1985, 64 MIN. COLOR.

**Of Great Events and
Ordinary People**
  (DES GRANDS EVENEMENTS ET DES GENS
  ORDINARIES).
DIRECTED BY RAOUL RUIZ.
FRANCE, 1979, 60 MIN. COLOR.

One Way or Another
  (DE CIERTA MANERA).
DIRECTED BY SARA GOMEZ.
CUBA, 1974, 87 MIN. COLOR.

The Promised Land
  (LA TIERRA PROMETIDA).
DIRECTED BY MIGUEL LITTIN.
CHILE, 1973, 106 MIN. COLOR.

Reed: Insurgent Mexico.
DIRECTED BY PAUL LEDUC.
MEXICO, 1971, 110 MIN. B&W.

9457